Anonymous

History of the Irish People

Anonymous

History of the Irish People

ISBN/EAN: 9783744734479

Printed in Europe, USA, Canada, Australia, Japan

Cover: Foto ©ninafisch / pixelio.de

More available books at **www.hansebooks.com**

HISTORY

OF THE

ISH PEOPLE.

BY

W. A. O'CONOR, B.A.

SECOND EDITION.

JOHN HEYWOOD,
Deansgate and Ridgefield, Manchester;
and 11, Paternoster Buildings,
LONDON.
1886.

PREFACE.

To Francis W. Newman, Emeritus Professor of University College, London.

Dear Mr. Newman,

I do not offer this dedication to you as a tribute of friendship, nor on a calculation of reflected literary fame, but rather because, differing from each other widely in country and creed, we are united in the assertion of principles without which religion and patriotism are dangerous in the very degree that they are sincere.

The Irish difficulty must be settled by the English party of progress. All the attempts to hinder this consummation, by whomever they are made, and in whatever form they appear, come ultimately from the enemies of both countries.

Organised Christianity has made for itself out of the deadliest vapours of earth a doctrinal heaven, from which it looks complacently on all human wrongs. Abjuring merit, it reprobates Ireland. The lever that can move it must be planted on a secular fulcrum.

I have come to those two conclusions unexpectedly, and avow them unwillingly; but in proportion to the force of the reasons that overcome my prepossessions must be the distinctness of the avowal.

Some persons, not indisposed to act fairly towards Ireland, are of opinion that it is inexpedient and unnecessary to revive or make known the history of the past. Concessions that are not acknowledged reversals of an evil policy are acts of impatience, not of justice, and convey by the manner of their bestowal a charge of unreasonable agitation. The tone of haughty superiority that prevails between rival nations should have no more right to exist in England towards Ireland than in Lancashire towards Yorkshire.

The first thing to be done is to substitute in the national conscience and in all public utterances the necessity of a real and willing union with Ireland, for the necessity of a mere union. When this position is taken, the end is in view and almost gained. I am sure you are ready to take it, and that you represent a large and increasing body of Englishmen.

I am, dear Mr. Newman,

Sincerely yours,

W. A. O'CONOR.

CONTENTS.

CHAPTER I.
PEACEFUL SETTLERS AND WARLIKE INVADERS.

SECTION | PAGE
I.—Introductory 1
II.—The Irish People 3
III.—Norman Invaders 7
    The Scoti 7
IV.—The Attacotti 9
    Moran 10
    The Boarian Tribute 11

CHAPTER II.
PEACE SUPERSEDES WAR.

I.—Scotic and Irish Influences 12
    Scotland Founded 13
II.—Early Irish Christians 14
    Pelagius 15
    St. Patrick 15
    The Irish Converted 16
III.—The Irish Convert the Scoti 17
    St. Columbkille 20
IV.—Irish Missionaries 23
    Irish Character 27
V.—Growing Peace and Prosperity 28

CHAPTER III.
PEACE ASSAILED BY NORMAN INVASIONS.

I.—Norman Invaders 30
    The Eugenians and Dalcassians 30
    Turgesius 31
    Irish Patience 32
II.—Fresh Invaders 33
III.—A Twofold Ireland 35
    Erigena 37
IV.—Fresh Invaders 37
    The Founders of Dublin 39
V.—Brian Boru 40
    Battle of Clontarf 43

CHAPTER IV.
PEACE AGAIN SUPERSEDES WAR.

I.—The O'Briens 45
    The O'Conors 47
    Dermot MacMurrogh 48
II.—Mystery of Irish History 49
    Source of Irish Distractions 50

CHAPTER V.
THE NORMANS.

I.—The Normans at Home 51
II.—The Normans in France 52
III.—The Normans in England 53
IV.—The Normans in Wales 56

CHAPTER VI.
SECTION   PEACE DISTURBED BY ANGLO-NORMAN INVASION.   PAGE

I.—Capture of Wexford 59
    Surrender of Dublin 60
II.—Landing of Raymond 61
    Terrorism 62
III.—Landing of Earl Pembroke 63
    Abolition of Slavery 64
IV.—The Faithful Norman 66
    Pembroke Recalled 66
V.—Landing of Henry II. 67
VI.—Possible Results of Henry's Stay 69
    The Real Question 69
VII.—Murder of O'Ruark 70
    Treaty of Windsor 71
VIII.—Landing of Prince John 72

CHAPTER VII.
THE O'CONORS.

I.—Cathal Crovderg 75
    Battles between Armed and Unarmed Troops 76
    Distinct Classes in Ireland 77
    Similar distinction in England 78
II.—King John in Ireland 79
III.—Hugh O'Conor 83
IV.—Mildness of Irish Law 84
V.—Edward Bruce 87
    Felim O'Conor 88
    Battle of Athenry 90
VI.—O'Neill's Letter to the Pope 91
    Battle of Faughard 92

CHAPTER VIII.
THE FITZGERALDS.

I.—Consequences of Bruce's Invasion 93
    Exaggeration of Irish Character 94
II.—Statute of Kilkenny 97
III.—Richard II. in Ireland 98
    His Second Visit 100
IV.—Dawn of Liberty in England 101
    Corrupt Deputies 103
    Disintegration of Irish Chieftaincies 104
V.—English Civil Wars 106
VI.—Irish Civil Wars 109
    Anglo-Norman Feuds 110
VII.—Lambert Simnel 112
    Battle of Stoke 113
    Poyning's Act 114
VIII.—Rebellion of Silken Thomas 118
IX.—Revolution in English Land Tenure 120
X.—Reformation in England 121
    Reformation in Ireland 122
XI.—England and Ireland 126
    Ireland a Corn-growing Country 127
XII.—The Anglo-Norman seeks Foreign Aid 129
    Rebellion of Desmond 129

CHAPTER IX.
THE O'NEILLS.

I.—Shane O'Neill 131
    His Character 135
    His Government 135

CONTENTS. vii.

SECTION		AGE
II.—The Earl of Essex		136
	Rory O'More	137
	The Irish People	138
III.—Hugh O'Neill, Earl of Tyrone		139
IV.—Battle of Yellow Ford		144
V.—Retrospect		146
	Carew in Munster	147
VI.—Lord Mountjoy in Ulster		148
VII.—The Spaniards at Kinsale		151
VIII.—The Flight of the Earls		154
	Confiscation of Ulster	155

CHAPTER X.
THE CATHOLIC CONFEDERATION.

I.—Confiscation in Leinster		156
II.—The Graces		157
III.—The English Rebellion		158
	Wentworth in Ireland	159
IV.—Puritan Governors		161
	Loyal Insurrection	162
V.—Reported Massacre		163
VI.—English Parliament Foments the Insurrection		165
	The Adventurers	166
VII.—Convention of Kilkenny		166
	Owen O'Neill	167
VIII.—Irish Troops in England and Scotland		168
	Puritanism	169
IX.—Duplicity of the King		170
	Battle of Benburb	172
X.—Dublin Surrendered by Ormond		172
	Execution of Charles	173
	Death of Owen O'Neill	174

CHAPTER XI.
CROMWELL.

I.—Drogheda		177
	Storm of Clonmel	180
II.—Collapse of the Royal Cause		181
	Confiscation	183

CHAPTER XII.
THE REVOLUTION.

I.—The Restoration		185
	Act of Settlement	186
II.—English Catholicism Forced on Ireland		187
III.—King James in Ireland		189
	Treaty of Limerick	190
IV.—Macaulay's Account of James' Parliament		191

CHAPTER XIII.
PARLIAMENTARY DEPENDENCE.

I.—Object of Penal Laws		198
II.—Prohibition of Irish Imports		200
III.—Protestants Aspire after Independence		202
	Confirmation of Articles of Limerick	203
IV.—Whigs and Tories		204
	Bill to Prevent the Growth of Popery	205
	Trade and Tillage Suppressed	208
	Molyneux	210
	Resumption of King William's Grants	210

SECTION	PAGE
V.—Swift's Writings	211
Froude's Interpretations	213
Berkeley's Writings	215
VI.—Wood's Halfpence	217
Swift's Modest Proposal	219
VII.—Land Monopoly	220
Irish Landlordism	222
The Whiteboys	224
Father Sheehy	225
VIII.—Irish Protestantism	228
Catholic Industry	229
Catholic Association	231
Catholic Relief Bill	233
IX.—Definition of Political Liberty	235
State of Irish House of Commons	236
Legislative Union Contemplated	237
Irish Volunteers	239
Independence of Irish Parliament	241
Catholics and Protestants	241
How Freedom is Won	242

CHAPTER XIV.
PARLIAMENTARY INDEPENDENCE.

I.—Grattan and Flood	245
Grattan Quarrels with the Volunteers	245
II.—Police Bill	246
Orde's Propositions	248
English Trade	249
III.—Parliamentary Reform Sought	250
The Volunteer Organisation Dies Out	251
IV.—Fresh Conquest Provided For	251
United Irishmen	252
Orangeism	253
Irish Leaders Seized	255
The People Goaded to Rebellion	256
The French at Killala	256
Good Conduct of the Rebels	257
V.—The Union	258
Emmett's Insurrection	261

CHAPTER XV.
CATHOLIC COMMITTEE.

I.—The Veto	265
II.—State of England in 1815	267
State of Ireland	269
III.—Catholic Association	272
Clare Election and Emancipation	274

CHAPTER XVI.
REPEAL OF THE UNION.

I.—Repeal Association and Free Trade League	275
Clontarf Meeting Forbidden	277
O'Connell Prosecuted	278
Tenant Right	279
II.—Young Ireland	280
Mitchell	282
Famine and Feasts	284
Encumbered Estates Act	285
III.—Tenant League	285
Disestablishment	286
Manchester Rescue	287
Phœnix Park Murder	287

HISTORY OF THE IRISH PEOPLE.

CHAPTER I.

PEACEFUL SETTLERS AND WARLIKE INVADERS.

SECTION I.

I SHALL attempt to sketch the history of a people who, dating their origin from a period anterior to the common distinctions of race, have been able to accommodate themselves rapidly to every phase of enlightenment, and deriving their rights from a source unreached by the usurpations of power, could never reconcile themselves to any form of slavery; who have triumphed over the hindrances that have always been considered fatal to virtue and progress; who protected themselves against the vices which political servitude engenders by a greater measure of that individual independence which the most liberal Constitutions often fail to produce; who, debarred from taking their place among free States, aspired nevertheless, amidst unequalled disasters and discouragements, to discharge all the functions which mankind expect from self-regulated communities; who, deprived of the air and light in which the fruits of civilization are ripened, successfully strove to supply the deficiency by the vigour of their genius and the warmth of their affections; who, without a government of their own, have sent forth colonies to aid in founding vast republics, and rulers to hold the reins of empire when they proved too weighty for the grasp of ordinary kings; without an army of their own, have directed the tide of conquest in every land; without a parliament, have laid all legislative assemblies under obligation by the wisdom of their statesmen and the unrivalled eloquence of their orators; without a press, have added the choicest ornaments to the classic literature of the world; without religious freedom have guided theological thought; and without political freedom have taught other States, vainly calling themselves free, what freedom means, and how it may be permanently won.

And it will be necessary to remind the reader when presenting him with this outline, that while it reflects only the dawn of a popular life struggling through slowly dissolving clouds, it is the repetition of what once and again has already taken place in the career of the same people,—that a former day of brightness commenced for them and was overcast; and yet another day arose with brighter promise and was turned into blood; and that therefore any temporary defeat or dull procrastination can be to their children only as the short night of repose that invigorates them for the morning of unrepressed development that will come at last.

B

We have two ancestries—one retrospective and human, the other progressive and divine. In dark and barbarous ages man classed himself with the lower orders of creation, which were made after their kind, and follow in the steps of their parents by an unconscious instinct. He supposed that he too was made after his kind, and he took pride in the brutal strength and passions of his forefathers, the objects of his emulation marking the lowness of his estimate of human destiny. He is gradually learning that he is made after the image of the just God, and that his true political birth dates from the hour when he becomes conscious of this immediate parentage.

The cherished and blazoned reminiscences of ancient barbarism that from the pages of a few modern writers throw their lurid glare into our purer day, may serve to warn us from the worship of antiquity. They exhibit the habits of former generations more truly than laboured dissertations on their virtues, because they set before us the standard of ambition which their descendants have actually inherited. The savage deeds which we boastfully ascribe to our forefathers are likely to be true, because we must have received from them the savage disposition that can feel complacency in such a retrospect.

Very different from those survivals of anarchy is that loving reverence which seeks to endow the elders of our race with the pious and peaceful attributes that are to mark the era of our ultimate civilization. We are reminded by its tendency that the character of a people is made up of what the national mind originates or selects, as much as of what it indiscriminately inherits. Aspiration is more potent than transmission. Men of higher type differ from men of lower mainly in having an ideal apart from their actual lot; and if they have fed their eyes on some bright prospect of future glory until, when they look backwards, they behold its vision glowing in the dense obscurity of the past, we have no uncertain promise that, even if they fail to realise it, they at least will preserve it undefiled. And this in itself would be a great achievement, and worthy of record.

The biography of an individual does not chiefly relate whether his days sped in happiness, or were stagnant in misery, but whether his mind was beautiful, and whether it grew to greatness alike on his prosperous or adverse fortunes. So it is with the lives of nations. The tale of a career broken and deformed by calamities, or of a series of brilliant and uninterrupted successes, is not a nation's history, but whether its purpose was noble or ignoble, whether its spirit rose or sank under the blows or caresses of fortune, whether the shout of its triumph or the sigh of its disaster has most of hope for the world.

The task of the historian is to help in shaping and refining the mind of his country, and in raising it above the shocks of earthly vicissitudes by training it into conformity with the unchanging purpose of creation. He must be the representative in his work of its best qualities. He must embody its dearest and loftiest hope. By being filled with the purest national life he deciphers the past and more than prophesies the future. The presumption of undertaking to write history is not excused by the possession of great abilities, but by a motive that acts with the force of duty.

Whatever origin be assigned to man, the distinctions of race must ultimately be traced to local and political sources. The historical writer who proposes to himself any useful object, does not properly engage his thoughts on the collisions of rival sections of the human family whose separation has been effected, but rather on the causes that produced, and are still widening their differences. It may be the part of the short-sighted politician, or of the hired literary bravo, to pile fuel on the flame of national animosities and to assume the immutability of race. But any person who can conceive an idea of man, and not merely of Kelt or Teuton, must prefer considering what unruly passion of the soul, matured into a principle in a long season of anarchy, or what abnormal correlation of interests, preventing the conclusions of reason, has warped the common children whether of heaven or earth, into a hating and scorning dissimilarity.

The two influences that most powerfully affect the disposition of individuals and the organization of societies, are the family tie and conquest. The wounds inflicted by conquest may cease to bleed, but they never cease to deform. Claiming irresponsible authority, it stamps a repulsive likeness to violated virtue on its bastard progeny of laws and standards. The systematizing faculty which it arrogates it employs only to make its wrongs indelible. Devastating in liquid fire, it cools and petrifies in legislation. The patriarchal form of government not only establishes the natural origin of all just rights, but modulates the tone in which they are to be asserted, and supplies the weapons with which they are to be recovered when lost. To this form of government the Irish people unfalteringly aspire. Deprived of its shelter, they have never forfeited its characteristic virtues.

To trace back the history of a country that has lost its liberty, and no longer pines for its restoration, is a melancholy and a worthless task. No encouragement can be won by demonstrating the high lineage of a prerogative whose very grave has not left a scar upon the soil. It is in every respect different to contemplate, as we now propose doing, the past of a people in whose veins still runs the warm blood of the world's youth, and who cannot endure the loss of their self respect. When we examine their earliest annals, we see preparations for contests which are still future; when we enter on the period of actual conflict, we view another part of the battle-field of to-day. The unbroken continuity of the struggle is not, however, by any means the most interesting and momentous fact that claims our notice. They who have never surrendered their freedom, hold it and defend it by its original title of reason and nature. It is because Ireland has always striven that she now strives with the arms of argument. She remonstrates to this hour with the robber, who, before the dawn of history, ravaged her shore. We are reviewing no battle of races, but a struggle between the rational right of self-government and the irrational and inhuman wrong of conquest.

Section II.

In very ancient times a medium-sized, dark-haired people proceeded from the eastern cradle of our kind, and gradually spread over the west of Europe. Some of their descendants, known as Iberi or Basques, still occupy the mountainous regions of France and Spain; and others form a considerable though not distinct element in the population of Ireland, and in a greater degree, and with a nearer approach to distinctness, of Great Britain. From the evidence furnished by their sepulchral mounds, we learn that those primeval colonists possessed at the remotest date accessible to investigation, remarkable capacities of refinement and intellect. In those districts where their race survives in its purity, the inhabitants are distinguished by grace of manner, gentleness of disposition, and a deeply marked religious temperament.

The physical distinctions of race are produced by differences of climate and peculiarities of region, operating during many centuries. There are probably few natural divisions of the surface of the earth which have not a tendency to mould distinct types of men by the continued influences of sun and soil. However long a people may have lived in any particular country, however indelible may seem the constitutional bent which they may have received from its conditions, they cannot become dwellers in a foreign land without slowly and inevitably growing into the likeness in shape and colour of its original and indigenous inhabitants.

We are, therefore, not accountable for the hue of our skins, nor for the measure of our stature, nor for those accidents of mood which have no ethical value. Here nature meant that there should be variety as unquestionably as elsewhere she meant that there should be uniformity. While all that is unimportant is beyond our control, the formation of our political bias is voluntary, and our moral standards can always be corrected by our reason. It is the especial privilege of man that he can substitute right for precedent, and truth for tradition. Even if the sacredness of antiquity have its undeniable claims, the responsibility of selection still remains. Most modern nations have a varied stock of progenitors from any of which they may trace their descent. The choice proceeds from, and strongly re-acts upon, our moral bias.

We shall only acknowledge an obvious fact and recognise a providential arrangement, if we adopt as the earliest representatives of our people, a tribe who took possession of our fields without human opposition, whose progress was unmarked by bloodstained and burning homesteads, whose children were neither disciplined in cruelty by the arrogant relation of their father's crimes, nor reconciled to injustice by enjoying the proceeds of another's toil, nor perverted from the pursuit of excellence by inheriting the fictitious and ready-made superiority of caste. The first ancestry of the Irish people is represented by justice.

Those first settlers were followed at an unknown but very remote date, by some tribes of the great Aryan family who, issuing still from the east, and travelling by some immediate route so that they did not suffer transformation into Kelt or German by the way, brought with them their arts, their customs, and their religion.

The region of unshadowed skies and vast horizons is suggestive of one infinite Deity by the homogeneousness of the sphere which an intuition of the soul conceives to be His dwelling place. The Aryans worshipped light, the Heaven-Father. This sublime primitive creed degenerated into gloomy and cruel rites as it slowly filtered through the dark and savage scenery of the north, and the God of light was changed into or associated with the god of the thunder and the tempest. No such depravation took place in Ireland. As the earth rolls its plains and mountains towards the dawn, so rose the spirit of the western isle from the mists of the far Atlantic, to greet the message from a brighter clime. The west embraced and enshrined in all its kindling splendour the promise of the east. The fact symbolises, if it has not helped to shape, the story of our land. While other nations have lowered religion to the meanness of their desires, Ireland through all the rigours of fortune has preserved the ideal of her youth, and with unmatched fidelity has scornfully turned from the taunting challenge with which her jealous enemies would tempt her from her grand devotion.

A rich crop of sacred emblems and edifices sprang from the soil at the first breath of this spiritual spring-time, and became perennial. A new style of architecture to which a happier future will do justice was invented; a new style of ornamentation which modern art has not rivalled was elaborated. Temples limited in size, but compact and perfect, intended to stimulate worship, and not like later structures to stand as exhaustive expressions of zeal, substitutes for holiness and monuments of human vanity, grew from the rocks. Towers of incomparable workmanship, pre-Christian crosses, veritable tokens of the nation's mind, stone circles and pillars, whose ruins seem more natural than the tempest-riven crags that stand beside them, literally covered the island, and silently testify to this day of a once prosperous, peaceful, and abounding population. No mountain is so bare, no islet so rugged, no headland so sequestered, no forest or morass so inaccessible, as not to possess imperishable relics of thronging worshippers.

The imaginative Greeks gathering hints from Phenician traders of mysterious islands in an unknown sea, and yielding to that clinging belief in some blessedness as yet unattained, which, too easily attracted by earth, droops its wearied flight towards any spot that is hallowed by distance, conceived that here were situated the Elysian fields. In the "Argonautics," a poem written 500 years before Christ, the name of Iernis occurs. In the record of an expedition, which took place as some suppose 500 years earlier, the island of the Hyberni is mentioned as having been known from ancient times as the "Sacred Isle."

At a time when the most celebrated states of history did not yet exist, Ireland in her ocean solitude was running the cycle of a peculiar civilization, possessed a literature, wrought in metals, and was directing all her resources to the cultivation of a religious sentiment which was to fit her when the appointed time came for the reception of a sublimer revelation. Her actual readiness in after days, notwithstanding the incessant inroads of barbarians which remind us of the Satanic wiles, that as legends tell us, sought to distract medieval saints from their dreams of heaven, proved that her discipline was not in vain. The unquenchable fervour traceable in part to that mystical past, was only faintly figured by the everlasting fires that burned on her shrines. The island of Anglesea, the part of South Britain nearest to her shores, borrowed her light and spread it onwards. The old myth which relates that the masses of Stonehenge were transported from Ireland has a meaning as real as the rocks themselves. Religion represents our second ancestry.

A craving for the infinite is the depth in which the immortality of a people must be fixed, and a deathless sense of justice is the corner stone of its foundation. Believers in the present, and worshippers of success, have but a feeble vitality, even in their best hours. It is the encounter with adversity that tests the toughness of a nation's life. In a world of changes like ours where the race is only beginning, and the goal and the prize are only dimly discerned, the final victory, whatever it be, can more surely be predicted as in store for those who have survived the storm, than for those who with selfish violence have monopolised the sunshine. Far-seeing ingrained justice alone can withstand and out-live triumphant injustice.

States founded on wrong, and hungering only with the senses, derive all their strength from immediate success, and if they are deprived of its support, they die. The vanquished giant drew fresh vigour from contact with his mother earth, and perished when held aloft from her embrace. The people who trust in right, which alone is immortal, when overthrown in the struggle, always fall upon heaven, and they will never perish while their nature remains unchanged.

According to the ancient Irish chronicles the original owners of the country were the Fomorians, a people of prehistoric arrival and extraction, who supported themselves by fishing and fowling.[1] They were found in possession of the island by Partholan and his followers, who, steering their course through the Mediterranean sea, and leaving Spain on their right, at length reached Ireland about 2,200 years before Christ. The four sons of Partholan bore names, whose meaning was Government, Inheritance of Property, Division of Land, and Chieftainship; and the names of his Druids signified Intelligence, Knowledge, and Inquiry.[2]

Such is the account given by the bards of the earliest colonizations of Ireland: the first by a primitive and uncultured race, whose habits are recorded in the flint weapons, most incorrectly termed Kelts, found buried in the soil; the second by a people of whose advanced civilization the golden ornaments dug from the same source are unmistakable tokens.

The united Iberian and Aryan tribes (from the former of which the country was called Hibernia), known in Irish history respectively as Fomorians and Partholanians, were the first occupants of the land, and their descendants ever afterwards formed the bulk and basis of its population. When we speak of the Irish people, distinguishing them from the Scotic or Norman chiefs, we really refer to that portion of the inhabitants of our island who are sprung in part lineally, but altogether politically and morally, from the earliest settlers.

This original people of Ireland, its rightful owners and first civilizers, were reduced to inferiority and obscurity by successive hordes of barbarian invaders. Those invaders one after the other were trodden down to the level of those whom they themselves had each helped in turn to

[1] Keating, p. 116. [2] Ibid, pp. 119, 121, Notes.

subjugate and despoil. But when compelled to share their fortunes, they became participators and heirs of their rights, their virtues, and their genius; and if we would seek for the men who, at home or abroad, have been an honour to their country, we shall not as a rule discover them either in the rank of the last conquerors, or in any preceding tribe who have gained or maintained a position in that rank, but we shall find them, in all tribes and races alike, after they have been purified by the sufferings and inspired by the faith of the Irish people.

Section III.

Foremost of the assailing hordes, who destroyed the ancient institutions of the country, were the Nemedians, so called from their leader Nemedius.[1] They established themselves on the northern coast, and employed some of the Fomorians to build forts for them; taking care immediately afterwards to put the architects to death, lest they might undo their work. They then made war on the natives, and defeated them in three battles; but were totally overcome in a fourth, and forced to leave the country, with the exception of a remnant, who were allowed to occupy a separate district under their own chiefs.

The successful resistance made against the invading Nemedians, a rare occurrence in early history, proves that, though the sensitive nationality of later times, which regards every inch of the soil as sacred, was as yet unknown, the Irish were capable of making a united effort, and when taken together with the tradition of their being builders, while their enemies were ignorant of the art, affords a confirming proof of their superior civilization. Marauding or invading tribes are by the nature of the case compelled to combine for the purposes of attack. Nothing but a growing spirit of enlightened union will induce even two tribes, much less all the tribes of a country, to act in concert for self-defence.

The conspiring instinct of invasion was as yet, however, stronger than the patriotic sentiment. A simultaneous inroad from three different quarters by the next assailants, the Belgæ, brought one half of the island under their sway.

The political disintegration which naturally follows on the settlement of foreign tribes in the heart of a country and the constant and harassing attacks of fresh enemies from without, soon took place. Ireland, hitherto one, fell asunder into five States, North and South Munster, Leinster, Connaught, and Ulster, each governed by its own ruler.[2]

But the distracted land was not permitted sufficient time to contemplate its condition, or to devise means for repairing its losses. A new body of invaders, the Danans, overthrew the Belgæ in one great battle, and the Irish in another, and became masters of the island. The conquered Belgæ obtained a free territory in Connaught.

The next successful invaders, and the last until the time of the Anglo-Normans, were the Scoti (from whom the island was named Scotia). As all the bardic compositions which treat of ancient Ireland were written at their dictation; and to gratify their pride and vainglory, we must explain the strange tales which are told concerning their

[1] Keating, p. 121. [2] Keating, p. 129.

immediate predecessors, the Danans, as fables invented to exhibit the prowess and magnanimity of those who overcame them, as well as to give a sort of moral right to their conquest.

The Danans, we are told, were not only warriors who fought with the weapons of ordinary warfare, but they were moreover magicians armed with talismans of super-human efficacy. They had overcome the Belgæ by investing themselves with a magical mist, and thus penetrating unseen into the country until they could engage the enemy under conditions of their own selection. When the Scoti, who were also known as the Milesians, from Milesius, the father of the leaders of the expedition, approached in their ships, the Danans first wrapped the island in a fog, so as to render it invisible, and then by their spells drove the fleet from the shore, so that they were forced to sail all round the coast before they could find a secure landing place. Undaunted by those difficulties they succeeded in disembarking their troops, and having met the Danan leaders, attended by their chief magicians, they challenged them either to resign the sovereignty of the island, or meet them in immediate fight. The Danans replied that they would submit to the decision of one of the Scotic leaders, whom they named, and do whatever he pronounced to be just. The umpire thus appointed gave the chivalrous sentence that his people should again go on board their vessels, and dare the perils of a second landing, which if they could successfully accomplish, they should possess the country. Both parties consented, and the Scoti went on board their ships. But as soon as they had put out a short distance from land the Danans by their incantations raised a terrific storm, in which a great portion of the fleet was destroyed. Eber and Erimhon, the only sons of Milesius who escaped, landed the forces that remained to them, and having overthrown the Danans in two sanguinary engagements, succeeded to the dominion of the island. Eight chiefs and eight principal ladies perished at this time. One of the latter, who had survived the perils of shipwreck and battle, died of shame at being seen unclothed by her husband as she came from bathing.

According to the native annals, the Partholanians, Nemedians, Belgæ, Danans, and Scoti, were alike descended from Magog the son of Japheth, and with the exception of the Partholanians, who came from Greece, were Scythians by nation. Under this adaptation to Biblical and classical nomenclature are couched the simple facts that they were all branches of the Aryan family, that the Partholanians sailed directly from the East, and that the other tribes had been for a long time settled in the north-west of Europe, commonly known as Scythia, where they lost their religion and sank into savagery, and from whence they successively made their descents upon Ireland.[1]

SECTION IV.

It is related that Eber and Erimhon divided the island between them, the former taking the Southern, and the latter the Northern half;

---

[1] The dates of those invasions can be conjectured by comparing them with cotemporaneous revolutions on the Continent. See Sullivan's Introduction to O'Curry, and the Appendix to "Cambrensis Eversus," Vol. I.

that in a short time they quarrelled, and a battle having ensued, that Erimhon slew Eber, and became sole monarch.

Those general statements must not be understood in the sense which modern ideas would assign to them. The actual occupation of the country by the Scoti must have been limited for some time after their first success. It is most probable that while they overcame all resistance and made their name formidable at the point where they landed, their arrival was unheard of in the distant parts of the island; that as time advanced, they gained a nominal sovereignty over the five provincial kings, and that they sought no further advantage until their predatory impulses were stimulated anew, and their growing passion for warlike renown inspired fresh aggressions.

The swarms of redundant or ejected populations who issued from the place of their birth in search of new dwellings, had but the vaguest ideas of a home or a country as objects of permanent attachment. As they had no national associations when they started on their expeditions, we cannot expect to see them forthwith proceeding to the establishment of a nation. They had as little conception of the conquest of a whole country, as an abstract intention, as a tiger has of the subjugation of a herd of cattle. The instincts of the restless plunderer, and not the comprehensive scheme of the organising conqueror, directed the course of events. They landed, slaughtered, robbed, enjoyed their booty, and extended their ravages according to the exigency or the caprice of the day.

The original Irish and the several settlements of successive invaders remained still separate and hostile, so that when the last conquerors sought to increase their territories, or to assert their authority by the exaction of tribute, they found no difficulty in overcoming their disunited and desultory attempts at self-defence. But it is only in keeping with the character of the times to infer that the Scoti, for a considerable period after their arrival in Ireland, made incursions by sea rather than by land, and found a more congenial scope for their adventurous spirit in plundering the coasts of Britain, than in systematizing their conquests in their lately acquired home.

A wide-spread insurrection of the native races, while their principal strength was occupied in those foreign wars, compelled them to think of consolidating their acquisitions, and strengthening the base of their future operations. This rising was made by the rent-paying tribes, the Attacotti[1] of Roman writers. The normal progress in possession of land is from the common occupation by the tribe to the more or less independent ownership by its individual members. It would seem that this latter stage had been partially reached when the ancient usages of the country were broken up by repeated invasions, and that the Attacottic revolution was occasioned by the universal impatience of the people at the imposition of rent or tribute which conquest had introduced. The Danans and Belgæ had imposed similar exactions when they had the power, but now when they found themselves under the same yoke, they rose in rebellion with the rest of the nation against their tyrants.

The events of this troubled period are obscure in the distance, and confused by the studied misrepresentations of the Scotic historians, who,

[1] Attacotti is a Latinized form of an Irish word, which means "rent payers."

as usual in such cases, have described this effort for freedom as a massacre. But the true lineaments of human nature in its grandest proportions can be dimly yet unerringly discerned through the clouds of prejudice. A native monarch was raised to the throne by the aggrieved people, and on his death his son Moran was appointed his successor.

The man who is fittest to rule is always unwilling to wear the vain insignia of power, and prefers to serve the state. Moran, anxious only for the nation's welfare, and for settled government, sought to reconcile conflicting interests by restoring the heir of the Scotic line, and accepting the office of chief judge for himself. The son of the stranger reigned, but native justice and piety presided in his councils, and a period of wise government produced its immediate harvest in the gratitude of an easily contented people. The monarch by universal consent was styled The Righteous.

His successor was a ruler of that vulgar type which, conscious of selfish ends, desires independence of the people's hate, and not the free homage of their love. Measures suggested by jealousy and suspicion were taken to consolidate the authority of the dominant tribe. As a preventive against popular insurrections for the future, the subject people, who were massed together in distinct localities by the encroachments of successive invading bodies, were distributed through the whole country; and thus weakened by dispersion, were further kept in check by the erection of numerous strongholds from which their movements could be watched, and mutual support afforded in case of attack. In the prosecution of this policy a general resistance was provoked, and countless so-called battles were fought; but the advantage a central power possesses when its plans are unsuspected, and its measures instantaneous, gained an easy victory in every case over a population unaccustomed to war, and naturally but prematurely reliant on the claims of merit and justice.

Having established the Scotic supremacy, the monarch, whose name was Tuathal, convened the national assembly, which according to custom met periodically at Tara, and exacted an oath of fealty to himself and his family. He further increased his resources, and strengthened his dominion, by adding as an appanage to the crown a territory formed from portions of the four provinces at the point where they met, which is now known as the County of Meath. By assuming the regulation of public worship, which already under royal patronage had begun to degenerate into idolatry, and making it a source of revenue to the provincial kings, he bound them more firmly to his dynasty.

A tragic event which occurred in his own family, was fabricated under his management into an additional buttress of his throne. He had two daughters, one of whom was espoused to the king of Leinster. Not long after his nuptials this prince appeared again at the palace of his father-in-law, and falsely asserting that his wife was dead, asked for the second daughter to take her place. His request was granted, and he returned home with his new bride, who, unexpectedly meeting the first wife when she arrived, was so overcome by shame and indignation that she fell dead on the spot. Her sister soon after died of sorrow at her untimely end. When the monarch heard of the fate of his children, and of the fraud that had caused it, he appealed to all the chieftains of the country for aid in punishing misconduct signalized by such mournful results. A general meeting of forces answered his summons, and the people of Leinster, moved too strongly by sympathy with the suffering father, instead of throwing the sole responsibility on the guilty prince, undertook that they and their posterity would pay a large biennial tribute of cattle and other property to the monarch and his successors in compensation for the wrong which had been done. By bestowing this fine equally among the kings of the other three provinces, the monarch hoped to oppose a continual obstacle alike to rivalry and combination among the nobles.

A plan for stabilitating a throne, that neglects or undermines the happiness of the people, resembles an attempt to make a building safe by increasing the strength of its materials and the complexity of its joinings, without giving any attention to the foundation on which it is raised. The whole island during centuries was embroiled in savage wars that arose from the enforcement of the celebrated Boarian[1] tribute. In less than half a century after the death of Tuathal, a contest arose between the monarch and the king of Leinster of that day, which ended in a partition of the island between the two combatants. This division, as before, lasted only a short time, but it gave a proverbial designation to the southern and northern portions as Mogh's half and Conn's half, and left a tempting track for the strides of future ambition.

Other similar encroachments of the ruling class on the original rights of the nation were equally disastrous in their consequences. By the tribal custom the king or chief was chosen by popular election from the family which represented the tribe. A wide-spreading fount of discord was opened by the efforts of the various kings to forestall the popular voice, and limit the area from which a successor was to be appointed.

One consoling thought greets the student of this tangled maze of conflict. The long period of the nation's life that elapsed before the northern invasions began is without record, because there were no intestine wars to celebrate. The dark clouds pregnant with fires of civil discord that hang over Ireland's history were wafted from foreign skies.[2]

[1] So called from the great number of cows it included, *bo* being the Irish word for cow.

[2] About the year 1774 the workmen in the collieries on the coast of Antrim unexpectedly broke through the rock into a cavern. This was found to be a complete gallery with branching chambers, and pillars left at intervals to support the roof, the work of people as expert in this business as the present generation, who must have lived before the times of the earliest warlike invaders of Ireland. See Hamilton, "On the Coast of Antrim," p. 33. The same writer says that under the turf bogs, and on the summits of mountains to which the great population of the country had not yet come (1786), the marks of the plough can be traced. He adds that within his own knowledge golden ornaments of unknown use have been found to the amount of near one thousand pounds in value.

CHAPTER II.

PEACE SUPERSEDES WAR.

SECTION I.

FROM the time of Tuathal we may date the commencement of a new amalgamation of the different peoples, and a reversion to the more primitive and ruder form of the tribal system. The Scoti assumed the headship of the various tribes, restricted the inheritance of the tribe lands to their own race, and forbade all historical mention of the conquered people.[1]

But though the native inhabitants were thus eclipsed by their conquerors, we must not suppose that their real strength was lost or greatly impaired. Large numbers of them continued no doubt to dwell in the mountainous and forest regions out of the beaten paths of war. Others became followers of their chiefs in their contests with each other. Nor was their influence unfelt in winning their rulers to a wiser and more appreciative line of treatment.

That the ancient worship was occasionally recognised if not protected by the rulers, we gather from an incidental mention of an outrage which is of the kind usually committed by youthful insolence against the institutions of a subject race. In the reign of Cormac, a son of the king of Leinster, with several companions, made an attack on a convent of virgins, whose duty it was to keep the fires of the Sun and Moon burning, and having failed to violate, slew them. The monarch put twelve of the Leinster princes to death for their crime, and increased the regular tribute. This act of severity affords a proof that the virtues of the people had won the respect of their rulers, or at least that it was thought expedient to conciliate their good will by a display of impartial judgment.

The preservation of the Round Towers, in which sacred fires continually burned, during so many tumultuous centuries, is inexplicable unless we ascribe it to a prudent tolerance, or a sincere reverence for the popular religion.

It was from the page of history, not from the order of living facts and potent influences, that the Irish people passed for a space. The crash of arms and the cries of warriors are the only sounds which the annalist has recorded, but the deeds of a simple life and the rites of a simple creed, which need neither the poet's panegyric nor the historian's notice, pursued their course in silence and awaited the day.

The primitive inhabitants of Ireland had never molested their British neighbours, nor been molested by them. Ireland was a constant place of refuge for the Britons, when oppressed by the Romans or the Saxons. There is good reason for concluding that relations of the most amicable kind, religious and commercial, existed between the two islands. But the Scoti began to infest the coasts of Britain very soon

---

[1] It has been assigned as an additional explanation of the disappearance of the Plebeian tribes, that they mingled with the early Anglo-Norman and English settlers, and took their names.

after their settlement in Ireland. After the suppression of the Atta-cottic revolt, their invasions assumed the method and dimensions of permanent conquest. Cornwall and a large part of Wales became Scotic, and paid tribute to the Scotic kings. The Isle of Man was also conquered and colonized by them. In the reign of Constantine, in conjunction with the Picts, who had come to Ireland about the same time, and from the same region with them, they occupied London, and were overcome and expelled from the province only after a severe struggle. The Roman poet who celebrated the victory, describes "Ierne as mourning over the heaps of slaughtered Scoti." They renewed their attacks in 397 under Niall of the nine hostages,[1] on which occasion Claudian represents Britannia as trusting to the protection of Stilicho, the Roman general, when the "Scoti moved all Ierne, and the sea foamed with hostile oars." In 405 Niall was treacherously slain by a son of the king of Leinster on the banks of the Loire in Gaul. The Romans left Britain in 410, and the final invasion of that country by the Scoti took place under the successor of Niall, Dathi, who is said to have reigned over Erin, Alba (afterwards called Scotland), Britain, and as far as the mountains of the Alps, in which latter region he was killed by a flash of lightning.

A portion of the Picts migrated to Alba, and gradually extended themselves till they founded the Cumbrian or Strathclyde kingdom; proceeding from whence under Cynedda, they overcame the Scoti in Wales (450). On the other hand, a body of the Scoti settled in Alba at the close of the second century, were reinforced by fresh colonists in 503, and finally having overcome the Picts, founded the Scottish kingdom under Kenneth Mac Alpine in 849. The name Scotia gradually passed to the colony, and the parent country retained only its ancient appellation.

Those movements would have little interest for us were it not that bodies of native Irish formed the rank and file of the colonies and invading parties. The Scotic name remained dominant in North, and was submerged in conquest in West Britain, but we may in part ascribe the religious fervour that has never ceased to characterize both countries, as well as Cornwall and the Isle of Man, to the influence of their Irish occupancy, and to the men of Irish blood who remained after the Scotic leaders had disappeared before the jealous pride of the victor. Multitudes of the Attacotti or native Irish were also led by the Scotic monarchs in their remote invasions, and a large proportion of them preferred entering into the Roman service to returning to serfdom at home. They took share in the great wars of that period, and were stationed at Rome and in various other parts of Italy.[2]

The imagination is wrought upon with all the vividness of a tale of yesterday, when we think of those ancient sons of Ireland, who from no restlessness, no predatory habits of their own, were severed from their land, and compelled to make their home in a foreign clime. The simple-minded children of the glen and the mountain! Did their hearts sink

[1] So called because he received nine hostages, five from Ireland and four from Alba or Scotland.

[2] See Sullivan's Introduction to O'Curry.

as the world disclosed its wonders to their inexperienced eyes? Did they stand before the Colosseum in reverie, and hear the ripple of the rivulet by the grey cairn, and the song of the lark over the green fields, and see before them through their starting tears the hills of their childhood wrapt in tender mist? O our countrymen and our kindred, vanguard of the army of exiles whose ranks are still leaving our shores, may your path have been made easy for you in those dark days, may friends have come to you instead of those you left behind, may loving voices have cheered you when memory was too busy, may loving hands have smoothed your pillow in the dread hour; and oh! may heaven have granted to you before the worst temptation had befallen your race, to be true to one another in presence of the stranger and the foe!

SECTION II.

The homage which a subjugating people pay to conscience is the depreciation, and, if possible, the political extinction, of their victims. The slave is oppressed not only by the degrading circumstances of his lot, but by the jealous sensitiveness of his master, who silences the clamour of remorse by making him, and of public opinion by declaring him, degraded. The arts and learning of the ancient Irish were ignored, and even their names suppressed by the Scoti, who regarded their own deeds of violence as the only becoming topic of commemoration, and the wild rhapsodies of their professional bards as the sublimest of human compositions.

The bent and affluence of the nation's intellect first displayed themselves, therefore, at a distance. Christianity had been sent to guide mankind into the path of virtue by the light of immortality. As the earliest invaders of Ireland of whom formal notice is left found the successors of previous ante-historic colonists in occupation of the land, so the earliest organized Christian mission came there to preach Christ to a people already through unknown sources not unacquainted with His name. In those virgin days of the Church the universal air was full of winged seeds of truth that floated on its currents, and here and there fell on fertile spots where they struck root and flourished. No land was so ready for the Sower as Ireland. But that section of the community which was specially prepared for the reception of the Gospel consisted of the ancient inhabitants, whose spiritual activity, even if tolerated by an unwilling measure of policy, would still be looked upon with secret dislike by the ruling class. The alliance of heaven with those whom we struggle to suppress and affect to despise is always distasteful to us.

The mind of the nation was forced to work in secret. Channels destined to direct the currents of thought through future times were hollowed out by the deep tides of irrepressible native energy, while all that caught the world's eye was a surface rippled by the combats of rival chieftains. It was the reverberation from the Continent of the beatings of her own heart that brought Christianity to Ireland in such a form as recommended it to the whole nation. The island was the sender before she became known as the receiver of missions. St. Mansuetus, first Bishop of Toul, in Lorraine, an eminent Christian Missionary of the apostolic age, is expressly said by his biographer to have been an Irishman. His companion, St. Beatus, the apostle of Switzerland and first Bishop of Lausanne, was probably his countryman. In the second century, during the reign of a Scotic king whose title distinguishes him as the hero of a hundred fights, St. Cathaldus is said to have issued from his Irish home as from the stillness of a monastery, to preach the Gospel to the people of Italy. The Christian poet Sedulius, who flourished in Italy about the end of the fourth century, was a native of Ireland.[1]

But the learning and ability that lay hid under the Scotic domination, were prominently displayed by the celebrated Pelagius.[2] Appearing at Rome in the beginning of the fifth century, and assisted by his compatriot Celestius, he taught in opposition to the depraved doctrines under which a widely prevalent immorality was sheltering itself, that obedience is better than abasement, that faith is to be tested by its strength to work and not by its mystic quality, that salvation is a state of attainment to be laboured for by all who will, and not a favour arbitrarily bestowed on a few, and that Christianity was meant to restore and not to stifle man's original constitution. Opinions such as these, tinged with a kindred Orientalism, and contrasting with a system framed in accommodation to a corrupt stage of society rather than for the correction of man's fallen nature, could not but arouse a fierce opposition in the Western Church. The scriptural and rational proofs by which they were supported being beyond the power of refutation were pronounced heretical. The lavish abuse of St. Jerome and the genius of Augustin were but feeble opponents to the blameless lives and calm reasonings of the Irish reformers. It was by imperial edicts and not by the force of argument or obloquy that their efforts were at last arrested, and their doctrines prevented from being either developed or rightly understood.

Having checked the heresy at its source, the orthodox party then proceeded to root it out wherever it had effected a lodgment. Britain was one of the regions particularly infested with Pelagianism, and accordingly in the year 429, Germanus, Bishop of Auxerre, and Lupus, Bishop of Troyes, were sent by the Gallican Church, with the approval of Pope Celestinus, to assist in its overthrow. Palladius, the deacon of Germanus, who had been sent to Rome to obtain the Papal sanction to the British mission, was himself consecrated by the Pope, and sent to the Christian Irish as their first Bishop. Patricius, one of those who had accompanied the Gallican Bishops into Britain, offered himself as an assistant to Palladius. He received his commission as a missionary priest from Germanus, and was on his way to Rome to receive consecration, when news of the death of Palladius, whose labours had not been successful, reached him. He was immediately consecrated Bishop, and proceeded to Ireland.

The country, family, and early life of St. Patrick are hidden in great obscurity. He was born most probably at Dumbarton,[3] where his father held the office of Decurio in the Roman service, went from there with his parents to Armoric Britain, where his family originally resided, and was thence carried captive to Ireland with many others by King Niall. He became the slave of Michul, an Antrim chief, and for six years

[1] Todd's "Life of St. Patrick," p. 190. [2] Neander, Vol. IV., p. 313. [3] Todd, p. 356.

herded his flocks on the mountains and in the woods. His mind thrown upon itself in his long hours of solitude, and stirred, it may be, at other seasons by the affectionate solicitations of the natives, who would have him join in the rites of their national worship, recurred to the forgotten creed of his childhood. The Christian doctrines he had then learned, whose meaning he had never properly apprehended, he nursed now by incessant prayer into a glowing and conscious life. No thought of spreading the Gospel seems to have occurred to him. Perhaps he did not consider himself sufficiently instructed in the facts and principles of Christianity to venture on becoming a teacher; and he may have even dreaded the contagious effect of the prevalent religious customs on his own overwrought feelings and unformed zeal.

There are no obscure indications in his autobiography that the imposing forms of sun-adoration left an impression on his memory which he could neither explain to himself nor quite cast off. The faith of his riper years has the comprehensive outlines of a true Christian pantheism. His vague unfolding belief leaned back into sympathy with the pure nature-worship that was reaching forward for further light. Thus he was prepared during his captivity by his intercourse with the people, and his acquaintance with their modes of life, to make known to them the God whom they worshipped in ignorance. Moved by dreams, he made his escape and returned to his own country, being at the time twenty-two years of age.

But a deeper affection than the associations of country or home had fixed itself unchangeably in his heart. The pleading voices of the loving people whom he had left haunted his slumbers, and besought him to come back and walk amongst them once more. After many years the wishes which his visions so faithfully interpreted were gratified. Fully instructed, formally authorised, and attended by numerous Irish Christians, he returned to Ireland, and planted the religion of the Cross from sea to sea. He not only made Ireland Christian, but he struck forth fountains of Christianity from every hill-side that have never ceased to flow. He filled the land with Christian seminaries. No like work was ever done. The Apostles planted churches on the way-side, over which the world's traffic passed and crushed out their existence. The labours of the Saint of Ireland were answered by a perennial harvest.

When we compare the result with the aspect of the country as described by writers of history, our first suspicion is that the conversion was only nominal, that the preacher merely gave a fresh name and more exciting variety to the inveterate habits of the people, and that the celebrated promulgation of the Christian faith was only a pagan revival. The slightest examination of the indisputable writings of St. Patrick leaves no shadow of pretext for any such supposition. We seem to behold what St. Paul would have been, had he laboured among kindlier and more responsive natures. Strength modulated by tenderness, zeal tempered by the tact of love, intimate acquaintance with Scripture irradiated by an inner spiritual perception that transformed the hard letter into a vehicle of light, marked the character of Ireland's great apostle.

There is only need to recognise and duly estimate one or two circumstances in addition to the temperament of St. Patrick's mind, and the special training it had undergone, in order to understand fully the secret of his exceptional success. He and his companions taught after the manner of the first teachers of Christianity. It matters little whether they were or were not the children of an elaborate ecclesiastical method, or believers in a complicated creed. The fact of all facts to be remembered by us is that together with the form and the symbol, they communicated the genial breath of heaven by which the seeds of truth are vitalized. In whatever reservoir the doctrines of their Christianity were formerly contained, in whatever channels it was taught to run, it was as a life that they poured it into living hearts.

And they did not come arrayed in the garb of power or wealth, but as poor and humble men they spoke to the lowly and the afflicted. For this is the second circumstance to be noted. It was to the ancient Irish people that the Gospel was first proclaimed, and among them that its first success was achieved. When the Christian religion was preached in Judea, kings and rulers refused to receive it. When in subsequent ages kings and rulers are said to have received the message in other countries, it was not the same message that had been preached in Judea, but a corrupted one. St. Patrick pointedly distinguishes the Hiberionaces, as he always calls the native Irish, from their conquerors the Scoti. He uses the word Scoti as synonymous with rulers and idolators.[1] He refers to the conversions that took place among them in terms of astonishment, such as the Baptist employed when he saw the Pharisees coming to enroll themselves under his banner. When Coroticus, son of Cynedda, having landed with a band of his followers in Ireland, slew some neophytes on the very day of their baptism, and carried others away to be sold as slaves, St. Patrick wrote with his own hand denouncing the barbarous deed, and declaring the men who did it to be not fellow-citizens of saints, but fellow-citizens of devils and associates of the Scoti.

The Scotic conversions are individual cases. The first of them is noted as a singular occurrence, and its subject, Dichu, was supposed to have acted in such marked contrast to the general conduct of his race, that a divine communication was said to have been made to the dying saint, specifying among other particulars that the descendants of Dichu should receive mercy and not perish. Michul, rather than submit to the humiliation of receiving spiritual freedom from his former slave, set fire to his house and perished in the flames. While the ordinary rule therefore has been that the people have accepted Christianity on the recommendation or authority of their rulers, the fact in Ireland from the commencement has been that the rulers have had no voice in dictating the popular faith, and have themselves in a large measure been dependent for their religion on the popular example. The dominant caste did not interpose any serious obstacle to the labours of the preachers of the Gospel, their conception of conquest not having reached that stage in which liberty of conscience among the conquered is considered an insult to the ruler. Still St. Patrick was not quite unopposed. He tells us

[1] Todd, p. 380.

that he was in some cases forced to conciliate hostile kings with gifts; and on one occasion at least his life was in danger from an attack made by an enraged chieftain.

Having travelled through the island, everywhere meeting a joyful reception from the lower classes, having established various religious and educational institutions, and founded the See of Armagh, he retired to an unpretending building erected on a spot which was consecrated by one of his early triumphs, and there he died.

After his death a feud arose between two clans for the possession of his remains. An attempt was made to terminate it by choosing two untamed oxen to carry the bier, and agreeing that wherever they stopped the body should be deposited. This device had only a temporary success in interrupting the contest, which soon burst out afresh. At length, when the rival hosts were about to engage in battle, their attention was arrested by the vision of a bier borne by two oxen, which appeared to lead each tribe into its own territory. The deception which must have been practised on one or either party by this contrivance need not be suffered in reference to the rival claims which are made by two contending ecclesiastical societies for the more precious inheritance of the saint's spiritual power. Both may enjoy it. It was unworldly devotion. It was fidelity to Ireland and Ireland's people. It was not to the claims of heaven represented by the tinsel of earthly rank that the Irish knelt for the boon of salvation. They received it from men of their own kind, speaking their language, and living their lives. No one, of whatever rank or race, has come to Ireland with these credentials who has not met a generous reverence and a loving gratitude.

Section III.

Some nations are set apart by Providence for the cultivation of the religious sentiment. Judea was one of these; Ireland is another. Christianity made no lasting impression on the communities whose names are associated with its original promulgation. They were only as lodging places where it rested on its way to a permanent residence. Like a train of light fuel they conveyed the flame to spots where it was destined to shine with inextinguishable radiance. From the hour when the religion of Christ was committed to the Irish people it grew and flourished. No vicissitude of power, no art of the enemy has availed against it. When the plain became too luxuriant for its purity, it sprung up in the wilderness and on the mountain. When the tyrannous torrent swept away the genial soil of learning by which it was fed and adorned, it struck its roots into the bare rock and defied the storm.

Whatever was the nature of the preceding worship it could not have been a cruel or an enslaving superstition. It was wholly transformed into Christianity; and so complete does the process of absorption and assimilation seem to have been, that no trace of the ancient gods or of the mode of their adoration remains. It had temples, towers, crosses, and monastic institutions which readily gave themselves to the new usage. When the national laws, known as Brehon laws, were formulated and purified after the time of St. Patrick, a continuous line in descent was allowed between the decisions which were guided by the written Word of God, and those of a prior date which were ascribed to the dictation of God's Spirit acting amid the darkness of heathenism.

There is also an essential principle of religion which is common to Christianity and the natural aspirations of the soul towards its yet unrevealed Creator. This principle must have existed in unusual force in the ancient creed. Its unconquerable influence struggling to maintain itself against oppression had pervaded every class and communicated a tinge of stoic sublimity even to the profession of arms. The rules of the Fiann, an ancient order of warriors, were replete with Christian chivalry. No man of their order should wed a dowered wife lest he might not choose her for her virtues. No man should use his strength against a woman. No man should assert his own rights selfishly against another's wants.

Christianity coalescing with a natural disposition such as this was never in circumstances more favourable for fostering that pure and comprehensive equity which is the very heart-throb of its life. Success was so subordinated to honourable effort that it ceased to be a desirable end in itself. Men became more sensitive of insult than of injury, and of general injustice than of personal suffering. When the Jewish monarch was guilty of a crime that outraged every obligation of positive law, the prophet who was sent to rebuke him appealed only to that intuitive sense of right which stoicism fixed in language and Christianity hallows, namely, that the greatest wrong on earth is not death or torture, or anything of that description, but that one man's gain or enjoyment should be achieved at the cost of the gain or enjoyment of another. The story of the rich lord who spared or slighted his own flocks, and plundered the poor man's single lamb, appears repeatedly in Irish history under various guises, testifying to the thoroughness with which the national conscience had become impregnated with the divine hatred of oppression. In the reign of king Diarmid a female recluse came to him complaining that the king of Connaught had taken from her the only cow she possessed. The monarch immediately made war on the offender and overcame him in battle. A son of Diarmid proposed to make a feast for his father, and disdaining his own herds, capriciously resolved that an ox, the solitary property of a nun in the neighbourhood, should be procured for the occasion. He sought to purchase it, offering eight beasts for the one, and when she refused he took it by force and had it dressed for the banquet. But during the festivity the wronged woman appeared and made her complaint. The king forthwith put his son to death.[1] The monarch Fergal, with more than twenty thousand men, made war on the king of Leinster, who was followed by less than half that number. Nevertheless the monarch was routed, several thousands of his men were slain, and a large number ran mad. The cause of these misfortunes was that as his troops were marching to battle some of them plundered a little church, and carried off a cow which formed the sole possession of the hermit who dwelt there.[2] The purport of these narratives is to show might subservient to right. Never to act from a sense of power, never

---
[1] Keating, 489. It may allay the reader's uneasiness to learn that Columbkille restored him to life.
[2] Ibid, p. 484.

to be even conscious of mere power, but always to act from a sense of right, and to be always and only conscious of the power of right, is the point from which true religion starts and the goal to which all good government runs.

The firm and lasting hold which Christianity has ever taken on the minds of the Irish people may in a certain degree be accounted for by the circumstances of their history. The ardour with which they gave themselves to its dissemination may be ascribed to its inherent expansiveness. But we must not leave out of the account the increased confidence which Irishmen would gain in knowing themselves to be members of a great spiritual organisation that aspired to rise above the disputes of kings, if not to control their movements. This sense of associated strength would be doubly welcome to men shut out from all command at home by the jealousy of class government. They now found themselves possessed of an authority greater than that of the sword, and eligible to offices of higher dignity than those which their masters withheld from them. The contest of centuries entered on a new field, and a marked change in the aspect of affairs testified to the completeness of the moral victory which the natives were wresting from their conquerors. The noise of battle ceased and the voice of psalmody echoed through the land. Armies of monks and missionaries appeared on the scene from which the marshalled hosts of opposing warriors had vanished.

The spread of Christianity upwards from the people to the chiefs and kings had a tendency to found society on a new and equable basis. About half a century after St. Patrick's death the monarchs began to give way to the increasing pressure, and to acknowledge themselves Christians. The reluctance with which they yielded and the species of persuasion to which they were compelled to succumb may be illustrated by a single incident. Tara had been from time immemorial the residence of the monarch and the seat of the National Triennial Council. A criminal who had fled for sanctuary to the monastery of St. Ruan was torn from the sacred precincts and put to death at Tara. The abbot and his monks went in procession to the palace and pronounced a curse upon it. From that day no monarch resided at Tara, and the national assembly was discontinued. The event amounted to a formal disruption of the confederation by which the Scoti maintained their supremacy, for the Tara meeting was not a popular assembly, but a convention of the kings and chiefs of the Milesian line.

The career of one eminent missionary chieftain furnishes an instance of the peaceable victories which Scotic genius could accomplish when separated from the contagion of habitual warfare. Columbkille was born about the year 531, and was closely related to the royal families of Ireland and Alba. He gave the vigour of his youth to the study of Christianity, rather with the view of bringing a more vivid inspiration from heaven into human hatreds than as the preparation for a new life. The Western Church, with a distinctive if not an exclusive bias, has always sought to gratify the greed of gold or the lust of power under the usurped patronage of religion. When Constantine was presented with the supposed nails of the Cross by Queen Helena, he had one of them forged into a bit for his war-horse, and the other into an ornament for his helmet. A life-time dedicated to the embodiment of an idea in practice could not more adequately illustrate it than does this single action represent the theory of the Christian religion that has been passionately held by a large portion of Christendom. In this spirit the bell of St. Patrick served as the battle-standard of one Irish sept, and the crosier of their patron saint answered the same purpose for another. A copy of some portion of the Scriptures made by Columbkille was similarly used. "Jesus and no quarter" were the words emblazoned on the banner of a Scottish clan in more modern times. It was thought that the name of Christ is mighty to strengthen an evil temper or purpose, not to change it.

While the accustomed din of battle rang in the ears of Columbkille, his faith served only to inflame his natural disposition. He was desirous of possessing a copy of the Sacred Scriptures belonging to St. Finnian, and when refused permission to write it out remained daily in the church where a volume containing the psalms was preserved, and made a hasty transcript of it. The owner of the volume when he discovered what had taken place demanded the copy as his right, and had his claim confirmed on appeal to the monarch Diarmid. Columbkille denounced the verdict as unjust and threatened vengeance. Soon after a criminal who had fled to him for sanctuary was torn from his refuge and put to death by the same monarch. Roused to fury by this act of defiance, Columbkille incited his powerful relatives to go to war with Diarmid. The monarch was repeatedly overthrown with a great slaughter of his forces. Those victories, we are told, were won by the prayers of Columbkille, though the prayers of Kinnion were offered up on the other side.

This contest was an ordinary feud of the Scotic kings under a new name and pretence. But the existence of a power by which the rights of birth were no longer held in awe was now able to assert itself. Columbkille, as the instigator of so much bloodshed, was menaced with excommunication, or was actually excommunicated. It is certain that he was compelled to leave the island, with the understanding that he must never reside in it again. The readiness with which he resigned himself to the inevitable justice of his sentence, as well as his whole subsequent life, point to the inference that the turbulent spirit he had hitherto manifested was owing less to hereditary bias than to the force of surrounding customs.

Though exiled from the land of his birth he could not be alienated from the best interests of its people. He resolved to settle on one of the Hebrides, from whence he might spread the kingdom of heaven to his kindred in North Britain. He passed island after island, but found none suitable for his purpose while Ireland was in sight. His passionate love for his country could not be brought to accord with the new line of duty that opened before him until she ceased to be anything more than a memory. At last he landed at Iona with twelve followers, and having obtained a grant of the island from his relative Conal, king of the Albanian Scoti, founded a monastery and commenced his missionary labours.

We are concerned for the moment as much with the character of the man as with the triumphs he won and bequeathed to his successors.

He is represented to have been a violent and ambitious priest while girt with the associations of home. When freed from those associations and from the dominion of a personal aim, all the attributes of his nature fell into a new order and grouped themselves under a calm far-sighted prudence, and a love for men that never waned in repose nor flickered in action. The conversion of a great part of Europe to Christianity is the monument of his devotion and his toils. It is a monument not greatly altered from its original proportions, save in the rank weeds of later growth that conceal the characters with which it was inscribed. The Gothic and Gallic kingdoms that are now Christian, owe their Christianity to Irish apostles of whom Columbkille was chief. During seven hundred years all the abbots of Iona were Irishmen. Messengers of life went forth from thence to every region, and during more than a thousand years dead bodies of kings and chiefs were brought to be buried in its sacred soil. When King Conal died Columbkille was selected to officiate at the coronation of his successor and to give his blessing. This is said to have been the earliest instance of royal consecration in Christian times.

Once he revisited Ireland to attend a national assembly at which two subjects that appealed to his sympathies were to be determined.[1] One was concerning the bards or literary class. Neither genius nor the moral character of its possessors has ever been improved by state direction or patronage. The Irish bards had long been engaged to laud the valour and prowess of the Milesians, and to depreciate or conceal from notice the milder virtues of the ancient inhabitants. The result would have been fatal to the independence of the literary character and to the authenticity of the bardic records under any circumstances. Since the introduction of Christianity the assigned staple of poetic praise had been falling in value and the topic whose very mention had been forbidden was engrossing the prospect. Dowered and privileged, yet with no duty left them to perform save silence, the bards grew so insolent and increased to such a degree that steps were about to be taken for the total suppression of their body. By the interposition of Columbkille their order was allowed to continue under certain limitations.

The second subject was the claim which the monarch of Ireland made for tribute on the colony which had migrated from Ireland to Alba. This important question was referred to the decision of Columbkille, and on his declining the office of arbitrator, to St. Coleman, who gave sentence against the Irish claims. Thus peacefully was launched on the stream of independent history a people who have run the cycle of a distinguished career while the parent state still struggled with an obdurate fortune, and whether on their own soil or in colonies returned to their ancient home, but never without being from time to time refreshed by pure draughts from the fountain of their race, have contributed their full share to the progress of the human intellect.

Columbkille returned to Iona and remained there until his death. In the thirty-fourth year of his sojourn a recurring presentiment admonished him that his end was near. While we read the accounts

[1] Keating, p. 452.

that have been transmitted of his last hours, we feel as when wrapped in the natural melancholy of a summer eve we gaze on the pathetic grandeur of the setting sun. But all the sadness is in our own hearts. The orb that inspires it is in the dewy freshness of its dawning on another world. There was no self-pity in the consciousness of Columbkille. On the last day of the week he went with his favourite attendant to the storehouse of the establishment, and rejoicing to find it well supplied, told his people that he was to depart from them that night.

An incident that occurred as he returned to the monastery teaches how close heaven lies to earth, and how simple a thing is true sublimity of soul. The aged saint paused to rest midway, and as he sat, the old white horse of the monastery moved near and rested its head on his bosom. More than twelve hundred years after, as another Irishman who did a world-wide work and won a world-wide fame, sat under an English sky musing sadly on the vanity of earthly pursuits, the old horse of his son, whose death had been the blight of his most cherished hopes, approached, and after viewing him for a few moments as if in sympathy, deliberately repeated the action of the superannuated servant of the brotherhood of Iona. Never did the divine eloquence of Burke produce such an effect on his hearers as this token of instinctive pity produced on himself. He flung his arms over the animal's neck and wept long and loudly.

After resting for awhile Columbkille ascended a little hill that overlooked the monastery, and standing there he blessed it with raised hands, and prophesied that small and poor as the spot was, kings and peoples and churches of distant lands would hold it in great reverence. In some verses which tradition ascribes to him his prophetic vision looks into a still remoter future. In the isle of his heart, he said, instead of monks there should be lowing of cattle, but ere the world comes to an end Iona should flourish as before. Going back to his cell, he resumed his favourite occupation of transcribing the Holy Scriptures. He reached the ninth verse of the thirty-fourth Psalm, and the words brought him to the bottom of the page. Then he stopped and said that Baithan, one of the twelve who accompanied him to Iona, and his appointed successor, must write the remainder. He lay on his stone bed till the bell sounded for midnight prayers, when he hastened to the church and was found dying before the altar. He feebly signed a benediction with his hand on his brethren who stood weeping around, and so left them.

SECTION IV.

The ecclesiastical establishment at Iona[1] was an advanced post in the operations which the Irish Church was conducting against Heathenism, or the still more obdurate error, corrupt Christianity. Her successful efforts among the Scots and Picts of North Britain opened ever-widening fields of labour to her view. Some kings of the Saxon Heptarchy who, chiefly at the persuasion of their wives, had avowed their belief in Christ, were imitated by many thousands of their subjects. But when their successors relapsed into Heathenism, the royal example was equally

[1] Neander, Vol. V., p. 12.

influential. The Roman mission which had commenced under Augustine was abandoned by several bishops, and merely held its machinery together in hopes of help from Providence, under circumstances that to human enterprise seemed desperate.

In the seventh century Oswald, King of Northumberland, who during a period of banishment in Ireland had been instructed in Christianity, applied to the Irish Church for a teacher. Aidan, a monk of Iona, was sent in answer to his request. The first step taken by the new missionary was to make himself master of the English language. He then travelled on foot among the people, and in this manner became acquainted with their condition. He preached the Gospel to them, and carefully explained that it was not a magical form of words but a rule of conduct whose efficacy must be evidenced by its results. Whatever presents he received from the king or the nobles, he distributed among the poor, or spent in redeeming captives. He rebuked evil conduct in rich and poor alike. He zealously promoted the study of Scripture. By his labours and his example the Gospel was firmly planted in Northumberland, from whence it spread to the other tribes of the Heptarchy.

Troops of Irish clergy, whose disinterestedness won universal admiration, entered the country and enlisted the affections of its inhabitants on the side of truth. The permanency of their work was their reward. Some differences of form between the Roman and Irish Churches, which no one had noticed during the heat of the fight against the common foe, stood displayed to view in the calm that succeeded victory. The time of celebrating Easter was one of these. A conference was held in the presence of King Oswin at Whitby, to decide which custom was to prevail. Colman, an Irishman, the successor of Aidan, pleaded the example of Columbkille. Wilfred on the other side cited the authority of St. Peter, who held the keys of heaven. The king, not daring to dissent from an apostle who could exclude him from eternal happiness, gave his verdict for the Roman usage. Thus the Irish bestowed pure religion on the Anglo-Saxons, and kingly influence decided the question of external observances and church communion. Colman and his monks returned to their own country.

Gaul and Germany had become indoctrinated in Christianity at a very early period, but in the convulsions that followed, every trace of it was obliterated, or so blended with paganism as to be no longer discernable. In the midst of scenes of lawlessness and violence that might be taken for the moral death-throes of the world, there appeared suddenly and silently bands of civilizers and instructors, who, judged by the work they came to do, and contrasted with the men among whom they came, were as angels from heaven.[1] To describe them as Christian teachers, interpreting the term by ordinary experience, would convey no true idea of their self-imposed duties or of their method of discharging them. They consisted mainly of Irish monks[2] who, under wise and judicious abbots, at a juncture in the life of mankind that was pregnant with religious and political precedents, were sent to infuse some elements of justice and love where wrong and hatred alone prevailed. They sought to mitigate the horrors of warfare, and to allay the spirit of strife at its source in the

[1] Neander, Vol. V., p. 37. [2] Ibid, p. 37–49.

heart. By voluntarily enduring all the hardships which necessity imposed on others, by entire disregard of wealth, by condemning the violence of barbarous chiefs, by dedicating themselves and their whole means to the deliverance of captives and healing the wounds of the broken-hearted, they manifested the power of truth, and recommended the religion of Christ. They were the world's vanquishers, and rulers of men after the divine model. Their dominion consisted not in the visible trappings of power, nor in the prostration of slaves, nor in the establishment of tyrannies, but in the enthronement in the human conscience of principles of righteousness which were of the essence of their own souls.

About the year 590 Columban, with twelve companions, crossed from Leinster to the Frankish kingdom. He chose a spot in the wilderness which he reclaimed and cultivated, and thus initiated the savage inhabitants into the first stage of social progress. By a discreet blending of the contemplative with the practical life, and a union of exact knowledge with genuine piety, he regenerated the Gallic church. Families of all ranks sent their sons to be educated by him, until, in order to find room for their increasing numbers, he was obliged to distribute his monks into three monasteries. Although he never identified the truth with the peculiar customs of the Irish church, his success raised enemies among the worldly ecclesiastics who made uniformity the substitute for every virtue, and he was thus brought into collision with the Papal See. We miss in him as in others of his countrymen, when engaged in controversy, that subservient spirit by which those who only seek their private ends humiliate principle in order to worm themselves into position. When Gregory the Great deferred too much to the authority of Leo his predecessor, Columban warned him that humility might run into extremes, and by quoting the inspired proverb that a living dog is better than a dead lion (*Eccles.* ix. 4), showed him that his own judgment could be exercised in opposition to great names without any assumption of personal superiority. When a Frankish Synod met to deliberate on the diversity that existed between ecclesiastical forms, he wrote to them expressing his hope that they would employ the too rare occasion of a Synod for a really useful purpose. Men, he said, would never differ about traditions and customs if they thought less of themselves and more of their Master; and he anticipated the prejudice which is always roused on such occasions to justify a corrupt decision by adding that the church does not know nationality, and that Gauls, Britons, and Irishmen are members of one family.

The anger which this honest speaking excited, smouldered until Columban felt himself compelled to rebuke the unchaste life of the king, when the civil powers joined the ecclesiastical in the effort to silence and restrain him. He remained firm to his sense of duty amidst threats and promises, refused to alter either his standard of moral rectitude or the discipline of his monasteries, and was eventually banished from the kingdom.

Men always suspect themselves of exceptional imperviousness to truth by the jealousy they display lest others should have an opportunity of accepting the lessons which they reject. The sentence pronounced on Columban was that he should be conveyed to his own country. This was only a suggestion with which they thought he might comply under feelings of discouragement and depression. They had no power to enforce it. He retired to Zurich, and after labouring in various parts of Gaul and Germany, whither in each case the zeal of his enemies pursued him, he finally settled in Italy, where, in the shelter of the Apennines, he founded the monastery of Bobbio.

His disciple Gallus, another Irishman, laboured among the Swiss and Suabian populations, and founded the monastery which afterwards became so famous under his name, St. Gall.[1] When a vacant bishopric was offered to him he declined it, and procured the appointment for a native of the country, who had been brought up under his direction. The consecration of the new bishop drew together a large concourse of people, and Gallus used the occasion to remind them that their baptismal renunciation was not to be the form of a moment, but the practice of their whole lives, and he specified by name the sins they were to shun.

These men are merely instances of the continuous multitude that streamed from the schools and monasteries of Ireland, and made their country known over the whole Continent as "the island of saints." Their influence was not exercised through their own immediate labours only. With that contagious force of character which belongs to the combination of strength with simplicity, they inspired with their ardour all with whom they came in contact. At the close of the seventh century numbers of young Englishmen seeking knowledge and holiness resorted to Ireland. They were not only entertained as honoured guests, but gratuitously instructed.[2] Some of them caught the spirit of their hosts, and burning with missionary zeal, went forth to give freely the knowledge they had freely received. One of them, the Presbyter Willibrord, having first visited Rome, was instrumental in fixing the German Church on a firm basis. When the breath of life had been inspired by Irish piety, the German people were massed into one religious community, and closely connected with the Church of Rome by the organised energy of the Saxon Boniface.

No religious Irishman in his higher patriotic mood, no patriot in his hour of calm religious consciousness, will raise a question as to the formal creed or ecclesiastical system of his ancestors. They were not characterised by their system. As on a sudden alarm men seize on whatever arms are next to hand, and never pause to change them till the danger is past, so they rushed to the field of Christian warfare under such conditions as presented themselves, and no doubt regarded the proposal to alter their mode of tonsure, or their time of celebrating Easter in presence of the advancing foe, as soldiers would regard an order to change their uniform in the crisis of battle. They shrank from making a surrender which would imply that the unity of the Church rested on externals. Their attachment to their own customs was founded not on any power they supposed them to possess, but on their association with the hallowed and beloved names of St. Patrick and St. Columbkille. The subjects on which they differed from, and those in which they agreed with the Church of Rome, had no analogy or

[1] Neander, Vol. V., p. 47. [2] Neander, Vol. V., p. 57.

connection whatever with the polemics of a later period. They were in communion with the Roman Church, but as was natural at a time when Christendom was not yet disrupted into rival bodies, the bond that held them in union was the blending of lofty motives and the pursuit of similar ends, and not a deliberate and indiscriminating partizanship.

The leading minds of the mother Church were on a level with this independent co-operation. It was discovered that an ignorant German priest had been in the habit of administering the baptismal rite in ungrammatical Latin. Boniface, who was then Archbishop of Mentz, considering that the ceremony was invalid, ordered the Irish Virgilius to perform it over again. Virgilius, feeling that the efficacy of Baptism consisted in something quite different from a legally correct form, referred the matter to Pope Zachary, who at once countermanded the order of Boniface.[1]

The startling modernness of Irish modes of thinking at this remote date fills us alternately with hopefulness and despair, as we see the world as it were on the threshold of a knowledge in whose renascent light we are now painfully struggling for happiness, and then behold it driven forcibly back against the tide of Providence into ignorance and barbarism. If the efforts of a beneficent Deity for the amelioration of our lot are interrupted by the wiles of a malignant principle, why may we not detect the evil at work in the sudden fury or the sober selfishness of nations, as well as in the actions of individual men? Why may we not recognise the presence of God in the spiritual aptitude of nationalities, in the bias they show whenever foreign interference is relaxed or withdrawn? When all other Churches were fixing themselves on earthly foundations, entrenching themselves with wealth and power, and laying up stores of future corruption, Irish Christians alone were intent on knowing what better wisdom and what higher life Christianity had to bestow, and on communicating the knowledge by precept and example. They studied Scripture till its meaning kindled and shone in their hearts and lives. They brought an unsophisticated common sense to the interpretation of its rules. They penetrated to the marrow of its doctrines, and incurred the charge of heresy because they deviated from the pedantic and darkening terminology of theologians. Accustomed to rate right above power, and preferring that rank should be lowered within reach of the many, rather than that merit should be subordinated to mere official rule, they conferred the higher ecclesiastical titles on exceptional holiness wherever it was met. The charges brought against them are a revelation of their characters and of the standards by which their accusers judged. They are said to have been guilty of every kind of blasphemy and immorality, and when the details are stated, it is discovered that they multiplied their bishops, and shaved their heads after some fashion of their own.

It will take centuries to make the earth worthy of having borne those men. They represented all that is precious in modern civilization. Their religious independence was only one feature of a mental constitution that knew no guidance save such as reason and justice inspired. Their spiritual pre-eminence was in religion because religion was the

[1] Neander, Vol. V., p. 83.

science of the time. During many ages a few Irishmen were the only champions of free thought. To be the pioneers of the noblest liberty and the purest religion is the bequest of our ancient history. It matters little what our critics may assume or assert, provided we neither misunderstand our mission, nor misapply the privileges with which Heaven has dowered it; provided we do not allow our lofty forethought to degenerate into immediate improvidence, nor mistake our susceptibility to the transient joy of the hour for the detaining purpose of life, nor pervert our indigenous freedom into licence. With such guards upon ourselves we may pass the assailants of our national character in silence, and leave our achievements to speak in its vindication. The genius of a people must be estimated in accordance with their aspirations. Those families of mankind who seek some lower good may settle in sluggish contentment on their lot, but for the higher aim and the long delay, for the interval of forced inaction and the dark hour of temporary defeat, nature has her compensations. The nations that represent their own interests only must differ in temperament from the nation that represents the interests of all mankind, and of more than all time. A near and selfish ambition steadies the movements of the individual or the family. The narrow lake can present an unruffled surface, the meteor may pursue its short course in an undeviating line, but the weary sweep of ocean requires the relief of its waves, and the planet's eternal career must have the solace of its perturbations.

Section V.

During the centuries after the introduction of the Christian religion, the civil constitution as well as the usages and manners of the country had been gradually re-establishing themselves on the foundations of ancient freedom. War was giving way to peace. The obscurity to which the Scoti had condemned the Irish by forced enactments, now became their own fate by the changing necessity of events. The chronicling monks celebrated the triumphs of religion, and either omitted or barely recited the battles and violent deaths of the kings. Foreign attacks had almost wholly ceased, and were encountered on their rare occurrence by the arbitrement of reason. In 684 the King of Northumberland plundered the eastern coasts of the island, in revenge, it is supposed, for shelter having been afforded to his brother. This aggression on the new relations that had sprung up between the two countries was regarded as a sin, and when the king who was guilty of it was slain the year after, his fate was looked on as a judgment from heaven. Adamnan, the successor of Columbkille, was sent to the court of the new king to seek restitution, and returned with sixty restored captives.

The causes of intestine war were disappearing before religious influences. The Boarian tribute, which was an ever fresh source of bitter strife, had been remitted for ever by the monarch at the request of St. Moling, Archbishop of Ferns; and though an attempt to resume the claim was made by a succeeding monarch, ecclesiastical remonstrance discountenanced the enterprise. The traces of successful invasion were wearing away. Punishment of death, the claims of primogeniture, and manorial rights over the land, all unmistakeable relics of conquest, were yielding place respectively to fines, elections and possession in severalty. The gap that existed between the Milesian chief and the Irish tribesman was bridged over by spiritual affinity or gossipred, fostering[1] and livery.[2] Even a law concerning the legitimation of children, which causes scandal to the unthinking, is seen on consideration to be an assertion of one of the most vital of human rights, and a wise provision for the dignity of womanhood. Bastardy is a relic of the savage period which gave the conqueror a right over the wives and daughters of the vanquished. The child which the woman who had no property in her own person bore to the slayer of her husband or her father, could not take rank among the offspring of free women, and was declared illegitimate. An avowed laxity of morals among equals is a far more manageable evil than the prudishly ignored custom which makes a degraded caste of women the creatures of privileged lust, and condemns the fruit of illicit intercourse to social ignominy. In ancient Ireland, if the power of the monarch gave him opportunities of corrupting the virtue of his people, a special law guarded his victim from destitution, and her child from infamy.[3]

All those early customs, it must be remembered, were in their initial stages. They must be judged by the direction in which they point. They contained in them the springs and germs of purity, equal justice, and freedom. They were not allowed to reach their full growth or their true development, but their influence and the bent of the national spirit that conceived them, in spite of persecution, vituperation and contempt, has produced a peasantry whose men are courteous, hospitable, and free from servility, and whose women are the most virtuous in the world.

At the period which we have now reached, the island was thickly peopled, and abounded with wealth. It was covered with schools and seminaries. Its libraries were stocked with manuscripts. A comprehensive code was promoting the advance and securing the fruits of learning and culture, and the example of ecclesiastical synods would inevitably have soon suggested a central representative authority, emanating from the bosom of the people, to modify or replace the declining power of kings. The Irish people were conquering their conquerors. At such a time trouble came. It came as ever from abroad. The rising hopes of the nation were overwhelmed by a sudden torrent of invasion that threw all things into confusion, and ended in restoring the power of the sword, the popularity of the bards, and the supremacy of the Milesians.

[1] "Children were mutually given, from different families, to be nursed and brought up in others; and inferiors, instead of expecting any reward for their care, purchased the honour of fostering the children of the rich." Leland, Vol. I., p. 38.

[2] "Even the lowest of the people claimed reception and refreshment as an almost perfect right; and so ineffectual is the flux of many centuries to efface the ancient manners of a people that at this day the wandering beggar enters the house of a farmer or gentleman with as much ease and freedom as an inmate." Leland, Vol. I., p. 35.

[3] Keating, p. 329.

CHAPTER III.

Peace Assailed by Norman Invasions.

Section I.

The Scandinavian races, from which the Scythi or Scoti were sprung, have always exhibited a passion for complex legislation in the disposal of their violently acquired possessions. One of the Irish monarchs, Niall of the nine hostages, left his throne in alternate succession to the descendants of two of his sons, who were known as the Northern and Southern Hy-Nialls. Again, the first king who ruled the two provinces of Munster, Desmond, or South Munster, and Thomond, or North Munster, divided his kingdom between his two sons and their descendants, with the further proviso that the sovereignty of the entire province should descend alternately between them. The two families, the Eugenians of Desmond, and the Dalcassians of Thomond, soon came to regard each other with feelings of bitter rivalry. It is remarkable that those attempts to supersede popular by personal rights were still forced to conform to the old tribal institutions, for in every case the succession was to be finally settled by an election at which the fittest person out of the eligible candidates was determined on. The ancient division of the island into two independent kingdoms gave continual occasion to the King of Munster to lay claim to the whole Southern half, and the attempt, if successful, opened the prospect to the monarchy. The monarch's claim on the King of Leinster for the Boarian tribute, though it had been surrendered under the growing influences of Christianity, was certain to be re-asserted whenever those influences were removed or weakened. The kings of Munster in assertion of their right to half the island claimed the Boarian tribute for themselves.

Those dynastic provocations to strife had been gradually disappearing from view as the heavenly light of Christianity waxed clearer, but their fading characters were ever ready to stand out in vivid distinctness whenever the atmosphere was heated by the congenial flames of war. The Norse or Danish invasions supplied the requisite incentive. The sole difference between the Norsemen or Normans and the Irish Scoti was that the latter had been for some centuries associated with a peaceful, domestic and Christian community, while their northern congeners had been strengthening their native propensities to restlessness and rapine by ages of violence, and the invention of a religious belief which fostered their worst vices.

There are grounds for the belief that intercourse of a more or less friendly nature had always been preserved by the Scoti with their original northern home, and that it was the knowledge of the unwarlike habits which were increasing among them, and of the stores of treasure that were piled in their religious houses, that turned their allies into marauding foes. The Normans hated and despised Christianity. Their own creed held out to them the prospect of an eternity during which they should quaff their favourite liquor out of cups made from their enemies' skulls, served to them by nymphs, and fed on the lard of a wild boar that ever resumed its full proportions; relieving the monotony of such enjoyments by combats in which they were to cut each other in pieces, and then recover their former shapes and appetites. There was no difficulty in believing in a heaven for which they ardently longed, stimulated as their faith was by the indulgences of their ordinary lives. They believed in it fanatically, and the courage nurtured by such a prospect remained in their descendants after the immortal side of it had waned away in scepticism, or been modified by a spurious Christianity.

In the year 795 the Normans began their attacks, confining themselves at first to the islands off the coast. In 802 they plundered Iona, and repeated the raid in 806, slaying sixty-eight of the monks. The next year they entered the mainland. They sought the monasteries and scholastic establishments chiefly because they offered the greatest booty and the least resistance. So thoroughly did they accomplish the work of ruin that in many cases the scenes of their depredations can no longer be traced.

Opposition was organised in a little time, and the invaders met a check from the Eugenians of Killarney. But the revived dissensions of the Scotic kings invited them to renewed and more systematic efforts. An immense fleet under the command of Turgesius, supposed by some to be the same as the celebrated Ragnar Lodbrok, arrived in 832, and poured a torrent of invasion over the northern half of the island. Three other fleets simultaneously landed bodies of pillagers in different parts. Turgesius was recognised by all the Normans in Ireland as their sovereign. Having fixed his head-quarters in the north, he attacked Armagh, and only after a third assault succeeded in taking it. For nine years he was content with secular authority. After that period he banished the bishops and clergy, and assuming the primacy himself, attempted to substitute his national heathenism for Christianity as a necessary step towards the establishment of the Norman power. He extended his conquests to Meath and Connaught, and taking his station at Lough Ree, plundered from thence all the religious houses of the surrounding district.

During the usurpation of Turgesius every sorrow that policy could devise and power inflict were endured by the Irish. All the native magistrates, civil and ecclesiastical, were displaced, and Normans appointed instead. Norman officers presided in every town and village, Norman privates in every house. Each had irresponsible and unlimited sway in his own sphere. Every right of property was violated, every province of life intruded on. The best food that the district produced was seized for the captain; the best that the household possessed for the private soldier. Whoever concealed his cattle or secreted food for his children was, on detection, chained and imprisoned until he made satisfaction. Resistance was prevented by forbidding martial exercises among the youthful nobles. Every head of a family was taxed an ounce of gold annually. On every marriage the Norman captain had a right to defile the bride. The delicacies of every banquet were borne off for the foreigners.

It is possible that this description is overcharged by the annalists, who had an interest in rekindling the warlike spirit. Yet the whole account only relates what might be reasonably expected under the circumstances. Men do not undertake the risk of conquest as amateur statesmen, nor yet to quench a vampire thirst for blood. Many persons are of a domineering temper, but as a rule the lust of power is only the servant of a hundred other lusts. Many persons are naturally cruel, but as a rule bloodshed is only the accident of war, and the instigating motive is the enlarged field of sensual gratifications that remains after the slaughter. The direct and naked use of power that shocks our sensitiveness and strains our credulity, in the initial stage of conquest, exhibits the reality that in various disguises flows to the remotest times from its polluted source.

But there can be no doubt that the most strenuous and insidious attacks were directed against the religious and intellectual life of the nation. The abbey churches and monasteries were assigned to Norman priests, and the praises and orgies of Odin prevailed where Christ had been sincerely worshipped. A law prohibited any of the natives from entering a school or church, or from employing a teacher or priest. The precious manuscripts on which such loving pains had been expended, which it had taken so many years to collect, and which were the intended heirlooms for coming generations, were sought out, as men might seek the germs of a deadly plague, and burned.

We are struck by a remarkable difference of character displayed by the two sections of the nation under those insults and impositions. The monks and lesser ecclesiastics, representing for the most part the original people, with unfailing patience and courage set about repairing the injuries they suffered. No repetition of disaster daunted their perseverance. When their church was burned they rebuilt it. When the spoiler a second time sacked and ruined the restored edifice, they raised it again. When a third time the flame consumed the work of their hands, nothing remained for them but to erect it once more. When the sword turned a spot where a happy religious community dwelt into a desert, fresh aspirants for holiness and martyrdom crowded to the vacant post. The peace lovers and peacemakers displayed the unconscious heroism of single-minded conviction.

The warlike classes, on the other hand, stood amazed for a while at the novelty of the spectacle that met their view. They saw the powers which they had been accustomed to reverence outraged with impunity. When they roused themselves to action their impulse was rather to imitate than oppose. The sight of unconcealed lawlessness blew the smouldering fires of their nature into an emulative conflagration. The King of Munster, himself an ecclesiastic, asserted his claim to the monarchy, and in prosecution of his object, while the Normans were devastating and murdering in another part of the country, plundered the religious establishments of the north, and put their inhabitants to the sword. In 826, and again in 833, he spoiled Clonmacnois with fire and slaughter, and after years of similar outrage elsewhere, plundered it once more in 846.

Contests arose among the higher ranks of the clergy. Rival Abbots of Armagh, supported by the monarch and the King of Munster, were alternately expelled and restored according to the chances of battle. The Normans gave a new direction to the strife by occupying the seat of the primacy. The monarch marched to its rescue, and after successfully encountering the enemy, perished in endeavouring to save one of his friends who was drowned while fording a flooded stream at the head of the army.

The forces of Turgesius were continually increased by fresh accessions. Every wave that beat on the coasts added to their numbers. Fears for their own position at length compelled the Irish kings to unite. The new monarch and the King of Ulster, assisted by some chief ecclesiastics, met in deliberation and determined on a vigorous resistance. The enemy was overthrown in two battles, in one of which they lost twelve hundred men and one of their principal commanders. This success was but temporary. The Normans, having concentrated their forces, again stormed and took Armagh. An insult meditated by Turgesius against the daughter of the monarch finally brought about the decisive effort which the thousand wrongs of the people could not produce. The Norman leader was taken prisoner by stratagem, loaded with chains, and flung into a lake.

Section II.

The power of the foreigners collapsed only for a period after the death of Turgesius. A fleet of a hundred and forty sail repaired their strength and developed a new element in the strife. Whatever restraints Christianity had hitherto imposed on the Scotic rulers, whatever ties of affection long intercourse had created between them and the people whom they had so long governed, were sacrificed to the expediency of the moment. The common origin and the common aim of the earlier and later invaders displayed themselves in their readiness to enter into any combination that promised the immunities and indulgences of dominion. Aided in each case by Norman allies, the monarch Malachy gained a victory over his own countrymen; Hugh Finlath, a prince of the Hy-Nialls, ravaged Meath; and a prince of Meath wasted the territories of the Hy-Nialls. Normans, on the other hand, supported by Scoti, fought against Normans. Robbers whose claims were sanctioned by time, and robbers who had no prescriptive rights to plead, combined on equal terms. Every sentiment gave way before the instinct of their race to rule, that is, to live in idleness and pleasure on the spoils of a conquered people.

In the middle of the century a newly arrived army of Normans attacked Dublin, which was then in the possession of some of their own tribes, and made themselves masters of it after great slaughter. The next year the dispossessed party, having obtained reinforcements from their own country, attacked the victors, and after a battle of three days and three nights' continuance, drove them from the city. Thus the last variety was added to the already sufficiently entangled discord by which the island was disfigured. As the dissensions between the Scotic chiefs hindered them from either offering a single object on which attack might be successfully concentrated, or from uniting in a triumphant defence, the want of harmony among the Normans prevented them from risking their fortunes on the issue of a conclusive battle, and thus from conquering or being conquered. Neither side could even win any such decided advantage as would force the other side to forget their personal ambition and mutual animosities. It was a tedious, unprincipled, and disunited warfare over a lengthened frontier, in which each man fought for himself, and defeat was impossible, because help could always be obtained from across the line. An interminable series of inconclusive conflicts drained the blood of the country, and poisoned that which remained unshed.

On the death of Malachy (863), Hugh Finlath, with one hand polluted by the murder of his countrymen and the other by coalition with their deadly enemies, succeeded to the throne. During his reign the Normans, having exhaustively stripped the shrines of the living of their treasures, ransacked the monuments of the dead in search of the golden ornaments which they heard or conjectured were buried there. They did not leave, we are told, a sepulchral cave from Leinster to Kerry, or from Limerick to Cork, which they did not rifle. Those ancient cairns and the Christian churches were apparently classed together by the Scoti as unconnected with their own glory, and as deserving of protection only for the sake of the people with whose cherished recollections they were associated. But when the more recent invader, undeterred by any kind of scruple, cut his way with the sword into the sanctuary of the grave, the descendants of the former conqueror saw only a privilege which they had neglected to use, and so far from resisting, countenanced, if they did not share in, the desecration.

The chief of the district which included the plundered cemeteries was in league with the plunderers, and his son a few years after was slain while fighting in their ranks against the forces of the monarch. In the same battle the heir to the monarchy, and the son of Olaf, the Norman chief, were slain. Olaf avenged the death of his son by once again devastating Armagh, and putting a thousand of its inmates to death. The monarch retaliated in what he supposed to be the most effective manner, by ravaging the territory of the Leinster allies of the Normans. He died deeply lamented by the bards in the year 879, and was succeeded by Flan Siona.

Flan began his reign in the royal fashion of those days by pillaging Munster with the aid of Norman mercenaries, and exacting hostages as a means of establishing his authority over that province. He next made good his supremacy in Ulster, and finally succeeded in reducing the tribes of Connaught to submission. The latter years of this century were passed in comparative quiet. This was partly caused by the vigour with which Harold, king of Norway, repressed the plundering expeditions of his subjects, and partly by the superior attractions offered in France and Italy to those lawless spirits who could not be confined within the limits of civil obedience. It was at this period that Rolf or Rollo, having brought destruction on his father and brothers by abstracting the goods of his own countrymen in addition to his foreign robberies, was banished from Norway, and founded the Norman settlement in France; from whence in subsequent years were effected successively those conquests in England and Ireland whose chains the peoples of both countries have to this day been endeavouring to unbind.

It is one of the commonplaces of history to ascribe the foundation of Dublin, Waterford, Wexford and Limerick, as centres of commerce, to Norman enterprise during this century. There cannot be found a single fact to justify such an opinion. Commerce flourished in Ireland from an immemorial period. The selection of the most favourable localities on the coasts as its depôts must have been its initial step. The Scoti tolerated and encouraged establishments which supplied them with the produce of foreign countries without obliging them to engage personally in an occupation on which, as on the other pursuits of the natives, they looked with contempt. The Normans seized on those positions, and erected fortresses in them in order to conduct from thence their hasty raids, or their plans of conquest. As those projects were continuously frustrated, they became incorporated with the original founders, and entered into their peaceful pursuits.

Section III.

As already intimated, we cannot receive the traditions that have come down to us from contemporary sources as furnishing a trustworthy account of the condition of the country in the centuries succeeding the Norman invasion. As the fortunes of the two competing interests, peace and war, learning and barbarism, Christianity and heathenism, the Irish and their invaders, rose or fell, there were two rival sets of chroniclers, the monks and the bards, who were each ready to hail with acclamation the emergence of their own side to the surface, and to magnify its triumphs with all the one-sidedness of professional enthusiasm. As in a previous century, when religion flourished in peace, the record of the ecclesiastic omitted the achievements of exceptional warfare, as undeserving of transmission, so now, in a century when war was on the ascendant, one set of facts only is related as forming the staple of annalistic composition, and all besides is passed over in silence. The bards were the historiographers of the Milesians, and as their patrons prided themselves on deeds of violence and took pleasure in narratives of destruction, we cannot be at a loss in understanding the exaggerated accounts, the multiplied epithets, the rude licence of poetic embellishment, and the at once exclusive and exhaustive selection of events of a violent character, descending even to the slaughter of a dog and the drowning of a cow, with which their memorials abound.

The effect that can be produced by limited and partial delineations may be seen at the present day exemplified by the reports of murders, which, without any sinister intention, but merely by the nature of the circumstances, form the only representation of Irish intelligence in English journals. The local politics and provincial incidents of Ireland have no interest or attraction for the English reader. A fundamental rule of journalism demands the insertion of murders. As they appear in the Irish newspaper they are only in fair proportion to the whole amount of ordinary occurrences, just as in England similar offences do not present any startling phenomenon when hid in the mass of parliamentary, municipal, and commercial information. But when appearing in English papers exclusively and constantly, at whatever intervals, under the heading of Irish intelligence, they naturally but most illogically cause Ireland and murder to become associated in the mind of the English public. And to render the parallel more complete, a habit has of late been adopted in exact correspondence with the inflamed language of the Irish bards, of describing all Irish crimes as brutal and savage, while denominating English offences of the same type not as murders, but as tragedies. As the crime of murder is less frequent in Ireland at the present day than in any other country, if it may not be said to be totally absent, if the term be limited to its strictly civil meaning, but appears to the English people to be more so because it is the only item of Irish news which is brought before their notice, so the turbulence and bloodshed of ancient Ireland were not greater than in other countries, nor by any means greater or as great as the victories of peace that were won in their midst, but appear to be greater because they were more carefully published.

Moreover, if we accept the bardic relations as in any degree worthy of credit when they present us with catalogues of depredations and slaughter, we must accord the same belief to the monkish historians, when they celebrate periods of tranquillity during which the fruits of industry were secure, and weakness was unmolested. Perhaps we shall not greatly err if we conclude that the dignity and the joy of a virgin life went on unbroken beneath the complicated net-work of civil and foreign war in all those bygone times; and that it is not a fervid imagination merely which bears, when the clash of arms has ceased for awhile, the echoes of melody or mirth from the crowded valley, and which sees the temple thronged with worshippers, and the seminary with aspirants for knowledge, when the smoke of battle has been wafted from the scene. It may be that we must reverse our modern ideas in order to reach a true estimate of those primitive ages. As now, like gilded insects hovering over some decaying substance, a few monopolists of pride and pleasure flutter in ignoble peace over an abyss of pauperism that reeks with vice and violence, so then, it may be, a few restless leaders smote each other in deadly feud, while the mass of the people fed their flocks and tilled their fields, and breathed the atmosphere of unbought affection in their rude habitations.

It is matter of positive historical inference that two distinct Irelands then co-existed; one boisterous and warlike, greedy of vulgar applause and jealous of any encroachment on its aristocratic pride; the other peaceful, studious, and tender-hearted, pursuing knowledge in its native wilds, and sending forth its sons, disturbed and slighted at home, to reanimate the lapsing nations with more vigorous modes of thought, and to be the associates of mighty kings. In the ninth, the tenth, and as far as the first half of the eleventh century, Irishmen who had learned Greek and Latin literature in their boyhood at home were honoured teachers on the Continent, Irish books were the vehicles of instruction, and Irish works of art were gifts most highly prized.

It was the peculiarity of Irish monasteries that they did not confine themselves to the writings of the Latin church fathers. The works of Origen and other Greek thinkers were also read, and hence a more liberal and comprehensive theology was spread over the land.

One man gathered to himself the best characteristics of this school and of his country, and has bequeathed his fame to his countrymen as an illustration of the possibilities of the past, and of the hopes of the future. John Scotus Erigena left Ireland in the middle of the ninth century, and was received by Charles the Bald, King of France, as his companion and friend. He was an unrivalled dialectician, and at the same time possessed an intellect that by its own unstrained capacity comprehended the whole circle of knowledge and science. Standing between two worlds of thought, he separated the light from the darkness, and sent it onwards as from a new source. The confusion of imperfect, partial, and fragmentary ideas, each of which had been the product of the toils of some preceding mind, met in his, and by the touch of his disposing genius, was marshalled into the order and system of a new creation, from which have been developed all the philosophies of modern Europe. Starting from the fundamental maxim that nature and the human reason are both, in their different growths, impresses of the Creative Power, he concluded that God and nature are intelligible to reason. The immensity of his resources, the constructive force of his understanding, a moral sense preserved from all corrupt bias by the purity of his life, and a spirit of devotion that brought illumination from on high upon every stage of his inquiries, enabled him to re-combine the phenomenal contradictions of nature, philosophy, and religion into one consistent scheme. The vastness of his scope exposed him to the misconception of persons who, through inability or indolence, never enlarged their views sufficiently to judge him correctly. As rash investigators who endeavour to mount up to the mystery of the universe, failing in their effort, confound their own shortcoming with the discovery that there is no God, so those who strove to master Erigena's system, unable to grasp it in its entirety, and forced to consider it only in fragments, have imagined that they found traces of atheism in his writings. As might be expected, he did not transmit his system to a band of scholars. His doctrines included the subjects of all the schools. There is no form of modern philosophy that is not traceable to his writings. Descartes, Spinoza, Kant, Fichte, Schelling, and Hegel were among his followers. The outline of Spurzheim's system is found in his works. In his character he was more or less a representative of his country. While the grandeur of his conceptions, and the largeness of his views, rendered him an inhabitant of the far-distant future, his personal qualities endeared him to his contemporaries, and the attractive playfulness of his wit made amends for his intellectual isolation.

Section IV.

Flan died in 916. The closing years of his reign were shadowed by domestic troubles and the renewal of Norman attacks. Dublin, which had been taken in 879 by the Irish, was retaken by the Normans in 912. The next monarch, Niall IV., after a reign of three years passed in constant warfare with the foreigners, was slain in an attempt to recover Dublin. His successor was Donchad, but his son Murkertagh, who, according to the compact of alternate succession between the Northern and Southern Hy-Nialls, held the recognised privileged position of heir to Donchad, was the leading spirit in war and council while he lived. The crisis was one that demanded all the best properties of a soldier, as the general circumstances of the country required the self-devotion of a true patriot. Murkertagh was equal to either necessity. The ravages of the Normans were renewed with redoubled fury. Their vessels surrounded the whole coast, and penetrated into the interior by every river-mouth and estuary. Landing suddenly at those retired spots of calm loveliness which men of deep religious feelings had chosen as retreats from the world of strife, they consigned the buildings to the flames and their peaceful inmates to slaughter. The cold ferocity of their deliberate carnage can neither be accounted for by the calculations of policy, nor the drunken phrensy of bloodshed. They were merely intolerant of a system that would not pander to their passions, and they hated a mode of life that reflected censure on their own. Clonmacnois and Kildare rising from their ruins, and collecting again the scattered fugitives who had escaped former attacks, were dismantled and desolated with a cruelty which was exasperated to fury by the pious resignation of their victims, as the energies of other men might be called forth by a vigorous resistance. It was only when they united their bands, and appeared near the haunts of public life, that they met with enemies capable of offering opposition. In 926 Murkertagh attacked a northern division commanded by a son of Godfrey, King of Dublin, and inflicted a signal defeat, in which eighty of the Norman chieftains and their leader were slain. In 933 he won another victory, and in 939, joining his forces with those of the monarch, he attacked Dublin, whose strength was diminished by a defeat which the Normans had suffered in England,[1] and reduced it to ashes. Not content with waging a defensive warfare, he assailed the enemy in the Hebrides, and in their settlements on the coast of Alba, and returned laden with spoils.

During his absence, Callaghan, King of Munster, in alleged prosecution of the rights of his crown, attacked the Ossorians in order to punish them for having given hostages to Murkertagh. The latter, on his return (940) made a circuit of the whole island, proceeding from his own district in Ulster, and received hostages from the other three provinces, as well as from Dublin, which the Normans had rebuilt. Callaghan w s the Munster hostage, and was alone subjected to the indignity of fetters. The next year Murkertagh handed over those hostages to the monarch, thus setting a much needed example of subordination under circumstances that would have overcome the loyalty of any other Milesian prince of the day. In 943 he fell at Ardee in an engagement with his old enemies, who, reinforced from abroad, had resumed their ravages, and were marching under Blakair to Armagh.

Murkertagh was never in league with the foes of his country; he never fought against his lawful sovereign, and never withheld from him

[1] At the battle of Brunsbury, under Ethelstan.

the glory of the victories which his own hand had won. He passed his years in successful resistance to the invaders, and lost his life on the battlefield before he reached the throne of which he was heir not less by merit than by law. And yet so fascinated is the gaze of men by the mere flash of the warrior's sword, irrespective of the cause in which it is drawn, that this brave career of uniform honour is coldly recorded, while the faithless and versatile actions of Callaghan, who pillaged monasteries, and always fought with Normans on his side, have left a hundred reflected rays on the chronicler's page, and have descended to us surrounded by the halo of romantic fiction.

The year after the battle of Ardee, Congal, who was now heir to the monarchy, took Dublin, and soon after succeeding to the throne on the death of Donchad, fought another battle at that city, which had meanwhile been retaken, and slew Blakair and sixteen hundred of his men (947).

The exceptional rancour with which Dublin was made the object of repeated Milesian assaults can neither be explained by the national animosity against the Normans, nor by the commercial pursuits of which it is said to have been the centre. The secret vindictiveness which the memory of civil strife alone is capable of producing may perhaps account for it. It has already been suggested that the ancient Irish, with whom war was not a passion, employed themselves in commerce, which the Scoti despised, and were in reality the founders and chief inhabitants of Dublin and the other mercantile cities. When the Normans seized on those cities they did not obstruct, but rather took share in the existing trade, and thus the original inhabitants, engaged in the congenial arts of peace, were gaining a consideration which they were never allowed to enjoy in other parts of the country. Had any such state of things existed, and all the circumstances are favourable to the supposition, the Milesian chiefs would have hated the Irishmen of Dublin with all the bitterness and jealousy of inferiority, and would never lose an opportunity of gratifying their spite under the pretence of patriotic ardour against the Normans. It is certain that the annalists dwell with a peculiar relish of repetition on the number of "plebeians" who fell, or were led away prisoners with the "women and children," at successive captures of Dublin by the Milesian kings. We may ascribe the sacking of monasteries and the slaughter and scattering of their inmates by native rulers to the same cause. The motives of political action are nearly similar at the most distant periods. In the vigorous resentments and strong desires which we behold working naked and not ashamed in the dawn of civilization are to be found the keys of history. Under the decorous garb that clothes the politics of to-day, we may assume the knotted muscle and strained sinew that displayed themselves a thousand years ago.

The Scandinavians have never been able to regard religion otherwise than as a weight in the scales of battle, in field or cabinet. They were ready to profess any creed which fortune favoured, provided it could place no efficient check on their actions. In England, they habitually became Christians when outnumbered, and resumed their ancient faith when recruited by fresh levies of their countrymen. One of their leaders boasted in Winchester Cathedral that he had been baptised twenty times without any alteration being produced in his mode of life. There is nothing remarkable, therefore, in the fact that the Normans of Dublin were converted to Christianity in 948, immediately after their crushing defeats at the hands of Congal. They are said to have founded the abbey of St. Mary in this year. Their observation of the Christian Scoti may have satisfied them that in dedicating a portion of their substance to religious use they were not parting with it irredeemably. As if to test the efficacy of the baptismal rite, Godfrid, successor to Blakair, the very year after he became a convert, rifled the churches of East Meath, and found no apparent moral obstruction to burning a hundred and fifty persons in the Oratory of Drumree, and carrying off three thousand captives.

The surrender of their national belief by the Normans added another complication to the hopeless tangle of interests that was only gathered into a tighter knot by every strain for solution. A division henceforth took place between the foreigners of later arrival, who still retained their old religion, and the Christianized descendants of former immigrants. Intermarriages between the leading families of the Scoti and Normans became frequent. All combinations and all oppositions became possible and common. Congal waged an incessant double war against Munster and the Normans, and was at last, while spoiling Leinster, surprised and slain by Godfrid (955).

Domnal, son of the brave Murkertagh, succeeded him. He was commonly called Domnal O'Niall, by which was implied that he was grandson of Niall. During this reign the course of spoilings of monasteries, hurrying off of captives, and battles of inextricable alliances and counter-alliances, seems to have run with accelerated rapidity. The monarch made incursions into the south, was driven back and returned to the charge again and again, alternately aided and resisted by the Northmen of Dublin under Olaf. He was the first who transported boats overland to employ them on the lakes. At the close of his reign he suffered repeated and severe reverses from the Normans, which were, however, redeemed by a signal victory won by the heir-apparent, Malachy, at Tara, after a battle which lasted three days. The victor pressed on to Dublin, which opened its gates and yielded to all his demands. The King of Leinster, who was in captivity, was surrendered without a ransom, together with a thousand other prisoners. Olaf fled to Iona, and died there.

SECTION V.

Domnal died the same year. Malachy came to the throne in the year 980. Two years before this date Brian had become King of Munster. He was of the Dalcassian family, and had fought under his brother Mahon, who was king before him, from his early youth, having been present at the battle of Sulchoid, in which the Normans were defeated with immense loss, and at the siege of Limerick, where great spoils were taken. The splendid successes of Mahon blew the chronic envy of the Eugenians into a blaze. Unable to cope with him in an open fight they lured him to a pretended conference, seized him with violence, and bearing him off to a mountain recess slew him. When he saw the coming blow, he snatched up a copy of the Gospel which was to have sealed the proceedings of the conference, and held it before him as a shield. The assassins drove their weapons home, and stained the sacred volume with his blood. Such was the kind of help that was claimed from religion, and such was its weakness against any evil passion united for the moment with power. Brian's lofty spirit was wrung with anguish and indignation at his brother's cruel death. He first went against the Norman allies of the murderers, whose king, with two of his sons, he slew in the sanctuary of Scattery. He then turned his fury on the murderers themselves, and in two fights, in which they were assisted by the Normans, utterly overthrew them. After these victories he was unanimously chosen King of Munster.

The dissension between North and South Munster having thus terminated in the established supremacy of the Dalcassians, that between the northern and southern divisions of the whole island pressed forward for settlement. In the very first year of his reign, Malachy marched into Thomond, and in the course of his raid dug up the oak tree under which the Dalcassian princes used formerly to be inaugurated, and cut it into pieces. The criminality of this reckless act has been somewhat magnified by modern writers. It was unimportant save as an indication of the monarch's impolitic and somewhat irreverent character, which left him little probability of success against his more statesmanlike rival. A contest of twenty years' continuance began, in which the monarch showed himself daring, generous, scrupulous in his alliances, and single if immediate in his aim; while in Brian we find, in addition to courage and generosity, that strong and steady grasp with which the weight of present discordant influences can be hurled at a distant mark, and that widening prospect of ambition which ceases to discern as it soars the nice distinction between means. Malachy was always ready to join Brian against the Normans, and more than once conceded the point in dispute rather than fight against Brian. The King of Munster, when it suited his purpose, could induce the Normans to join him against Malachy, and one occasion refused to fight against the foreigners when Malachy was almost at their mercy. The monarch was fond of dashing exploits, and has won lasting celebrity by carrying off from Dublin a golden collar and a sword, which were valued as sacred heirlooms by their owners. He amused himself with games of chess, and breaking wild horses. Brian rendered himself popular with his contemporaries by munificent gifts to the Cathedral city. The monarch lost his sons in battle. One of Brian's daughters was married to the King of Alba, another to the Norman King of Dublin, and one of his sons survived to marry the sister of Harold, King of England.

In short, the time had come when the numerous independent and rival chieftaincies of Ireland might be fused into each other by the pressure of one central power, and the warrior, politician, and diplomatist had arisen who was able to collect and apply that power. A free constitution had been in course of peaceful development among a people regenerated by Christianity from conquest, when the eloquent murmur of the schools, and the growing song of peace, were drowned by the trump of war. Ireland went through the fresh trial to which she was called without the extinction of her characteristic qualities. The atrocity of her warfare was perhaps not so much less than that of other nations as the inextinguishable brilliancy of her intellect was greater, but it was at least directed by a less sordid motive, and was dashed by a stormy ray of chivalry elsewhere wanting. The problem whether the country possessed the formative instinct that moulds its several parts into the symmetry of a consentient life, was now about to be worked out under the recognised ascendancy of military and aristocratic ideas.

Brian, by steady uniform steps, established the kingdom of Munster in his own family, extended his sway to the ancient moiety of the island, had his claim to the Boarian[1] tribute allowed, and finally, with the consent of Malachy, and in presence of the Irish princes and the Norman lords of Dublin, Waterford, and Cork, was proclaimed monarch at Tara. This event took place in the year 1001.

The new monarch immediately on his accession devoted himself with unabated industry to the consolidation of the empire he had won. That he ruled with the sword, that the maintenance of order depended on his personal vigilance, and that the permanent success of his enterprise was contingent on the ability of those who might come after him, are conditions inherent in the initiation of all new dynasties. They who charge Brian with usurpation must first of all settle at what stage and within what limits in the reign of force the right of force is to cease. To insist on the stability of relations seized and maintained by violence is the merest superstition. The sword of the conqueror never ceases while it is unsheathed, to be double-edged. The union of an inviolable prescription, whereby the sovereignty of the island was attached to a particular family, with the almost unlimited but equally sacred title of the nominally subordinate kings and chiefs, clamoured for some extrication by the chronic disturbance which it produced. The right of the monarch and that of the provincial king rested on the same foundation, and neither could assail the other without undermining itself. It was necessary to break the charm of an artificial line of succession to the sovereign throne before the petty rulers could be awed into common loyalty or mutual peace.

Brian had no need to make his authority felt by any unusual severity. He went through the various provinces in assertion of his rights, and was received with unquestioning submission. The instances of resistance were so few and insignificant that they were put down without an effort, and required no stronger measures than the imprisonment of their instigators. But the forcible suppression of revolt was not the method on which he rested his best hopes, or consumed his most strenuous endeavours. He sought chiefly to engage the nation in the pursuits and enjoyments of peace. He built and endowed churches and schools, he repaired roads and bridges, he facilitated and enforced the execution of just laws. He practised a lavish hospitality. On one occasion he entertained at Christmas-time in his house at Kinkora three thousand guests, including the Norman lords of Dublin and the Isle of Man, the Earl of Kent, the King of Alba, and the four provincial kings of Ireland. The results of his government read like the wish of the patriot, or a poet's

---

[1] From having re-imposed this tribute on Leinster, as a punishment for its adhesion to the Normans, Brian was called Brian Boru.

imagination. Life, property, and chastity were everywhere secure. A beautiful and richly jewelled damsel traversed or might traverse the island from end to end without insult or injury.[1] If we confront this picture with the more current ideas of Irish character, and treat it as a product of the imagination, we must then receive it as the end to which Irish efforts and aspirations are tending. Fancied memories are hopes. But in testing the accuracy of the delineation we have to take into account that a profoundly pacific and religious people formed the base of Irish society. They were forbidden a history. They became known only as the blue of heaven is momentarily seen through a rift in the clouds. Their virtues were studiously ignored. It was high treason against Scotic dominion to record their actions. When Brian quelled the turbulent nobles and brought them under the terror of his laws, a rich and lovely maiden might walk unharmed through the land. This is the unconsciously revealed home history of the people of Ireland. It is no fable, no melancholy vision haunting the ruins of a nation's hope. It is sober fact. It was as true then as at any time since, and it has been as true at all times as at the present day. Were the experiment to be made now, two things would happen. No peasant, whether of Irish, Norman, or Anglo-Norman extraction, would sully his country's fame. This is certain. But it is equally certain that the spirit of envious ascendancy, more crafty than of old, would, through the very guardians of order, either invent a falsehood, or impute a crime of their own commission.

Only during a few short years was Brian permitted to prosecute his work, and to strengthen the new constitution against the wear and the accidents of future ages. The Normans, enraged at a peaceful triumph, greedy of accumulating wealth, emulous of their countrymen's success in England and France, longing insatiably for the fertile plains and green hills of Ireland, and prompted by traitors of Scotic race, after having made several desultory efforts in 1012, which were easily repelled, withdrew in baffled rage to gather their strength for one supreme effort. Messages were sent in every direction, and to all distances, to rally auxiliaries. Wherever the Scandinavians dwelt and had disposable forces, or adventurers who could be tempted by the prospect of booty, urgent applications and glowing descriptions of Irish affluence were forwarded. An immense armament answered to the call. Norway and Denmark sent their chosen warriors. The advancing fleets gathered contingents from Scotland, the Isle of Man, the Orkneys, the Hebrides, and the Shetland Isles. Intent on the enjoyment of a conquest, which in imagination they had achieved, they brought with them their wives and children. The King of Leinster joined them with all the forces he could muster; Sitrick, King of Dublin, who was Brian's son-in-law, kept aloof. The aged monarch at the head of forces from most parts of Ireland, marched to Dublin, and at the battle of Clontarf almost annihilated the invaders, but perished in the fight with his eldest son and grandson. So overwhelming was the defeat of the Normans that it struck terror into their people in their distant homes, and the project of

---

[1] Keating, p. 568.

conquering Ireland vanished from their thoughts for ever. But Brian's scheme of government fell with him.

The religious and intellectual victory of the native Irish had been arrested by the wanton aggression of Norman robbers. The second alternative, a united Scotic ascendency, was now frustrated. Ireland's hope had bourgeoned again, and again the cruel northern blast withered it to ashes. Yet the union of strength which Brian effected was not in vain. Had the island been divided as at other times, and had the Normans in their usual fashion poured in successive billows from every sea, the inhabitants would have been wearied out in a thousand fights, and finally overrun and subdued as England had been. For the occasion Ireland was as one man, and though her prospect of fixed laws and a firm centre of government was postponed, she remained unconquered.

CHAPTER IV.

PEACE AGAIN SUPERSEDES WAR.

SECTION I.

ON the death of Brian and of his eldest son, political relations returned to the state they had been in previous to his accession to power. While he lived, his pervading sway held the subordinate rulers in their respective orders; when he was removed they fell into collision. In the remoter region of his attraction the more ponderous bodies paused for awhile before they swung from their orbits. Among the smaller dynasts, and in his own family, the disorder was instantaneous. As the Munster army marched from the scene of its sorrowful victory, at the very first encampment the Eugenians demanded hostages from Brian's son Donchad as an acknowledgment of their right to the alternate succession, and only refrained from enforcing their claims with the sword, because a dispute arose among themselves concerning the distribution of the advantages which success in the fight would bring. After escaping this danger, Donchad and his Dalcassians were challenged by the Ossorians,[1] who refused to allow them a passage through their territory unless they gave tokens of submission. Only when their refusal was so determined and unanimous, that even their wounded men insisted on standing in the foremost rank, supported by stakes fixed in the ground, was the ill-timed interference withdrawn, and their army allowed to continue its march. Even then impediments were thrown in their way, and their stragglers were cut off by skirmishing parties.

When the Eugenians reached their own country they decided their differences by combat, and the victors were themselves defeated immediately after by the Dalcassians under the two sons of Brian, Donchad and Tadg, who had also quarrelled and fought, but were temporarily reconciled by the clergy. They afterwards reigned in partnership over the southern half until 1023, when Tadg was treacherously slain at the instigation of his brother.

After the battle of Clontarf, Malachy resumed the duties in which he had been superseded by a more vigorous mind. He took the command of the army which had been led by Brian's eldest son Murrough, and followed up the victory by attacking the Normans in Dublin, and destroying the greater part of the city. He was kept busy during the remainder of his reign in exacting hostages, repressing the crimes of his chiefs, and repelling the desultory attacks of the Normans. Having conquered the latter in a great battle in 1022, he retired into religious privacy, and died a few months after. His last act was the institution of an orphanage for three hundred children. During his reign the son of that King of Leinster who had assisted in the Norman coalition against

---

[1] Ossory comprised almost the whole of the present county of Kilkenny, with parts of Tipperary and Queen's County.

Ireland, was blinded by Sitrick, an act of cruelty which brought upon him the indignation and vengeance of the people of Leinster.

On the death of Malachy there was no claimant for the throne. The arrogant brawlers, who without any other fitness than pride of birth, were ever struggling to rise above each other, did not dare to aspire to a post so lately occupied by a sovereign who had illustrated the uses of power, and discharged the responsibilities of a throne. During seventy-two years there was no monarch in Ireland. An attempt was made to conduct the central government by appointing as regents two men, Corkran and Cuan, venerable for character and profession, rather than for their elevated rank or family connections. Where the conception originated, who made the selection, and who were the parties whose assent gave validity to it, there are now no means of judging. The political self-consciousness evidenced in the contrivance of such a remedy, more Irish than Norman in its form, is a symptom of the times worthy of careful record. On the death of Tadg, Donchad reigned as king of the southern half. In the year 1051 his brother-in-law, Harold, son of Earl Godwin, took refuge with him, and on his departure was furnished with a fleet and army. In 1063 Donchad was overcome by the friends of his nephew Terence, son of his murdered brother, and deposed. He went to Rome, and is said before his death there to have delivered his crown and sovereignty of Ireland into the hands of the Pope. He had no crown or sovereignty to dispose of, but the report has a significance of its own. In the twilight passage from rule by force of arms to rule by force of mind, we must be prepared to meet with monstrous forms partaking of the nature of both. They are the first rude acknowledgment of a public opinion.

Terence, the first who bore the name of O'Brien,[1] or grandson of Brian, succeeded Donchad immediately as King of Munster, and eventually as king of the southern half (1072). The principal event in his reign was the expulsion of the Norman King of Dublin, and the appointment of his own son Murkertagh in his stead. This step marks the arrival of the period when the amalgamation of the different tribes was almost complete. Terence received complimentary letters from Lanfranc, Archbishop of Canterbury, and Pope Gregory VII. The people of Man sent to him for one of his family to rule them during the minority of the native heir.

On his death in 1086, his son, Murkertagh, claiming the southern half of the monarchy as well, was embroiled in a long and bitter contest with his brother Dermot, and the monarch Domnal O'Lochlen, the head of the Hy-Nialls. A settlement was made in 1090 by which the old division of the island was made the condition of peace; the southern half being assigned to Murkertagh, and the northern to O'Lochlen.

The renewed experiment was less likely than ever to prove successful now that the monarchy was an open prize. A long war and a series of mutual invasions took place between the two kings, in the course of which the two royal residences were taken and demolished. On the

---

[1] Before the time of Brian each person took the name of his father or grandfather as a surname, the prefix "Mac" meaning "son of," and "O" "grandson of." Brian established the arrangement that the patronymics thus formed should be permanent in families. To the present day every surname is prefixed with "O" in the Irish language.

capture of the northern palace, Murkertagh ordered all the stones that composed it to be borne away by his soldiers. Immediately after thus wreaking vengeance on his rival he made a perpetual gift of the city of Cashel to the Archbishop and clergy of the southern province (1101). In 1103 the rival kings, when about to resume hostilities, were induced by the Archbishop of Armagh to enter into a truce for a year. In 1110, and again in 1113, they were reconciled on the eve of combat by a similar intercession. At last, after a struggle of a quarter of a century, they entered on a better competition. Murkertagh went into religious retirement, and died in 1119, and in 1121 Domnal followed his example.

In 1102, Magnus, King of Norway, is said to have sent a pair of shoes to Murkertagh, with the command that he should place them one on each shoulder, as a token of submission. The story grew into circulation that the prince quietly complied with this arrogant demand, and when remonstrated with by his indignant nobles, made answer that it was better that such a form should be gone through by one person than that whole provinces should be exposed to devastation. Such a story must have owed its origin and credit to a generally felt and freely expressed desire, that if kings must be amused with an interchange of ceremonies, they would choose some mode of conducting them less ruinous to their subjects, even if less dignifying to themselves, than rapine and slaughter. The other version of the affair is that the king ordered the ears of the ambassador to be cut off. This is more likely to have been the fact. It is certain that Magnus attempted an invasion, and was killed in an ambuscade soon after landing.

Murkertagh ranks in written history as monarch of Ireland. During his lengthened struggle with Domnal, a new aspirant for power, a son of his half-brother, had been actively making preparations, and on his death laid claim to the monarchy. This was Terence O'Conor, whose family was of the same stock as the Hy-Nialls, or O'Neills, and took its name from Conor, a king of Connaught in the tenth century. He was an able and politic prince, and when released from the engrossing calls of war, engaged with equal aptitude in the works of peace. He constructed roads, coined money, celebrated games, maintained regular fleets at sea, and was inflexible in the distribution of justice. By force of arms, by sowing discord between the Eugenians and Dalcassians, and by employing the arbitration of the church, he gradually extended his sway until he became monarch in 1136.

His claims were disputed by Conor O'Brien, King of Munster, but were admitted after a desperate battle was fought, in which seven thousand Momonians,[1] including the flower of the Dalcassians, fell (1151). It was a point of honour with the Dalcassians never to retire from the fight, nor to ask for quarter. It is manifest that a rule of this kind, however it may seal devotion to a lost cause, is only a challenge for personal distinction, and must eventually sacrifice the public interest to individual fame. The destruction of those chosen troops at such a critical period was a national misfortune of the gravest importance; all the more to be lamented that it was incurred, not for their country or their religion, but merely that it might be said among their own people

[1] Men of Munster.

that they were brave men. The fate that secluded Ireland from the rest of the world during so long a period, and confined her theatre of warlike glory within the limits of her own shores, left a fatal bias on the minds of her children that has yet to be corrected. It is well that we should know each other to be brave : it is better that our enemies should know us to be united.

Dermot MacMurrogh, King of Leinster, fought on Terence's side in this battle. Two years afterwards he eloped with the wife of O'Ruark, of Breffni,[1] who appealed for vengeance on the seducer to the monarch. The petition was granted, and Dermot was compelled to separate from the partner of his guilt. Henceforth he espoused the cause of O'Lochlen, and became a bitter foe to the house of O'Conor. When Terence died, Murketagh O'Lochlen, who by land and sea had encroached seriously on the glory of the later years of his reign, succeeded him (1161). This prince became involved in quarrels with the people of his own province, in the course of which, having taken the lord of Down prisoner, he ordered his eyes to be put out, an act of cruelty which aroused a general feeling of resentment. A league was formed against him by the friends of his victim, and when he took the field he had not even the honour of an important battle to signalise his fall, for his tribesmen deserted him at the last moment, and only thirteen men were slain with him. The detestable habit of inflicting blindness on prisoners in order to prevent them from giving any further trouble makes its appearance about this time in Irish history, and seems to be of Norman introduction. It is one of the mongrel crimes that display themselves among aspirants for rule, as policy supersedes warfare, or religion checks the full sweep of its stroke without quenching its spirit. As long as men fought for the joy of the strife, war was graced by a generous temper that proves our nature to have a good side at its worst. But when wars were undertaken for a separate and distinct end, artifice and cruelty found their combined gratification in acts of physical torture that at once satiated vengeance and prevented retaliation.

On the death of O'Lochlen, Roderick O'Conor ascended the throne of Ireland (1166). Having received the submission of Dublin and of the northern half, he held a general convention of princes and clergy at which various regulations, temporal and ecclesiastical, were decided on. When he demanded hostages from Dermot, the latter, rather than submit, burned his city of Ferns, and retired into the interior of his territory. Roderick proceeded to the south, still securing the adhesion of the princes. Meanwhile O'Ruark had entered Leinster with an army, and was joined by the people of the province against their own prince, who had rendered himself detestable for his vices and crimes. When Roderick came back to enforce his demands, Dermot, deserted and desperate, but burning with guilty rage and thirsting for vengeance, fled to England for aid against the institutions of his country. He was publicly deposed and banished by the assembled princes, and a successor was appointed to take his place.

[1] Breffni comprised the present counties of Cavan and Leitrim ; the former of which was Breffni O'Reilly, the latter Breffni O'Ruark.

Section II.

The narrator of Irish events is beset throughout his task by an insuperable difficulty which perplexes, bewilders, and disheartens him. He at last ceases to struggle against it in despair of comprehending its nature or its origin, and is forced to proceed with the perpetually increasing burthen of its mystery on his spirit. It arises from the total lack in the materials on which he works of that human interest which he knows to be indispensable to his success, but which he can neither find, nor create, nor communicate. The personages are characterless, the facts are devoid of political significancy, the heroic deeds stand in high relief and are apparently no part of the edifice. The myths which in other histories have an ethereal grace and glow as they rise from a seething national life, here are spectral and inanimate, and shrivelled by their coldness into deformity. The line of kings might be the result of an arithmetical calculation. The legends resemble the borrowed decorations of an unimaginative compiler.

And yet within this lifelessness he well knows that there beats a tender human heart beseeching his patience, and capable of winning his warmest sympathy if he could only understand its muffled throbs. Under the clangour of spears and the hoarse shouts of brutal warriors, and the loud plaudits of the privileged bard, there ever murmurs a smothered voice, whose sweetness charms his ear, although it cannot make its story known. A rayless sun looms before him in a heaven without an atmosphere. It is only when the beams pass through the vacuum to the skies of other lands, and fill them with light, that the mystery is solved. The strained and unreal attitude of the Milesian rulers is produced by their secret jealousy of the native or plebeian population, and by affected contempt for them. That population, ignored at home and debarred from the exercise of their special faculties, sank into apathy or strayed into foreign lands to learn or teach or pray in peace. Iceland was first peopled by Irish anchorites. In the restlessness of their agony they discovered the Western Continent, which was to be the refuge of their descendants. There is scarcely an educational establishment in Europe in whose foundation Irish scholars had no share. Had there been a sufficiently extended time of peace their genius would have ruled and characterized the nations. Even the rhyme which echoes in our modern poetry is an Irish invention. England owes her alphabet to Ireland. The real battle of to-day is waged to determine which country is to supply the ideas of which that alphabet is to be the vehicle. The Irish Church, the most active, the most missionary, the most instinct with life, was the only one that did not rest its success on the accumulation of wealth and dignities. A despoiled shrine seemed all the holier to the Irish monk. No other church left to future times the example and the certain element of success.

It was not possible that the influence of such a people should be unfelt, or that the tendency of the society of which they formed a part, however wild its oscillations, should not be towards quiescence. One

E

invasion after another had hitherto mocked the prospects of repose when the haven was all but gained. At the period to which we have now come, the spirit of order is again distinctly and growingly discernible. The subtle essence of religion, while it ceased not to infuse all its olden power into the individual life, was embodying itself in the visible proportions of a powerful ecclesiastical union. A public opinion that leant with overwhelming weight to the side of right was pervading all classes, and drawing its inspiration from the best. Kings and chiefs, foreseeing the effects of popular detestation, counted the cost before they sacked churches or mutilated their prisoners. Ecclesiastical reform was promoted by men of zeal and enlightenment who would have been an honour to any period of the church's history. Synods and assemblies of clergy and princes were becoming more frequent, and were more numerously attended. The fury of contending armies was again and again compelled to submit to the remonstrances of religion. The struggle for the monarchy was narrowing to fewer competitors, and each new aspirant who made good his position was surrounded by a readier and a wider adhesion. The land was almost rocked to rest. But again the harvest passed, and the summer ended, and Ireland was not saved.

We must not turn from the retrospect with dumb impotent regret, nor give way to passionate protest against the traitor or the foreign intruder. We cannot too often imbibe the lesson that the native bent of the Irish people is to union and peace, and that all their troubles and distractions have come from without. Our country was advancing with quickened consciousness towards the goal which God has destined for her, when her progress was interrupted by a wholly unprovoked application of the vulgar and brutal method by which governments are too commonly stained at their fount. But we learn from the past that there are no elements so discordant or hostile as that the country cannot blend them into her own uniform and vigorous life, provided only that she be allowed a season of repose.

CHAPTER V.

THE NORMANS.

SECTION I.

THE people of Scandinavia and Denmark were descended from the same race as the Saxon conquerors of Britain and the Frankish conquerors of Gaul. From a very remote period the Northern extremity of Europe has been undergoing, from geological causes, a gradual elevation of its surface. The consequent changes in climate and productiveness would tend to force the population downwards from the Northern to the Southern regions. But before migratory movements, whether arising from diminished fertility of the soil, or from mere increase of population, took place on any large scale, the inhabitants of the two peninsulas strove for a long time to meet the inadequacy of their resources by piratical expeditions. Availing themselves of their maritime skill, they plundered the neighbouring coasts, or lay in wait for merchant vessels laden with agricultural produce, and carrying off the spoil to their homes, lived in idleness and revelry while it lasted. Habits of sensual indulgence, of settled aversion to industrious labour, of savage exultation in the infliction of injury, and of insolent pride in their unpunished lawlessness, were engendered, and became inveterate. Those qualities, thus acquired, constitute the boasted superiority of the Northern races.

The fictions of their bards perpetually stimulated them to fresh outrages. Their language lost the power of expressing moral reprobation. Terms denoting phrensy, treachery, and theft acquired a heroic significance, from which, if we may judge by the fondness with which some modern writers linger on them, the sweetness of their original wild flavour has not yet departed. They felt the glow of enthusiasm in the infliction of torture, and the satisfaction of magnanimity in the commission of rapine. As the skins of animals are supposed to retain their gloss if torn from the yet breathing carcase, so the wild revel on the spoil of the peaceful hamlet had a keener relish for the northern freebooter if the roof-tree still blazed, and the mangled frame of its owner had not yet ceased to palpitate. The growth of liberty and civilization in modern Europe is the struggle of humanity against the example and institutions of the Northmen.

In any ordinary period of history they would have been driven back to their savage dens; but the nations, at the time of their principal irruptions, were gasping helplessly on the strand from which the waters of Roman tyranny had ebbed, and found a relief from anarchy in every fresh wave of conquest. In the only country which the Romans had never penetrated the direct attacks of the Scandinavians were decisively repelled.

We are accustomed to hear those ferocious depredators spoken of as if they were the best and the bravest in an age when no other kind of enterprise but theirs was known. They are represented to us as criminals on a princely scale, while the rest of mankind grovelled in petty delinquencies. During the whole period of their history Irish monks were sedulously preaching the maxims with which we are still endeavouring to appease the world's distracted conscience. The rivalry was not between lordly violence and servile incapacity, but between ruthless crime and heroic piety confronting and condemning it.

At the end of the ninth century Harold, King of Norway, strove to repress the disorders of his realm. A number of chiefs, unable to relinquish their lawless practices, went on board their ships and put to sea. Rollo was the younger son of one of the king's favourite nobles. His obstinate violation of the laws lately enacted against robbery had caused his father's death and the exile of his brothers. Unaware or regardless of their fate, he repeated his offence on the Norwegian coast. He was tried, condemned, and banished. Having joined the discontented refugees, whose numbers were recruited by outcasts from every neighbouring state, he was acknowledged as their leader. They sailed up the Seine, and, aided in some degree by the Gallic people, succeeded in wresting from the Frankish conquerors, who at the time were absorbed in a contest between rival claimants of the throne, a small tract of land on the banks of the river, which, with additions afterwards made to it, became known as Normandy.[1]

SECTION II.

The rugged vices that had gained hardihood in the Norwegian winter sprang into exuberant growth and quick maturity under the warm sun of France. The Northmen transferred their unscrupulous and insatiable rapacity from the products of the land to the land itself, and with the crafty instinct that prompts the bird of prey to guard the entrance to its nest with an intricate maze of thorns, they secured their ill-gotten territories with every legal subtlety that an alarmed conscience could devise. Their coarse love of feasting was excited and refined by the ample supply of rich viands placed at their disposal. Intercourse with the pomp and politeness of the French court trained the outrageous bearing of the bandit into airs of supercilious haughtiness and disdain, through which the unchanged brutal nature was ever ready to break forth. Their cruelty was methodised by policy. Instead of compelling the affrighted peasant to prepare a feast for them, and firing his homestead after they had partaken of it, they kept him in slavery, debarred him from every manly exercise, and lived in wantonness on the proceeds of his toil. The cycle of wrong was completed when they drained the wealth of soil and sinew to some distant luxurious capital. Aware of the wrongs they inflicted, and deliberately bent on maintaining them unabated, they never sought to conciliate their subjects with any pretence of common interest, or admission of common humanity, but ruled by systematic terrorism.

[1] The received accounts concerning the power of Rollo and his obtaining the daughter of the French king in marriage are mere fables. The extent of territory ceded to him and his followers is also greatly exaggerated. See "Criticism on the Life of Rollo," by H. H. Howorth, Esq., author of the "History of the Mongols."

In the reign of Richard, great-grandson of Rollo, an awakening breath of consciousness passed over the benumbed Franco-Gallic people of Normandy. They saw how a few vicious and alien men, differing in no endowment of nature from themselves, reduced them to a bare subsistence by the imposition of services and taxes, debarred them from freedom of forest and river, and left them no mark of ownership in the land they tilled or the houses they inhabited. Measures were concocted for a general insurrection. Representatives from all parts of the country were appointed to meet in a general council and determine on its time and manner. The Normans, who had quietly watched all that was taking place by means of spies, came suddenly on the assembled delegates, and made them prisoners. Without condescending to any assertion of right, or form of trial, they put a certain number to death, in the sight of their fellows, by impalement, or by burning them with molten lead, plucked out the eyes or cut off the hands and feet of the remainder, and sent them back to their homes in this condition through the public ways and villages. For hundreds of years after this event the peasants of Normandy, the rightful owners of its soil, lived in unresisting misery, and submissively sacrificed their freedom, their happiness, and their families to the will of their foreign lords. Such is Norman rule. Its cares are lessened, its immunities increased, by crushing the spirit of resistance and complaint.

Section III.

A ruling class may allow its weak or superflous members to sink into the ranks of the people; a ruling race must find fresh places of command for its increasing numbers, by alliances or by war. The impoverished nobles and younger sons of the Normans were quite willing to accept the sweets of power on the easiest terms. Emma, sister to Duke Richard, was married to Ethelred, King of England. A crowd of greedy adventurers accompanied the princess to her new home, and were raised to positions of trust. A Danish invasion took place soon after, and those men, with the instincts of their origin, made common cause with the enemy, and surrendered to them the towns which they held. Ethelred was compelled to take refuge in Normandy with his sons Alfred and Edward. Alfred made an attempt to recover the throne, but appearing with a number of Normans, ready to monopolise the fruits of his success, was forsaken by the English and lost his life. Eventually the Danes were driven out of England (1041), and Edward, half-Norman by birth, and formed from infancy in Norman habits, was elected king. By distinct stipulation he came to England with only a few attendants; but in a little time he was followed by troops of courtiers and place-hunters, who, through his favour, got possession of all the principal military and ecclesiastical posts. They introduced the French language and French fashions at court, and created social distinctions before unknown in England. Foreign manners sparkled on the surface, and all the homely Saxon ways were precipitated, like dregs to the bottom. The chief nobles and the mass of the people were keenly sensitive of this contemptuous treatment in their own land. Earl Godwin and his son Harold roused the nation to resistance, but were betrayed by the king, and forced to leave the kingdom. Godwin went to Flanders, and Harold sought refuge with his brother-in-law, the King of South Ireland (1049).

The Normans now poured in like a flood that has burst an opposing embankment. Their Duke William, reputed son of their preceding ruler, was borne away by the tide of his subjects. He visited England, and saw a new realm of enjoyment, already in a great measure possessed by his own people, tempting his seizure. But Godwin soon after again appealed to his countrymen, and Harold returned with troops from Ireland. They were joined by the whole nation, and King Edward had no alternative but to yield to their demands. The Normans took to hasty and ignominious flight. The Archbishop of Canterbury did not return even to take his pallium. The last of the fugitives, as they left London, massacred several English children in the rage of their baffled rapacity.

The Irish were the allies of England in their successful opposition to foreign aggressors. Whatever enmity has since raged in England against Ireland had its origin in the hatred which William then conceived towards the friends of the people on whom he intended to lay his yoke.

Norman devices were not yet exhausted, and Norman appetite was only whetted by delay. Harold having fallen by shipwreck into the power of William, was surprised by him, during the unguardedness of social intercourse, into a promise that he would aid him to obtain the crown of England on the death of Edward. Having thus over-reached his guest, William next called on him unexpectedly to confirm his promise by taking an oath on relics laid on a golden cloth, in the presence of the great council of his barons. Unaccustomed to those wiles of policy, and lacking the coolness and readiness of resource by which they might be evaded, Harold took the required oath. The cloth was at once removed, and there was revealed beneath a large chest filled to the brim with the bodies and bones of saints, which had been secretly collected from all the churches in the neighbourhood.

The art of a great ruler seems to consist in his not being ashamed to employ in engagements between nations the fraud and falsehood which would be criminal and despicable in a petty bargain about a yard of stuff or a measure of corn. The burthen of his unintentional oath lay like a nightmare on the conscience of Harold, and paralysed the courage of the people of England. The page of history that follows is read to this hour under its shadow, which not all the suns which have since shone have been able to scatter.

When King Edward died (1066), he appointed Harold as his successor, and the nation enthusiastically sanctioned his choice. The new king refused to abide by the pledge into which he had been entrapped at the Norman Court. A storm swept the soul of William. As the raven urges its flight towards the region where the carcase taints the air, so did he fall on the people whom his artifice had made accursed. He hurled the charge of sacrilege against the English nation, induced the Pope by promises of submission to approve his undertaking and anathematise his enemies, enlisted under his banner all the beggared profligacy and fermenting social refuse of the Continent, removed by assassination every thwarter of his plans, prayed to heaven for favouring winds, sailed to England, defeated the English army more by his ban than his arms, slew Harold, denied him a grave, took possession of his throne, and divided the lands and men and women of the island among his troops. No crime so lawless, no sorrow so pitiful, is found in the record of all time. The men of England, who shrank from the intrusion of foreigners as an agony to their pride, were now compelled to yield their liberties, and all they prized on earth, to the offscouring of Europe. It was not so much a conquest as a multiplied sacking and violation of homesteads. It was not the establishment of a new dynasty, nor the introduction of a new government, but the perpetual consignment of an opulent home-loving populous nation to the will of an army of licentious robbers.

Some desultory attempts at organised resistance were made. The sons of Harold went to Ireland, and returning with troops, raised the standard of independence amongst such of the English as were not disheartened by their misfortunes. But their efforts were rendered abortive by the adhesion of the principal men of the Saxons to the side of the conquerors. They went back to Ireland, the last representatives of English rights, to blend with its population, and share its future fortunes.[1]

Then throughout the land of England commenced the convulsive struggle of dying freedom. The national life, no longer existing as a consentient whole, broke out in a thousand disjointed throes and aimless spasms, that lent an excuse to the tyrant for pursuing the work of subjugation and of death. The chiefs had submitted in order to secure their lands. The people who continued to resist were branded as rebels and assassins. Mutilation of limbs, and extermination of provinces, crushed the courage of individuals, and the spirit of the community. Sixty miles of Northumbria were left strewn with slaughtered men, ravaged fields, and burnt cottages, so that one hundred thousand persons, whom the sword did not reach, died of destitution, after those nameless horrors of famine, with descriptions of which exulting hatred, or harrowing pity, have defiled the records of mankind. When the people were sunk in despair, the helpless chiefs were plundered and executed. The island was divided among William's followers. No Englishman was allowed to own land under the crown, or to fill any office of dignity or trust.

William is said to have introduced feudalism into England, and to have caused a survey of lands to be made. He simply ascertained the amount of his revenue, and the extent of his hunting grounds, and took such measures as seemed best to him to secure the quiet enjoyment of his newly acquired power. He maintained his personal authority by temporary expedients, pregnant with future confusion. When dying he repented, not with the awed regret of disillusioned ambition, but with the vivid agonies of a criminal. His heartless sons haggled over his last bequests. His servants plundered and deserted his dead body. The interment was interrupted by one who claimed the grave as property of which the dead man had despoiled him.

[1] Eight years after the Norman Conquest Godwin and Edwin Magnus, sons of Harold, after defeating the forces opposed to them, ravaged Devon and Cornwall, and then retired with their booty to Ireland.—Gilbert's "History of Cornwall," Vol. 1., page 8.

During a century and a half England was scourged and fleeced by foreigners who spurned the name of Englishmen. When the conquerors lost their connection with Normandy, they were compelled to make England their country. A new contest then began. The descendants of the victors and the vanquished, gradually forgetting, or ignoring, their original quarrel, disputed as rival classes, the one insisting on the right of possession, the other on their sufferings and necessities.

The constitutional checks on absolutism that have grown during recent periods, have been gratefully assigned to the influence of the Norman invasion. It would be as reasonable to thank the ravager of a sown field for the surviving ears that reach maturity; or to ascribe to the waters of the ocean the bulwark of shingle that stops their encroachments on the land.

Robert was the eldest son of the Conqueror. His two brothers, William and Henry, successively usurped from him the throne of England, and supplanted him in the possession of Normandy. Henry at last took him prisoner, had his eyes put out, and confined him in prison for life. On Henry's death (1135) England was seized by his nephew Stephen, and Normandy came eventually into the possession of his grandson, who, on the death of Stephen (1153), succeeded to the English throne as Henry II. This prince inherited all the phrensy, the licentiousness, and the insatiable land greed of his race. He held the kingdom of England by arrangement with Stephen and his followers. As vassal of the King of France he succeeded to the Dukedom of Normandy in right of his mother. He kept possession of Anjou, his father's province, by an act of perjury. He obtained Aquitaine as the dowry of his wife Eleanor, whom he married six weeks after she had been divorced for incontinence by her previous husband. He became master of Brittany and Gisors by marrying his infant sons to the infant heiresses of those possessions. In a spirit of unlimited chicane he claimed Toulouse in right of his mother-in-law. He obtained in 1156 a Bull from Pope Adrian, entitling him to acquire Ireland, on the ground that its church needed reformation, but he had hitherto been too busy in urging his claims on the Continent to make actual use of it. Some writers say that it was sent to, and accepted by the Irish Church.

Section IV.

The people of Wales had ever found in their Irish neighbours faithful allies while defending their independence against the Saxons, and afterwards against the Normans. At the end of the eleventh century Griffith ap Conan, Prince of North Wales, and Rhees ap Theodor, Prince of South Wales, having lost their dominions, recovered them by the aid of troops brought by them from Ireland, whither they had fled in their distress, and where the former married a sister of the King of Ulster. The latter was slain in an engagement with the rebellious lord of Glamorganshire, aided by Norman mercenaries, who ended by seizing the territory of their employer. Tempted by their example, several Normans, reduced to want by their extravagancies, and finding no longer any harvest in England that the sword could reap, obtained permission from the English king to conquer lands in Wales at their own charges. Among these was Gilbert de Clare, created Earl of Pembroke by King Stephen. A colony of Flemings, who had been driven to England from their own country by an inundation, and become a cause of uneasiness through their increasing numbers, were sent by Henry I. to settle in South Wales, where they formed a valuable soldiery for the Norman nobles.

On the death of Rhees, his son, Griffith ap Rhees, went to Ireland, and his daughter Nesta, after being mistress to Henry I., by whom she had two sons—Robert Earl of Gloucester, and Meyler Fitzhenry—was married to Gerald, governor of Pembroke Castle, and then to Stephen, castellan of Abertivi. The sons of these marriages—William, Maurice, and David Fitzgerald and Robert Fitzstephen, engaged in an insurrection against their cousin Rhees ap Griffith, the son of Griffith ap Rhees, who had come from Ireland, and regained his ancestral principality. At the time to which our history has now come, Fitzstephen was a prisoner in the hands of the Welsh princes.[1]

[1] Girald. Camb., p. 187.

CHAPTER VI.

PEACE DISTURBED BY ANGLO-NORMAN INVASION.

SECTION I.

WHEN Dermot left Ireland he sailed to Bristol, and finding that King Henry was in France, he followed him to that country, and offered to acknowledge him as his lord on condition that he reinstated him in his kingdom of Leinster. Henry was prevented by more urgent concerns from at once giving the needed assistance, but he could not absolutely refuse the tempting request. He directed Dermot to return to Bristol, and there await further intelligence from him.[1] To render the delay as little irksome as possible, he wrote to Dermot's host at Bristol, instructing him to treat his guest and his attendants with all the hospitality in his power.[2]

The ardour of a dethroned king seeking restoration could not be expected to loiter with the deliberate policy of a potent monarch absorbed in adding province to province, and giving attention to each as regard to his own interests dictated. After waiting for a month without receiving any communication from Henry, Dermot began to look around for speedier aid. He made his wants known to Richard, Earl of Pembroke, a discontented and embarrassed man, whose father, having failed to keep the confidence of either party in the late civil war, bequeathed impoverished resources and a mistrusted name to his son. Pembroke expressed his willingness to lend his services, but declined to engage in active operations until he obtained the king's permission.[3] In order to enlist his hopes and stimulate him to immediate measures, Dermot promised the hand of his daughter in marriage, and the succession to the throne of Leinster, as the price of success.

Unable to obtain anything more than contingent promises of support the exiled king made one further provision, on which he might fall back in case his greater expectations failed. Having learned, or already known, that there were in South Wales certain Norman relatives of the prince of that country, men of a restless turn, who would regard the disapproval of their king and the scruples of honour as matters of equal indifference in any enterprise that seemed likely to gratify their thirst for gain, he resolved to secure their friendship, and use it as circumstances might suggest. He succeeded in obtaining the liberation of Robert Fitzstephen from prison, and filled the minds of the Fitzgeralds with alluring pictures of the vast estates he would be able to bestow on his followers if he could only recover his kingdom.

[1] Giraldus Cambrensis says that Henry gave Dermot a letter, addressed to all his subjects, English, Norman, and Welsh, authorising them to assist the King of Leinster in the recovery of his territory. The existence of such a letter is inconsistent with subsequent events. Regan makes no mention of it.
[2] Regan, p. 13.
[3] Regan, p. 13.

He then returned to Ireland, accompanied by a son of the Welsh Prince and a body of Flemish mercenaries, with whom he resolved to make a first experiment against his enemies. As soon as he took the field the monarch and O'Ruark came to meet him, and an engagement ensued, in which the young Welshman was killed.[1] Dermot possessed the faculty of turning all the tumult of his soul into the repose of a dissembling policy. He threw himself on the compassion of Roderick, did homage for a small portion of land, with which he declared himself content, and paid a fine to O'Ruark, in acknowledgment of his long-standing offence. He then secretly sent his secretary, Regan, to Wales, with offers of unmeasured recompense in lands or money to all who would come to serve under him.[2]

This bait did not fail in producing the calculated effect. Volunteers, knights, and common soldiers flocked together, and placing themselves under the leadership of Fitzstephen, proceeded to Ireland, where they landed in the month of May, 1169.[3] With them came Hervey de Montmorres, a relative of the Earl of Pembroke, who was sent by him to watch the course of events, and to maintain some connection with the enterprise.[4] They numbered about five hundred men, horse and foot, and were joined on their arrival by Donald, the son of Dermot, with a like number of cavalry, and soon after by Dermot himself. The united forces marched against Wexford, then inhabited by an industrious commercial population. On the first attack eighteen of the foreigners were killed,[5] whereupon they prepared for a fresh assault by publicly celebrating the most solemn rite of religion. Overcome by the sight of the sacrament, or unable to resist a movement that they supposed to be sanctioned by the Head of the Church, or yielding, it may be, in part to Dermot's legitimate claims, the clergy of the town, among whom were two bishops, persuaded the garrison to surrender. The inhabitants renewed their oath of allegiance to Dermot, and were received into favour. The lordship of the town was bestowed on Fitzstephen and Maurice Fitzgerald, though the latter had not yet arrived in Ireland. An adjoining tract of land was given to Hervey, who colonized it with Flemings.[6] The descendants of these men were in long subsequent struggles the foremost and boldest asserters of national independence.

After three weeks' rest at Ferns, Dermot led his forces, now amounting to more than three thousand men, into Ossory, to punish the former defection of MacGillapatrick, the prince of that district. So long as the Ossorians fought within their natural fastnesses, where the want of armour did not expose them to disadvantage, they defended themselves successfully.[7] They were drawn into the open plain by

[1] Annals of Four Masters.
[2] Regan, p. 14.
[3] Hume's account of the first connection of English and Irish affairs is very suggestive— "Dermot lurking in the monastery of Ferns, which he had founded (for this *ruffian* was also a founder of monasteries), prepared for the reception of his English allies. The troops of Fitzstephen were first ready. That *gentleman* landed in Ireland with thirty knights."—Hume, Vol. i., p. 428.
[4] Girald. Camb., p. 189.
[5] Regan, p. 15.
[6] Girald. Camb., p. 192.
[7] "'We are well armed and they are naked,' were the words addressed by one of the Norman leaders to his soldiers on this occasion."—Regan, p. 17.

stratagem, where they were easily thrown into confusion by the foreign cavalry, and then slain by the native foot soldiers. Their chief obtained peace by submission.

An incident which occurred at this time throws some light on the character and aims of Dermot's foreign auxiliaries. Maurice de Prendergast, one of their leaders, taking some offence, went over with his men to the Prince of Ossory, and was employed by him in a private quarrel with a neighbouring lord.[1] As soon as he grew weary of this service he returned to Wales. His conduct provoked no censure, nor was it any hindrance to his afterwards resuming his place in the Irish enterprise. The men who joined Dermot from Wales were soldiers of fortune, unrestricted by any Royal warrant, who fought for money or lands, and were at liberty to transfer their services wherever and as often as they pleased.

Having reduced Ossory, Dermot marched against Dublin, and laid waste the adjacent districts until the townsmen sued for peace and gave hostages.

It was mainly by the action of his subordinate chiefs that Dermot had been deposed. Their submission and return to allegiance reinstated him on the throne. The sovereign right of Roderick over the province of Leinster, as represented by its restored king, now came into question. The monarch marched against Dermot and his allies; they retreated before him into the woods. Roderick had now an opportunity for the second time of arresting the danger that threatened his country. But it was not an Irish custom to press hard on a fallen enemy, and the idea of national subjugation has never as distinct an existence in the apprehensions of mankind as in the mind of the tyrant who conceives it. A series of negotiations and intrigues commenced which, by the intervention of the clergy, resulted in a peaceful settlement. The kingdom of Leinster was conceded to Dermot, on condition that he did homage to Roderick as his liege lord. The compact was ratified by the usual formalities. Dermot gave his son as a hostage to Roderick, and Roderick promised to give his sister in marriage to Dermot. By a secret understanding the King of Leinster engaged to dismiss his foreign troops. Everything that was due to the rudimentary principle of national unity, which then existed only in the titular dignity of the monarch, was accomplished.

SECTION II.

The recovery of his kingdom was thus achieved on much cheaper terms than those on which Dermot had calculated. He had been at first anxious to secure his object at the price of his daughter's hand, and the succession to his crown. He now found himself recognised as King of Leinster at no greater cost than the town of Wexford, and with his daughter and his kingdom still at his disposal.

The supreme throne of Ireland, to which he imagined he had a claim through his descent from a former monarch, became the object of his ambition. With the concurrence of his Norman-Welsh allies he sent letters to the Earl of Pembroke, reminding him of their agree-

[1] Regan, p. 21.

ment, and acquainting him with the new and wider field of advancement into which their former aim had widened. It is not stated that he offered any other prize than that which had been at first proposed, but no specification of details was necessary to suggest that the rights of Dermot's son-in-law and successor must increase with every fresh acquisition that might be made.

Pembroke, who knew through private channels all that was taking place in Ireland, and the prospects of success that awaited a more extensive armament, perceiving that the enterprise was entering on a new phase, immediately repaired to King Henry, who was then in Normandy, and sought his permission in general terms to engage in an Irish military undertaking. The king, who saw no immediate opening to the execution of his own designs concerning Ireland, thought that he could gain his end best by giving such a consent as he might afterwards, if it suited his purpose, declare to have been a refusal. Too eager to discuss ambiguous sentences, Pembroke returned home and commenced his preparations. His intentions were evidently as dishonest towards the king whose permission he sought, as towards him whose invitation he accepted.

That no time might be lost in taking possession of his intended prize, he sent Raymond, a nephew of Fitzstephen and the Fitzgeralds, with an army of knights and archers, accompanied by Hervey, who had returned to Wales in execution of his commission. In the spring of 1170 this vanguard of the Earl of Pembroke's invading army landed near Waterford. They erected a fortress on the shore, and collected a vast spoil of cattle from the neighbouring country. Waterford was then inhabited by Danes, immersed in the pursuits of commerce, and aboriginal Irish, unaccustomed to the use of arms.

At the present day a crowd of Irish townsmen or peasants, forbidden all their lives the sight of a sword or a rifle, save in the hands of their enemies, are seized with a panic when charged by a few disciplined and armed men of their own race. They enter into a foreign service, and in an incredibly short time, masters of their weapons, and sanctioned by authority, hurl back the very torrent of victory wherever they may appear in the field, and astonish the world by their systematic bravery.

Inexperience in arms was then, in cause and consequences, almost the same as it is now. The people of Waterford and the owners of the plundered cattle, to the number of three thousand, went forward to question the right of strangers to occupy their land and seize their herds. The intruders retired towards their fortifications. As the Irish pressed on them, Raymond suddenly turned and slew their leader. His party, taking advantage of the pause of consternation that ensued, opened the enclosure in which the cattle were confined, drove them with loud cries on the astonished multitude, and put them to a tumultuous flight.[1] They then fell on the bewildered fugitives, and after an unresisted slaughter, took a large number of prisoners, among whom were seventy of the principal citizens of Waterford.

Those captives had committed no crime, violated no engagement, broken no parole. They were simply possessors of rights which the

/. Regan, p. 25.

invaders meant to disclaim, and owners of property, of which they meant to deprive them. Ransom to any amount was offered and refused. A council of war was held, and it was determined that they should be put to death in order to strike terror into the Irish nation. The prisoners were carried to the summit of a precipitous rock, their limbs were deliberately broken, and they were flung into the sea.[1]

It would be useless to condemn as criminal what is maintained as expedient. Yet if expediency be a guide for the conduct of human beings, there must be a depth of criminality where its light ceases to exist. The plea for instantaneous and overwhelming severity is that it prevents continuous bloodshed. That is not want of mercy, it is said, but mercy in disguise which cuts off the necessity of future cruelty.

But why assume the necessity of continuous bloodshed and future cruelty? The man who is resolved on gaining a certain end, at any cost, may decide on what is the easiest course, which he may also suppose is the least guilty; but he is reasoning within the narrow limits of his own will and his own imagined interests. He is arguing about the comparative guiltlessness of the means of a pre-determined end, about which he does not argue at all, but assumes it to be necessary and right.

But the means he uses expose and condemn his object. His proposed method is to economise bodily at the expense of mental death. He inflicts one crushing physical blow, and justifies it by pleading that it will crush the spirit for ever. The carnage that is intended to subdue the souls of men, to make the thought of the past a horror, and that of the future a despair, is an attempt to make power irresponsible by destroying the tribunal before which it is judged.

That statesmanship stands self-condemned which confesses that its aim is to produce a community palsied by affright into abject quietude, and contented to be wronged out of every ennobling joy, and every generous aspiration. Perennial rebellion and massacre would be infinitely preferable to such a condition. But in reality, when the danger of repeated insurrections is thus provided against, it is the repose of a consciously usurping government and not the happiness of the people that is considered.

To rule rightly is an arduous and necessarily a self-forgetting office. The task may be made easy by benumbing the faculties of the governed. But the ruler who adopts this method puts himself on a level with the burglar who stuns his victim that he may despoil him with greater safety.

The deadliest part of those inhuman acts is the perverted sympathies and antipathies to which they give rise. Modern Irishmen are distracted between loyalty to their cause and allegiance to humanity and justice. They either execrate England as the parent of a cruel system, or they are tempted to adopt this system as expedient, because they identify it with the friends of the English connection. It should be remembered that the men who initiated rule by terror in Ireland, had no claim to the name of Englishmen, and did not even act in the interest of the Norman rulers of England. They represented no nationality and no legitimate authority. They were faithless subjects of Henry, and faithless allies of Dermot.

[1] Girald. Camb., p. 211.

SECTION III.

Meanwhile the Earl having selected and equipped a force of fifteen or sixteen hundred men, including two hundred knights, was on the point of sailing from Milford when an order came from King Henry forbidding his leaving the kingdom. Kings act in great affairs as ordinary men do in trifles. Henry, who looked at any accession of territory as a personal matter, could not endure that another should reap the first fruits of conquest. But Earl Pembroke was now acting on the impulse of his own ambition and his own hopes. His mind was too much engrossed by the brilliant visions presented to it, to be affected by the king's interdict. He set sail and joined Raymond at Waterford.

The united forces attacked the town, and after one or two assaults took it. A merciless slaughter was made in the streets. Two Danish leaders were taken prisoners and put to death. The Danish Governor and an Irish Chief were about to meet the same fate, when Dermot arrived and saved their lives. The invaders had not yet set up their own interest and policy in direct opposition to those of their Irish employer. Dermot had brought his daughter with him, and her ill-omened marriage with Pembroke was celebrated amid the desolation of homes and the reek of carnage.

Leaving a garrison at Waterford, the allies marched for Dublin. Hasculph, the Danish Governor, had revolted from Dermot, and anticipating an attack, called Roderick to his aid. The latter with a large army advanced to Clondalkin, within a few miles of the city.

While Dermot was intriguing for foreign aid Roderick had reduced the North and South of Ireland to order, made provisions for the security of church property, and the dissemination of learning, and solemnized the national games on so vast a scale that six miles in extent were covered with the encampments of those assembled. As usual, no domestic insubordination availed against the consolidating pressure of the central monarchy.

But the inability of the provincial kings and chieftains to combine against the monarch, or resist him singly, was no measure of their willingness to unite with him in exterminating a foreign enemy. On the contrary, they saw in external aggression a release from their allegiance and a licence for mutual strife. The precedent of one of their own order successfully opposing his suzerain by the help of mercenaries brought from a distance, was not repugnant to their habits of thought. Accordingly, when Dermot led his forces by mountain paths within Roderick's lines, the petty kings were not eager to obstruct him in the reduction of his own capital. They separated, and returned home to engage more hotly than ever in their private feuds.

The monarch was forced to retire, and Dublin was left to defend itself. The clergy, the chief of whom was Laurence O'Toole, brother-in-law of Dermot, and uncle, by marriage, of Pembroke, proposed a treaty, and Dermot, though he had received bitter provocation from the citizens of Dublin, his father having been assassinated and buried with circumstances of studious insult by them, consented to a truce. The common termination of Irish wars, the promise of future allegiance, and the giving of hostages, was at hand.

But the plans and interests of Pembroke and his companions could no longer wait on those of the King of Leinster. The peaceful settlement of his demands would neither answer their end nor secure their safety. They were acting in opposition to the orders of their king, and their only hope lay in such a prosecution of the war as would place them beyond the reach of his vengeance. While Dermot and the citizens of Dublin were arranging about hostages, Raymond and Milo de Cogan treacherously attacked an unprepared part of the city, and having gained an entrance massacred all on whom they could lay hands, and gorged themselves with spoil. Numbers of the miserable inhabitants, affrighted at this unknown warfare, rushed into the river and were drowned. Hasculph and some of the leading citizens escaped to the shore, and sailed to the Orkney Isles. Dermot was henceforth a mere instrument in the hands of the Anglo-Normans.

Leaving the plundered city under the command of de Cogan, the allies proceeded to devastate Meath. They swept like a tempest over the devoted region, marking their passage by a wreck of rifled churches and violated homes. Nothing remained for Roderick but to appeal to an allegiance whose sanction had departed. He threatened Dermot with the death of his son, whom he held as hostage, unless he fulfilled the terms of his engagement and dismissed his foreign auxiliaries. His demand was met with defiance, and a claim of the monarchy. Carried away by rage and forgetting the brutal indifference of his enemy, Roderick ordered the execution of the hostage, and a thrill of regret passed through the land at the useless sacrifice.

The signs of the times seem to have been more correctly read by the ecclesiastical than by the political rulers of the country. The English people had been in the habit of selling their children to the Irish as slaves. The only inference we can draw from this otherwise incomprehensible proceeding is that the parents knew they were not consigning their children to an unkindly fate. A Synod which now assembled at Armagh resolved that all English bondsmen in the country should be set at liberty.

Whatever the motive of this act may have been, whether it was meant to propitiate heaven, or to smooth the way to those relations with England which the Head of their Church recommended, it must have emanated from men, who, even in those dismal days, felt that slavery, however mitigated, was the crime that weighed heaviest in the balance of a nation's offences, and that freedom is the most precious gift that man can give to man in the sight of heaven. Ireland must not lose the credit of the first authoritative measure that loosened the chains of the slave.

Section IV.

The jealousy of King Henry was thoroughly aroused when he learned that the Earl of Pembroke was prosecuting the conquest of Ireland. He issued an edict recalling his English subjects from that country, and even seized on the estates of the Earl, as forfeited. Raymond was sent to appease him with assurances that nothing was won in Ireland, save in his name and for his glory. Henry had little faith in those professions, but his affairs were then in too complicated a condition to admit of his showing his discontent in any other way than by a disdainful silence. The murder of Becket, probably by his order, certainly in his interest, left his hands free, but for a moment he was paralyzed by the recoil of the blow.

The death of Dermot in the spring of 1171, though it simplified the attitude of the adventurers, was at first equally embarrassing to them as the death of Becket was to the king, for it was followed by the defection of a large portion of the Irish force.

When men are in doubt about the legality of their position, nothing is more to their advantage than a sudden necessity for immediate action. Hasculph attacked Dublin with a small army of his Northern countrymen, under the command of a chief who was known as John the Furious. But the Northern nations had for some time been learning the rudiments of industry and civilization, and the remnant of the phrensy that inspired their victories in former times was no match for the order and artifice of disciplined warfare, in which their kinsmen were so long and so exclusively conversant.

While the assailants were thundering at one part of the walls, they were attacked in the rear by a party who had issued from a different quarter, and thrown into confusion. An Irish king, connected by marriage with the adventurers from Wales, who watched the battle for the fittest moment to lend his aid, fell on them as they fled, and completed their destruction. John was slain and Hasculph was taken prisoner. When brought before de Cogan, the Danish officer declared that he would soon repeat his attempt with a different result. A legitimate ruler, or an honourable foe, would have met this bold sally in a corresponding spirit of generosity. Men engaged in a lawless and selfish enterprise are not magnanimous. Hasculph was immediately beheaded.

While the King of Leinster was alive Roderick did not put his authority over the Kings of Ulster and Munster to so severe a test as calling on them to join him in resisting the recovery of his throne. He now summoned them to take part in recapturing Dublin from strangers. They so far recognised his sovereignty as to march to the capital with their forces.

While their army was encamped near the city, a body of Irish brought intelligence to the Normans that the garrison at Wexford had been slain, and Fitzstephen taken prisoner. Disheartened by this event, de Cogan and his knights commenced a negotiation with the besiegers, but not meeting with favourable terms, they suddenly, with the aid of several Irish chiefs, followed by large bodies of native soldiery, made an attack at a very early hour on Roderick's camp, at a time when, according to the Irish accounts, the monarch was absent, and scattered them without a contest. The other kings at once withdrew.

The easy success that would have attended any concerted action is shown by the fact that O'Ruark of Breffni soon after attacked the capital with only his own troops, and was not repulsed until he had inflicted much damage on the enemy, and been disheartened by the loss of his son.

F

Pembroke marched from Dublin to the relief of Fitzstephen, and was very nearly defeated and destroyed with his army by the forces of O'Ryan, chieftain of Hidrone,[1] through whose district he was passing. A monk named Nicholas who accompanied him, singled out the Irish leader and slew him with an arrow, on which his men fled.

The Irish fought hand to hand, and were in consequence both unaccustomed to weapons that slew from a distance, and dependent on the presence of their chief, who always fought at their head.

When Richard reached Wexford, he found that the townsmen had carried their captive to an island in the harbour, where they threatened to put him to death if an attack were made on them. This difficulty was increased by the arguments with which those men defended their conduct. They declared that they held Fitzstephen in custody as one who had violated the commands, and lawlessly assailed the allies, or subjects, of the King of England. Not daring to employ his arms against men who put forward such a plea, he was forced to proceed to Waterford without accomplishing his purpose. When he arrived there he was persuaded by O'Brien, King of South Munster, or Thomond, to attack Mac Gillapatrick of Ossory for alleged treason.

O'Brien was formerly under the authority of Roderick, but when he had seen the success that attended Dermot he entered into alliance with him, and received his daughter in marriage, so that he was now brother-in-law to Pembroke. When Mac Gillapatrick knew of the impending danger, he sought a safe conduct in order that he might exculpate himself in person. His old friend Prendergast was appointed to escort him to the Norman camp. On his arrival, O'Brien insisted that he should at once be put to death, and his treacherous malice would have been gratified had not Prendergast drawn his sword and sworn by its cross that no harm should befall the man who had confided in his honour. He conducted the Irish chief to his home, spent the night with him, and returned next day to his people. In this action began and ended the actual Norman Conquest of Ireland. Men's voices falter to this day, when after the lengthened enumeration of perfidy and wrong they recount the deed of Prendergast. He is known popularly and distinctively as the Faithful Norman.

Raymond, who had been sent to allay the suspicions of Henry, came back without fulfilling his task. Hervey next undertook the office, and was equally unsuccessful. The king had managed for the time to extricate himself from his difficulties, and was preparing to visit Ireland. He disowned all that had been done by Pembroke and his companions, and ordered him to appear in his presence.

No alternative remained for the earl. He was compelled to turn away from the visions of independent monarchy in which he had begun to indulge. He went to Pembroke, where the king then was, surrendered his Irish acquisitions, and was restored to favour and the possession of his English estates. The king retained Dublin and the other maritime towns, and the Earl was allowed to hold the remainder under fealty to the English crown.

[1] Now Idrone, in the county of Carlow.

Such was the manner and the degree in which Ireland first came into the possession of Henry. The distrust and disunion that existed between the Irish monarch and his provincial kings and nobles was henceforth supplemented by a foreign dominion, liable to the same infirmities.

SECTION V.

At the same time several delegates from Wexford presented themselves before Henry, informing him that they held in their custody the person of Robert Fitzstephen, who, after having excited rebellion in England and Wales, had, contrary to every principle of right, ravaged the lands and slain the people of Ireland. The king received them with cordiality, thanked them for their services, and promised that he would punish Fitzstephen according to his deserts when he reached Ireland.[1]

His sincerity is sufficiently vouched for by the immediate and decisive steps which he took to guard against the recurrence of inroads such as that of which the people of Wexford complained. He severely censured and threatened the princes of South Wales, who had assisted the earl in his expedition against Ireland, and withdrew his anger only on condition that they allowed him to place royal garrisons in their castles.

On the eighteenth of October, 1171, King Henry landed near Waterford with a force of five hundred knights and four thousand men at arms. His arrival occasioned neither protest nor surprise. By one portion of the nation he was understood to have come with the sanction of an authority which had all the kingdoms of earth at its disposal, by another he was regarded less as a conqueror than as a restrainer of a band of ravagers, whom the perfidy of one of their own princes had introduced into the country.

The people of Wexford brought their prisoner Fitzstephen and besought justice against him as a disobedient subject and a lawless depredator. Henry attended to their accusations, publicly reprimanded Fitzstephen, and ordered him to be sent back to prison.

The failure of Pembroke's independent claims opened the way to the recognition of Henry by the Irish chieftains. Mac Cartie of Desmond was the first who acknowledged his sovereignty and promised to pay tribute to him. O'Brien of Thomond and Mac Gillapatrick of Ossory quickly took the same course, and the inferior chiefs of Munster soon imitated them, making their submission as the king advanced to Dublin. Even O'Ruark abandoned Roderick, and became the vassal of his rival.

Kings and great lords are rarely patriotic in the sense of suffering for their country. They belong to a caste which is not separated by natural boundaries, and generally feel at liberty to maintain their rank by changing their allegiance.

Roderick alone, for whom terms with the enemy meant loss of dignity, kept aloof. He collected his forces, and posted himself on the banks of the Shannon. Messengers were vainly sent requesting him to do homage. Henry did not venture to attack him, either doubtful of

[1] Regan, p. 56.

success, or unwilling to confound his claims with the violent and illegal measures of Pembroke and his companions, or, perhaps, preferring that the power of his Norman lords should be checked by the influence of a native monarch until he should have time to consummate his plans. The feast of Christmas was celebrated at Dublin with all the display and sumptuousness that distinguished the official banquets of the Normans from the hospitality of other nations.

The terms on which the Papal Bull, authorising the conquest of Ireland, had been granted, were that Henry would correct the irregularities of the Irish Church. It was necessary that some form of fulfilling this engagement should be gone through. At a Synod held at Cashel early in 1172, it was enacted that marriages should not be contracted within the seventh degree, that infants should be baptised within the Church, that tithes should be paid, and that ecclesiastical property should be free from all impositions and fines.

Those were the reformations in the name of which Henry laid claim to the kingdom of Ireland. Before he could make any further progress in his undertaking, he received intelligence that his sons had rebelled against him, and that two cardinals had entered Normandy to call him to account for the murder of Becket.

He had been five months in Ireland and had done little more than establish a nominal right, by the voluntary submission of the Irish chiefs, over the territories which Dermot and his Norman auxiliaries had won.

The King of Leinster in proposing to become the vassal of Henry, and the Kings of North and South Munster in submitting to him as their liege lord, acted under the impression that they were changing the duty they owed to Roderick for a looser and remoter tie. Henry, on the other hand, while he entered into engagements with the Irish chiefs by receiving them as his feudatories, claimed the disposal of the soil of Ireland. Following the method which had been adopted in Wales, he executed charters assigning the entire land of the island to ten of his adherents, to be conquered at their own cost, with the exception of the towns on the eastern coast, which he held in immediate possession.

Thus a simultaneous attack and unanimous resistance were both prevented, the original vices of an independent chieftaincy on the side of Ireland, and of unregulated freebooting on that of the Normans, were inflamed, and a universal and endless contest initiated. Ireland was made to resemble one of those modern ships in which the danger of wreck is guarded against by dividing it into several water-tight compartments, any one of which, while it resists the sea, can keep the vessel afloat. There was always some region to which the foe could not gain an entrance; and such is the sacredness of freedom, that a single resisting district, or unyielding right, preserves a whole country unconquered.

Before leaving Ireland, Henry liberated Fitzstephen at the intercession of his companions. He deprived him, however, of the town of Wexford, and obliged him with Maurice Fitzgerald and others of the first adventurers to reside at Dublin. Having appointed Hugh de Lacy governor of the capital and viceroy of the kingdom, he sailed from Wexford, and landed in Wales on the seventeenth of April, 1172.

Section VI.

Those writers who fondly speculate on the good results that would have followed if Henry had prolonged his stay and completed the reduction of Ireland, start from an impossible hypothesis, and proceed to an inference opposed to the general experience of mankind. Had he been free from the passions that eventually produced his recall, he never would have invaded Ireland. And those who have watched the growth of governments will not imagine that the product of centuries could have been secured against circumstances unfavourable to order and happiness by the visit of a foreign king, even if protracted to a lifetime.

England was still enduring, and had no prospect of deliverance from, as great if not greater anarchy and misery than Ireland ever suffered. The first stages of constitutional administration did not commence in that country until the kings had been long expelled from their Continental dominions. The invasion of Ireland by Henry II., regarded politically, proceeded from Normandy. It had, in consequence, a corrective and restraining influence on the English or Anglo-Norman attempt made by the Earl of Pembroke. It is very questionable whether Henry would have undertaken his Irish expedition if he had not been moved to it by jealousy of his Anglo-Norman subjects. His so-called conquest was rather the modification or repression of conquest undertaken by others; and there is no doubt but that the power of the Kings of England would have been exerted in the same direction so long as they continued to be Dukes of Normandy. But the moment that England became a separate kingdom, and her Norman rulers condescended to display their pride and rapacity under the name of Englishmen, it was inevitable that Ireland should fall into the same relation towards England which England had before occupied towards Normandy, and that the name of Irishman should be despised and abhorred by Englishmen, just as the name of Englishman had previously been by the men of Normandy. This was the lot in store for Ireland. There is no provision against the tendency of circumstances, except the possession of a spirit that resists their pressure with a power and a patience greater than theirs.

The probable results of Henry's stay in Ireland might be computed on the supposition that he and his successors gave their undivided attention to her fortunes. This is almost identical with speculating what the fate of Ireland would have been had she been left to the government of her own kings.

The real question to be solved is what the consequence is likely to be when a conquered nation, with its resentments and its jealousies held in the leash by its crafty conquerors, is involved in the subjugation of another country, equal to it in tenacity of purpose, and in the integrity of its traditions. The answer is to be found in the history of the two islands from Henry's time to the present day. Ireland has had her peace disturbed and her development delayed by perpetual invasions, and England has had her ideas of freedom and happiness hopelessly confused by successful outrage.

Under Roman rule Britain was supposed to be stimulated to hopes of freedom by the sight of free Ireland.[1] Under Norman rule England has always been betrayed into connivance with her own enslavement by the sight of enslaved Ireland. As a nation she has, by an inconceivable delusion, imbibed the spirit without the privileges of her ruling caste. For substantial equality at home she has accepted a superiority abroad that to the mass of her people exists only in idea. Making common cause with her masters in destroying Irish freedom, she has inferred that she was herself free; zealously co-operating with them in disposing of the lands of Ireland, she imagined that she was in possession of her own. Her rulers have artfully diverted her attention from her natural rights by identifying them with the clamours of a race with whom sympathy was rendered impossible.

The disunion between the peoples of England and Ireland is the standard specimen of Norman statesmanship in its subtlest form. The blind fury of a sorely oppressed nation was engrossed on the spectacle of another nation constantly struggling against oppression. Englishmen were taught to see in Ireland a claimant for the liberties they had lost, and in Irish resistance an insult to their own easier subjugation; and so mechanically did their embittered feelings turn towards that devoted land, that the moment their own invading brothers were lost to sight as they crossed the channel, they were confounded with the people whose rights and properties they assailed, and became equally with them the objects of indiscriminating and unreflecting hatred.

SECTION VII.

Henry left the traces of his distracted counsels and warring passions on the administration of affairs. He deliberately embroiled his nobles with the Irish, and set them at rivalry among themselves. His object was to keep the fortunes of Ireland in inconclusive warfare until he could return to reap victory with his own sword.

Some writers state, as has been mentioned, that when he obtained the Papal Bull in 1155, assigning to him the sovereignty of Ireland, he sent it immediately to the Irish clergy, and that they confirmed it by their written consent. Trusting, as it appears, to the impressions thus made, he neither promulgated the Bull, nor engaged in any military undertaking. He received the submission of the Irish princes in the name of the Pope, and then handed over their territories to his followers to be conquered for the crown.

He had acknowledged O'Ruark, King of Breffni, as lord also of Eastmeath, which had been bestowed on him by Roderick. This did not prevent him from assigning the same district to de Lacy. Two lords of the same territory, deriving their immediate titles from the same sovereign, stood face to face. It might be an act of disloyalty for either to make war on the other. They agreed to discuss their rival claims at a conference. It was the Irish custom to meet on such occasions on an eminence, as a provision against possible treachery. On the night before the meeting, Griffith, a nephew of Maurice Fitzgerald, had an opportune dream, in which he saw a herd of wild boars,

[1] Tacitus, "Life of Agricola," 24.

headed by one of vast proportions, rushing on de Lacy, whom, according to his vision, he saved by slaying the monster. On the appointed day O'Ruark presented himself on the summit of the hill without attendants. De Lacy on the other side was accompanied by Fitzgerald, Donald O'Ruark, and an interpreter. Fitzgerald, without any provocation, drew his sword. Griffith with seven knights appeared on the scene. O'Ruark, now an old man and half blind, must have acted only in self-defence against his numerous opponents. He killed the interpreter, twice smote de Lacy to the ground, though defended by Fitzgerald, and at last, when his people rushed to his assistance, was run through with a spear while attempting to mount his horse and off his guard, by Griffith, who had already rehearsed his part in his dream.

This occurrence removed a troublesome competitor, and furnished occasion for blackening the Irish character. The treachery and the inception of the attack were imputed to O'Ruark. He was declared to have been a rebel, his head was cut off and sent to Henry, as a proof of his treason, and his body, with the feet upwards, was exhibited on the gate of Dublin, conclusively establishing the same charge. De Lacy then distributed the lands of Eastmeath among his followers.

A similar contest arose concerning the province of Leinster. Henry had ratified Pembroke's acquisition of it, but had also received the homage of Donald Cavanagh as Dermot's heir. The Earl, who, on Henry's departure, resumed his kingly style, and created his son-in-law, Robert de Quincy, Standard Bearer of Leinster, got the son of Donald into his power as a hostage, and put him to death. A war ensued, in the course of which de Quincy was slain and the Earl himself defeated at Thurles by the troops of Roderick and O'Brien, with a loss of seven, or according to other accounts, seventeen, hundred men. Hastening from the scene of this disaster to Waterford, he was driven by the townspeople to an island in the river, where he was kept in a state of siege until Raymond came with a large force from Wales, and rescued him. Waterford was then strongly garrisoned, and Limerick, which had been taken by O'Brien after the battle of Thurles, was recovered. About the same time Donald Cavanagh was treacherously killed.

Henry had not been inattentive, meantime, to the affairs of Ireland. He had impeded the projects of de Lacy and the Earl of Pembroke, by summoning them successively to his aid in France, from whence he sent back the latter to assume the Government with Raymond as his partner (1173). Having succeeded in getting absolution from the Legate for Becket's murder, he moreover procured from Pope Alexander a confirmation of Adrian's grant. The Bull of Adrian was now for the first time publicly read in Ireland, with the further authority of the confirmatory document. Roderick, who had hitherto maintained his independence, yielded to the solemn requisition; he sent three prelates to Henry at Windsor, and an agreement was made, whereby he promised fealty to the King of England, on condition that his title as King of Connaught and Monarch of Ireland should be acknowledged, and made good, if necessary, by the aid of Norman arms. The Papal sanction was thus formally asserted and admitted. Henry retained under his immediate dominion the portion of the island known afterwards, with varying dimensions, as the Pale. It now comprised Dublin, Wexford, Waterford, and the districts surrounding them—a considerable tract of Leinster. The Irish who had fled from those parts were allowed or expected to return, and pay tribute, or render services, as their lords might require.

The grants which Henry made of Irish territories bestowed almost kingly power on their holders. Those powers were irregularly qualified by immediate interferences on the part of the crown with the sub-feudatories. The English king had no standing army in Ireland, but he could generally reckon on the services of his vassals for his French, Scottish, and Welsh wars. Risings in Ireland were met, not by the soldiers of the great lords, who could rarely be depended on, but by fresh importations of troops from England. Thus under a Papal grant and a form of feudal government, the wound of conquest was kept raw for ever.

SECTION VIII.

On the death of the Earl of Pembroke, which event took place in 1176, the Norman chiefs elected Raymond, their most popular and successful soldier, to the office of deputy. Henry refused consent to their choice, and sent William Fitzaldeln de Burgo, or Burke, who was descended from a son of William the Conqueror's mother by her prior husband, as his representative. When Raymond, surrounded by a number of the Fitzgeralds, all clad in bright armour, and bearing the same device on their shields, went to resign his charge, the new Governor, either heedless of concealing what he knew to be the king's desire, or indulging in the jealous pride incidental to the occasion, muttered in an audible voice that he would soon put an end to this brilliant display, and scatter those shields. During his government he discouraged the extension of the Norman territory, and strove to conciliate the natives by kindness and justice. He was in consequence detested by the rapacious colonists, who urged his leniency to the Irish and his unpopularity with the Normans so effectually on the king that he was withdrawn, and de Lacy appointed to take his place (1179). A grant of all Connaught had been previously made to him, notwithstanding the treaty with Roderick.

Still dissatisfied, Henry obtained the Pope's consent to make his youngest son John, King of Ireland. Startled at the significance of the title he had created, he hesitated to send John to the seat of his newly-appointed authority, nor did he allow him to be styled King of Ireland in any public document. While he delayed, word was brought that de Lacy had married a daughter of the Irish monarch, and had thus laid a foundation for claiming the throne in case the O'Conor family should fail to offer a direct heir, a contingency at the present rate of their mutual slaughter by no means improbable or remote. Henry immediately recalled the suspected deputy, and then after three months, reassured of his fidelity, or believing that he had sufficiently foiled his plans, sent him back accompanied by a priest, John of Salisbury, who was expected to keep a watch on his proceedings (1181).

His distrust again reviving, he sent his son John to undertake the government. The Prince landed at Waterford on the first of April,

1185, with four hundred knights and a large army. When the Irish chieftains who lived within the English settlement came to pay their respects they were received with mockery and derision. The young Prince and his companions saw only persons clad differently from themselves, and wearing their hair in a fashion unknown to them. They scorned the kiss of peace proffered according to national usage. They amused themselves by tapping on the head with poles, sticking with pins, and plucking by the beard, the men who came to offer friendship and goodwill after the ceremonial of their country.

The chieftains retired in disdain, and communicated their indignation to the independent princes, who were actually on their way to pay their respects. The Irish combined, and in a little time the forces of Prince John were almost annihilated.

But no sense of personal dignity or national honour could unite the Milesians for the final expulsion of the common enemy. They might be roused by the exasperation of the moment to avenge an insult, but they quickly subsided into their usual mood, and felt more pride in perpetuating the venerable feuds and ancient hatreds of their tribes, than in contending against an upstart enemy of yesterday.

Prince John was recalled when he had been eight months in Ireland. The disasters that had occurred were ascribed to the treachery of de Lacy, who had gone so far, it is said, as to order a crown to be made, and was, beyond question, commonly regarded as king. Henry commanded him to appear before him, and defend himself. The accused man was busily engaged in perfecting his preparations, whatever their object may have been. In the course of superintending the erection of a castle on the site of a monastery dedicated to St. Columbkille, he stood giving directions to his workmen and stooped over the entrenchment, as he indicated some work to be done. Prompted by, or awaiting for, the opportunity, a young man of a good family, who was at hand, raised his axe and with one well aimed blow cut off his head, so that it and the body fell together into the fosse.

Modern historians to escape the responsibility of pronouncing on the quality of the deed, dispute about the name of the man who did it.[1] It is not by any means intended as commendation when it is said that the act was conceived and executed in the truest spirit of the race against whose profane usurpation it was directed.

The conquest of Ulster had been committed to de Courcy by Henry when leaving Ireland. He entered on the undertaking during the deputyship and contrary to the orders of Burke. With a few hundred men he is said to have scattered armies of ten and fifteen thousand Irish enemies in successive battles. That large bodies of unarmed peasantry, suddenly called to the defence of their fields and homes, were thrown into confusion by de Courcy and his mailed knights is very probable. The native wars of the Irish were confined to the Milesian or military class, who fought with each other for glory as a privilege of their rank. When a foreign enemy appeared this class was exhausted in numbers, and still prone to disunion, and the mass of the people were wholly

---

[1] As his name is not likely to become a household word, it may be given. It was Guilla-gon-inathor O'Miadhaigh.

unaccustomed to war. The men of Ulster were not, however, daunted, but returned again and again to the charge, until, eventually, the Norman leader was forced to make his escape, scarcely with his life, and with an almost total loss of his troops. He stood at bay, near Strangford Lough, protected by fortifications, and aided by contributions from the people of Dublin, and from his father-in-law, the King of Man.

When Henry heard of de Lacy's death he appointed de Courcy to succeed him as Viceroy. He had already bestowed on him the title of Earl of Ulster.

CHAPTER VII.

THE O'CONORS.

SECTION I.

By the treaty of Windsor the Normans were pledged to maintain Roderick and his successors on the throne of Ireland.[1] As the succession was frequently decided by battle, the Normans, when such a contingency arose, were liable to be allied with one faction against another, or to be ranged on both sides, and encounter each other in the field.

Murray, the eldest son of Roderick, claimed that, according to the ancient custom, Connaught should be resigned to him. The change that had taken place in the circumstances of the monarchy justified the refusal with which the demand was met. Murray and Milo de Cogan, commissioned by Burke, who was Viceroy at the time, invaded Connaught to make good the claim by force. They were resisted and defeated. Murray was taken prisoner, and deposed from his rights by being blinded. His brother, Conor Mounmoy, succeeded to his place, and urged the same demand. Roderick at last resigned in his favour, and retired into the monastery of Cong.

The resignation of Roderick, the absorption of King Henry in the narrowing vortex of his fortunes, and the accession of the restless and impolitic de Courcy to the chief command, removed every obstacle and increased every facility to universal dissension.

De Courcy entered Connaught to depose Mounmoy, on behalf of another of Roderick's sons, who accompanied him. Mounmoy, with O'Brien of Thomond, drove him back with great slaughter. The Kings of Thomond, Desmond, Ulidia,[2] and Breffni united in support of Mounmoy. His death, by accident or assassination, prevented the advantages that might have been expected from the combination.

Crovderg, a brother of Roderick's, appeared as a new claimant to the throne. This prince, illegitimate by birth, and persecuted from infancy, had passed a life of hardship and peril among the peasantry. He was engaged, with his companions, reaping a field of corn, when the news came that opened his path to greatness. In words that became proverbial, he bade farewell to the sickle and welcomed the sword. From the moment of his entrance on the scene of strife he was the central figure, around which all the movements of military and political life circled. As if under the spell of a master mind, the Norman chiefs became alternately and successively his allies or his foes, as his needs required or his attacks compelled.

His rival was Cathal Carrach, son of Mounmoy. The clan, to stay, if possible, the unnatural contest, brought Roderick from his monastery,

[1] Leland, Vol. I., p. 104. MacGeoghegan, p. 276.
[2] Ulidia comprised the present county of Down and part of Antrim.

and surrounded him with the emblems of royalty. An attempt was made to settle all differences by a compromise ; it failed, and Roderick retired finally from the throne to the cloister. The two Cathals brought their claims to the decision of the sword, and Crovderg remained master of the field and the crown.

Shortly before Roderick's last retirement, Henry II. died, defending his ill-got possessions against his sons with his death-grasp, and yielding his life to the wrench that tore them from him. The proclamation of Richard I. was followed by the appointment of the younger de Lacy to the viceroyalty (1189), and the return of de Courcy, sullen and discontented, to Ulster.

If the Milesians had arrived at the sentiment of nationality they now had an opportunity of asserting it with every prospect of success. Donald O'Brien of Thomond defeated the Normans decisively at Thurles, but, instead of pressing his advantage, immediately connived at their invasion of Desmond. On his death (1194) two claimants strove for the succession, one of whom, aided by the Normans, devastated the district and took Limerick. The other, aided by Crovderg, swept the Normans, who had acted with characteristic cruelty and vindictiveness, out of Thomond, and rested on his work as if it were complete. Cork was the only city of Munster that remained in the hands of the enemy. The Kings of Connaught and Ulidia and the two chiefs of Munster laid siege to it. The old jealousy between North and South broke up the coalition. O'Conor and O'Lochlen withdrew; Cork yielded to the Prince of Desmond alone, and what might have been a national triumph became the barren victory of a solitary chief.

Crovderg made peace with Cathal Carrach, and assigned him a portion of land. A dispute however, arose, and Carrach, aided by William Burke, a relative of the former viceroy, dethroned his rival. A contest of such violence commenced that all parties and interests are undistinguishably confused in the rapidity of its movements. Crovderg sought the assistance of de Lacy and de Courcy. Carrach, assisted by Burke, surprised and defeated them. De Courcy quarrelled with Crovderg about the pay of his army, and made him prisoner. The Irish Prince, when released, contrived to detach Burke from his competitor, whom he attacked and slew. He then assailed de Courcy so hotly, that the latter to strengthen his position in Ulster sent for his companion in arms, Armoric St. Lawrence, who immediately marched to his assistance with, according to English accounts, only two hundred foot soldiers and thirty knights. Crovderg intercepted them on the way and cut them off to a man.

Even Irish historians show an extraordinary partiality in recording this transaction. They represent all the heroism and devotion as being on the side of the foreigners, and charge Crovderg with want of mercy in annihilating so inconsiderable a force, and with undue elation at so ignoble a victory.

When de Courcy first invaded Ulster, he is said to have easily beaten armies of twenty thousand men with a few hundred followers. Recent writers tell in terms of brief disdain how with a few warriors, one Norman Knight scattered hosts of Irish Celts, almost without rising in his stirrups.[1] But if the Irish had withstood and overthrown their insolent foes, the same friends of the vanquished men would have invoked the commiseration of heaven and earth against the cruelty of the resistance. Such are the claims of the invader, and so profoundly have they imposed on the imagination of mankind.

It must be remembered that the Normans, clad in impenetrable steel armour, fought against Irishmen dressed in linen. Under any disproportion of numbers this must ever be an unchivalrous kind of warfare. There is no reason whatever why a few hundred warriors fully armed and organised, should not resist the assault and complete the destruction of any number of unarmed and undisciplined men, unless it be found in the superhuman courage of the attack. Such a fight can only be compared to a crowd of willing martyrs rushing on a death-dealing engine of war, and quenching its fires in their blood. Numbers here do not describe the power to kill, but the readiness to perish. A thousand Irish are said to have fallen in this fight. They did not fall in vain, for their cause or their fame. They helped to vanquish, by their numbers and their devotion, men superior in discipline and arms, and as this is what is generally required of a people fighting for their country's freedom, it must be distinctly insisted on that it displays the rarest and truest courage.

But it cannot be pretended that the Milesian leaders fought consciously for national freedom, or that their efforts can be associated with subsequent popular aspirations for self-government. There are two ways in which the question of Irish regeneration may be viewed. We might desire to see the Milesian independence restored, with its deep class distinctions and its warlike instinct; or we may contemplate an Irish nation set sufficiently free to develop its predominant character, and shape its indigenous career. Modern patriotism in its generous impatience blending those two views in its visions of the future, fails to see how widely they are separated in the past. The contemporaneous annalists who represented the oppressed religion and literature of the day, did not forget the highest interests of a people in their blind admiration of a caste of mere fighters. They tell how Cathal Carrach and William Burke and the two O'Briens, with their foreign and native troops, ravaged and destroyed Connaught from Sleive Aughty in the south, to Dun Rossarach in the north, and from the Shannon westwards to the sea; and how neither the inviolability of the sanctuary, nor the sanctity of the priest, nor the weakness of woman, nor the strength of man, was any protection against their demoniacal host; so that the people of Connaught had never before known so dire a scourge of nakedness and famine. And they tell us again how Cathal Crovderg, and the same William Burke with the two sons of O'Brien, and the heir of the Mac Carties, and their followers, took up their residence in the Monastery of Boyle, and during three days polluted the hospital and the cloister, and every holy place of the building by their licentiousness, and wantonly broke and burned every structure, save the roof that covered them. And they tell us, moreover, how, after the desecration, the soldiers were scattered to levy their hire from the people whom they had outraged, and how a miracu-

[1] See Macaulay's "History of England," Vol. I., p. 12.

lous report got abroad, whether through a man, or through the spirit of God in the form of a man, was unknown, that William Burke had been killed, and how on hearing the news the tribes arose as one man, and slew the spoilers of their shrines and their homes, to the number of nine hundred. So little were the people influenced by the alliances of their chiefs. The kings and chieftains regarded the Normans only as their opponents or partners, it mattered not which, in the game of war; the peasants, or rent-payers, saw in them the oppressors of their fields and the enslavers of their country.

In England there was the same distinction of interests and sympathies. While the turbulent Richard slaked his thirst for blood, and butchered his prisoners in a holy war, and the treacherous John massacred his guests in pursuance of his personal ends, the Saxon people were ground to the earth by lawless taxation, and insulted by wicked and obscene forest laws. The assumption of modern historians and novelists that they felt pride in the martial deeds of their lords, is the device of a present policy.

The population of London raged and swayed in loose but infrangible chains. Their leader was torn from the sanctuary and executed. In a last wild appeal to heaven they made his memory a religion, and fondly endowed the gibbet, on which he suffered, with miraculous powers; just as the Irish ascribed the death and misfortunes of their tyrants to the vengeance of the saints whose altars they had robbed.

Rural England was a scene of smothered and unorganised warfare carried on by homeless men from the hidden recesses of mountain and morass. Denounced and treated as assassins and robbers in their own day, they figure in ours as bold and licensed freebooters, whose innocent pastimes were viewed with indulgence by their congenial lords. Victims of bitter Norman hate, they are with us objects of poetic fancy. They were hunted as wild beasts, and when no refuge remained for them in their own land, numbers of them fled to Ireland, and filled the neighbourhood of Dublin with their insurrectionary movements. Here, once more, were sown the seeds of the most vigorous plants in the crop of Irish discontent and future rebellion.

SECTION II.

The coming of the Normans had accomplished nothing but the frustration of the natural progress towards union and order which was being made in the island, and the loss on the part of the intruders of whatever habits of patriotism and reverence for law they had acquired since they left their homes in the north. The Milesians and Normans were literally fighting each other back to the manners of their common ancestors; and as the Normans had descended from a somewhat higher superficial refinement, their downward impetus became more rapid, and they distanced their competitors in retrogression. Their example reacted on their antagonists, who naturally impatient of the restraints of settled government, were not averse to the introduction of a new element of discord.

The Normans having experienced kingly authority, were more

anxious to escape its pressure than the Milesians were to avoid incurring its obligations, accustomed as they had been to an empty subjection to their native monarch, and supposing that a distant dependency would be less felt. The Milesian was learning to dissociate protection of the peasantry from lordship of territory, and the Norman found free scope for his habitual licence in the laxer customs of Ireland. Both parties discovered a more congenial occupation in ravaging each other's lands than in superintending the culture of those under their control; and in consequence, the unhappy natives or plebeians were condemned to the task of rearing cattle, like larger game, to furnish an interchange of plunder between their common spoilers.

The troubles that reigned in England, and the evil influence of King John, had characteristic results in Ireland. William Burke flung off his allegiance and ravaged Connaught. Crovderg, aided by Fitzhenry, now deputy, besieged him in Limerick, and compelled him to submit. De Courcy refused to pay homage to the murderer of Prince Arthur. He was made prisoner at John's command by de Lacy, who succeeded to his title of Earl of Ulster. Soon after he succeeded to his treason and its consequences by giving shelter to the wife of Broasa or Bruce, Lord of Brecknock, and possessor, through the daughter of Dermot, of large estates in Ireland, who had also provoked the king by taunting him with his nephew's death. John, beset with difficulties at home, was glad of an excuse for proceeding to Ireland (1210). De Lacy fled to the Continent as he approached. The wife and child of de Broasa were taken and starved to death.

As the English Monarch's visit was meant for the correction of his Norman subjects, and not for the conquest of the Irish, the native chiefs attended his court in large numbers, and made formal submission. He was in reality deposed in England, and for a brief period acted as if Ireland constituted his sole dominion. He rode side by side with the Monarch O'Conor, at the head of their joint troops. He dismounted to meet the Northern chief O'Neill, and no longer refused the kiss of equality. He addressed himself to the pacification of the country, the redress of wrongs, and the introduction of English laws. He divided the district in which his subjects had any possessions into twelve counties, and appointed sheriffs and other officers for each. Throughout the remainder of this reign, while England was the scene of tumult, Ireland was comparatively at peace. Thus the very worst of English kings, by ruling Ireland apart from English interests and jealousies, succeeded in effecting what ability and honesty, hampered by rival claims, have always failed to accomplish.

After John's departure a rival branch of the O'Conors, indignant at the relation in which Crovderg stood to the foreigners, invaded Roscommon, but were defeated by his son Hugh. They then made an inroad into Delvin, and were resisted ineffectually by the Normans until Crovderg appeared on the scene. The monarch's fidelity to his engagement with the King of England at length involved him in such difficulties with his subjects that he applied to John for support according to the terms of the treaty. John gave the promised aid, and at the same time sent a quantity of scarlet cloth to be presented to the King of Ireland, and the provincial chiefs who acknowledged the English supremacy.

It was an old Irish custom that the superior kings should bestow garments of rich materials on their tributaries, who by receiving them made submission and claimed protection. In the year 1014, when Brian was sovereign, his brother-in-law the King of Leinster accidentally tore the silver clasp from a satin mantle adorned with a border of golden tissue, which Brian had presented him with a short time before, and gave it to his sister, Brian's wife, requesting her to refix it. The Queen, as the old historians relate, took the mantle and cast it into the fire, reviling her brother for having consented to be vassal to any man on earth.[1] John had become acquainted with this national usage, and by adopting it, entered into a solemn engagement of mutual obligation with the rulers of Ireland.

On the accession of Henry III., at the age of ten years, to the throne, the Normans of Ireland requested that a member of the Royal family should be sent to reside among them. It is natural to the peculiar connection between the two islands that, except in moments of extreme exasperation, the inhabitants of the one will not explain what they mean by their requests, nor the inhabitants of the other what they imply by their refusals. The king's advisers gave no definite reply, but took measures to soothe the discontented nobles, and engage their minds in the important events that were passing in England. The de Lacys were recalled, and taken into favour, and a copy of the great charter was sent to Ireland. This document applied only to the English of the Pale, and ignored the very existence of the native princes and people.

Meanwhile Cathal Crovderg was faithfully fulfilling his agreement according to its true meaning. He acknowledged the sovereignty of the English crown, but resolutely and successfully resisted the encroachments of the Norman nobles. In 1219 Walter de Lacy marched with an army to the Shannon, and commenced building a castle between Longford and Roscommon. Cathal compelled him to retire, levelled the castle to the ground, and returned home in peace. This was the last of his achievements.

A new spirit was infused into the O'Conor family from the reign of the peasant-bred king. Of simple tastes, virtuous life, and transparent honesty, he stands in glaring contrast to his vicious and deceitful enemies. Trusted in a time of universal duplicity, and true amid discordant interests, he had the happiness of finishing a career of prosperity, achieved by strength of hand and brain, on the blending confines of earthly and heavenly triumph. He died in 1224, while the skies poured a heavy and awful shower to mingle with the tears of Ireland, in the habit of a Franciscan monk, at the Abbey of the Hill of Victory, which he had founded forty years before to commemorate the defeat of Armoric St. Lawrence.

Apart from the wars or friendships of their lords, native or foreign, the people of Ireland, who were not entrusted with the defence of their country against the invaders, maintained a distinct national existence

[1] Keating, p. 569.

in their intercourse with the Court of Rome. The great offices of the Church were generally filled by members of the ruling faction, but the rank and file of the ecclesiastical army belonged to another muster roll. They organised their forces, repaired their losses, and provided for future contingencies with the steadiness of an instinct. In 1203 some illegal innovation was made at Iona. The clergy of the North of Ireland sent deputies to the spot, who remedied the abuse, and guarded against its recurrence by appointing an Irishman to the abbacy of the metropolitan island. King John appointed an Englishman to the vacant see of Armagh. The Irish elected Eugene, and Innocent III. confirmed their choice. Eugene presented himself before the king in England, and while pleading for his Church did not forget to complain of the ill-usage his countrymen suffered from the avarice and tyranny of the Normans. When John was deserted by his own clergy he sent for Eugene to assume the duties of the diocese of Exeter.

SECTION III.

Hugh, son of Crovderg, was elected to his throne, and persisted in his policy. O'Neill, who might be said to represent the independent Irish party, forcibly raised a rival to him in the person of Terence, one of Roderick's sons. Hugh appealed to the English at Athlone. It now appeared that some years before, the King of England, influenced by Hubert Burke, his justiciary, had promised that Richard Burke, his nephew, should succeed to the kingdom of Connaught on the death of Crovderg. An order came that this promise should be fulfilled. William, Earl of Pembroke, the deputy, unable to execute an order made in complete ignorance of the circumstances of the country, espoused the cause of Hugh, and helped him to drive Terence from his territories.

The act of spoliation only glanced from Hugh to fall upon his people. In the wars of the Irish with each other, herds of cattle formed the conventional objects of prey, and they were swept backwards and forwards from province to province, as either side gained the advantage. The Norman soldiers made a closer scrutiny as they passed through North Connaught, and glutted themselves with spoil. The Normans of Munster and Leinster, headed by the sheriff of Cork, fired by the accounts of the rich harvest their friends were reaping, invaded South Connaught, without invitation from Hugh, and stripped the region so bare, that multitudes of women and children died of famine and cold. Pestilence followed, and in whole towns not a living soul was left.

When Connaught was drained of its wealth, Hugh was invited to a conference at Dublin, and made prisoner on his arrival. The Earl of Pembroke delivered him and escorted him home. He made an attempt to retaliate the wrong he had suffered, and provoked a multiplied attack. Burke, with one of Roderick's sons, marched a large army into North Connaught, and Geoffry de Maurisco, with another son, marched to Roscommon. Hugh fled to O'Donnell, and on his return was attacked by both his cousins, who took his wife prisoner and gave her up to the Normans. The next year he was once more invited to a conference at Dublin, and treacherously murdered there.

His two cousins contended for the vacant crown. Richard Burke, though he was now deputy, and had married Hodierna, a granddaughter of Cathal, did not venture to assert his own claim openly, but sought to gain his point indirectly by aiding one of the competitors. His interference produced such dissatisfaction among the people that his assistance was disavowed. He offered his services to Felim, son of the late monarch, who had already asserted his claim, and made it good by a victory. Repulsed with scorn in this quarter also, he made Felim prisoner by a dishonourable artifice, and again attempted to attach himself to the other side. Felim made his escape from prison, rallied his followers, and slew his rival. Hubert fell into disgrace with King Henry; his nephew was in consequence removed from the deputyship, and Maurice Fitzgerald appointed as his successor. Felim seized the occasion of making a complaint to his suzerain of Burke's lawless conduct. Henry, who was officially informed that Felim had rebelled, and been conquered with a loss of twenty thousand men, made further inquiries, and confirmed Felim's title. Hubert was soon after restored to favour, on which his Irish relative went to England, and being civilly received at court, took that as a sufficient warrant for resuming his attempts on Connaught, in which he was assisted by the deputy. Felim repaired to England, and had an interview with the king, the result of which was a letter from Henry to Fitzgerald inveighing in strong terms against Burke, and commanding that the title of Felim should be respected.[1]

Henry, being about to make war on Scotland, summoned the Irish chiefs to his assistance. The list of the names of those to whom this requisition is addressed is headed by that of Felim, who is styled successor to the monarchy of Ireland. Peace was made with the Scots before this levy was put to the test, but the following year (1245) a similar request was made for aid against the Welsh, and was obeyed by Felim alone, who gave a powerful assistance, and was suitably honoured by Henry.[2]

The bad faith and disobedience exhibited by Fitzgerald on this occasion caused his removal from the deputyship. He engaged in a war with the O'Donnells on his own account, and slew the chief of the enemy with his own hand. Ten years afterwards he met a brother of this chief in personal conflict, from which both were borne mortally wounded. While O'Donnell lingered at death's door, O'Neill entered his territory. The dying chief ordered himself to be carried in his coffin to the battlefield, where his clan won a decisive victory. When they laid down their burthen at the close of the day, they found their chieftain dead.

The most memorable deeds of the Milesians were displayed in fratricidal strife. Yet in comparison with their enemies their warfare was honourable, and their courage unique in its kind. They fought for fame, were ready to yield their lives, and were only careful to avoid infamy. They prided themselves in fighting in the open field, and without armour, and persisted in this tradition of their forefathers against men who employed every wile, knew not generosity, and took without stint all the advantages that their coats of iron gave them.

During the deputyship of Maurice Fitzgerald, Richard, Earl of

[1] Leland, Vol. 1, p. 219. [2] Ibid, p. 220.

Pembroke, having fallen under displeasure at the English court, was ordered to quit the realm. He went to Ireland, and with a force collected there, returned and possessed himself of the castle of Pembroke. Letters were sent by the English ministers to the Irish deputy, Hugh and Walter de Lacy, Richard Burke, Geoffry Maurisco, and others, offering them the Earl's Irish estates if they could destroy him. They lured him to Ireland by lying accounts, trapped him into a conference with elaborate artifice, and murdered him with circumstances of unexampled treachery. The brother of the murdered man was restored to the king's favour before his assassins could obtain their full reward.

The remainder of Felim's reign was a vigorous and successful struggle to hold good against foreign and native opposition, the part which he inherited under the protection of the English king. His son Hugh, a man of true northern type, and not unaffected by collision with the later tactics of his race, was so carried away by instinctive patriotism that he consented, during his father's life-time, to forego his personal rights, and to serve under O'Neill, who claimed the monarchy, in the cause of resistance to Norman encroachments. The Ulstermen and a contingent from Connaught marched against the enemy at Down. They were met by Stephen Longespe, the new deputy, and an obstinate battle was fought. At last O'Neill fell and the Irish were routed (1260).

It is constantly said that the Irish make good soldiers everywhere but at home. This is only part of a universal truth, stated as if it were an exception. The Irish, speaking very moderately, have won as many victories in their own country as any other people have in theirs. What they differ from other countries in is this, that they have never been conquered by any number of defeats on their own soil.

In the reign of King John an army of barbarous foreign mercenaries devastated England, from Dover to Berwick, reduced villages and castles to ashes, and drove one portion of the nobles to purchase safety by doing homage to the King of Scotland, and compelled the remainder to offer the sovereignty of their country to the eldest son of the King of France. Military glory is won in the enemies' country. Men lose their presence of mind when they see an armed foe occupying the scenes that are associated in their minds with peace and happiness. The strongest passions of our nature, hatred, pride, and cruelty, are called into full activity in perpetrating an invasion, while outraged tenderness unnerves the arm of the defender. This is so strongly felt, that a wise general will always anticipate invasion, if only by a few yards' march.

Hugh succeeded his father in 1265. For a few years he was prostrated by illness, and the enemy overran his territories unopposed. Then he rose from his bed of sickness as one who feels that there is work to be done, and that life is short. Two armies came against him, commanded by the deputy and Walter Burke, now Earl of Ulster, the son of his father's life-long foe. They marched to Roscommon, thence to Elphin, and were crossing the Shannon when a small division of Hugh's army drove them back. Then for two days and nights he stormed round their camp, as a lion rages round a fold, and did not allow them a moment's rest. They invited him to a conference, sending William Burke, the earl's brother, as a hostage for his safety. Hugh seized William and slew his attendants. Earl Walter passed the night in impotent rage and grief. Next morning he advanced to the Shannon, where he encountered O'Brien coming to Hugh's assistance, and killed him in battle. Hugh watched for an opportunity, dashed on the enemy with his whole force, drove them in headlong flight with countless slaughter, and took an immense booty of horses and armour. Gauging exactly the nature of the men he had to deal with, he added blow to blow, and put William Burke to death to appease the shade of O'Brien. The Norman appals by the prodigality of his lawlessness, and is terrified only by his own image in the blood mist. For once the tyrant was smitten with his chosen weapon, and sank beneath the stroke. Earl Walter sickened and died at Galway. Hugh reposed in the glory of his victory. He was satisfied with ravaging his enemies' lands, and destroying their castles. He had never quite recovered from his illness, and died in 1274.

SECTION IV.

Maurice Fitzgerald was deputy on the accession of Edward to the English throne. He marched against a body of Irish who had penetrated into Leinster, and were demolishing the castles of the Normans as they went. He was seized and imprisoned by the enemy, with the connivance of his own people. On his release he made war on the O'Briens in aid of his son-in-law, Thomas de Clare, son of the Earl of Gloucester, to whom, with the usual recklessness of right and result, a grant of land in Thomond had been made by Edward. The native inhabitants were not recognised by English law. Their lands were given away as freely as if they were part of a desert.

Two O'Briens were already at war for possession of the same territory. The new claimant entered into a confidential compact with one of them against their common rival. They were totally defeated in battle. De Clare appeased his mortification by having his ally torn asunder by horses. A fierce war arose, and after de Clare and Fitzgerald had been repeatedly overthrown, they were driven into the mountains, and starved into unconditional surrender. The O'Briens remained masters of Thomond.

De Clare reaped the benefit of the mildness of Irish laws. Instead of being treated with retaliative cruelty for the detestable murder he had committed, he was only adjudged to pay a fine.

The fidelity with which the two nations clung to the spirit of their respective criminal codes gave the Normans a decided advantage. The Irishman whom they murdered with impunity was the victim of his own freer and more merciful institutions. But inequality of civil privileges, caused by the exceptional mildness of their laws, was not the especial disadvantage under which the natives laboured. The English Government in Ireland altogether ignored the Irish, just as the settlers in a new land would ignore the herds that grazed its fields. If an Englishman murdered an Irishman it was not considered a murder. In the year in which Edward hanged Wallace, Sir Piers de Birmingham invited O'Conor of Offaly, with his brother and twenty chieftains of their house, to his castle, where he murdered them all. He got a chieftain named O'Flynn into his power, a few years before, under the pretence of projecting a matrimonial alliance, and treacherously killed him. He was always defeated in open fight, and at last was slain in battle against an O'Conor and an O'Flynn. This man was esteemed a hero among his own people, and their song writers relate how he hunted the Irish as if they were hares, and took off their heads in payment of their lodgings. The invaders persuaded themselves that the lands of Ireland were their property, even to the rocks amid which the true owners sheltered themselves from their pursuit.

There is nothing remarkable in this attitude of mind. It is one that is seen to exist between all nations foreign or hostile to each other. The singularity is that it should prevail in reference to a people living on the same soil, and protected by political treaties and religious engagements. It does not matter that there are no laws in a European nation guarding the inhabitants of an Asiatic or African village from extermination. It becomes a matter of great importance when armed members of the European nation find themselves in close contiguity to the Asiatic or African village. It is nothing strange that a nation should exalt itself by partial and one-sided records, and by misrepresenting and depreciating the people of every other country. All nations, more or less, do this. The singularity is when of two nations united by law and equal in theory, one should persist in lowering and slandering the other, just as if it were a foreign, distant, and hostile region unrecognised by law.

A request sent by the Norman element of the Pale to the Government of England for a member of the Royal family to reside among them had received no attention. A petition was now sent by the commonalty of the same district to Edward for an assimilation of the laws of the two islands. They supported the request with an offer of eight thousand marks. Edward recommended the proposal to the Irish Council; they simply took no notice of it. After a lapse of two years, the king again urged the subject on their attention. They disregarded it as before. To grant the petition would be to forego the gains and consciousness of conquerors. It never was granted.

England had undertaken to introduce order and good government into Ireland. During now more than a century, she was fully occupied in moderating the disorders of her missionaries of reformation. If the Irish could not unite in repelling the Normans, it is equally true, and more to the point, that the Normans could not unite in conquering the Irish, either by force or example. The Barretts and Cusacks, two English families, settled in Connaught by the Burkes, drew their swords against each other, and never sheathed them till one of them was destroyed. De Verdon of Meath and Fitzmaurice of Offaly engaged each other in a long and desolating war. The death of Maurice Fitzgerald and de Clare in 1286 left Richard Burke, who by marriage obtained the Earldom of Ulster and the estates of the de Lacys, foremost in power. He set aside the authority of the Viceroy, and made war at his own will and for his own ends.

In 1296 de Cogan was sent to allay the distraction of the colony. The condition of the Pale, and the fatal influence it exerted over the Normans in other parts of the island, may be understood from the fact that when the deputy persuaded the heads of the Burke and Fitzgerald families to make a truce with each other for two years, after the manner of sovereign princes, a universal tranquillity ensued. A tax was then imposed on absentees, and the construction of roads and bridges was furthered. This tax was not intended to procure for the Irish tenant the protection of his lord's presence, but to provide arms for his subjugation; and the contemplated roads and bridges were meant not to throw open the resources of the land, but to facilitate the intrusion of hostile bands into the interior. Regulations were also made, forbidding the adoption of Irish manners, laws, and customs. The Irish were refused the laws of England, and the English in Ireland were forbidden Irish laws.

The mind grows wearied over the monotonous record of injustice and violence. It is at the same time irritated and alarmed at its own increasing insensibility. In the wintry hour, when life at its best is needed, a deadly lethargy invades its faculties. We lose sight of nationality, and justice, and human purpose and worthy courage as we read. We can see no merit in man, no design of providence in the accidental successes that were won, or the losses that were suffered. There is only one clue to guide us through the labyrinth, the indefeasible right of the just cause. This is the rainbow that God sets in the heaven when the confusion of warfare begins, and the deluge of blood threatens. There is no other science of history.

The nation did not forfeit by forgetfulness the right of appointing its monarch. General expectation or formal convention indicated from time to time the popular choice, lighting now on an O'Neill and again on an O'Brien. But besides the advantage derived from its treaty with England by the royal family of Connaught, that family in the line of Crovderg alone exhibited marks of statemanship and dynastic forethought in addition to warlike capacity. Richard Burke, known as the Red Earl, who in the generally relaxed relations with England sought to supersede the deputy, marched against Manus O'Conor in 1228, but finding him supported by the forces of the King of England, was compelled to retire. He then assumed absolute sovereignty in the North with such unquestioned success, that the King and people of Connaught were perplexed as to whom their allegiance was due.

On the death of Manus a contest arose between Sir William Vesey, the deputy, and Fitzgerald of Offaly, concerning the appointment of his successor, which, fanned by fresh disputes, culminated in mutual charges of treason and an appeal to the combat. Both lords went to England, but Vesey privately withdrew to France, and Fitzgerald returned in triumph. He attempted to depose Hugh, Vesey's nominee, but Burke, at the instance of the English king, came to the assistance of the threatened monarch, and the clan being appealed to, acquiesced in his title.

King Hugh was succeeded by another Hugh, who was killed at the instigation of William Burke. The prize long coveted by the Burke family seemed now within their grasp. But the royal glory was not to pass from the O'Conor family without a flash of dying splendour. The chief of the MacDermots, who was the hereditary marshal of Connaught, perceiving the policy of the Burkes, asserted the right of Felim, his foster-son, to the throne. He caused him to be inaugurated with all the ancient ceremonies that added solemnity to the dedication. In the language of those days the enthronement of a king was an espousal to the province over which he was to reign. Felim's wedding feast was celebrated with an unprecedented magnificence.[1] It was the fitting consecration of the last royal representative of the O'Conors. He had uttered a marriage vow, the meaning of which, if he were faithful to it, was death.

Edward I. diverted attention from the unsettled dispute between the throne, the barons, and the citizens of London, by engaging in the conquest of Wales, and then in that of Scotland. On three several occasions, during this latter war, troops were conveyed from Ireland to aid in subjugating a people who were of their own kindred, and spoke their language. It is generally taken as a mark of transcendant ability when a ruler succeeds in directing the arm of phrensied liberty against her own bosom.

Edward II. (1307) was of a different disposition from that of his warlike and politic father. Piers Gaveston, a French knight of good family, stood high in his favour. The polished manners, quick wit, and skill in arms of the stranger, roused the fierce jealousy of the coarse Norman nobles. The king was compelled to part with his favourite, and sent him as viceroy to Ireland. The brilliant qualities that provoked envy in one country shone with undimmed lustre in the other. Gaveston, faithful to his master's interests, and having no personal object in reserve, reduced the Pale to order, and extended its limits. He was successful in the field, won the confidence and admiration of the soldiery, and after victory exercised the abilities of an experienced organiser.

The Earl of Ulster, who had no desire to see the power of England established in a legitimate form, retired to his castle at Trim, and held his court there as an independent sovereign. Had Gaveston continued in office the insolence of the savage and disloyal baron might have been chastised, and a prospect of good government secured. He was recalled, and the discordant elements were left to their own wild motions.

Section V.

There was still one other ingredient in preparation for the bitter cup of discord which Ireland was fated to drink. A portion of the island was disordered and endangered by the mailed grasp of the robber, and the abnormal transactions of that portion pass for the history of Ireland. An indirect consequence of Norman aggression was now about to convulse the whole country with a new pang. When the attempts of England on Scotland's liberties were defeated at Bannockburn, some of the Northern Irish chiefs offered, it is said, the throne of Ireland to Edward Bruce. They had no authority to do so, save that which accrues to each individual in a time of anarchy. Bruce made an immature effort to land in Ulster with some troops, and thereby made known to

"[1] Annals of Loch Cé," Vol. I., p. 555.

England the design that was in contemplation. While Ireland was a spoil for the Normans alone the English Government allowed them to mangle it and each other at their leisure. The appearance of a fresh claimant excited instantaneous alarm. A regular Parliament was held for the first time in Ireland, and the great officials of the Pale were summoned to England to consult on the crisis.

Bruce landed on the north-eastern coast of Ireland in 1315, with an army of six thousand Scots. In their long contest with the Normans the people of Scotland had learned and adopted the secret of Norman success. Instead of being terrified by crime, they hurled it back in the teeth of their invaders. In dealing with the assailants of their liberty and the robbers of their lands, murder, assassination, bad faith meant only defeat and death to their enemy and freedom to their country. So they had preserved their independence. Robert Bruce deserted from the English service, and murdered Cummin with his own hands. The Irish Milesians had been accustomed to suffer murder, but had not retaliated. Now the land was doomed to feel the ravaging sword of Milesians trained under different circumstances. They plundered, burned, and slew as they went. At Ardee they set fire to a church filled with fugitives, and all perished. With such ceremonials Edward Bruce was proclaimed King of Ireland.

Richard Burke assembled his forces at Roscommon, and marched to Athlone, where he was joined by Felim O'Conor with twenty battalions. They could only follow in the footsteps of their adversaries. They spared, the annalist tells us, neither saint nor asylum, however sacred, nor territory, nor termon,[1] but wasted and utterly destroyed from south to north. Lord Edmund Butler, the deputy, who should have been the chief adviser of the campaign, was satisfied to play a subordinate part, and came to the Earl's assistance. The latter contemptuously rejected his offer, and refused to march with him, declaring that he was able to expel the Scots with his own troops.[2] Butler was forced to return to Dublin.

The two armies were now encamped on opposite sides of the Bann. Secret overtures were made by Bruce to Felim, promising him the secure possession of Connaught, if he would desert the Earl. The slightest consideration of the circumstances in which Felim was placed will acquit him of even formal treachery. The technicality of an obsolete and effaced engagement might be pleaded, or the irreversible and insurmountable law of nature be permitted to assert itself. His kingdom, guaranteed to him by a solemn covenant, had been surreptitiously and unjustly handed over to the enemy of his house. The supremacy of England, which his family since Roderick had recognised, was deliberately set at naught by the leader to whose army he was attached, and a king of native race was proclaimed by the Northern half of Ireland. His ultimate course was determined by events. Roderick, a pretender to his throne, availing himself of his absence, went to Bruce and sought his authority to drive the foreigners out of Connaught, which Bruce granted on condition that he should spare the lands and possessions of

[1] Termon lands were lands set apart for religious or educational purposes.
[2] "Annals of Loch Cé," Vol. i., p. 565.

Felim. Roderick, however, marched with a large army into Connaught, and having burned and demolished the towns and castles belonging to his rival, caused himself to be proclaimed king. Felim's clear duty was now at Connaught. Having in vain besought the Earl to return with him, he set out on his journey homewards. The people of the North, little interested in dynastic wars, but incensed at the devastation of their fields, offered him so much opposition on his march that his army was greatly reduced in number, and he was forced to disband those that remained, advising them to submit to Roderick rather than be wanderers with himself. He resolved, for his own part, to abide by the counsel of his guardian and foster father, MacDermot.

Meanwhile Richard Burke, deprived of Felim's aid, and weakened by desertions, began to retreat, but was immediately followed by the Scots, compelled to fight, and totally defeated. His brother William was taken prisoner. Bruce having afterwards decisively overthrown Roger Mortimer in Meath, and the deputy in Kildare, returned to Scotland. The Earl, after his defeat, fled to Connaught, where he was waited on by Felim and MacDermot, with many others, Irish and Norman, who had been driven from their lands and were seeking redress. When MacDermot, whose character affects us like a relic of human life in a desert, saw the house full of fugitives and supplicants, and reflected on the condition to which his country had been brought, he resolved that he would never again seek the stranger's aid, but abide by the result of his own efforts. The Normans, he thought to himself, having failed to rule Ireland, by their further failure to conquer Scotland, had poured the rage of an outraged and defiant people into the naked wounds of his country. Allegiance he did not owe to them, respect he could not feel, duty drew him from them. At first he felt inclined to own Roderick as king, but soon after having delivered Felim from danger incurred while making a foray, their old affection was restored, and he united with him and the Normans of Lower Connaught in wasting the lands of Roderick.

This was a year of untold woes and worse forebodings. The angry skies frowned on the sins of men, and famine and pestilence supplemented the deeds of the sword. The women of the royal family of Connaught inflamed the fury of their husbands when it slackened, and presided in person over sacrilege and assassination.

At last Roderick was slain (1316), and Felim once more assumed the sovereignty. He forthwith entered, under MacDermot's guidance, on the only course that duty could dictate, or prudence prescribe, or pride inspire. The land was without a government. Burke, Earl of Ulster, who had disposted the deputy, was a wanderer. A new monarch claimed the allegiance of Ireland, and the army of a kindred people defied the Normans. Felim might at least secure his own province as an immediate step. He went against the unprivileged intruders, who, in violation of solemn treaties, were sapping the basis of his kingdom, and overthrew them in a number of brilliant skirmishes, in which kind of fight personal skill and courage are more nearly on equal terms with the weight of mailed strength. Exeter, Cogan, Prendergast, and several others fell before him.

William Burke, the treacherous foe of his family, and claimant of his possessions, returned from captivity in Scotland, and arrived in Connaught. Felim mustered all his available troops, and called to his aid the lords of Munster and Meath. Undisciplined peasants and disorganised cattle drivers, and chiefs with linen garments and bare heads, prepared under the leadership of a boy to fight with mailed and disciplined soldiers, led by calculating veterans. The Milesians, intent as ever on personal glory, and forgetting that their country was at stake, fought against terrific odds; and the Normans, with the want of chivalry which they always exhibit in proportion to the helplessness of their foe, hurried from all parts of Ireland to the unequal combat. The first instinct of the wild beast, when attacked, is to crush the prey which it bears off in its fangs. Burke and Birmingham, and the English of the north, thought less of the enemy of their king than of the native prince who disputed their title to his lands. They turned their arms from Bruce against O'Conor. They had never brought together so large an army in Ireland. A long and desperate battle was fought on the tenth of August, 1316, at Athenry. A fight persisted in by the unarmed against the armed, is one in which men stand to be slain. The Irish would have stood to their last man, if that man were their leader. The Normans well knew this, and as in most other conflicts in Ireland, the Irish leader fell. A rout then took place and a countless slaughter. The O'Conor family never again rose to more than nominal royalty. Felim died in the twenty-third year of his age, undisputed heir presumptive to the monarchy of Ireland. He, and not Roderick, closed the line of Irish kings.[1] The last monarch of Ireland died fighting for his country's rights, in the dawn of his unreached manhood, and the full day of his unclouded honour.

SECTION VI.

The Scottish invader still remained to be subdued. The Earl of Ulster was his brother-in-law, and was thrown into prison by the mayor of Dublin on suspicion of favouring his enterprise, nor could the remonstrance of the English Government speedily obtain his release. Roger Mortimer landed at Waterford, as deputy, with fresh troops. To confirm the loyalty of the Normans, Irish titles were for the first time bestowed in Ireland. John Fitzthomas, of Offaly, one of the Fitzgerald family, was made Earl of Kildare, and Lord Edmund Butler, Earl of Carrick. The never failing and all potent aid of Rome was next sought and obtained.

The Papal Government gave England to the Normans, saved them more than once from France, gave, and again and again preserved Ireland to them, and yet among the nations Rome has no such foe as England, no such devoted servant as Ireland. The exp'anation of this singular fact is an important part of history. The Normans were mainly active in creating the temporal power of the Popedom, courted it for the sake of the temporal gifts it had to bestow, and when their ends were gained, flung to the earth the ladder whose top they had pretended to rear towards heaven. Ireland recognised Rome only as a spiritual power,

[1] "Annals of Loch Cé," Vol. I., p. 587.

and was faithful in her adherence, even when the temporal arm was lifted for her ruin.

When the Northern Irish heard that an application to Rome was contemplated, they prepared to meet it by a counter appeal. A letter was written by O'Neill, in which he laid the Irish statement of their case before the head of the Church. The document began by requesting the Holy Father not to be misled by slanderous accusations against the Irish, with which from the time that the murderer of Becket had deceived Adrian IV., the Normans had always covered their own detestable cruelties. It goes on to say that the Normans having entered their country in the name of religion, had by force and cunning deprived them of their habitations, and driven them into the wilds. It says that the Normans, with an inconceivable arrogance, which it calls insanity, asserted that Ireland did not belong to the Irish, but to themselves. This, it declares, is the cause of the famines and slaughters which depopulated the country. It solemnly complains that the Irish clergy are not only robbed of their temporal possessions, but are provoked by a sense of their wrongs into a mood injurious to their spiritual health and eternal happiness. It shows how Henry had violated every article of Adrian's Bull, and how the Normans, instead of introducing better laws, and better morals, had robbed them of every law, and polluted them by their evil example. It makes the memorable complaint that Norman tyranny was changing the dove-like simplicity of the Irish people into the malicious cunning of the serpent. It declares that the people of Ireland cannot be accused of perjury or rebellion, because they have never sworn allegiance to England. It proposes to make good its averments before a tribunal of twelve bishops, and points out how this offer differs from the conduct of the Normans, who appeal to Rome for help when they are in adversity, and when they are prosperous, despise heaven and earth.

The Pope who, influenced by misrepresentation, had already issued his orders to the chief clergy in Ireland, was so moved by the contents of this epistle that he forwarded it to the English king, with a strong remonstrance, and a recommendation of juster treatment of the Irish. Meantime the Papal name was cast on the side of the Normans. The archbishops of Armagh and Dublin excommunicated Bruce and his followers.

The deputy delivered Burke from prison, and drove the de Lacys, who had joined Bruce, from Meath, giving their lands to his soldiers. Bruce, who had come back from Scotland with fresh forces, began a new campaign. He took Carrickfergus, and marched to the walls of Dublin. But the tide of fortune had begun to ebb. The citizens of Dublin made such active preparations that a siege seemed hopeless. From the force of habit the Scotch ravaged indiscriminately, surrounded themselves with famine, and alienated the natives. They went to Limerick, but O'Brien declared against them. They were compelled to fall back on their old quarters in Ulster, and accomplished the retreat unopposed, though an English army of thirty thousand men was ready to take the field.

Early in the following year (1318) Edward Bruce again marched to the south, and had reached Louth, when at the hill of Faughard he was met by an army under Birmingham, sent from Dublin to oppose him. Robert Bruce was expected, and the chiefs of the army earnestly advised Edward to postpone the battle till his arrival. But he was desirous of winning the whole glory of a victory, of which he, not arrogantly, after eighteen successive victories, felt certain, and at once engaged. If he fought with men restrained by any law of honourable warfare, his confidence would have been well grounded. Scotland may thank him for rushing into danger alone, and not involving her heroic monarch in his fate. The Normans had planned to paralyse the Scottish enterprise by assassinating its chief. They had acted similarly, but with greater caution, in every important battle since they came to Ireland. In this case they plotted with a desperation that sought concealment only as a temporary element of success, and not as an evasion of infamy. A person named Maupas was the agent employed. According to some accounts he consummated his deed the night before the engagement. Others say that he disguised himself in the garb of a jester, sought out unsuspectedly the Scottish leader in the battle-field, and dashed out his brains with a leaden ball. The death of Bruce ended the battle and the enterprise.

The crushed head of the fallen chief was cut off and salted. It was carried to London by Birmingham, and placed on the table, at an entertainment, before the king. This was a graceful and appropriate way of asking for a title. Birmingham was made Earl of Louth. The disposal of Bruce's other remains carried out the system of sickening terrorism in which the Normans place their final trust. The body was divided into quarters, and exposed in different parts of the country.

This invasion, like most of the wars and alliances of the Milesian chiefs, was transacted in a region to which the sympathies of the mass of the people did not ascend. The native wars had been always carried on at the expense of the occupants of the soil; but transient forays, sustained by no abiding passions, swept over the land with comparative lightness, and the exactions that accompanied them were restrained by law and custom. The foreigners had forced on the country wars of life and death instead of the tournaments of rival chieftains, and habits of lawless plunder instead of regulated quarterings. We have seen how Felim's army was impeded in its march homewards by the peasantry whose lands it had ravaged. The annals of the time abound with complaints of the excesses committed in his subsequent war with Roderick. In a similar spirit the defeat of Bruce's army was popularly described as the best thing that had ever happened for Ireland. The people only desired to reap the fruits of their lands unspoiled, and to exercise their religion undisturbed.

CHAPTER VIII.

THE FITZGERALDS.

SECTION I.

THE first Anglo-Norman adventurers came to Ireland to acquire lands and independence. They had never cordially submitted to the authority of the English crown. The recent course of events threw independence into their hands.

The eastern counties of Ulster, and the richest parts of Connaught and Munster, where they adjoined in Leinster, were possessed by Norman lords and occupied by English tenants. The manner, half fraudulent, and half forcible, in which they were acquired, had not involved either the extermination or distant expulsion of the native owners, who had merely retired to the more sterile and mountainous districts. During Bruce's invasion, the Normans, adopting the ancient usage of the country, quartered their troops on the peasantry. This custom, which might be safely practised with a soldiery trained to it from immemorial times, grew into an intolerable outrage when permitted to an army whose only relaxation from rigid serfdom at home lay in the indulged excesses of foreign war. The tenants, unable to bear the violence and licentiousness of their own countrymen, fled to England or took refuge among the Irish, and the native tribes returned to their old homes.

Some lords of high position deliberately furthered this movement. Maurice Fitzgerald of Desmond let his soldiers loose on the English settlers in Kerry, Limerick, Cork, and Waterford, and filled with his Irish adherents the lands thereby depopulated. He then renounced all dependence on English law, and assumed the character of an Irish chief. Some time after the Earl of Ulster was murdered in a family quarrel. His widow in terror hurried to England, leaving her territories undefended. The strength and attention of England were engaged elsewhere. Two members of the Burke family[1] seized the portion that lay in Connaught, comprising the present counties of Galway and Mayo, and qualified themselves for its retention by adopting Irish laws and assuming the name of MacWilliam. Two other branches of the same family took the names of MacHubbard and MacDavid. Birmingham of Athenry took the name of MacYoris, and Mangle of MacCostello. These examples were extensively followed. The measures taken by the English Government to arrest the evil only gave it greater strength. They made Lord Carrick and Maurice Fitzgerald Earls of Ormond and Desmond, intending thus to secure their fidelity. They raised the existing numbers of Palatinates to nine. Carlow, Wexford, Kilkenny, Kildare, and Leix, parts of Meath and Ulster, and the territories of the two lately created

---

[1] From whom were descended, respectively, the Earls of Clanrickarde and Mayo.

earls, were all made almost independent principalities, whose lords exercised the privileges of royalty.

In adopting the character of Milesian chieftains the Anglo-Normans did not omit its vices. They rather improved on them. In this disastrous period the native chiefs continued their intestine strifes, as if they had no enemies outside their own families. The O'Conors fought a battle among themselves, in which four thousand men were slain. We are unacquainted with the cause that led to their contest, but whatever its triviality, and however deplorable the result, they were undeniably excelled in a contemporaneous quarrel of the Normans. Lord Arnold Poer called Maurice Fitzgerald, Earl of Desmond, a rhymer. A violent and sustained warfare instantly burst out between the insulted Fitzgerald, assisted by the Butlers and Birminghams, and Poer, aided by the Burkes. Great numbers of those families were slain; others were driven to flight, and their lands were devastated. The Earl of Kildare, the deputy, vainly interposed. Lord Poer was forced to take refuge in England, and the unappeased indignation of his enemies was at last quelled by a stern mandate from the king. Lord Philip Bodnet and one hundred and forty others were treacherously murdered by the Barrys and Roches. The Earl of Louth, the victor of Faughard, and Talbot of Malahide, with one hundred and sixty more, were killed by the Savages and Gernons. Maurice Fitznicholas, lord of Kerry, slew the son of the chief of the MacCarties as he sat on the bench in the assize court in Tralee. The Earl of Ulster, the year before his assassination, took Walter Burke prisoner and starved him to death. The son of the earl was captured by another Burke, and flung into a loch, with a stone tied round his neck.

The simple ways of an ancient civilization were liable to strange developments when adopted by persons untrained in their history and unimbued with their spirit. English chronicles relate with pride how when the son of Sir Robert Savage saw his father building a castle—a proceeding alien to Irish customs—he railed against the act, and how his father yielded to his remonstrances. This same knight was in the habit of deluging his soldiers with strong spirits before they went to battle, and he always prepared beforehand a sumptuous feast for their regalement on their return, avowedly satisfied that the enemy should have the advantage of it if they chanced to be victorious. This grotesque exaggeration of Irish life and hospitality was an instance of the proverbial pre-eminence of the Normans in Irish modes of thought and manners. In subsequent times the dispossessed lords of the soil aped the manners of their foreign masters, and such lineaments of truth as lay under the wild portraiture that passed for an Irishman in English scenic literature were only the reflection of the Irish character travestied by English imitation.

The accounts of Irish disorder would remain true in fact, but would lead to a worse than false conclusion if unaccompanied by some reference to the contemporaneous condition of England. The Great Baron was an independent potentate who knew no law but force. The king on one occasion required his nobles to show their titles to their estates. Earl Warrenne flung a rusty sword on the table as his title-deed. His fathers, he said, had won their lands with the sword when they came over with the Conqueror, and by his sword would he maintain them. The power that refused to recognise any legal origin knew no legal exercise. The noble who thus claimed the rights of a conqueror ruled over a conquered people. He had a number of retainers ready to execute his will. All who lived on his estate were absolutely at his disposal. The lesser nobles plundered the goods of the trader on the open highway. Once a band of country gentlemen attended a great merchant fair at Boston. At night they set the booths on fire, robbed and murdered the merchants, and carried off the booty. Lawless bands of club men lived by outrage, and aided the nobles in their robberies. By an Act of the fifth of the reign of Henry IV. it was made felony to cut out a person's tongue or put out his eyes, crimes which the Act says were very frequent.

The Irish of Leinster once more petitioned to be admitted to the benefit of English laws. The king recommended their request to the attention of the deputy. It was not heard of again. It was impossible to rest under a dominion that neither enforced its laws on its subjects nor extended them to the natives. The Irish of Leinster, Munster, and Meath ravaged the English settlements in their respective vicinities. All attempts to suppress them proved unavailing. Sir John Darcy, the deputy, sought the aid of the Earl of Desmond. The Irish still remained masters in the field. It soon became obvious that they were acting in concert with the old Normans for the independence of the country. A new deputy, Sir Anthony Lucy, having made unsuccessful attempts to assemble a Parliament, first in Dublin and then in Kilkenny, took a determined step, and made prisoners of Desmond, two Burkes, and two Birminghams. One of the Birminghams was hanged, and Desmond was kept in confinement for some time and afterwards sent to England (1332).

SECTION II.

King Edward III. manifested an intention of supporting the deputy's decisive measures by his presence. He summoned the Earl of Ormond and others to England to consult with them on the objects of his voyage, and ordered all the ships in the Irish harbours to be sent to Holyhead. When everything was ready he made known that his real purpose was the invasion of Scotland. Orders were issued that all the disaffected in Ireland should be admitted to the king's peace on easy terms.

Full of his prospects of personal ambition, and supposing that the inhabitants of Ireland would be bound to his service by mere careless lenity, the king next asked for help to carry on his French wars. When it was refused he recalled all remissions of debts due to the crown, and cancelled all grants of lands made by himself or his father. He further formally ordained that no person married or possessed of estates in Ireland should hold any office in that country unless he also held estates in England.

Later historians wonder why this scheme of government was not silently acted on without being openly proclaimed. They forgot that the charm of arbitrary government consists in its conscious power of asserting itself in extremities of passion or necessity.

The Anglo-Irish lords called a meeting at Kilkenny, at which they threw the whole blame of the admitted disorder on the incompetency, venality, and extortion of the deputies and other officers of state, and complained that, from the same causes, the conquered lands were rapidly reverting to the possession of the Irish enemy.

The real difficulty of their position with regard to Ireland now began to dawn on the minds of the English king and council. They seem to have assumed that a fragment of clay removed from England to Ireland could still retain the gravitation of the spot from which it had been taken. They expected that Englishmen settled on Irish estates would resist the growth of those feelings that identify home and country, and would perpetually remain Englishmen by the force of political imagination. They now saw that attachment to the land of their adoption must either be treated as an acknowledged factor in the government of the English in Ireland, or be resisted by violence or the substitution of selfish interest, as subversive of the designs of the sovereign dominion.

The examples of the public officers alone showed the possibility of detached love of country. The deputies maintained their English sympathies and prejudices during their temporary sojourn, formed no ties of interest or affection with the land that ministered to their promotion, and in consequence succeeded each other with suspicious rapidity, and generally escaped from Ireland by back doors, followed by the angry curses of unpaid creditors. The time was yet to come when every Irish landlord might stand as loose on Irish soil, during his fleeting visit, as an English viceroy; when the sense of obligation could travel with the coin that represented the tiller's labour, from the land where it was produced to the land where it was consumed; and when envenomed hatred of the fame and honour of his native land was to constitute the patriotism of the loyal Irishman.

Sir Ralph Ufford, who was appointed deputy in 1343, set himself to straighten the battle line between the two nations. He enjoined that the English of the Pale should have only one war and one peace, that is, that when one English lord went to war all should aid him, and that no one should make peace by himself. He then sought to reclaim the disaffected nobles. Desmond, who had been liberated from prison, was summoned to a Parliament in Dublin, and when he defiantly called together a counter assembly at Callan, the deputy issued a proclamation prohibiting it as an act of treason. He invaded the earl's territories with a large army, collected his rents, and having by stratagem got possession of some of his castles, hanged on a nominal accusation the knights who were in charge of them. The earl surrendered himself, and was bailed out by twenty knights, who, when he afterwards failed to appear, were deprived of their lands.

The Earl of Kildare was next assailed. An officer was sent with two writs, one calling him to join the king with his forces, the other authorising his seizure and imprisonment. When the unexpected success of the first writ prevented the execution of the second, the officer persuaded him to disband his troops and accompany him to Dublin. There he was arrested in the council chamber and committed to prison. On the deputy's death his rigorous rule was changed. Desmond and Kildare were received into favour, and served the king in France. Both earls were afterwards successively deputies in Ireland in 1355 and 1361.

The barest concert of the Irish chiefs would now have sufficed to recover the whole island. Ulster, Connaught, and Munster were overflowing into the Pale, and even in Leinster, in the midst of the English settlement, the native clans were growing strong and exhibiting hostility. In 1358 the O'Moores of Leix defeated the English of Dublin, slaying two hundred and forty of their number. But the Irish had no united plans, unless their attachment to their national customs can be so denominated. They elected their chiefs, and observed their ancient laws, not defying but utterly ignoring the English. This instinctive policy would have proved the next wisest had it been allowed time to work. The Anglo-Irish families were numerously and rapidly falling from the English connection, and blending with the native population.

In 1361 King Edward sent his second son, Lionel, who claimed in right of his wife[1] to be Earl of Ulster and Lord of Connaught, to Ireland, with an army of fifteen hundred men. By a Royal proclamation the Anglo-Irish were forbidden to approach the English camp. When his army was almost destroyed Lionel was forced to solicit the aid of the men he had thus insulted, and the king ordered all the Anglo-Irish in England to hasten to his assistance. Having celebrated his escape as if it were a triumph, he returned home, and a law was passed forbidding any mention of the difference between English-born and Irish-born residents in Ireland.

In 1367 Lionel again went to Ireland, and at a Parliament assembled at Kilkenny, a statute was passed declaring marriage, gossipred, or fosterage with the Irish to be treason, making it penal to adopt Irish customs, or dress, to hold intercourse with the Irish people, especially with their bards, and strictly prohibiting the admission of a mere Irishman to any ecclesiastical benefice within the English district.

Indications of an equitable and a pacific spirit have been sought for in this statute. We must interpret it with its historical context. English-born residents in Ireland, with pride violent in proportion as it was baseless, affected to abhor the Anglo-Irish, and called them Irish dogs. The latter retaliated, and called the former English hobbes. The English Court adopted the side and sentiments of the hobbes, and would not suffer the dogs, as we have seen, to fight with them against the common enemy. When it was found that England could make no way in Ireland without the aid of men born in Ireland, the law was passed forbidding any mention of distinctions of birth. The statute of Kilkenny aimed simply at turning the mutual hatred of the Anglo-Irish and the English resident in Ireland, on the mere Irishman. Eight bishops, two of them bearing Irish names, were present at this Parliament.

Section III.

On the departure of Lionel, who was created Duke of Clarence, to commemorate imaginary victories won in Clare, Desmond became

[1] She was daughter to the Earl of Ulster, who had been murdered.

deputy, quarrelled with the Birminghams, and was replaced by de Windsor, who adopted the desperate plan of taking some of the Irish clans into his pay, to prevent the inroads of their countrymen. In 1371 de Windsor was succeeded by Kildare, who held office only for a year. In the following year there were three successive deputies. Then de Windsor was re-appointed, and insisted on an allowance of eleven thousand pounds, though the revenue of the country was only ten thousand.

The English Parliament demanded that a sum should be raised in Ireland sufficient to defray the necessary expenses, and were met by a plea of poverty. The king summoned the Irish Parliament to England to debate on the subject. The Irish Parliament replied that they were not bound to send delegates to England, but that in deference to the king's wish they would send them, reserving, however, the power to grant subsidies.

Meanwhile the O'Neills of Ulster, the O'Conors of Sligo, the Mac Mahons of Oriel, and the O'Kellys of Galway, reduced the English in those localities. The Leinster clans were gradually narrowing and reclaiming the Pale. The Normans did not dare to meet their enemy in the field. They assassinated Mac Murrough, and having by treachery got twenty-five of the Tiernans of Cavan, who were marching against them, into their power, they beheaded them. Such was the condition of Ireland towards the close of a reign specially distinguished as glorious in English annals.

An established Government could scarcely be said to exist in England at this period. The nobles, for their own purposes, preserved the fiction of a sovereign whom they exercised the right of dethroning at their will. The kings, who by ability might have introduced settled order, betook themselves from the danger of the task to foreign wars. Those who were unambitious or desirous of enjoying the delights of power, found themselves beset with perils. The people were a dead weight thrown now into one scale and now into another, and despised when the momentary object of either party was gained. Edward III. was wholly occupied in his wars with France in his riper manhood, and in his later years was reduced to dotage by the wiles of a domineering mistress.

Richard II. was eleven years old on his grandfather's death. When he came of age he bestowed the absolute sovereignty of the Pale for life on de Vere, Earl of Oxford, with authority to conquer and appropriate the rest of the island. The Parliament ratified the grant and voted a supply of troops for two years. At the last moment Richard changed his mind and refused to allow de Vere to leave England. Sir William Stanley was appointed his deputy, and made a treaty of peace with the Mac Murrough, who was already in the pay of the Normans.

In 1393 the Duke of Gloucester, the king's uncle, undertook the viceroyalty, and was about to embark for the seat of his government, when the king countermanded his appointment, and announced his intention of going to Ireland in person. He landed with four thousand men at arms, thirty thousand archers, and quite a troop of dukes, earls, and other titled personages. The scenes of his projected victories were the parade ground and the palace. He brought with him all the royal jewels, and armed with their splendour, directed a whole artillery of sumptuous feasts against the unsophisticated senses of the enemy.

The Milesians have never shrunk from this species of encounter. O'Conor, O'Brien, O'Neill, and Mac Murrough, with seventy-five lesser chiefs, repaired to Dublin, and went through elaborate forms of submission, the display of which gratified their self-importance far more than the terms of the engagements into which they entered occupied their attention.

Richard wished to confer knighthood on the four provincial kings. As a preparation for the honour they were required to conform to the manners and dress of the English. The customs of the two countries first came into collision in the matter of taking food. The Irish kings had always been in the habit of eating and drinking at the same table with their minstrels and retainers. When their hosts, with as great solemnity as if they were performing a religious service, arranged separate tables, the kings looked at each other, smiled, and acquiesced. The court dress of the English, and the use of saddles and bridles, were further novelties to which they courteously resigned themselves.

But there is no boundary in the delicate inquisitiveness of conscious civilization when dealing with the ways of savage life. Their instructor, expecting no doubt some extraordinary revelation of heresy, questioned his guests on their creed. The Rubicon of good manners was now passed, and the Irish kings felt the insult for a moment, but with marvellous self-possession they immediately recovered themselves, and replied that they believed in God and the Trinity as he did. Which Pope they adhered to was the next object of enquiry. They answered without hesitation that they adhered to the Pope at Rome. They were asked if they would wish to receive the order of knighthood. They answered that they had already been knighted according to the national usage when children. And when they were informed that the King of England had no regard to such a puerile ceremony, they quietly concurred in the new proposal.

The Earl of Ormond some days after enquired whether they were satisfied with the treatment they had received, and they made answer with wonderful composure, that they were most obliged for the pains their instructor had taken with them in showing them the usages of his country. The historian of this event informs us that the reply of those Irish kings was agreeable to the Earl of Ormond because it showed sense.[1] When the Atlantic cable was laid at Valentia in 1867, the English newspapers told with surprise how the peasants actually manifested some knowledge of the principles of political economy in seeking employment and receiving remuneration in divers small ways from the distinguished visitors who were present. One history, at least, repeats itself. The four kings were knighted and, dressed in robes of state, sat at a grand banquet at the royal table.

In a letter to his uncle, the Duke of York, Richard gave an account of Irish affairs. Engrossed by what he actually saw, and not disturbed by the dominant interests of his English realm, he expressed the opinion that injury and wrong had goaded the people into rebellion, and that all that was needed to promote order was pardon and kindness. The Duke, writing in England and thinking only of England, reminded his nephew

[1] Froissart.

that severe measures were his original purpose, and recommended him, at least, to exact contributions to defray the expenses of his journey.

Richard seems to have been really desirous of pacifying the English district, and the simplicity of his aim was the surest warrant of success. He appointed trustworthy judges, and was engaged in reforming the laws, when the Duke of York and the Bishop of London arrived in Ireland, representing the danger to which the church was exposed from the preaching of the Lollards, and urging the king's return to meet the crisis. Richard sailed for England, after a residence of nine months, leaving Roger Mortimer as his deputy.

It was not possible that the intercourse of a few months with the courtiers of England could have changed the habits of the Irish chiefs. If Richard remained in Ireland it is to be presumed from the readiness with which they conformed to the usages of his court and entered into its enjoyments, that they would in a little time be attracted by new pleasures and form new ambitions, and seek permanent relations with the government through which those pleasures and ambitions could be gratified. It was by persistently employing the great Anglo-Irish lords in the royal service, and flattering them with titles and favours, that the fidelity of a portion of them was preserved to the crown, and they were prevented from becoming Irish. With the original Irish chiefs no such pains were taken.

The momentary excitement sent the visitors of Richard back to their ordinary pursuits with a double zest. The Leinster chiefs had engaged to quit the province, and surrender their lands. Apart from their having no power to make this promise without the consent of their clans, they could only have been reconciled personally to the loss of their homes by the prospect of a Royal reception at Dublin, to which they might occasionally repair from the more distant region to which they were to be relegated. Deprived of such an inducement, they delayed, then objected, and at last resisted. A general conflict began, in which the Normans, after having burned Glendalough, were totally defeated by the O'Byrnes and O'Tooles, and their leader, Mortimer, was slain.

Richard, who had got rid of his chief opponents, and made himself supreme master of England, was at this time leading a life of luxury, and spending the national revenues on his pleasures. When he heard of Mortimer's death he resolved to avenge it. At a grievous cost to his subjects, he raised an army of forty thousand men, and landed at Waterford in June, 1399.

Appearing in a new character, he found everything changed. MacMurrough denounced the wrongfulness of the original occupation of Ireland, and declared his determination to disown if not to undo it. When Richard marched against him he hovered round the vast armament with a body of three thousand men, whose disciplined activity kept the English in constant alarm. When the Royal army prepared for battle, MacMurrough disappeared. When they were off their guard he suddenly dashed on their path, the wild shouts of his men striking them with dismay, while their spears smote through shield and armour from side to side.

This harassing warfare continued till the king's forces were reduced to the direst distress by want of provisions. MacMurrough then proposed a conference. The Duke of Gloucester was sent to meet him. A long discussion was terminated by the absolute refusal of the Irish chief to consent to anything more than a nominal submission. The king protested that he would get possession of the rebel alive or dead before he left the island. He marched to Dublin with his half-starved troops, and offered a hundred golden marks for MacMurrough's head. News then came that a rival to his throne had appeared in England, and he returned to that country to find his kingdom lost, and to lose his life by unknown assassination.

Those events form the principal if not the only items of Irish history in the pages of English writers. They appear only as two or three obscure entries in the annals of the Irish historians. The death of Mortimer in Leinster ranks with the death of some undistinguished chief in Munster or Ulster. The arrivals and departures of Richard obtain no more notice than the founding of an abbey or the lifting of a herd of cattle.

Section IV.

The forces that were to become predominant in English history were now struggling, amidst repeated interruptions, to take definite shape. Slavery in its most absolute form still extensively prevailed. The Norman nobles and great Churchmen divided between them the wealth of the nation. Popular discontent, seizing on the rudimentary principles of religion as an argument for universal equality, directed them, as was natural, most pointedly against the luxurious and worldly-minded clergy, numbers of whom were foreigners. This was the first opening of the germ of the English Reformation and Revolution.

The nobles, who looked on the possessions of the Church with a longing eye, saw in the detachment of the people from the clergy a prospect of future plunder. The accession of the House of Lancaster strengthened the Church for the time, and offered the nobles a more immediate object for their insatiable avarice. A part of France had been seized by Rollo while the country was convulsed by rival claims to the throne. A similar dissension now tempted a similar invasion. The French wars of England were the expeditions of robbers. The king, holding his English throne only by a parliamentary title, sought to reign in Normandy by the stronger and more congenial right of conquest. The nobles, with the passions of bandits, thirsted for the plunder of country houses and the ransom of prisoners. The Saxon soldiers found freedom in distant service, and struck with blind rage against the country to which all their miseries were traceable.

Wars undertaken in sordid lawlessness were conducted with corresponding cold-blooded cruelty. The bravest captives were butchered, and the inspired maiden who foiled the enterprise was burned at the stake. We follow other men to the height of their ambition and find a barren rock; we trace the Norman to the summit of his victory and discover an outlet of hell.

Having succeeded only in making France united, the invaders returned to exhaust their inflamed and disappointed passions on the vitals of England, and thus to frustrate for a while longer the patient but unslumbering liberties of their country. Most Englishmen know the events of this period, abroad and at home, chiefly through the plays of Shakespeare.

The method of silent aggression, by which under the sanction of the Papal Bull it was intended to appropriate the lands of Ireland, was found to be a failure. The English settlers melted into the Irish life, and the Pale was tolerated just as any of the other tribes, in a state of general disunion. As the power of Rome insensibly declined in England, the Irish Council began to change their unconsciousness of the existence of an Irish people for acts of parliamentary attack.

Ormond was made deputy in 1403, and fought a desperate battle with Art Mac Murrough. To supplement a doubtful victory, the statute of Kilkenny was renewed. In 1408, the Duke of Lancaster, second son of Henry IV,, who had been deputy before Ormond, again succeeded to the office, having stipulated that one or two families from every parish in England should be transplanted into Ireland at the king's charges. He supposed that the colonists lost their nationality, not by change of nation, but by Irish infection. After some other undertakings of a similar kind, he concluded that a victory in the field was necessary for the support of his economical measures. He attacked Mac Murrough, and in a fight in which at least ten thousand men were arrayed on either side, received a total defeat under the very walls of Dublin. He escaped only with his life, wounded and humbled. The Council found their usual relief in an act of parliament. At a time when the former laws against gossipred, intermarriages, and mutual traffic were impracticable as they were inexpedient, they were re-enacted and flung as a kind of legislative excommunication against the Irish people. In order that not a single soul should escape the impending curse, it was further enacted that no Irish enemy should depart from the realm, and that the goods of any Irishman attempting to escape should be seized and forfeited. This was only idle bravado. None of the Irish were anxious to leave their own country, where there was ample room for them; and had they chosen to leave, there was no power to prevent them. When those laws were passed, several Irish chiefs were in receipt of annual tributes from the Normans as the price of peace, and the English settlement existed only by their protection. They were not eager to exterminate an enemy who flattered their importance, and ministered to their resources.

The Irish had no Parliament to fulminate retaliatory enactments against the foe; but they had bards who were formidable for their satirical power. Stanley, who was for some time deputy, offended the political family of the O'Higgins by his general contempt for poetry, and his particular ill-treatment of themselves. He was satirized by them with all due solemnity, and as he died a few weeks after, they had something to allege in proof of the efficacy of their art.

The English legislature, which by the deliberate exclusion of the popular element had ceased to be a national institution, exhibited with greater success the same spirit of intolerant insult towards its English subjects in Ireland that the Irish assembly had displayed towards the natives. The Pale was filled with a crowd of adventurers who had come from England in hopes of plunder, and foiled in their projects, had subsided into the vicious and dishonourable courses which are generally the alternative with persons of this description. There is no type of character so unlike the Irish disposition as this, yet Ireland has always been credited with the production of the degraded foreigners who have failed to win or retain a place among her aristocracy by fraud or rapine. The Parliament of England, shrinking from the sight of its own people defeated and degraded, passed a law that no inhabitant of Ireland should be permitted to live in England. When they found it necessary afterwards to leave an opening in favour of those who came to be educated, the exception proved of no avail, for the Anglo-Irish students were ignominiously excluded from the Inns of Court. When Ireland flourished as a land of schools and colleges, before her peace was disturbed by Normans and Anglo-Normans, her treatment of strangers who came to her shores, seeking knowledge, had been very different.

The continued successes of the Irish procured the appointment of Sir John Talbot, Lord Furnival, as deputy, in 1414. He made a show of activity by joining several of the lesser chiefs successively in attacks on each other; but he did not turn the tide of victory. The O'Haras defeated and slew de Exeter; O'Conor Faly overcame and despoiled the English of Meath; and Mac Murrough compelled the English of Wexford to give him hostages. This was the last of MacMurrough's long list of triumphs. He died the next year (1417), not without suspicion of poison. In 1418, Talbot, just before his departure, attempted to plunder Magennis of Iveah in Ulidia, but was repulsed, pursued, and utterly defeated by that chief.

This deputy is described by the native writers as a plunderer of chieftains, poets, and saints. He was charged by the English of the Pale with leaving the country without paying his debts. Desirous of making his conduct favourably known to the king, he contrived to obtain an address approving of his government. To counteract this document, a petition was drawn up by the Parliament, complaining of the intolerance and tyranny of the English deputies. Talbot afterwards went to the French wars, where he greatly distinguished himself, and became Earl of Shrewsbury. Time and place distinguish the hero from the swindler.

The Earl of Ormond was appointed Lord-Lieutenant in 1419, displacing Archbishop Talbot, whom his brother, Lord Furnival, had left in charge of the settlement. In the usual address from the Parliament to the king, all the governors sent from England were charged with extortion and fraud, while nothing but praise was reserved for those who were residents in the country. Indications in the same direction were visible in the request that the king should visit his Irish realm in person, and that there should be a permanent coinage of money as in England. The occasional residence of the sovereign in Ireland would at once equalise and distinguish the two islands, while the government by foreign lieutenants made Ireland an inferior, obscure, and dependent part of the kingdom.

Edmund Mortimer, Earl of Meath and Ulster, and heir to the English crown, having been appointed Lord-Lieutenant, did not proceed to Dublin, but nominated the Bishop of Meath as his deputy. Archbishop Talbot protested against this arrangement, on the ground that the deputy's commission bore only the private seal of his principal. When it was found that the objection could not be pressed, the contest was carried on by getting up an accusation against the Bishop of having stolen a chalice.

Some Scotch marauders appearing in the North, Ormond assumed the deputyship, but the Lord-Lieutenant, thinking his private interests concerned, now came on the scene. He was successfully engaged in prosecuting a conciliatory policy when he suddenly died at Trim.

Lord Furnival again became deputy, and pretending to continue the friendly relations of his predecessor, treacherously made prisoners of O'Neill, O'Conor, and a number of other Irish chiefs, and liberated them on conditions that mainly regarded his personal interests and those of his brother the Archbishop. Ormond succeeded to the vice-royalty, and came to friendly terms with O'Neill, who acknowledged himself liege man to the King of England. In 1438 he acted as deputy to Lord Wells, and was about to be raised to the higher office when Archbishop Talbot, the representative of English supremacy, drew up a series of condemnatory articles against him, and requested that the chief power should be bestowed on some great English lord, who could command greater confidence than any Irishman was likely to inspire. The Earl was, notwithstanding, raised to the vice-royalty, and entered into a close alliance with his cousin, the Earl of Desmond, who, having usurped the title and added to its territories by an illegal grant of one-half of what was called the Kingdom of Cork, now obtained patents from Government that gave validity to his claims, and exempted him during life from attendance at Parliament.

So greatly had the power of the Irish increased since the statute that forbad the mingling of the races, that Desmond could assign the difficulty of passing through the enemy's country as a reason for absenting himself from the capital.

The English inhabitants of the Pale, which at this time consisted only of portions of the four shires of Dublin, Meath, Kildare, and Louth, less than one half its former extent, were so harassed by incompetent and corrupt legal officials, and by the troops that were maintained for their defence, as well as by those of the enemy, that they wavered between flight to England, and the adoption of Irish laws.

Against this increase of native influence in the south two offsets must be made. The Earls of Desmond, Ormond and Kildare were establishing their power and independence, and winning the affections of the peasantry; and the disintegration of the native chieftainries was steadily progressing. The O'Conors were already divided under an O'Conor Don and an O'Conor Roe. In 1445, the O'Farrells partitioned Anally,[1] between two lords. In 1446, the MacDonoghs elected two chiefs and shared the territory of Tirerrill between them. A MacDermot of the Wood descended to joint equality with a MacDermot of the Rock,

[1] Anally is the modern Longford.

an O'Brien of Ara became rival or partner to the O'Brien of Thomond, and the nephews of Art MacMurrough disputed the superiority of his sons.

The north, on the other hand, was becoming united and aggressive. O'Neill reduced Anally and Oriel, paying stipends to the Irish according to the national custom, and receiving tribute from the English. He even extended his ascendancy by the employment of English troops.

Section V.

The constantly healing wounds of Ireland were added to by daily accessions of fresh invaders, and were torn open as fast as they closed by legislative enactments. The statute of Kilkenny, so far as its operations availed, turned an injury, whose smart would have soon subsided, into a perpetual festering sore. The bitterness of invasion, to reverse the prophet's figure, was not allowed to digest into sweetness, but must remain bitterness in the mouth for ever. The increase of the Irish, their encroachments on the Pale, and the lawlessness that pervaded all races and classes demanded, it may be, the raising of a barrier of separation as the only defensive measure of which England was capable at the time. But England was not defending herself: she was only defending an artificial and unjustifiable position in Ireland. Her helplessness in that position did not arise from its inherent difficulties, but from her neglect of Irish affairs in consequence of her absorption in foreign wars. She could not govern Ireland, and so the statute of Kilkenny was raised to keep the races apart until there was strength for more active measures. What else could England do? it is asked. We must not linger to contemplate a people passing through an interval in conquest, and expecting the angry waters to stand as walls on right hand and on left till firm land was gained.

It is always assumed in this discussion that the Norman king who first came to Ireland, and his successors, thought only of extending religion and good government. If we cast aside this palpable delusion the whole subject is clear as noonday. England, it is said, must conquer Ireland or succumb; she must sow disunion or fail; she must exterminate Irishmen or yield. The true statement is this: England must conquer Ireland, or leave it as God and nature meant every nation to be, unconquered; she must sow disunion in Ireland, or leave Ireland to grow into union and peace; she must exterminate Irishmen, or be human, and not exterminate them. Her attempt to govern Ireland had been practically only the delegation to Ireland of robbers of land protected by soldiers. Was it worth her while to persist in this undertaking till she succeeded in planting those men throughout the country, still protected by soldiers? She had transfused into Ireland some of the impure civil and ecclesiastical blood that was enfevering her own life; and when the vigour of the Irish constitution was assimilating this indigestible material the statute of Kilkenny arrested and forbad the process. It may be said that the French wars were the immediate cause of this necessity; but Ireland, and the same may be said of England, was not accountable for the French wars; neither was Ireland or

England accountable for the civil wars which we are now to see involving Ireland in still deeper confusion and wretchedness.

The Houses of York and Lancaster were descendants of two sons of Edward III. The Yorkists had the prior legal right to the throne, but the Lancastrian Henry IV. had deposed Richard II., avenging a personal wrong, and had taken his place. His grandson, Henry VI., was now King of England.

In 1449, Richard, Duke of York, nephew of Mortimer, and inheritor of his claim to the English crown, came to Ireland as viceroy. The motive of his appointment was that his removal might rid the reigning family of a danger. Its pretext was the outbreak of a general rebellion in Ireland against the English Government. This was a mere state fiction devised for the occasion. When the duke arrived, the Irish of the vicinity where he landed vied with the English in providing him with beeves for his kitchen. He encouraged this friendly disposition and sought it even on the battle-field. The MacGeoghegans and a body of English were devastating part of Meath; he made overtures and easily came to terms with them. He conciliated the Earl of Ormond, who was a Lancastrian partisan, and the Earl of Desmond, who was living apart from public interests as an Irish chieftain, by making them sponsors for his third son George, thus appealing to their Irish associations rather than to their English loyalty.

The insurrection under Cade, an Irishman by birth, which occurred at this time, was industriously ascribed to the duke's instigation, and it was reported that he was about to lead an Irish army to England. To allay those suspicions he went to London (1451) unattended, and the king being seized with insanity, he was made Protector of the realm by Parliament. The king recovered, took the field, was beaten, and taken prisoner at St. Albans, and the duke was again made Protector, during the minority of the infant Prince of Wales. The friends of the king re-asserted his authority, were defeated at Bloreheath, but gained a success immediately after at Ludlow by treachery, and the Yorkist leaders fled.

The duke took refuge in Ireland (1459). He was formally attainted by a Parliament held at Coventry, and writs were issued against some of his followers. The Irish Parliament immediately and unanimously explained their repeated request for a resident ruler by setting themselves in direct opposition to the English Government, and asserting their sovereignty and complete legislative independence. They declared the person of the Duke of York sacred, and executed according to the law of treason some emissaries sent by Ormond to make him a prisoner. They founded their claim to independence on a distinctively Irish characteristic, for they defended the duke on the plea that it had always been the custom in their land to succour and entertain strangers. Their intentions were made plainer by some further measures. They declared the lands of absentees forfeited, resumed all grants made during Henry's reign, and enacted that for every possession of twenty pounds, an archer, horsed and armed after the English fashion, should be maintained.

York was virtually king in Ireland, but he was a member of an English party, and was swayed by its movements. His son Edward, after visiting Ireland, joined the Earls of Warwick and Salisbury in Calais, made with them a descent on England, and won the battle of Northampton through the treachery of one of the king's generals.

The duke left Ireland, accompanied by numbers of Irish adherents, and was appointed virtual ruler during the lifetime of the king, and heir on his death. The queen raised an army in the north, in which Ormond held a chief command, and the duke, miscalculating its strength, was defeated and slain at Wakefield. His head was cut off, and, decorated with a paper crown, was fixed on the gate of York. His son, the Earl of Rutland, a youth of seventeen, was taken prisoner and murdered in cold blood by Lord Clifford.

Edward, the new Duke of York, when the battle of Mortimer's Cross drove the queen to the north, entered London, and was declared king by popular election (1461). The queen raised an army, and was defeated by Edward at Towton, where thirty-six thousand men were killed, and the Earls of Devonshire and Ormond beheaded after the fight. Edward was declared king by the Parliament. He appointed his brother, the Duke of Clarence, who was born in Ireland, viceroy, with Sir Edward Fitzeustace as deputy.

It was the Irish of the Pale, and not the native chiefs, who had aspired at national independence. The hopes of the former were absorbed in the success of the Yorkists; the latter were content to seize on the lands abandoned by the colonists who had followed Duke Richard in the expedition in which he lost his life, and to receive pensions from those who remained as the price for leaving them unmolested.

Sir John Butler, brother of the late Earl of Ormond, though attainted by the Irish Parliament, threw himself on the fidelity of his Irish adherents in Munster, and was zealously supported by them. The Earl of Desmond marched against him with superior force, overthrew him, and was appointed deputy. The representatives of the principal families, without distinction of origin, repaired to Dublin, and paid their respects to him as governor, with a cordiality inspired by affection for his person. Suspicions and jealousies were immediately excited towards a nobleman supported by the native population, in the breasts of persons who had proclaimed the independence of the island in the name of the Duke of York. Injurious rumours were circulated, and a bitter quarrel ensued between the earl and the Bishop of Meath, which was brought before the king, who decided it in Desmond's favour, and raised him to the rank of viceroy. But the Council at Dublin made such representations to the king that he was soon removed from office, and the Earl of Worcester installed in his stead. This was but the prelude to a more decisive blow. A Parliament was called, at which the Bishop of Meath and his friends had an Act passed charging Desmond, Kildare, and others with treason. Desmond appeared in person to meet his accusers, and was hastily seized and beheaded. The Irish chroniclers lament him in phrases identical with those employed in descriptions of the native chiefs.

Section VI.

The Earl of Warwick, provoked by the king's neglect, and, as is said, by some attempts against the honour of his family, fomented several insurrections, arising from petty causes, to dangerous proportions, all of which were marked by the cold-blooded inhumanity of the time. Lord Montague seized in a skirmish the leader of a popular commotion in Yorkshire, and put him to death. Sir Henry Neville and Sir John Coniers took his place. The Earls of Pembroke and Devonshire marched against them. Devonshire withdrew his forces; Pembroke attacked the rebels, took Neville and executed him, but was immediately after taken prisoner and executed in turn. The king ordered the instant execution of Devonshire. Coniers took the Earl of Rivers and his son, father and brother of the queen, prisoners, and put them to death.

In 1470 a rebellion broke out in Lincolnshire of thirty thousand men, headed by a son of Lord Willes. This lord took refuge in a sanctuary, from which he was lured by a promise of safety, and beheaded. The king defeated the rebels and put their leaders to death. Warwick, who had gained Clarence to his side, fled to France, whence, having formed a union with Queen Margaret, he returned, raised an army of sixty thousand men, by the aid of Montague's treachery, and drove King Edward to Holland. Henry was placed again on the throne, and the regency was given to Warwick. The Earl of Worcester was condemned and executed. The Irish, eager to detect an indication of justice, believed that he was punished for his severity towards Desmond. Edward returned to England, and, aided by the treachery of Clarence, defeated and slew Warwick at Barnet. Queen Margaret made a last effort at Tewkesbury, and was beaten. The Duke of Somerset and twenty other persons of distinction took refuge in a church, but were dragged out and put to death. The young prince was struck on the face with the gauntletted fist of Edward, and then despatched by Clarence and Gloucester. King Henry was murdered a few days afterwards by the latter nobleman. A Parliament ratified the acts of the conqueror.

The instant the civil war was settled the irrepressible spirit of robbery surged towards France. The Parliament granted supplies, and the nobles flocked to the expected plunder. Their hopes were dashed by the craft of Louis and the impolicy of Edward. Left to prey on themselves, the destruction of Clarence was as a wet finger applied to their unappeasable thirst. He was accused by the king, his brother, condemned by Peers and Commons, and permitted to choose the mode of his death.

On the death of Edward, another frantic struggle for the throne began. He left two infant sons, and appointed his brother Richard, Earl of Gloucester, regent. Richard, aided by an army from the north (for England, like Ireland, has always been divided into a north and south, hostile to each other in intestine wars), had the young king's guardians arrested and put to death. With an affectation of legal right, he pretended that the late king's marriage was invalid, and his children illegitimate. He supplemented this allegation by asserting that he himself was the only true offspring of the Duke of York, and that

Edward and Clarence were the children of adultery; and he procured the publication of this argument from the pulpit of St. Paul's. He was declared king. Not relying on the murdered reputation of his family, he ordered his two nephews to be put to death in the Tower. A marriage was now negotiated by the Lancastrians between Elizabeth, daughter of the late king, and Henry Tudor, or Theodor, Earl of Richmond, whose father (son of Owen Theodor and Catharine, widow of Henry V.) had married Margaret, the descendant of John of Ghent, and who was now the representative of the House of Lancaster. Richard proposed to marry the princess herself, though she was his niece, and gained her and her mother's consent, engaging that his present wife would die in a short time, an undertaking made good by the event. Fearing, however, the opposition of the people, and the condemnation of the clergy, he was forced to resign his purpose.

Richmond, with the permission of the French king, raised an army of three thousand Norman adventurers, with whom he came to England, and having defeated and killed Richard at Bosworth, declared himself king by right of conquest (1485). He married the Princess Elizabeth, ordered the Earl of Warwick, son of the Duke of Clarence, to be confined in the Tower, and erected an alabaster statue of his slain rival on his tomb. He took no steps to punish the murderer of the infant king and his brother. A papal decree gave the final ratification to his title.

The English civil wars almost destroyed the power of the nobility. The people, with that faith in eternal justice which always marks an oppressed but unsubdued community, saw the hand of Heaven in the misfortunes of their masters. The power of the throne became absolute. Respect for forms of legislation was professed and enforced in proportion as injustice prevailed. Parliamentary law was superseding the authority of the church, and becoming the favourite governmental superstition in England. Religion was moral and fixed, while law could always be used to make wrong appear right. A servile Parliament was preferable to a Pope who rested his claims on the immutabilities of Heaven.

As we consider epochs of internal strife, we may feel a solace as we catch troubled rays of dawning freedom struggling through the tumult, or yield ourselves to despair at the sight of seemingly barren suffering. The instantaneous character of the Norman Conquest of England left the great mass of the Saxon people a distinct and unbroken element in the state, with the same hatreds and the same hopes. In the wildest commotions, apparently irreducible to any law of order, that interrupt the career of a people free from foreign influence, there is always a central principle by which the mass of confusion is regulated, and its forces guided to a beneficial end. During the intestine wars of England, tens of thousands of men were slain; but the blood from every wound ran in the same direction. Rival families battled for the throne; and the prize they strove for became more precious, and drew the attention of the people until they became one in the oneness of the object they contemplated.

The character and the tendency of the Irish civil wars before the Anglo-Norman invasion had been the same as those which England was now experiencing. They were no longer so. There is no natural limit or end for the disturbances that are influenced from a foreign source. The piecemeal acquisition of Ireland never disengaged the people from their chiefs in sufficient numbers at any one time to feel a common interest, or to form a public opinion. The various modifications of nationality and religion that existed among the lords affected the tenants, and are scarcely yet disappearing. The wars of the clans prevented them from knowing that they had a country. The O'Byrnes, Mac Geoghegans, and O'Donnells slew each other in haphazard contests about cattle. Nachtan O'Donnell, chief of Tyrconnel, was killed by Donnell and Hugh, sons of his brother Neill. Donnell usurped the lordship. He was taken prisoner by O'Doherty, and confined in the Castle of Inis. Rury, son of Nachtan, assailed the castle, and set it on fire. Donnell was released from his fetters in the extremity of the peril, and ascending to the battlements, flung a stone on the head of Rury and killed him on the spot. Two years after the sons of Nachtan attacked and slew Donnell. Terence became chief, and after a few years was taken prisoner by the sons of Neill, and mutilated to unfit him for the chieftaincy. Such is an unprogressive period of Irish history under foreign control. May no Irish Shakespeare falsify those brutal wars. May no lyrist succeed in winning men to weep or glow over the graves they have left. Bare and sterile and bloody may they remain, till freemen walk over them. Let what flowers may spring up in their path.

Yet Ireland was not without indication of the course that things would take if they were only allowed to shape themselves. In 1460, O'Brien of Thomond asserted his claim to the Monarchy of Ireland, ignoring rather than opposing the English Government. He united the Munster chiefs in his favour, gave gifts to the lords of Leinster, and entered into an alliance with Desmond, a step that mainly contributed to the downfall of the earl. The enterprise was defeated by the ancient jealousy of the north. Again in 1475, O'Donnell began to extend his expeditions towards Connaught, and though resisted by the O'Conors and the Burkes, succeeded in laying Lower Connaught under tribute, and recovering some ancient manuscripts which had been taken from the north ten generations before. Aided by Maguire and O'Ruark, and the chiefs of Lower Connaught, he made a circuit through the whole province, reconciling the feuds of his friends, and exacting hostages from those who resisted. The tides that set towards national integrity were faint and fitful, but the law that governed them was eternal.

The quarrels of the Anglo-Norman lords were as purposeless as those of the Milesian chiefs. But they also from time to time swelled to the dimensions and followed the direction of a high national policy. Kildare, escaping the fate of Desmond, fled to England and made his peace with the king. He was afterwards made deputy, and took measures, nominally for the maintenance of English authority, that were resented by the officials in Dublin as encroachments on their province, and acts of secret self-aggrandisement. Sir John Butler, who accompanied the king to France after the battle of Tewkesbury, and won a high place in his favour, was made the vehicle of representations to the throne, that resulted in his removal from the deputyship, and the appointment of the enemy of his family, the Bishop of Meath (1475). The Parliament summoned by this prelate restored Butler to his title and estates. A violent contest arose between the two earls, and continued till Ormond went on a pilgrimage to the Holy Land. Kildare soon after died. The king appointed the young Earl of Kildare as deputy, and then changed his mind and substituted Lord Grey. Kildare refused to resign his office, and was supported by his father-in-law, Lord Portlester, the Lord Chancellor, who carried away the great seal, and Keating, Prior of Kilmainham, who declined surrendering the castle of Dublin of which he was constable. The rival deputies summoned rival Parliaments, which annulled each other's decrees. On the death of Clarence, who was Lord-Lieutenant, the office was conferred by the king on his infant son George, and Grey by a new commission was appointed his deputy. Meantime an assembly calling itself the king's council, proceeding on an ancient custom of choosing a chief governor on a vacancy, elected Kildare. The king eventually concurred in this latter choice. Ormond, who had recovered the title of Earl of Wiltshire held by his father, took up his residence in England. Kildare, whose manifest aim was independence of the English Crown, was obstructed by rivals rather than opponents. Both the Pale and the far more important English interests of Munster and Connaught were ready to seize an occasion of severing the English connection. But if this end were accomplished, the Irish enemy would still remain to be dealt with. Kildare took the most politic and patriotic course that was possible under the circumstances. He resolved to identify himself with the native Irish, and to make them partners in his enterprise, and sharers of his success. He secured the alliance of O'Neill, the chief of Tyrone, by giving him his sister in marriage.

SECTION VII.

On the accession of Henry VII. (1485), his uncle Jasper Tudor, Duke of Bedford, was appointed Lord-Lieutenant of Ireland, and the Earl of Kildare, though a zealous Yorkist, was allowed to continue in the deputyship. The entire council, though attached to the Yorkist interest, remained in office. The changes attempted by the king were only sufficient to show how his disposition lay. He deprived Keating, Prior of Kilmainham, and appointed an Englishman to succeed him. When the latter landed, Keating seized him and took away his credentials. He was excommunicated, on which he threw his competitor into prison, where he died. The king next summoned Kildare to England, to consult with him on Irish affairs. The deputy assembled a Parliament and pleaded his engagement with it as an excuse for disobedience. The king took no further trouble in the matter. The cause of his singular forbearance seems to have been no other than the knowledge that the Yorkist interest was too strong in Ireland to be provoked by open resistance. He may also have calculated that any opposition to his authority that might arise, by being made to originate in Ireland, would be regarded by his English subjects less as a just assertion of legitimate claims, than as an arrogant and unfounded interference of a rebellious dependency. It is certain that the Yorkist zeal of the Anglo-Irish attracted the attention of Henry's enemies to that country.

The choice of a pretender to the throne seems to have been decided by the popularity of the Duke of Clarence with the inhabitants of Ireland. It was reported that the Earl of Warwick had escaped from the Tower, and when a youth named Simnel, answering in all particulars to his description, appeared in Dublin, he was received with universal favour. Two thousand soldiers arrived from Flanders with some English noblemen, and the adventurer was solemnly crowned at Christ Church, and conveyed to the castle on the shoulders of an Anglo-Irish chief. For it is remarkable that this movement, though confined to the Pale, was made in the name of Ireland, and under the sanction of Irish customs. In fact the Irish in this district outnumbered the English. A Parliament was called, by whose decrees the enemies of the new king were driven from the country, and all the forms of orderly government were initiated.

Had Ireland been a conquered country the whole fighting population would now have risen and flocked to the standard that was raised in the capital, and Henry might have thought himself fortunate in retaining his English throne. Ireland had not been conquered. A small space of territory around Dublin had been imperfectly inoculated with an exotic form of government, and the inhabitants, Irish and Anglo-Irish, of seven-eighths of the island, remained undisturbed in their ancestral customs, and were ignorant of or wholly indifferent to the revolutions of their neighbours. The native annals of those years are unusually copious, but they do not even allude to the arrival of Simnel, or the preparations for a contemplated invasion of England from the Irish shores. We are told how one Macnamara slew another Macnamara, how Felim Finn O'Conor made himself tributary to O'Donnell, how the chiefs transferred their lands from one to another, how the English adopted Irish usages and names, and left rival heirs to their chieftaincies; how Neidh O'Mulconry, head of the inhospitality of Ireland, a new title indicating the only successful inroad of foreign manners, or growth of indigenous economy, won by its wearer's having sworn that he would never give both bread and butter to the same person, died; and how Leery O'Mulconry, head of the cheerfulness and jocularity of the men of Ireland, still kept the balance of family characteristics equal by dying the year after. The jesters were amusing themselves by writing elegies on salt, which had become so scarce that a poetic imagination could regard it as wholly departed. Its scarcity may perhaps account for the unwonted churlishness of O'Mulconry. Without insisting on this point, or enlarging on the merits of the poems composed on the occasion, it is enough to remark that these topics engrossed the historical muse at a time when the part of Ireland supposed to be exclusively English, instead of owning the supremacy of England, was undertaking to give that country a monarch.

In the beginning of June, 1487, the invading army left Dublin, and landed near Furness in Lancashire, accompanied by Thomas, brother of the deputy, who had resigned the chancellorship for the purpose. An army of Irish and Germans coming from Ireland was not likely to gain much countenance from the English. They marched to Yorkshire, in hopes of gaining some adherents, but the Northern spirit of insurrection, which had so constantly risen at any summons against the South, gave no response to an Irish invitation. The little army then resolved on a battle, and advanced to meet the king. Henry prepared as for another Hastings. He dazzled the approaching foe with ecclesiastical fulminations, and made a pilgrimage to our Lady at Walsingham. The two armies met at Stoke, and notwithstanding the immense numerical majority of the royal forces, the victory was won only by the advantage of their armour. We are familiar with battles in which a few men in coats of mail have routed thousands of disciplined but unmailed warriors. In this fight the mailed soldiers were the multitude, and the unprotected the few. The Irish had never been induced to adopt the protective armour of their English enemies. On the contrary, they had by some inexplicable means brought the English to adopt their military garb and their notions of warfare. The Irish and Anglo-Irish at Stoke fought (1487) as the Irish have always fought, more to display their courage and signalise their devotion, than to win victory and to secure its material gains. They stood their ground, and suffered themselves, without flinching, to be cut down in their linen vests by men clad in invulnerable steel, until the sight sickened and horrified their German allies, who had never before witnessed a conflict between men offering themselves to be slain, and others ready to reap the bloody harvest to the last sheaf. All the Irish leaders were killed. The young adventurer, Simnel, fell into the hands of the king, who, fearing less from his claims when living than from a new pretender to them if he were dead, placed him in a menial position in his kitchen.

His conduct towards Ireland was equally politic. He issued a Papal Bull of excommunication against the clergy who had countenanced Simnel. The intestine jealousies of the Anglo-Irish nobles, and their readiness to combine against the natives on any emergency, relieved him from the necessity of taking coercive measures against the former, or any aggressive movement against the latter, for the present. He seems even to have contemplated adding fuel to the existing discord by permitting the people of Waterford, who had remained true to his cause, to seize on the ships and merchandise of Dublin; but he did not persist in this intention. Sir Richard Edgecomb was sent with five hundred men to receive the allegiance of the rebels and confer the royal pardon. So incommensurate was his power with the magnitude of his office that he did not dare to land until his safety was made certain; and in holding an interview with Kildare, instead of assuming a high attitude and dictating terms, he was glad to take a secondary place and acquiesce in such terms as were proposed. The surest pledge of loyalty, within certain limits, was the tenure of high office, so Kildare was continued in the deputyship, and presented with a chain of gold. Keating alone was marked for punishment and exile. The Archbishop of Armagh, rating his fidelity as equal in value to Kildare's hesitating strength, asked to be made chancellor, but the king estimated things differently, and did not deem it prudent to grant the request. The deputy and the principal lords of the Pale were invited to England, where the king entertained them at a sumptuous banquet, and took the only revenge he could venture on by making Simnel officiate as waiter.

A new claimant to the throne appeared in the person of Perkin Warbeck. The king removed Kildare from his post, and made the Archbishop of Dublin his successor. In the absence of the Earl of Ormond, who was in France, Sir James Ormond, an illegitimate son of the late earl, was appointed treasurer, and repaired to Ireland as the representative of the family. The Butlers and Fitzgeralds immediately flew to arms. Warbeck arrived in Cork and was openly acknowledged by Desmond, and not disavowed by Kildare (1491). Before he could take any active steps, he accepted an invitation to the court of France. Henry at once made peace with the French king, with whom he had been at war, and assured him that he was about to establish order in Ireland.

Sir Edward Poynings was sent as deputy with a thousand men. An English Lord Chancellor and Lord Treasurer were appointed, and English lawyers were substituted for the former judges. Kildare was made prisoner on the charge of entering into secret negotiations with the enemy. The deputy summoned his first Parliament in December, 1495. Acts were passed forbidding the holding of Parliaments in Ireland until the heads of the intended measures were transmitted to England and approved of there; and extending to Ireland all statutes made in England.

Had the Irish Parliament been a really representative body, had the attempt to conquer Ireland been a success, or had the English settlers scattered through the country retained their political connection with the Pale, and not been absorbed into the native population, those suicidal acts could never have been even entertained. If the English interest had become strong and the Parliament had grown with its strength, the legislative independence of the country would have been permanently rooted in the soil. Paradoxical as the statement may seem, it is yet absolutely true that England's failure to conquer Ireland has been the chief, if not the only, ground of her success in crippling Ireland's resources and wounding her pride.

The growth of freedom in a native assembly had not taken place in the past; it was now determinately forbidden for the future. We too often give rulers credit for intending all the consequences that flow from their measures. There was no astuteness or profundity in the Act known as Poynings'. Danger to the Tudor line from the free action of a body of deputies was apprehended; the rude remedy was adopted of destroying its freedom altogether. It was only by a blunder that in saving a dynasty the Parliament of a small colony was gagged and a nation was enslaved.

No subtle skill in governing was needed while the hackneyed thunder of the Vatican was at command. An order was procured from the Pope, authorising the English archbishops and bishops to make such appointments to the Irish sees as they might choose, and to pronounce the censures of the Church on the rebellious and refractory.

Section VIII.

Kildare was sent to London and detained a close prisoner in the Tower (1494). His wife died of grief during his incarceration. Brought at last with his accusers into the king's presence, he overcame the royal mistrust by the simplicity of his address. He familiarly seized the king's hand, and declared he would take him as his adviser against his enemies. When charged with having burned the church of Cashel, he innocently pleaded that he had done so because he thought the Archbishop was inside. His adversaries warmly protested that all Ireland could not govern the earl, on which the king, finding an escape from his perplexity in an antithesis, replied that in this case the earl must govern all Ireland. Kildare was sent back as deputy, having first contracted a new marriage with a cousin of the king.[1]

Whatever his feelings of gratitude and obligation may have been, they could not neutralise the necessities of his Irish position. Ruling the Pale in the name of England, he unconsciously adopted the style, gathered the interests, and provoked the jealousies of a great Irish chieftain. O'Neill, the toparch of the North, was his nephew, owing his supremacy over his rivals to his aid, and yielding him a deference which he never would have conceded to a foreign power. In the South he asserted the king's authority by taking hostages after the Irish fashion. He made no attempt to withdraw the tribute paid to several Irish chiefs, nor to check the universal adoption of Irish customs.

A contest for the chieftaincy arose between the Butlers, which he turned to his advantage by establishing the power of the weakest claimant, and giving him his sister in marriage. He sought to extend his family influence still further by marrying another sister to Burke of Clanrickarde. The result of this marriage led him further than he contemplated. Burke ill-treated his wife, and Kildare entered as zealously on the vindication of the dignity of his house as if his authority were supreme. He was followed by the lords of the Pale, aided by O'Neill and the Northern chiefs. O'Brien and his Munster friends rallied around Burke. The two armies met at Knocktow (1504), and Kildare was successful. After the battle Lord Gormanston, one of his followers, proposed that, having slaughtered their enemies, they should finish their work by cutting the throats of their Irish friends. This saying showed the spirit which each fresh arrival brought into the country. Kildare died in 1513; the Council elected his son to succeed him as deputy.

Ormond's position at the English Court gave him an opportunity of prejudicing the mind of Wolsey so strongly against Kildare that the latter was removed from office, and summoned to England (1518). The Earl of Surrey was appointed Lord-Lieutenant. O'Neill, instigated by Kildare, proposed to O'Donnell that they should unite against him. O'Donnell, knowing that the supremacy of Kildare would elevate his rival, O'Neill, gave information to Surrey, and thus gained his confidence. O'Neill, ready to follow O'Donnell into any kind of contest, sent an embassy to Surrey, professing warm attachment, and requesting to be taken into favour. The king (Henry VIII.), mistaking intestine

[1] "The Earls of Kildare" p. 58.

emulation for loyalty to a distant sovereign, presented O'Neill with a collar of gold, and invited him to England. O'Donnell, not to be outdone, entered into immediate communication with Henry. Disturbances arose in the South, and Surrey sent for the assistance of the Northern chiefs. The instant O'Neill marched, in compliance with the call, O'Donnell invaded his territory, and compelled him to return for its defence. Surrey collected what force he could, and proceeded to Offaley, where he was badly beaten by O'Conor. A united rising of Irish and Anglo-Irish in the South now seemed imminent, when O'Neill and O'Donnell settled their differences, and came to the aid of the Lord-Lieutenant. The Southern leaders were forced to submit. We are reading the history of a people never allowed to emerge from their political childhood.

Surrey was recalled to take the command in a French invasion. In a letter to the king he confessed that the Irish chiefs were more disposed to orderly government than the English, and he advised that the island should be conquered throughout and colonised with English inhabitants. The suppressed premise in this reasoning is either that the Irish should never obtain orderly or just government, or that it was not in the interest of England that Ireland should be tranquil and united.

When leaving his post he recommended Sir Piers Butler, now Earl of Ormond, as his successor. Henry followed his counsel, but compromised matters by declaring his intention of sending back Kildare, who had contrived to obtain a daughter of the Marquis of Dorset and first cousin of the king in marriage[1], and to ingratiate himself with the king during his visit to Calais.

That tide in Irish affairs which perpetually in every pause of foreign attraction bore some native ruler into prominence now set in favour of O'Donnell. Though opposed by the Irish and English of Connaught, he defeated them, and compelled O'Neill to submit to his terms.

On Kildare's return, in 1522, he set himself to the work of supplanting Ormond, by representing him as surrounding himself with Irish adherents in his own interests. He succeeded in his object, and was sworn in as deputy (1524), on which occasion Con O'Neill carried before him in procession the sword of state. His loyalty was soon put to a severe test. Henry declared war against France; the French king negotiated a league with the Earl of Desmond, treating him as a sovereign prince. Orders were sent to Kildare to seize the earl. His enemies accused him not only of failing to do so, but of concerting measures of common resistance with Desmond. He was summoned to England, and committed to custody.

Successive deputies were appointed. O'Conor Faly took one of them, Delvin, prisoner, as a summary method of procuring the payment of tribute which was due to him. He openly threatened if his demands were not complied with to fling off the authority of the English crown.

Sir Piers Butler, who had resigned the Earldom of Ormond to Sir Thomas Butler, and was now Earl of Ossory, was nominated by the king to the vacant office. The Irish Council had in the meantime elected Sir

[1] ",Earls of Kildare," p. 84.

Thomas Fitzgerald. The Emperor of Germany now entered into negotiations with Desmond, and proposed landing a Spanish army in Ireland.

Even Wolsey, Kildare's personal enemy, saw that only one course could save the English interest from destruction. Yet it was felt that Kildare's appointment as viceroy would be a virtual surrender of the island. A middle line was taken. Skeffington was made deputy, with Kildare as chief director, and manager of war against the Irish.

O'Neill assumed a threatening attitude. Whatever his object may have been it was frustrated by O'Donnell, who immediately offered his services to Skeffington against him. The deputy and Ossory undertook an expedition, in which they were accompanied by Kildare, but it ended in a sanguinary battle between the two earls, in which Ossory was defeated.

In 1532, Wolsey being now dead, Kildare went to London, and returned with power to supersede Skeffington. He took instant steps to secure his power—he substituted Cromer, Archbishop of Armagh, a friend of the Fitzgeralds, for Allen, Archbishop of Dublin, as Chancellor. He gave two of his daughters in marriage to O'Conor Faly and O'Carrol. The lands of Ossory were invaded and ravaged.

In these proceedings Kildare does not seem to have contemplated any nobler end than a permanent tenure of the deputyship. If ever the thought of freedom from England crossed his mind it was regarded only as the alternative choice to the supremacy of the Butlers. He preferred power and pre-eminence as a subject to the obscure independence of Desmond. Ormond relied on England as the source of his authority. Kildare took his claims from England, but rested them on alliances with the Irish chiefs. Desmond became one of the native rulers, and competed with them successfully for the affections of the people. The three houses represent three grades of union with Ireland. The fortunes of their descendants corresponded with those relations.

Ireland was not a passive prey between those foreign competitors. Whatever danger Kildare might offer to the imperial dignity of England, or the pride of the Butlers, he was utterly unable to cope with the smaller native clans of the South, who now represented the national rights, and were gradually transmitting them to a larger and truer body of conservators. The O'Tooles surrounded three of his brothers as they were encamped on the borders of the Pale, and compelled them to make their escape in disguise with the loss of all their men. Another brother was beaten and put to flight by the Mac Mahons. His son Thomas was defeated by the O'Reillys.

The Archbishop of Dublin the Earl of Ossory and Skeffington forwarded complaints to the king of the decline of the English interest, the contraction of the Pale, the alienation of the king's land, the diminution of the English and the increase of the Irish race. Kildare was summoned to London. He armed his castles from the royal stores; appointed his son Thomas, a youth of twenty-one years, his deputy, and sailed for England (1534). He was committed to the Tower on his arrival. It was falsely reported by the partizans of Ossory and Skeffington that he was executed. Lord Thomas, who from the gorgeous apparel of his body guard, was called Silken Thomas, flung down the sword of state before the council in a phrensy of grief, and declared himself the king's foe. His feelings were worked to this result, it said, by the improvised strains of a native bard, who followed in his company. The so-called degeneracy of his race is exemplified more distinctly in his subsequent half measures. A Norman would have instantly seized Dublin, and put all his enemies to death.

The insurgent army laid siege to the castle of Dublin. Archbishop Allen, fearing the vengeance rather than calculating the strength of his enemy, embarked secretly for England. His ship was driven ashore at Howth, where he was seized and murdered by the Fitzgeralds. A lowering excommunication flashing with angry curses was launched against the perpetrators of the deed, and blasted their cause on the threshold. When the fatal step was taken, Lord Thomas began to measure his resources. He proposed to the Earl of Ossory to join him in conquering Ireland, and dividing it between them. Ossory, who had in the preceding month obtained the government of a large territory, on condition that he helped to reduce Desmond and resist the Pope, haughtily rejected the offer.

The people of Dublin, encouraged by promises of aid from the king, overpowered the besiegers of the castle. Lord Thomas exchanged some prisoners he had made for his captured soldiers, and stipulated with the citizens that they should help him in recovering the king's favour. His enterprise and its guilt were qualified by this hope.

The ill health of Skeffington, who was now deputy, dwarfed the war to a tangle of small demonstrations, in the course of which the country was mercilessly devastated. In one day the royal army burned thirty towns, and the garrison of Trim, ten. At last, assisted by an army from England, Skeffington attacked Maynooth, the principal fortress of the insurgents, took it by treachery, and hanged the garrison. Immediately after the deputy intercepted and captured a hundred and forty of the enemy, and apprehending that an attack was about to be made by the main body, took the precaution of ordering them to be slaughtered.

But the council at Dublin desired still more vigorous measures, and wearied the king with their importunities. Lord Leonard Grey was appointed to the chief military command. He found the scene of the war an unpeopled desert. Through a whole day's journey there was seen neither beast to graze, nor man to till the land. O'Moore joined the English, and led them to surround Lord Thomas, who was accompanied by O'Conor Faly. The prehistoric but unextinguished Irish mistrust of the Milesian was now manifested. O'Moore's people would not fight against the soldiers of Lord Thomas, but showed no such reserve towards O'Conor's men. They took Lord Thomas prisoner in ignorance, and released him when they discovered who he was.

Lord Grey, seeing no end to this kind of contest, offered conditions of personal safety, and the possession of his lands to the insurgent lord. Relying on those engagements, Lord Thomas surrendered himself prisoner, was taken to England by Grey, and committed to the Tower. Only then he discovered that his father had not been put to death, but had died of grief at the tidings from Ireland. The king was eager to have the rebel lord executed at once, but the Duke of Norfolk represented to Cromwell, Wolsey's successor in the confidence of the king, that Irishmen would never put themselves in the power of England again, if faith was so speedily broken, and that the slaughter should be deferred at least till the trap was better filled. Lord Grey returned with a list of victims, invited five uncles of the captive Kildare to a banquet, and arrested them in the height of the festivity. The six Fitzgeralds were executed on the third of February, 1537[1]. This delay would inspire the Irish with confidence in future engagements.

SECTION IX.

The rebellion of Kildare was a contest between a family of the Fitzgeralds and the Anglo-Irish Government for possession of the lands of Ireland. This object was growing every day more distinct in open declaration and characteristic measures. Projects began to be discussed for clearing the country of its native owners, and occupying the vacant tenements with colonists from England.

For the present the zeal of the council was engrossed on extirpating the remaining heirs of Kildare. This impatience grew into a fever. Skeffington died and was succeeded by Lord Leonard Grey, who went with an army to get possession of the person of Gerald, a younger brother of Lord Thomas, then staying with O'Brien of Thomond. A Parliament accompanied him from place to place, ready to appropriate on the instant the fruits of success. The army mutinied for their pay, and the expedition, military and legislative, failed.

The inhabitants of the Pale refused to make a grant. The relations between the two islands was producing a party almost without precedent. The Anglo-Irish were beginning to calculate that their extravagant profession of loyalty was a sufficient price to pay for the advantages they expected from the reduction of the country by English forces. Men placed in a position of unnatural guilt towards their native land are insatiably exacting. A violated conscience feels that it has given what cannot be recompensed. Englishmen, more Irish than the Irish, were already known. Irishmen, more English than the English, were now to appear.

The aunt of young Kildare, who was the widow of MacCartie, married O'Donnell to secure his protection for her nephew. The lady and the youth travelled in safety, with only a slight escort, to Donegal. The council mistrusted and blamed the deputy for this escape, and drove him to the adoption of perfidy. He appointed a meeting with O'Neill and O'Donnell, at which Gerald was to be present, intending to take the latter dead or alive. The Irish chiefs saw good ground for not keeping the engagement. The council importuned the king to hasten the destruction of the young heir, mingling their entreaties with descriptions of the enchanting scenery to the possession of which his life remained a barrier. The deputy made a second attempt at treachery and again failed. The cause of the fugitive was becoming the nucleus of a national confederation. Desmond, O'Neill, O'Donnell, and O'Brien

[1] "Earls of Kildare," p. 177.

were united in a common object. A rival Desmond was sent from England to sow discord, but was almost immediately murdered. The unslumbering rivalry of North and South foiled the growing hope. O'Neill claimed the kingdom. O'Donnell put young Fitzgerald on board a vessel which bore him to Brittany, where he was received by the governor with honourable welcome. In the reign of Edward VI. he came to London in the train of a foreign ambassador, made a fortunate marriage, and was received with favour by the king. Queen Mary restored him to his earldom in 1554.

The tenure of land was at this time undergoing a radical change in England. Hitherto it had been identical in its main features in both countries. The tenants held their farms conjointly by a perpetual ownership, dividing a part yearly for tillage, and using the grazing part as a common. In Ireland the right of the clans was as good as that of the chief. In England the tenant held from his immediate lord by the same title as that on which the lord held from the Crown. In the reigns of Henry VIII. and Edward VI. the great landlords of England, violating various Acts of Parliament, persisted in enclosing the commons and turning the tillage grounds into parks, expelling by force the real owners. The dissolution of monasteries was a cognate proceeding. Multitudes of people became outlaws. In Henry's reign seventy thousand persons were put to death. In the reign of Elizabeth from three to four hundred persons were hanged annually. An insurrection spread through the whole of England. The manner of its suppression may be gathered from a single instance. The rising in Norfolk consisted of twenty thousand men. They were fighting for their fields and homes, but they were poorly armed and quite undisciplined. A small army, consisting of little more than a thousand German troops, for they could not trust English soldiers with the work, was led against them, and exhorted to take them not for men, but for brute beasts.[1] The peasants were put to flight, and their leaders were hanged from the tower of Norwich.[2] This scene was repeated in other counties; all resistance was crushed; the enclosure of commons and the dismantling of villages went on without interruption, and the system of land tenure that now prevails in both islands, whereby the tenant holds at the will of the lord, was established. In England the evil was alleviated by the arrival of foreign manufacturers, who settled in the country and united themselves, under royal patronage, into corporations protected by exclusive privileges. In Ireland every attempt at trade or manufactures was ruthlessly crushed in the bud.

The defeat of the Norwich rebels took place on the 27th of August, 1549. In the preceding year, 1548, as we read in the Annals of the Four Masters, O'Conor and O'More went to England at the king's mercy; the king gave their patrimonial inheritances, namely, Leix and Offaley, to the Lieutenant and his kinsman, who built two large mansions in those territories, and proceeded to let these lands at rents to the

[1] "Lord Edward..when caught in his lair, fought with the ferocity of a wild beast."—Froude's "English in Ireland," Vol. iii., p. 334. "Father John..when seized, struggled like a wild beast."—*Ibid.*, Vol. iii., p. 449.

[2] See Strype's "Memorials," Vol. II., Part I., chap. xxi., and Russell's "Kett's Rebellion in Norfolk," pp. 144, 145.

English and Irish, as if they were their own lawful patrimonial inheritances, after having banished and expelled their own rightful, original inheritors, O'Conor and O'More, from thence, with all their adherents and descendants.

The revolution in land tenure was identical in time and manner in both countries, and was effected in each case, against the law of the land and the will of the people, and by the aid of foreign troops. The only difference was that the English lords, in England, took immediate possession of the lands, while in Ireland, before doing so, they murdered or expelled the Irish lords. In England again the deed was done once for all, like the original conquest, and was then designedly hidden in a blaze of class glory, while in Ireland it was prolonged over an endless period, and was accompanied by unrelieved and unbalanced atrocities, which their perpetrators have endeavoured to excuse by slandering the characters of the miserable sufferers. England has two histories; the history of her people, and the history of her lords. Ireland has only one history, because the history of her lords is that of the extermination and robbery of her people.

SECTION X.

Henry VIII. now became ambitious of completing the engagement made by Henry II. with the Pope, in a very different manner from that contemplated. The aim of Christianity is to fit man for a future state of existence by establishing a kingdom of heavenly justice on earth. Under all other forms of government the people are impoverished and degraded for the sake of the rulers; under the kingdom of heaven the ruler must die for the people, in the sense of always consulting for their lives and happiness, and not for his own. The Norman kings systematically used the name and authority of Christianity to frustrate its end. Through the Pope they sought to command the resources of heaven. They surrounded their palaces with titled and opulent priests, whose services to the Divine Being were weighed down to earth by gorgeous pomp and superhuman magnificence that glorified only their employers. They built stately temples, in which worship was paid to earthly pride. The Church half recoiled from and half took advantage of this prostitution. In mistaken self-defence it extended its power and its territories, and became corrupt. Whenever the moment came that it disobeyed the king, it would be deserted by the people who associated it with their political tyrants, and by the nobles, who longed for its rich stipends and fertile grounds.

The king made himself head of the Church when the Pope refused to divorce him from his wife, and for the future exerted immediately the power that was formerly sought for from the Roman See. The right to conquer in order to spread the Gospel is the regal form of the Papal claim to bestow kingdoms. Henry poured the wealth of the religious houses into his own coffers, and bestowed their lands on his nobles. The deluded people, plundered once more in the plunder of the monasteries, got for their share a translated Bible, qualified by a declaration of man's duty to his Maker, that has sealed it more effectually than Greek or Hebrew.

Wolsey may be taken as a representative of the English Church. In the guise of a minister of God, he worshipped Henry VIII., and to render his worship more gratifying to kingly arrogance, he was raised to the proportions of heavenly dominion. He was made Bishop, Archbishop, and Cardinal. His household furniture, his clothing, and the trappings of his horse were of gold. He drew revenues from the whole field of ecclesiastical preferment. His retinue was an array of gentlemen, knights, and nobles. His cardinal's hat was borne before him by a person of rank. One cross was carried before him as Cardinal, another as Archbishop, by two priests of remarkable stature and beauty. He was appointed Chancellor and then Legate, with absolute authority over the Church. When he said mass bishops and abbots served him, and noblemen of the first rank waited on his ablutions.

A member of an old bardic family, named O'Daly, born at the close of the sixteenth century, entered a Dominican convent in Kerry, went from there to Louvain, and thence to Madrid, where he gained the friendship of Philip IV. His abilities were so great that he was sent as ambassador to Louis XIV. of France, and to Charles I. and Charles II. of England. He won the favour of the Pope, and was the intimate friend of monarchs. Yet he never departed from the simple life of his youth. He never confounded the parade of earth with the service of heaven. While in Paris nothing could induce him to reside outside the walls of his convent. He was offered bishoprics and archbishoprics, and declined them. The only thing he asked for was that he might be allowed to found a convent in Lisbon, where his Irish brethren, persecuted in their native land, could study in peace.

All the churchmen in England were not like Wolsey, nor were all the churchmen in Ireland like O'Daly : but the two men represent the characters of their respective churches. When the pride of the English church was humbled, and the people acquiesced in its humiliation, and in a corresponding change of doctrine, it was not doubted for a moment but that the Irish church needed humbling, and that the Irish people would acquiesce.

The great monasteries of England were regal in their wealth and luxury. In the South of Ireland, on a little island in a dark lake, among high and savage mountains that shut out the world, and leave the heavens only open to the eye and mind, many miles away from town or village, an abbey was rudely built, where eight or ten humble men lived in stone cells, and slept on beds of stone, and prayed, and taught such of the wild inhabitants of the rocks and glens as visited them, to cherish a better hope than earth afforded. Because it was deemed right to pillage the English religious palace, it was also deemed right that the humble abode of contemplation and beneficence should be torn down, and that its inmates should be scattered.

The Irish people did not receive their religion from kings or chiefs, yet, now, when an English king gave a new religion to his people, it was assumed that the Irish people would surrender their religion which man never gave them, and accept that offered by such a man as Henry VIII. There is nothing specially tyrannical in this circumstance. It is only what naturally happens when one country attempts to force its wholesale rule on another.

An Englishman named Browne, who had distinguished himself in London by his zeal for the Reformation, was advanced to the see of Dublin, and charged with the task of obtaining an acknowledgment of the royal supremacy. The secular pride of the reforming prelate contrasted unfavourably with the modest sacerdotalism of the native clergy. The claims of the king were treated with ridicule. Cromer, Archbishop of Armagh, an Englishman, to confirm his clergy in the old faith, reminded them that Ireland from the earliest times had been called the Holy Island.

Browne recommended that the work should be committed to a Parliament. To expedite matters, the king ordered the suspension of Poynings' Act for this occasion. A Parliament was called, from which the clerical element was carefully excluded. Browne made a speech in favour of the king's spiritual authority, ending with the argument that those who differed from him were not loyal subjects. This was the very point at issue. If the things due to God are not distinct from, but are included in, the things due to Cæsar, religion is an element in loyalty, and men acknowledge their God when they own their king. Acts were passed declaring the king head of the church, suppressing several religious houses, and vesting their lands in the crown. At the very moment when the introduction of a new creed was provided for, an ancient law abolishing the Irish language was revived.

Sir Anthony St. Leger was made deputy in order to carry out a policy of conciliation. The Cavanaghs were the first to consent to resign their Irish title and to hold their lands from the king. O'Conor Faly and his allies next yielded. O'Toole, who on a late occasion joined the deputy because all the other chiefs were against him, now that they were all with him felt bound in consistency to resist, and was induced to submit only on condition that he should treat with the king in person. Ormond and Desmond became friends. O'Brien came to terms. Mac William took the name of Fitzwilliam, and Mac Gillapatrick of Fitzpatrick. St. Leger assured the king that the Irish chiefs could be permanently reconciled to his rule by kind treatment and refraining from spoiling their goods. It was thought that the adoption of the title of King instead of Lord of Ireland, would flatter the pride of the Irish. At a Parliament held in June, 1541, attended by Irish and Anglo-Irish chiefs, this measure was passed, with a vote of thanks to Henry for extirpating the power of the Pope.

In the following August, O'Donnell applied for apparel, a request which the deputy, not understanding its political meaning, thought very strange, seeing that when he made it he wore a coat of crimson velvet with twenty or thirty pairs of aglets, under a double cloak of rich crimson satin, corded with black velvet, and a bonnet of equal splendour.

O'Neill, who was the last to yield, offered his submission on the condition of receiving English honours. He sought the Earldom of Ulster. The king, reserving this title for the royal family, made him Earl of Tyrone. By the same patent, his son Matthew was created Baron of Dungannon. O'Brien at the same time was created Earl of Thomond, Fitzpatrick Baron of Ossory, the previous holder of that title having resumed the family title of Ormond, and Uliac Burke, Earl of Clanrickarde. Those titles were made more acceptable by grants of monastic land which accompanied them.

There was no opposition of moment to the steps taken for the abolition of the old worship. When shrines were violated and emblems of worship destroyed, the chiefs acquiesced, the great ecclesiastics protested, but the people made no sign. If the king imagined that this apparently voluntary surrender of their religious endowments and edifices was equivalent to an acceptance of the Reformation, he deceived himself. The religion of the Irish people had always been independent of kings. Contrary to the almost universal rule they gave religion to their chiefs. In immemorial times they had worshipped the God who dwells in a temple made without hands. This habit of their souls remained unchanged after they had received Christianity, and it survived without a shock the removal of the symbols with which Christianity was associated. Their forefathers had worshipped under the expanse of heaven, on mountain sides, and in savage glens, and they now reverted as to a familiar way of youth.

It has been charged on them that under Christian forms they retained the old Paganism. The truth is that they were forced to carry back, now and through long bitter penal days, their Christian faith to the simple and primitive forms of a dim ancestral creed. The tall grey rocks reared by unknown hands on the wild moor, the mysterious cave, and the Druidic circle have left an indelible impression on the mind of the Irish peasant. His plain chapel with its bare walls and earthen floor is dear to him, not only because it is connected with times of peril and persecution, but because it recalls the shadowy reminiscences of the childhood of his race.

The pacification of the country by grants of abbey lands, and titles to the natives, was not the end for which the council at Dublin had been working. The growth of loyal feelings would disappoint their hopes. Skeffington had been too lenient in their eyes, and they had never ceased complaining of him to the king. Lord Grey sought to unite the leaders of both islands by intermarriages, and they urged their accusations against him till he perished on the scaffold. St. Leger was striving to conciliate and pacify the country by the creation of an Irish nobility, and immediately intrigues and disputes arose, which reached such a height that the deputy and his enemies, Ormond and his partisans, were summoned to England. Before his departure, the deputy called together the lords of the Pale and the Irish Chiefs, and urged them to fidelity during his absence, or till the appointment of his successor. They lamented that he was leaving them, with tears, and ascribed the new prosperity, on which the island was entering, to his gentleness and wisdom.

The charges made against him before the king were that he had shown confidence in the faithless Irish, and had not reduced Leinster. This meant that he had endeavoured to reconcile the Irish to English rule, instead of exterminating them and leaving their lands a prey for adventurers. The deputy, in his answer, showed that peace, order, and loyalty were making rapid strides through the island, and that the breaches of faith lay not with the Irish but with the English. He was sent back to Ireland, and his accusers were punished. The policy of conciliation triumphed. When Henry died, in 1546, the annalist of Loch Ce says of him that there came not in later times a better king than he. Anxious to promote the Reformation in Ireland, Henry had discouraged for a time the projects of material conquest.

Under the new reign the Fitzgeralds were first to disturb the public tranquillity. They sent emissaries to France, soliciting assistance. Desmond withdrew to his estates and resumed his isolated independence. Two nephews of the late Earl of Kildare raised an insurrection, but were defeated by the aid of O'Toole, and with fourteen of their party were hanged at Dublin.

O'Conor Faly and O'Moore of Leix, led by their sympathy with the Fitzgeralds, took some share in this disturbance. They met with no support from their own people, surrendered to St. Leger, and were taken to England, where O'Moore died in prison. Leix and Offaley were violently and unjustly torn from their owners and added to the Pale.

The degeneracy of their people which the English complained of in Ireland had particular reference to the adoption of the Irish system of land occupation. The Irish had succeeded in maintaining their ancient right to the land under the Milesians. The Norman lords were ready to adopt the existing system, and the greater indulgence they practised in administering it was probably a cause of the preference manifested for them by the natives. The new custom that had arisen in England gave an increased intensity to the contest against Irish manners.

When Queen Mary came to the throne the Catholic religion was formally restored, but no restitution of property, civil or ecclesiastical, on behalf of the deprived Irish was attempted. The people were firm Catholics, needing no propitiation, and the queen felt herself at liberty to consult for the temporal interests of her throne and her followers. Henry had borne heavily on the Fitzgeralds and Butlers as hinderers of his purpose. Mary sent the young Earl of Ormond to Ireland, and reinstated young Kildare in his title and estates. O'Conor was restored to his country, but the triumph of his religion was considered a sufficient consolation for him, and his lands and those of O'Moore were reduced to shire ground. Catholicism was re-established, but the Church land remained alienated.

Section XI.

The reigns of monarchs are secondary in Irish history to the rule of principles or passions, which alone affords a chain of continuance, where all else is broken and irregular. Even through the sudden changes that took place on the throne, each involving, it might be supposed, a revolution, Irish Catholicism, always deeper than forms of religion, and Norman greed for Irish land, always stronger than its reality, went on undisturbed. When the Catholic religion was restored by Mary, there was not the slightest attempt at religious persecution. An English ecclesiastic, whose aggressive Protestantism must have been a galling provocation, can lay no greater charge against the people on the renewal of their old ritual than that they rang the bells, flung up their caps, and laughed most dissolutely. Their innocent exultation was neither checked nor driven to outrage by the fact that nothing but the freedom to worship God as their conscience dictated had been given back to them.

The seizure and confiscation of lands went on as before. The real owners of the territories of Leix and Offaley, the chiefs of which had been imprisoned and deposed, pleaded that their rights could not be affected by the conduct or the fate of their leaders, inasmuch as the lands belong to the clan and not to the chief. The Irish Government sent an army to expel the people from their possessions, and to punish with martial law all who resisted. The fires of the burning huts, we are told, were slaked by the blood of the inhabitants. Some of the neighbouring lords saved, with difficulty, the lives of a miserable remnant. Leix was named Queen's County, and Offaley, King's County; and their chief towns become Maryborough and Philipstown.

Elizabeth came to the throne in 1558. England's mind was strung, and her heart was hardened by the experiences through which she had passed. A new nobility took the place of those who had perished in the civil contest, and were vividly conscious of the fate of their predecessors. Prosperous merchants and traders, protected and favoured in their industries, and with the old baronial estates now thrown into the market as prizes for their success, abhorred the thought of fresh intestine disturbance. The landlords had got the country into their immediate ownership, and were jealously unwilling that any other tenure should exist wherever English law claimed dominion. The struggle through which the nation had gone left behind it an intense hatred of Catholicism, which only by an artificial association of ideas was fixed on its doctrines. The classes under those influences gladly submitted to absolute government, even in matters of religion, for their own security, and did not reflect that it was the very essence of tyranny to compel another nation to adopt political and religious conclusions to which their history had not led them. It did not occur to them as an argument for tolerance or leniency, that Ireland differed from England, that her Catholicism was not the Catholicism which England rejected, and that her traditions, the balance of her industries, and her ancient and immediate experience unfitted her for the reception of usages which in England were the creation of events, and if they bore heavily on one class, made recompense by giving wider scope, and opening a more splendid career to another. England was partly proud of, partly terrified at, the novelty of her position, and was ready to exhibit her zeal, and hide her mistrust, by an unflinching proselytism of the sword. The nation had shaken off her old religion at the very time when she was almost consciously entering on a path of unrivalled temporal prosperity. It was never intended that Ireland should share in that prosperity; all that was insisted on was that she should wear the uniform of her rulers, feel proud of the glory in which she was to have no share, and not offer a contrast over her plains to the beggared but dazzled yeomanry of the governing island. It is only part of the ordinary course of things that such feelings should arise under the circumstances. The fault is in the circumstances, not in the feelings.

If England and Ireland had not been locked in a death embrace for so long a time, no occasion would have existed for those exciting apprehensions of foreign interference which we shall now see maddening and misleading the two countries. It was because Continental nations regarded Ireland as the weak point of England that they commenced intriguing with, or listened to the overtures of the Anglo-Irish lords. But why was Ireland the weak point of England? Had she invited the invasion? And had she not petitioned repeatedly for equal laws, real union, and uniform strength? If Ireland were united with England on equal terms no foreign nation would ever have turned a glance in her direction. If Norman England meant honestly and fairly to Ireland she never would have been so feverishly apprehensive of foreign intervention. Having failed to plant a colony in Ireland governed by the same fears and illusions that swayed her own people, she imputed to Irish influence what resulted from the nature of things, and resolved on the extermination of the Irish and Anglo-Irish population. It was this avowed purpose that created her sensitive jealousy of French and Spanish interference. Norman England knew that in any other hands than her own Ireland would be prosperous and happy. She had, moreover, a discontented population at home, whose dangerous turbulence might be engrossed on the suppression of a rebellious colony. Some movement of this kind was suitable to the stage at which her history had arrived. Her hands and her conscience were free. She was full of unoccupied energy pressing on all sides for an outlet. Ireland was the nearest and readiest field, and the torrent of England's fury rushed where the peculiar policy of her rulers wished it to flow. The fear of a foreign invasion was a palpable pretence. How could a depopulated Ireland stay the march of a Continental enemy? Were not the Anglo-Irish the first to invite the foreigner to come to their aid? Whatever hatred of England ever existed in Ireland has always burnt fiercest in men of English extraction. The constitutional efforts of Irishmen for their country's welfare have always been exceeded and foiled by the violence of Anglo-Irishmen. The Milesians were and are ready to coalesce with the Normans in ruling the two countries. The rebellious spirit that has so obstinately prevailed in Ireland is the old Saxon resistance to the Normans renewed on Irish soil.

It is neither reproach nor praise to Anglo-Norman statesmanship that it overlooked or calculated on those results. That statesmanship keeps possession by present force, and force calculates on nothing but force in the future.

Ireland was at this time studded with dense woods embowering lakes of unsurpassed loveliness; ample rivers dashed over mountain falls, and moved in broad and stately volumes along the plains; waving fields of corn and verdant pasturages rivalled each other in richness and extent. The gift of Heaven and the labour of man had made the land fair to the eye and grateful to the heart, beyond what falls to the common lot of earth's surface. The project was deliberately entered on of destroying the woods, because they harboured the Irish, and of devastating the corn fields and carrying off the cattle, because they fed the Irish. The Irish would then perish by the sword and by famine. The present conventional assumption that Ireland is not a corn-growing country is the verbal crime, answering to the former destruction of corn fields; and the Irish emigration of to-day corresponds with the Irish extermination of the past. The remorseful rage at failure in the impossible, joined with a dogged resolution that the world should never know what the attempt had cost Ireland, as it must know whenever Ireland has even a single generation of self-government, gave rise to the common wish that Ireland was sunk beneath the sea, and keeps it still fervent in the hearts and on the lips of all inheritors of the Norman spirit. The wish, perhaps, is inevitable to the occasion, but the occasion is not inevitable.

It had become a point of honour with England that Ireland should not be free or prosperous. It is a point of interest with the satraps who govern her, that she should not become loyal. The English council were always ready to wage an exterminating war in Ireland, because, if the country were allowed to follow her own instincts she would become powerful and achieve her independence. The Irish council always created and encouraged rebellion, because the establishment of order would put an end to confiscation and the perquisites and privileges obtainable in troubled times. England is not desirous that Ireland should be unhappy or discontented. Her intention is that she should be weak and dependent. Whenever the struggle grows perilous to the connection, the English council appeals to the lowest motives of their Irish instruments. Queen Elizabeth stimulated the courage of her Irish agents during a dangerous rebellion by telling them that the hotter the war raged, the more lands there would be for them to seize. The representatives of English power in Ireland have never been satisfied with the insignificant position which Irish prosperity, limited by loyalty, would assign to them. They prefer a strong Ireland in chronic rebellion, and an exasperated England. Whenever the peace is too profound, and the Irish officials are subsiding into unimportance, crime is simulated or agitation is provoked. This is the history of the past; in a modified form it is the history of the present.

SECTION XII.

Elizabeth found the Irish nation more tranquil than it had been under any of her predecessors. Whatever disturbances existed in the south, were occasioned by the wars of the Fitzgeralds and the Butlers in Munster, and of the two families of the Burkes in Connaught. The attempt to spread and enforce the reformed religion gave those wars a new character. Lord Sussex, the deputy, summoned a Parliament in 1560. The acts of Mary's Parliament were repealed. In addition to the spiritual supremacy of Henry's time, an Act of Uniformity was proposed, by which the Prayer Book, as then established in England, was introduced; its use made compulsory by imprisonment for life, on a third act of disobedience; and all persons were compelled to attend the new services by a fine of twelve pence for each absence. A strong resistance was offered, but Sussex appeased it by pledging himself, that if the Act were passed, it should not be enforced. It was passed and enforced. The greater ecclesiastics, with a few exceptions, veered with the wind. The lesser clergy, who were one with the people, were true to their faith, and were expelled from their cures. Their places were filled up with the refuse of the English churches, recreant ministers, and rejected candidates. Those men were the Protestant rivals for the confidence of the people with priests of irreproachable characters, many of whom came from abroad at the risk of their lives to teach the Catholic religion.

The war with Shane O'Neill, which will be subsequently referred to, occupied the Government from 1558, till the time of his murder in 1567.

A Parliament was summoned for January, 1569. Its designs were anticipated by the enemies of the Reformation, and its constitution objected to; but only so far successfully as left the objectors still in a minority. An Act was passed for the attainder of Shane O'Neill, which lays the right of England to conquer Ireland on quite a new ground. The right given by the Papal Bull was no longer valid, but it was now discovered that King Gurmonde, son of a King of Great Britain, had possessed Ireland before the coming of Irishmen to the island.

The Anglo-Irish lords retired from this Parliament with feelings of discontent that strained for an outlet of open rebellion. The Butlers joined the Fitzgeralds and the Earl of Clancarty, who were in the field, and entered into communication with the King of Spain for the restoration of the Catholic religion. The Earl of Ormond came from England and induced his brothers to submit, but the Fitzgeralds and the Burkes, sons of the Earl of Clanrickarde, laid waste the whole region bordering on the Shannon, and destroyed every town or castle that belonged to the English or their allies. When firing the town of Athenry, the Burkes were reminded that their mother lay buried there. One of them answered that if she was alive he would burn her rather than that the English should possess the place. The Earl of Clanrickarde at last persuaded his sons to submit. They were taken by Sir Henry Sydney, the deputy, to Dublin, and released after a while on condition that they would not return to their province. They immediately called their followers to arms and burned Athenry once more. They broke in pieces the queen's arms which had just been completed over the gate by the workmen who were restoring the town.

The Earl of Desmond, who had been suddenly made prisoner by Sydney a few years before, was brought from England, still in custody; but while the authorities were in doubt how his influence could be most safely employed, he made his escape to his own territory, asserted his independence, and re-established the Catholic religion. Sir William Drury was appointed President of Munster, according to a late arrangement, and announced his intention of holding a session for the trial of offenders. Desmond protested against this infringement on his palatinate rights, and then pretending to assent, invited Drury to Tralee, but laid an ambuscade of eight hundred men to cut him off during his journey. Drury discovered the plot and put the ambushed troops to flight. The Countess of Desmond sought pardon for her lord with tears, and succeeded in gaining a temporising policy.

James Fitzmaurice, cousin to Desmond, went to the Continent, seeking aid to wrest Ireland from English dominion. He returned with Spanish troops paid with Papal money, and landed at Smerwick, where he was joined by two brothers of the earl. It was expected that the people would gather enthusiastically around the Catholic champion. But the religion of the people was beyond the reach of law, and the need of ascendancy, and they kept aloof. Desmond had neither the ability to make a vigorous use of his position, nor the heroism to risk its

K

loss by a bold exploit, and hung in sullen self-importance on the skirts of treason. Like many proud men, he humbled himself through his wife. She gave up her son as a hostage to Drury, who had brought a large army into Munster, probably hoping by this step to determine the loyalty of her irresolute lord. Fitzmaurice was killed in an attempt to seize some horses for the use of his men. A Papal Bull raised Sir John Desmond to the chief command. The insurgents risked a battle, and were defeated. The newly-appointed commander was only a spectator of the fight, and the earl and Fitzmaurice of Lixnaw viewed it from an eminence. Papers were found on the field that incontestably incriminated the earl. After vain protestations of loyalty, complaints to the Council at Dublin, and efforts to induce the Irish chiefs and even the deputy to join him, he was compelled to take the field openly, and was proclaimed a traitor.

The command of the English army was given to his rival, Ormond. The Fitzgeralds burned Youghal to the ground, and did not leave a living soul in its ruins. Ormond entered Desmond's territories, and destroyed towns and villages wholesale, with their inhabitants. In the beginning of 1580, Pelham, the deputy, came to the South to glean the remnants of slaughter. Desmond's castles were taken one by one, and their garrisons hanged. Sir John Desmond, attempting to join an insurrection raised in Leinster, was seized by the Sheriff of Cork, Sir Cormac MacCartie, given up by him to the military authorities, and hanged.

Towards the close of the year, eight hundred Spaniards landed at Smerwick, and fortified the place. Ormond and the deputy cut off all communication with the land, and the ships of Admiral Winter completed the investment. The garrison surrendered, and were massacred in cold blood. Sir Walter Raleigh was principal in the achievement, and the poet Spenser was present, and approved. English reputations became reversed by touching Ireland. Though the feuds of centuries were reaching their climax in Munster, Raleigh extemporised his part so as to transcend the hereditary actors in the long tragedy. Men burned their castles rather than fall into his hands.

The Fitzgeralds were not always defeated, but their occasional successes were followed by inhuman reprisals. The garrison at Adare were cut in pieces by David Barry. The forces at Kilmallock butchered a hundred and fifty women and children in retaliation. The shedder of most blood must win in the end. Barry and Lixnaw at last sought and obtained pardon. Desmond was left alone as leader, and Ormond was appointed governor of Munster. In November, 1583, the protracted agony was finished, and Desmond fell by the hand of a kerne, in a miserable hut, pleading his name and calling for mercy.

The earl and one hundred and forty of his adherents were attainted, and their estates vested in the queen. The re-peopling of Munster with an English colony was undertaken. The attempt failed through the dishonesty and incompetency of those concerned, and merely introduced a number of foreign landlords. Sir Walter Raleigh secured forty-two thousand acres in Cork and Waterford. The confiscated lands amounted to five hundred and seventy-four thousand acres. Nearly three hundred and fifty thousand of these remained in the hands of the old possessors.

CHAPTER IX.

THE O'NEILLS.

SECTION I.

THE condition of the independent parts of Ireland varied in the several provinces. The tendency of the national feuds throughout the island, before the Norman invasion, had been gravitating upwards and narrowing to a point. Since then the direction had been broadening downwards, breaking the lesser chieftaincies into rival fragments, and giving the lowest a greater power of irresponsible action. In Munster the great power and popularity of Desmond overbalanced and denationalised the authority of O'Brien, driving it for support to the shelter of the English crown. In Ulster, where foreign influence was least felt, the national life asserted itself with full vigour in the family of O'Neill. The O'Donnells were their only rivals. These two families preserved to the last the spirit of domination and defiance, characteristic of their race and history. Send me tribute, or else—was O'Neill's imperious demand. I owe you none, and if—was O'Donnell's reply. Milesian pride never freely scintillates till it comes into collision with Milesian pride.

Con O'Neill, the first Earl of Tyrone, was son and grandson of sisters of Earls of Kildare. He accepted a grant of all his lands from Henry VIII., to be held on knight's service, and secured the barony of Dungannon, and the succession to his earldom for Matthew, reputed to be his illegitimate son, but, in reality, a member of a different family. By Irish law, no chief could take the tribal lands to himself, and though an English title would descend lineally, the tribe were not bound to choose its inheritor as their chief.

Shane,[1] the earl's eldest legitimate son, worked on his father's national feelings and sought to revive in him the ancient spirit of his clan. Matthew, fearing the result, entered into communication with the Government at Dublin, and the earl was in consequence arrested and imprisoned. Shane, incensed at this outrage, declared war against the Baron of Dungannon and his English supporters, having reinforced himself with bands of Scots, who at that time were making settlements in Antrim. The deputy, Sir James Crofts, three times invaded Ulster, and was each time disastrously repelled. Matthew marched to his aid, and was driven back in a night attack by Shane in precipitate flight. Crofts at length advanced into the north with an overwhelming army, but his wily opponent sheltered himself in his fastnesses, and the baffled deputy was forced to retire.

The following year (1558) Matthew was killed in a fight with some of Shane's men, and the Earl of Tyrone died in prison. Shane was elected the O'Neill by his clan, and so set in opposition to English law

---

[1] Shane is the Irish for John.

and government. His territory comprised the central half of Ulster, and he claimed the headship of the tribes of the other portions. Of these the most powerful was that of the O'Donnells.

Sir Henry Sydney was now acting as deputy. He invited Shane to visit him at Dundalk, but Shane excused himself, and in turn requested the deputy to become sponsor for one of his children. Sydney consented, and used the occasion to expostulate with Shane on his rebellion. The Ulster chief in reply made a forcible statement of his case, and persuaded the deputy to convey to the queen an explanation of his claims and his conduct. In this document he expressly dwells on the prosperity he had introduced into his district. The English Government could not deny the rightfulness of his position, were unwilling, and just then unable, to resist it by force, but were determined not to suffer it to be established. The method they resorted to was one usual with them. They entered into negotiations with the Scots, and with Calvagh O'Donnell, whose wife was sister to the Earl of Argyle, and other Ulster chiefs. The Earldom of Tyrconnel was offered to O'Donnell, and that of Brenny to O'Reilly. Presents were sent by the queen to the Countess of Argyle, O'Donnell's wife. Shane was summoned to London to explain his claims. He knew that the object was to make him prisoner, but he wrote a long letter to the queen in which he pleaded want of money as the cause of his not making the journey. Meantime the negotiations were carried on with the Scots through the Earl of Argyle, and troops were despatched to Ireland.

Shane suddenly attacked O'Donnell at his residence near Lough Swilly, and took him and his wife prisoners. He kept O'Donnell prisoner for some years, and eventually ransomed him for a large sum. Having gained the affections of his wife, he made her the instrument of winning over the Scots from the English side to his own. He now proclaimed himself Lord of Ulster, and built a fortress on his border which he called the Hate of Englishmen.

The Earl of Sussex, the deputy, with Ormond and other nobles, invaded Ulster, and having turned the church at Armagh into a fortified camp, marched against O'Neill, who, with a force not more than half in number that which they led, routed them so thoroughly that Sussex described himself as dishonoured and wrecked. The Earl of Kildare came with fresh forces from England, and there were no less than five earls in the deputy's camp. O'Neill proposed holding a personal interview with the queen, but refused to leave Ulster while an English garrison remained at Armagh. Sussex made an attempt through O'Neill's servants to have him assassinated, and the Government, so far from disapproving, recommended its repetition.[1]

Kildare, standing on his right as a kinsman, produced a letter from the queen, inviting O'Neill to court. A peace was concluded (1561), the Ulster chief was furnished with a protection from the deputy, and it was agreed that the soldiers at Armagh should be withdrawn. Sussex wrote to the queen acquainting her that though the removal of the troops from Armagh was in the agreement, there was no word forbidding others at any time to be brought there, and that O'Neill had unknow-

[1] "Calendar of State Papers relating to Ireland," p. 179.

ingly, but formally, committed himself to such an interpretation of the terms.

Shane went to England, disregarding in contemptuous unconsciousness the obstacles and delays interposed by Sussex, who was now bent on thwarting him in whatever direction he moved. He appeared in London with a bodyguard of Irish soldiers armed with axes, and clad in saffron vests, and by his lofty bearing drove the mortified superciliousness of the courtiers to relieve itself in affected ridicule. When he was in the power of the Government he discovered that the safe conduct specified no time of his return, and that he was a prisoner at their will. He was told that he must await the arrival of the young Baron of Dungannon, and private instructions were given that the baron should be prevented from coming over.[1]

O'Neill, in the toils of his enemies, was like Samson, bound with green withs. He addressed himself to the queen, and won her friendship, involving himself in a debt of gratitude to her, which afterwards lost him his life. He began to treat with the Spanish Ambassador.[2] News arrived that the Baron of Dungannon was killed. The queen issued a proclamation in Shane's favour, and he left England (May, 1502). Hurrying through Dublin, he reached Tyrone in safety.

Aided by Hugh O'Donnell, he set about the reduction of the lesser chiefs, and when the deputy remonstrated with him, he replied that he meant to assert the birthright of his family, and extend his sovereignty over all Ulster.

The deputy requested his attendance at Dundalk, and prepared a safe conduct so worded as that he might be arrested without violating its literal meaning.[3] When the intended victim wisely kept away, the deputy wrote to the queen complaining of his refractory conduct. The expectation of tyrants requires a distinct metaphysical study. It was by implication demanded that Shane should shut his eyes to perfidy and falsehood, and meet betrayal or assassination as defeat in honourable strife.

Shane had suggested while in London marriage with an English wife as a means of confirming his loyalty and helping his adoption of English customs. The sister of Sussex was mentioned to or by him. Sussex now wrote to him proposing that he should come and see her. At the same time he informed the queen that if he came he should never return.[4] A modern writer,[5] well qualified to judge, tells us that he meant to hang him.

In September, 1563, articles of peace were signed between Shane and the Queen's Commissioners, by which all former agreements were cancelled; the title of O'Neill, with all its hereditary rights, was conceded to Shane; he was to have exemption from attendance on the deputy; and the garrison was to be withdrawn from Armagh. Confidence being thus established, a present of poisoned wine was sent to

[1] "Calendar of State Papers," p. 190.
[2] Ibid., p. 205.
[3] Ibid., p. 202.
[4] Ibid., p. 205.
[5] Froude's "England," viii, 30.

Shane from Dublin, which brought him to the verge of death.[1] The assassin, an Englishman named Smith, was arrested, and quietly discharged without punishment.[2]

The Ulster chief was now left for a while in peace. He ruled his province so successfully that no part of Ireland or England could compare with it for freedom from crime, and general happiness. He then went straight at the measures that would have given to his country the good government which he won for Ulster. He subdued Tyrconnel, and invaded Connaught, claiming the tribute formerly paid to the chief of Tyrconnel by the chiefs of Connaught. He made one mistake. In order to please the queen, who had always continued his friend, he severed his connection with the Scots, who were her open enemies, and overthrew them in a series of exterminating battles.[3] The sense of power and the habit of success reduce all things to the level of instruments which may be taken up or cast away at pleasure.

Sir Henry Sydney was sent over as deputy. In the spring of 1566 he summoned Shane to Dundalk. Shane answered the call with an army of three thousand men. The accounts here grow confused, but we learn that Randolph, who had come with fresh troops, was slain, and that Derry, which was held by an English garrison, was accidentally burned. When all else failed, the ever unfailing plan of sowing disunion was busily employed. The Northern league was broken up. The native order and principle of subordination were secretly assailed and loosened. Faster than the fall of Shane's foes was the defection of his friends. The reduced chiefs joined the enemy. Maguire bound himself to the English cause. MacCartie was received into favour, and made Earl of Clancarty. The O'Ruarks cast off their chief of Shane's appointment, and elected one who was his enemy. Hugh O'Donnell, raised on the death of Calvagh to the chieftaincy, and with the prospect of an earldom, joined the English and invaded his territory. Shane sprang forward to avenge the insult. The forces of Tyrconnel were stationed near Lough Swilly. Shane marched across the sands, and drove them back; but reinforcements just then coming to their assistance, he was forced to retreat. The elements had fought with him against the English, but all nature goes wrong in fratricidal strife. The tide had come in, and nearly his whole army perished in the waves. He escaped to his own territories, whither the deputy, with a powerful army swollen by Irish tributaries, hastened to finish the work. Shane, with unwavering boldness, snatched at the weapon he had blunted and flung aside. He demanded the alliance of the Scots, some of whom had just landed. His wish was granted, and he went among them with a retinue of fifty men. But an Englishman named Piers was busy in the Scotch council. A banquet was prepared, and O'Neill was slaughtered in the season of fancied security. He fell in no fair English fight. His own countrymen arrested his patriotic

---

[1] "Shane clamoured for redress with the fierceness of a man accustomed rather to do wrong than to suffer it."—Froude's "England," vii., 49. This language is worthy of careful consideration, not to produce angry feelings, but to understand a peculiar phase of mind. It would be a very mild remonstrance which privileged guilt would not consider fierceness. The mere fact of making a remonstrance in any form would be more than a crime. An act of self-defence against the silently assumed privileges of a caste is a far more serious offence than any violation of law.

[2] "Calendar of State Papers," p. 224.

[3] *Ibid.*, pp. 263-270.

instincts, an Irish sea engulphed his army, and Scotch and English perfidy slew him when he was a fugitive and a guest.

The O'Neill's history is the best exposition of his character. His enemies have credited him with every vice; but men who would have taken his life by cowardly assassination would not scruple to assail his character by lying. He is charged with pride, and is known historically as John the Proud. To comprehend the nature of this charge we have only to distinguish the attitude of a high-spirited man towards base and unscrupulous enemies, from the wretched affectation of a low nature, availing itself of a fancied superiority of nation or rank. He is accused of incontinence. He did not blindly rush to his capture when the sister of Sussex baited the trap. His conduct in the matter of O'Donnell's wife proves him not to have been a man of strict virtue; but all the circumstances point, not to profligacy, but rather to a reckless and contemptuous retaliation on his enemies with the weapon of their own choice. They were intriguing against him with the lady; he seized her, and overcame their wiles by her agency. His conduct must be condemned, but the condemnation should rest on the true nature of the offence. He is said to have been a drunkard. He was temperate in the use of the poisoned wine sent from Dublin, or he would have drunk his death. He is called a barbarian. He was abler and honester, and a far truer gentleman, and even a more successful courtier than the men who were arrayed against him. Had his imperious nature not been weakened by the relentings of honour and mercy, notwithstanding the desertion of the Milesian chiefs, he might have swept his country clear of the outcasts of all nationality, who afterwards crawled it into horror-stricken slavery. But this is the failing or virtue of all his countrymen. They cannot strike against the body that is still paralysed by the first blow. They await some greater triumph. When Shane was murdered, the deputy bought his head and placed it on a pole over the Tower of Dublin.[1]

It is not only the personal character of O'Neill that compares favourably with that of his traducers. The contrast between Ulster, where the native rule and the native population predominated, and the South, where English influence was prevalent, is still more striking and significant. In O'Neill's district the undiluted national life was invincible in honest warfare, and was checked at last only by the opposition of the adjoining septs, whom it had infected with its vitality, though it could not inspire them with its example. Sir Henry Sydney confesses that Shane's territory was better inhabited than any other Irish county. An English historian admits that all that was needed to good government in Ulster was Shane's submission to the English queen; thus, with singular infatuation, maintaining that loyalty to a foreign crown attended

---

[1] In reading the history of Shane O'Neill we are constantly reminded of Moore's lines:—

    And when they tread the ruined aisle,
      Where rest at length the lord and slave,
    They'll wondering ask how hands so vile
      Could conquer hearts so brave!
    "'Twas fate," they'll say, "a wayward fate,
      Your web of discord wove;
    And, while your tyrants joined in hate,
      You never joined in love."

with misery and starvation, is better than thriving prosperity under an independent native ruler.

In the South the Fitzgeralds and Butlers in Munster, and the Burkes in Connaught, in petty contests fomented by the pride of their wives, and the violence of their idle younger sons, changed every spot where they set their feet to a scene of desolation. Sydney describes the region in 1567 as presenting a horrible and lamentable spectacle of burned villages, ruined churches, wasted towns and castles, and fields strewn with the skeletons of the starved and murdered people.

SECTION II.

An Act of Parliament was passed by which more than half of Ulster was declared to be forfeited to the Crown. Another Act abolished the title of the O'Neill. It was not considered possible or prudent to enforce those statutory rights. The inferior chiefs, who had taken part against Shane, not in submission to England, but in assertion of their independence, were allowed to remain for the present undisturbed on their lands. The people elected a successor to Shane, and his claims were not disputed by the queen.

But though the right of conquest was not formally insisted on, its ends were sought under various new pretexts. An illegitimate son of Sir Thomas Smith obtained a grant of the long peninsula between Strangford Lough and the sea, with the view of teaching the barbarous people civility. The O'Neills, knowing only that they had lands to lose, and unaware that the strangers had civilisation to give, put a violent termination to the enterprise. In 1573 Walter Devereux, Earl of Essex, undertook to plant another district in Antrim with English settlers, in order, it was pretended, to expel the Scotch. Brian Mac Phelim O'Neill rushed to the defence of his territory with such vigour that several English lords who had accompanied the Earl became disheartened and returned home. Essex made an alliance with the O'Donnells, and when one of them was in his camp, he took him prisoner and seized his castle. He next made a treaty with Brian Mac Phelim, and being entertained by him at a feast, took advantage of the occasion to slay his people, make himself and his wife prisoners, and send them to Dublin, where they were executed and quartered. The island of Raghlin, the stronghold of the Scotch, was taken; two hundred men who submitted were, at the soldiers' request, given to them to be killed; and three or four hundred others, found hidden in caves and cliffs, were also put to death. Those actions provoked such detestation among the Irish that Essex was compelled to pause in his design. He went to England, and on his return with reinforcements was poisoned, it is said, by the Earl of Leicester, who immediately got a divorce and married his widow.

The Franco-Norman character, under the influence of British literary culture, had reached a new phase. A thin iridescence, reflecting all the brightest hues of heaven, disguised natures that knew neither the obligations of justice, nor the tenderness of humanity. They were conscious of no hypocrisy. The beauty of their theatrical ethics, and the utter baseness of their acts, had the same motive and end. The inflicted miseries of earth and the asserted principles of divine virtue alike amused their fancies and contributed to their gratification.

Among the varieties of warfare that sprang up around the fatal stem of foreign growth, one species, characteristic alike of the nation's earlier military contests, and its modern political strifes, is deserving of notice. Equally distinct from the haughty prowess of Shane O'Neill, and the hesitating rebellion of the Munster lords, was the light-hearted chivalry of Rory O'Moore, the chief of the dispossessed O'Moores and O'Conors of Leix and Offaley. The ejected owners fought as men will fight who have no hope, but cannot give way to despair. They did not seek to destroy, but to disquiet. They found a refuge from the depression of those whose natural career is taken from them, in the excitement of guerilla war, and the charm of a wholly unshackled life. Rory attacked Naas on a holiday, when the inhabitants were sunk in gluttony and drunkenness, set fire to the town, watched the conflagration from the market cross, and returned without taking a single life. He entrapped two English officers, and found a pleasure in taking them with him in his perilous ventures, and showing them the kind of existence to which their countrymen had driven him. He could not have devised a line of conduct more exasperating to his enemies. Negotiations were entered on for the restoration of the captives, and they were on the point of being given up unhurt, when the English came dishonourably on their place of confinement, and carried them off in triumph. Rory escaped, but his followers were slaughtered. The English then invited the Irish chiefs of the two districts to a conference at Mullaghmast, suddenly surrounded them with soldiers and massacred four hundred of them. The murderers and murdered were Catholics. Among the former was at least one Irish family, the O'Dempseys. A curse is said to hang over their descendants. Sydney connived at this deed. Rory was killed the year after in a rencontre with Fitzpatrick, Baron of Ossory.

Where were the people of Ireland while these invaders of various dates battled over the spoil? At one time we know that they still existed, from the impatience of those who desired their destruction. When Admiral Winter was off the coast in the South, the surviving inhabitants of the place hastened to seek protection from him, as if the land could afford them no protection from their destroyers. The English soldiers were aggrieved at this proceeding, for otherwise, it is said, they would have slain them all. At another time we catch their broken accents as they bid a tearful adieu to some humane ruler. When Sir John Perrott, President of Munster, left the island, his departure, as we read in the Annals of the Four Masters, under the date 1573, was lamented by the poor, the widows, the feeble, and the unwarlike of the country.

A few passages from those celebrated Annals will help us to understand the character of the Milesian and Anglo-Norman wars, and the relation of both to the Irish people. In this same year a civil dissension broke out between two members of the O'Brien family, in the absence of the Earl of Thomond, aided on the one side by the Fitzgeralds, and on the other by the Butlers. The assailing party marched through Upper

Thomond, and the cries and the shrieks of the unfortunate people whom they plundered, gave warning of their march in every place through which they passed. They pitched their camp at night, but the place was not "adapted for rest, on account of the crying and wailing of women and widows, who came bewailing their wrongs after being plundered." A battle subsequently took place, after which it is intimated that notwithstanding great provocation the prisoners were spared. This is an account of an intestine quarrel. The plundering was of the wholesale description introduced by the Normans, but there was no cold-blooded slaughter. The cries of the women broke the slumbers of the encamped army. In 1579, when Sir William Pelham was deputy, the sons of the Earl of Desmond proceeded to destroy, demolish, burn, and completely consume every fortress, town, cornfield, and habitation, lest the English might get possession of them, and dwell in them; and on the other hand the English consigned to a like destruction every house and habitation, and every rick and stack of corn to which they came, to injure the Geraldines; so that between them the country was left one levelled plain, without corn or edifices. In the following year Sir William got a supply of provisions and great ordnance from England, and accompanied by the English of the Pale, and Ormond, with an immense host, went to Limerick, and set to work vigorously for the dispossession of the Fitzgeralds. Wherever they went they showed mercy neither to the strong nor to the weak. "It was not wonderful that they should kill men fit for action, but they killed blind and feeble men, women, boys and girls, sick persons, idiots, and old people." No cries of women, we may assume, disturbed their slumbers. From Limerick, we are told, they passed to Kerry, and after taking Carrigafoyle and slaughtering the garrison, returned to Limerick, where, as a specimen of the thoroughness of their operations, they killed Ulick Wall, a man who had been blind from his birth, and "John Supple, a man whom it was not becoming to have killed, for he was upwards of one hundred years of age."

The Council of England in the first month of autumn sent, as the Four Masters continue to inform us, a new Lord Justice to Ireland, namely, Arthur Lord Gray. He was of a higher title and honours than Sir William Pelham, though there had never come to Ireland an Englishman who, during the time he remained, was more energetic in his expeditions, more nobly triumphant, or who had been more successful in his services than this William. He (Sir William Pelham) went to meet the new Lord Justice, who had arrived from England, and gave up the sword to him; and he then set sail for England, having been victorious over his enemies.

The annalists who wrote in these terms of one whom they had just described as a slayer of aged and helpless men and women, were the literary descendants and representatives of the bards, who were prohibited from ascribing any virtues or rights to the plebeian class, and accustomed to flatter the violent deeds of the Milesians. Trained in admiration of outrage and success, they naturally transferred their applauses to the most deserving. The worship of force and bloodshed is a very old superstition, yet its modern advocates, in consideration of the hostile light that has been long effacing its lineaments, deserve almost the credit of inventors.

That the accounts of the Four Masters may not be ascribed to flattery, it will be well to compare them with Sir William's own report furnished to the Queen in 1580. He says that they entered Connelough in two companies, Ormond towards the Shannon side, and Pelham himself towards Newcastle, and that they marched all day without offence of any enemy, wasting and spoiling the country to the foot of Slouloughor. The people and cattle flying before them in the mountains were followed by some horsemen and light footmen. Finding the country plentiful, and the people but newly fled, they left their camp guarded the next day, and searched some part of the mountains. There were slain that day, by the fury of the soldiers, above four hundred people found in the woods, and wheresoever any house or corn was found it was consumed by fire. A number of the rebels, he complacently adds, will starve.

The term, rebels, applied to simple clansmen who had no desire save to till their lands and worship their God in peace, and to lead harmless lives, justified every enormity. If any motive other than a phrensied spirit of murder can be assigned for the destruction of men, women, and children, it would be uncharitable to withhold it. The object that the Anglo-Norman leaders were fighting for could not be secured by the capture or death of the Earl of Desmond. If he and his family were utterly exterminated, the end aimed at would be no whit nearer. It was the land that was fought for, and the land was owned by the peasants. The murder of a peasant, young or old, removed an owner in possession. A war for land was waged against unarmed peasant owners by armed land robbers, making themselves landlords by the extinction of all rival claimants. That war modified by circumstances has gone on incessantly. Sometimes the victims have been driven forth on the road side to starve or beg. Sometimes they have been thinned by sword or famine. Sometimes they have been shipped to distant climes and sold as slaves. Sometimes they have been forced to emigrate. The manner has varied but the spirit has always been the same. Law and war acquired meanings and relations different from those which we ordinarily attach to them. Law pronounced every assertion of natural right or national custom to be a crime, and war became a wholesale execution of criminals thus created.

Section III.

Hugh O'Neill was the second son of Matthew, Baron of Dungannon, and reputed grandson of Con O'Neill, first Earl of Tyrone. He was brought up in England, and had served with the English in the war against Desmond. On the conclusion of that war Sir John Perrott, who then became deputy, stationed him with the troop which he commanded on the borders of Ulster, as a check on his relative who bore the title of The O'Neill. Sir Henry Bagnal, Marshal of Ireland, kept a watch on both. The power of the Ulster chiefs was further weakened by the treacherous seizure of the O'Donnell, who was lured on board a vessel, carried off to Dublin, and imprisoned in the castle. In 1587, Hugh O'Neill went to England, won the Queen's friendship, and obtained the earldom and the family inheritance. The deputy, though displeased that his own authority had not been made the medium of this transaction, acquiesced in it when accomplished. The Earl of Tyrone, as we must now call him, was intimately acquainted with the circumstances of England and those of his own country, and his first and abiding desire was to escape from the low and degrading entanglements of inferior tyrants, by the establishment of a direct understanding with the imperial government.

In 1588 Sir William Fitzwilliam was appointed deputy, and instantly turned his office into gain by wholesale venality. The crews of some ships of the Spanish Armada driven on the Ulster coast had been hospitably received by the Irish chiefs. It was supposed they had brought large treasures with them, and had confided them to the safe keeping of their hosts. The deputy having failed to discover this imagined wealth by means of a commission, pursued the search in person. Disappointed a second time he wreaked his anger on the chieftains whose only crime was their innocence. O'Ruark, one of them, fled to Scotland, was delivered by the Scots to Elizabeth, and was finally executed in England. His family was said to be one of the proudest in Ireland.[1] When brought up for trial he refused to plead unless before the queen in person, and bore himself through the terrors of his solitary doom with unmoved disdain. Mac Toole and O'Dogherty, both loyal men, were carried prisoners to Dublin, where the former died from the severity of his imprisonment. O'Dogherty was liberated after two years on the payment of a large bribe. In 1589 a dispute arose about the succession to the district of Monaghan, on the death of Mac Mahon, who held by English tenure. His brother, Hugh Roe, opposed by claimants who adhered to Irish customs, went to Dublin, was forced to promise a bribe of six hundred cows to the deputy, and was thrown into prison because he failed to complete the number. In a few days the deputy took him from Dublin to Monaghan, hanged him in his house, declared his territory forfeited, and parcelled it out to Sir Henry Bagnal and a number of other landowners who agreed to pay rents to the queen, and had already paid large bribes to the deputy.[2]

Tyrone must have distinctly seen that the part intended for him was connivance in the gradual ruin of the Ulster chiefs, and a share in their fate at last. On an occasion when he demonstrated his loyalty, the deputy openly threatened him as a traitor.[3] Every effort that he now made in self-defence was liable to the imputation of disloyalty. If he did nothing his inaction would be ascribed to duplicity and cunning. There is neither probability nor evidence that his mind ran on ambitious projects. He was Irish, not Milesian. The fortunes of his country in the future bore no fictitious hue imparted by personal expectations. The actual condition of things appealed, by the peculiar genius of his race, rather to the instinct of the statesman than to the impulse of the soldier. At this time he certainly did not entertain hostile feelings towards the English. Illustrating the only true and equal union that possibly can exist between the two islands, he fell in love with Marshal

[1] An O'Ruark bears the title of Prince in Russia.
[2] Fynes Moryson's "History of the Rebellion of Hugh, Earl of Tyrone," p. 10.
[3] Fynes Moryson, p. 12. Comp. p. 270.

Bagnal's sister, and asked for her in marriage. Bagnal, who regarded Ireland only as a spoil, and Irishmen as men to be despoiled, gave an insolent refusal. But the lady, who was very beautiful, preferred her Irish lover to her English relatives, and shared with him while she lived his home and her brother's undying animosity. The marshal's baffled greed and national contempt became a blinding hatred. He refused to pay the marriage portion to which the countess was entitled, shortened her days by his unkindness, and pursued his brother-in-law with incessant slanders.

In May, 1590, Tyrone suddenly sailed for England, and sought an interview with the queen. After undergoing a formal imprisonment for leaving the country without permission from the deputy, he was favourably received by Elizabeth, and agreed that his territory should become shire ground. On his return he found the English officials implacably incensed by his successful appeal to the Sovereign. Bagnal formally drew up an impeachment of treason against him, and laid it before the council. Tyrone replied in detail by letter; Fitzwilliam sent the accusation to England, but withheld the defence.[1]

Young O'Donnell made his escape from Dublin Castle. Another prisoner, one of the O'Neills, who shared his flight, perished from hunger and frost on the mountains. O'Donnell was found by the O'Byrnes, and brought to Ulster, with limbs dead from cold, but with a heart on fire. Tyrone strove earnestly to allay his just exasperation, to reconcile him to the English government, and to procure the recognition of his title as chief of Tyrconnel. The Maguires and O'Ruarks, maddened into open war by the iniquitous conduct of the deputy, won a victory over the royal forces. Tyrone aided Fitzwilliam against them, and was severely wounded in an engagement.[2] His enemies seeing that fidelity to Ireland was comprehended in his fealty to the English crown were far more enraged by his loyalty than they would have been by avowed rebellion. They detected in his policy the peace and free government of Ireland, and interpreted his intentions by their own selfish fears. Every improvement in the condition of a subject state is a step towards equal freedom. But the enslaver sees and dreads this far more clearly than the patriot plans it. That Tyrone should desire to see his people delivered from the grasp of the men who perpetrated the horrors of the war against Desmond, of which he had been a witness, would have been less the inclination of patriotism than the duty of manhood. But he was one whose designs were limited by the practicable, whose views of national independence were conditioned by wide consideration, and whose appetite for glory was much weaker than his desire to secure weighed and solid advantages for his country. In a mind such as his, fidelity to the English crown may have been loyalty to the best interests of Ireland.[3]

In 1593, the chief who bore the title of The O'Neill ceded to him his claims on Tyrone. Instead of being a mere blind from behind which the English intrigued and projected, he now occupied the whole of the

[1] Fynes Moryson, p. 12.
[2] Ibid., p. 13.
[3] For the true causes of the Rebellion see Fynes Moryson, p. 13.

coveted position and became the central object of covert and open attack. He stood, moreover, in his two-fold character of Earl of Tyrone and The O'Neill, between the Crown and the native population, the arbiter accredited by each of claims which the other would never recognise. He wrote to the queen complaining of the deputy and the marshal. Elizabeth, concealing her anger at his assumption of the Irish title, appointed a new deputy, Sir William Russel, and ordered that this fact, as well as her instructions that the marshal should cease his attacks, should be made known to him. On this Tyrone went boldly to Dublin, the den of his foes, and defended his conduct triumphantly. The queen, expecting that her dissimulation would be understood, angrily censured the Council for not having made him a prisoner.[1] It was observed that he henceforth cautiously protected himself against secret danger.

Fresh troops came from England, and the erection of a chain of forts separating the northern and southern halves of the island was commenced. Lest this gigantic insult should only daunt the Earl, the garrison at Blackwater offered him more pointed provocations, and by their outrages drove the neighbouring inhabitants to resistance, which of course was called rebellion. Tyrone vindicated his dignity, but neither lost his self-control, nor stained his cause by any deed of excess. He took the Castle of Blackwater, and sent the garrison to the south (1595). He then wrote to Sir William Russel, who had summoned him to Dundalk, entreating him not to persist in courses which must drive him to insurrection. His letter fell into the hands of Bagnal, who with despicable wickedness suppressed it. When Tyrone's reply was not received, he was proclaimed a traitor.[2]

By the queen's orders a conference was proposed. Sir John Norris, the English commander, took Tyrone's part, and refused to acquiesce in the deputy's measures.[3] Tyrone insisted that the meeting should take place in the open field. Neither now nor at any future time would he enter a town possessed by the English. Accompanied by O'Donnell and some other friends he met the Commissioners appointed by the English at a regulated distance from the respective armies. Between the Commissioners and their troops two mounted Irish soldiers were posted, to guard against any sudden attack; and between the Irish leaders and their army two English horse soldiers kept watch. On the second day of the conference the minds of Tyrone and O'Donnell were so pre-occupied, and their senses held in such strained attention for distant sounds, that they did not seem to catch the meaning of the words addressed to them. Nothing was effected.

The battlefield was chosen as the scene of the next meeting. In a skirmish that took place during the investment of the castle of Monaghan by the Irish, an English knight of vast size, named Seagrave, singled out Tyrone and bore him to the earth with overwhelming force. But even as he fell, in the grasp of his formidable enemy, the Irish chief slew him with his shortened sword.

[1] Fynes Moryson, p. 14. [2] Ibid., p. 15. [3] Ibid., p. 16.

Section IV.

It is not wonderful that a man thus beset should have sought the friendship of foreign co-religionists. If he over-estimated the power of Spain to help him, his hopes were not more visionary than the fears of the queen in the same direction. But we must judge men's conduct, not by the reserved and enforced alternative, but by the deliberate and persistent preference. Tyrone never ceased to declare his readiness to yield to the queen, and constantly protested against the local tyrants who with interested motives alienated her from the Irish, and drove them to rebellion. In 1595 he sent letters to London expressing his eager desire to comply with the royal commands, and in the April of the next year he formally submitted. The other northern chiefs followed his example. Soon after three Spanish ships arrived with troops and letters of promise and encouragement. Tyrone sent these letters to the deputy.[1]

The fort of Blackwater was re-built and re-garrisoned. The cruel and degrading outrages by which a hostile army can provoke resistance almost evade description. The soldiery had gone through the experience of the Munster war, and were left to exact their pay in plunder. A lawless miscreant invaded the sanctity of every home, and supported his demands by authority of the English throne. Every kind of property was seized and confiscated; and when the inmates fled for refuge from their houses, the soldiers pulled them down and compelled the owners to carry the timbers to be burned as fuel in the garrison. An English fleet hovered on the coast of Donegal and plundered churches and sanctuaries. It became known that Sir John Norris was about to be removed. Tyrone compelled the troops who held Armagh to remove to Dundalk. The English made overtures for a pacification. Tyrone would meet the Commissioners only in the open air. Holding his hat in his hand he protested before God that he honoured the queen beyond all other princes, and her people before every other people.[2] There cannot be a doubt of his sincerity. He desired to rule his province subject to England, but free from the corroding presence of foreign garrisons, and the plots of hungry adventurers.

He was urged after some time to resume negotiations. He answered that it was useless to come to terms which would, as always before, be violated by the queen's officers, that the honourable intentions of Sir John Norris would be counteracted by the deputy, and that he had less hopes than ever of just treatment since Sir John was about to lose the chief command. On two points he insisted unalterably, religious freedom and the withdrawal of the garrisons. He was willing to renew the conference, but the queen had given express directions that any meeting that took place should be held in a walled town.[3] To this condition he would not consent. Sir John was abruptly removed from his command, and died of the wound which his spirit had thus received (1597).[4]

Driven on one side by the violence of the English, Tyrone was drawn on the other by the example of the Irish chiefs. No work or enjoyment

[1] Fynes Moryson, p. 19. [2] *Ibid.*, p. 18. [3] *Ibid.*, p. 19. [4] *Ibid.*, p. 2

of peace in which his heart could rest was open to him, and he was summoned to the stormy duties of his rank, in which his genius was paramount. He was an Irishman flung by a billow of accident to the head of a Milesian dynasty. The deeds of his brother chiefs provoked him to rivalry. O'Donnell and Maguire had invaded the South, taken the port of Belleek from the English, and established one of the Burkes as chief of North Connaught, under the title of MacWilliam. He now saw O'Donnell with MacWilliam raging through Roscommon, taking Athenry, and defying the opposition of O'Conor Sligo, who fought for England. He saw him chasing the Earls of Clanrickarde and Thomond out of his territory. He saw young O'Conor Faly cutting to pieces at Tyrrell's Pass a thousand of the enemy. He knew that those were the actions that appertained to the O'Neill, and that the traditions of his class demanded from him. But he was not seduced by the spirit of emulation from the actual requirements of circumstances. He fought a successful battle with Lord Burroughs, who had been lately appointed deputy, in defence of his province at Blackwater. He followed it up by messages complaining of the wrongs that were necessitating rebellion, and asking for an honourable peace.

He was commanded to separate from his confederates and to give up his eldest son as a hostage. Knowing that the design was to ruin and rob the chieftains in detail, he would not engage to desert his compatriots till time was given them to come to terms also, and he refused to surrender his son.[1] He laid siege to the fort on the Blackwater, which was a constant and immediate menace to him, and a wall of division from the other half of Ireland. His brother-in-law, Marshal Bagnal, came to its relief with five thousand veterans. Tyrone went to meet him with inferior forces and overthrew him at the Yellow Ford with a loss of half his army and his life (1598). Of the Irish only two hundred fell. Armagh and Blackwater surrendered and their garrisons were escorted in safety to the English district. But final and complete success in war is not gained by brilliant victories and generous treaties. It is gained at a cost which the Irish have never been able to defray. Carrigaholt had been taken in an invasion of Thomond by O'Donnell. The Milesian Earl of Thomond, who was now in religion and feeling a warm adherent of Norman England, having received from the queen a charter of his territory and towns, and nearly all the church livings of Thomond, recovered it by the aid of ordnance and hanged the soldiers. He had fitly chosen the winning side. The English compared Tyrone after the defeat of Bagnal to Hannibal after Cannæ. He knew how to overcome, they said, but did not know how to improve his victory.[2]

After the Battle of the Yellow Ford O'Neill was regarded by the Irish and the Continental nations as monarch of Ireland. A crown of phœnix feathers was received by him from the Pope. He sent letters to the Leinster chiefs, recommending them to invade Munster. Acting by his authority, they raised James Fitzthomas to the earldom of Desmond, and established him in possession of the Fitzgerald lands. Yet Tyrone saw no grounds in the discomfiture of English officials and nominees in Ireland for breaking off the subjection which he owed to the queen. He never ceased his offers to submit.

[1] Fynes Moryson, p. 23. [2] *Ibid.*, p. 51.

The Earl of Essex, son of the earl who attempted the plantation of Antrim, came from England with full power as Lord Lieutenant, and twenty thousand men. By the advice of the Irish Council he marched against the new Earl of Desmond, but met with so spirited a resistance, and suffered so much from the harassing attacks of the Leinster chiefs, that he brought back only a wreck of his force to Dublin. Another division of his army, consisting of five hundred men, was decisively beaten by an inferior force of the O'Byrnes. Having received a reinforcement of two thousand soldiers from England he sent Sir Conyers Clifford, the President of Connaught, to relieve the castle of O'Conor Sligo, which was besieged by O'Donnell. The O'Conor Don was in Clifford's army, which consisted of over two thousand horse and foot. O'Donnell hastened to the Curlew hills, where the relieving army must pass, and joining his forces with those of O'Ruark, routed the English and slew Clifford.[1] The united army of the Irish was numerically much inferior to the enemy.[2] O'Conor Sligo surrendered his castle, and was settled in his territory by the victors. An incidental record in connection with this battle brings into view the true but generally unnoticed subject of our history. The people of Connaught, we are told, were not pleased at the death of Sir Conyers Clifford, and the reason given is that he was always generous to them, and had never told them a falsehood.[3] The peasantry had no interest in the wars of ambition that eternally harassed and ruined them, save so far as they affected the occupation of their lands. At this early period and during the confusion of the conflict the difference between the modes of tenure was unfelt. But any show of justice or kindness, from whatever quarter it came, they regarded as a beam from heaven. The native annals compare Ulster at the end of 1599 to a still pool, a gentle spring, and a reposing wave, without the fear of battle or invasion from any other part of Ireland.

Essex had now only four thousand effective men under his command; with these he marched to the north, and was met by Tyrone with a formidable army. The contest that ensued was one of knightly courtesies, in which the peasant-descended Irishman bore the palm.[4] He stated his grievances and terms of submission, which Essex promised to transmit to the queen. A truce of six weeks was agreed on. The proposed terms were that the Catholic worship should be tolerated, that the principal officers of state and the judges should be natives, that O'Neill, O'Donnell, Desmond, and their associates should enjoy the lands of their ancestors, and that one-half the army in Ireland should consist of natives. Elizabeth recalled Essex in anger, and imprisoned him (1599). Tyrone saw that his peaceful overtures were rejected, and that nothing remained for him but war. He issued a proclamation, calling on the people to rally to the defence of their religion, and made a circuit through the southern parts of Ireland, distributing justice and receiving submissions from English and Irish chiefs. At Cashel he was joined by the newly-elected Earl of Desmond. When near Bandon, the Mac Carties, who

[1] Fynes Moryson, p. 37.
[2] According to Fynes Moryson they were only two hundred in number, p. 38.
[3] "Annals of Four Masters."
[4] See Fynes Moryson, p. 38.

L

had emerged from obscurity on the downfall of the Desmonds, came to his camp and referred a dispute about the chieftaincy to his arbitration. He decided it by raising Florence Mac Cartie to the dignity of Mac Cartie More. Having appointed Dermod O'Conor, who was son-in-law to the late Earl of Desmond, commander of the Munster forces, he returned to the North. It is thought that the death of his friend Maguire in an encounter with St. Leger, the deputy President of Munster, in which both were killed, so saddened and dispirited him that he hastened his journey homeward. This was quite in keeping with his character. After he had marched past, Ormond and Thomond made a vain movement to intercept him.

Section V.

Four centuries had elapsed since England commenced the attempt to reduce Ireland. The present condition of things differed only in intensity from what it had been in the time of Henry II. The monarch was more absolute and arbitrary. The troops of adventurers were more numerous and more trusted by the monarch. In a military point of view the possession of large ordnance gave the invaders a greater advantage than that which coats of mail conferred on their ancestors. This new force was to be used in destroying the castles which it had been the long struggle of the early invaders to build. The notion that the lands of Ireland were their own, which O'Neill in his letter to the Pope had described as an insanity, had become a more blindly passionate delusion than ever. A religious difference had been added to those already existing. A large class, of ambiguous nationality, ready to hate England or to espouse her cause with a fierceness which no genuine Irishman or Englishman could emulate, was mingled with the population. A retrospect of the past produced rather the exasperation of failure than the wisdom of experience. The consciousness of injustice, so far as it existed, inspired a greater determination to win that complete success by which wrong is made to appear right.

The plans for the subjugation of Ireland had hitherto emanated from moods of which the human mind is ordinarily susceptible, and the power to destroy was limited by want of method. A horrible nightmare of the imagination had been conceived by the poet Spenser, just as he might have pictured wild visions of the cruelties of demons and the agonies of the lost, and without losing a single element of its dread maleficence was reduced to perfect working order. In an essay on Ireland, with the licence of his calling he had shown how the Irish people could be reduced by famine and then exterminated with the sword. That plan was about to be put into operation. Elizabeth, under whose protection Tyrone had hoped to free the country from the vampires that preyed on it, had been abused by falsehoods, and now regarded the northern chief with implacable resentment. Sir Charles Blount (Lord Mountjoy), who was secretly involved in treasonable practices and in daily terror of discovery,[1] and was in consequence ready to commit any enormity that could secure the queen's favour and his own safety, was appointed to the deputyship. Sir George Carew or Carey was made President of Munster (1599).

[1] Fynes Moryson, p. 80.

The President sowed dissension between the Irish and Anglo-Irish, employed spies in every direction, and offered bribes wherever any service in return could be expected. He sent for Florence Mac Cartie, and without infusing any love or loyalty to England into his mind, succeeded in detaching him from the cause of his country. He bribed Dermod O'Conor, commander of the Munster forces, playing on the credulous dreams of his wife, to betray the Earl of Desmond, dead or alive,[1] into his hands. He employed a person named Nugent, a deserter to and afterwards betrayer of the national party, to assassinate John Fitzthomas, the Earl's brother,[2] first lulling suspicion by charging him publicly before the Council with his treason, and dismissing him in pretended disgrace. Nugent attempted to execute his mission, failed, and was hanged. With his dying breath he asserted that several others had sworn to the President to kill the Earl and his brother. This confession so terrified the two brothers that they never dared to lodge together, or serve at the head of their troops, for fear of being shot by their own men.[3]

A method was devised by which O'Conor might perpetrate his treason without losing the confidence of his friends, and so becoming useless for further treachery. The constable of Lough Gur Castle, in Limerick, was induced to surrender his charge. The President then wrote a letter, addressed to the Earl of Desmond, thanking him for having secretly yielded Lough Gur Castle, and for undertaking to deliver Dermod O'Conor into his power. This letter was forwarded to O'Conor, who having seized the Earl, produced it, as if it had been intercepted by him, in justification of his conduct. The traitor, however, apprehensive that he might not receive his promised reward, failed to send his captive to Carew, and in the meantime the Fitzgeralds, Lacies, and Burkes arose and rescued him. The Earl could no longer trust O'Conor, and the army commanded by the latter, consisting of two or three thousand Connaughtmen, the only force on which the Irish could rely, entered into secret negotiations with the President, and finally went back to their own country. After reading Carew's false letter it becomes difficult to give credit to any document quoted in defence of the Irish Government.[4]

Carew having thus paralysed his enemy, in company with the Earl of Thomond, attacked the castle of the Knight of Glen, one of the Fitzgerald family, with his heavy guns, took it, and put the inmates to death, even the women and children. O'Conor Kerry immediately surrendered his castle of Carrigafoyle, and the other owners of castles or mansions either destroyed or abandoned them, and took refuge with their women and families in the mountains. James Fitzgerald, son of the late Earl of Desmond, who had been kept prisoner in London, was sent to Ireland to cause a further diversion in the Irish ranks. The only fortress that remained to them, that of Castlemaine, was given up

---

[1] "Pacata Hibernia," p. 65. Fynes Moryson, p. 92, describes the attempt as one of assassination.

[2] Fynes Moryson, p. 92.

[3] "Pacata Hibernia," p. 82.

[4] Fynes Moryson, p. 93. "Pacata Hibernia," p. 93.

to him, and was garrisoned by the President.¹ A pardon was offered by the queen, excepting the Earl of Desmond and a few others, on account, it is said, of the horrible murders and monstrous and unnatural outrages which had been committed in the rebellion. In the history which records this proclamation, the projected assassination by Nugent is characterised a few pages after as a bold attempt, and the general success of Carew's policy is quoted as a demonstration that God fought for them and directed their councils.²

All serious resistance was over. The President set about the process of starving the Irish at his leisure. The manner and spirit of the work will be best conveyed by giving the very words of a history written under his own instructions. The President having received certain information that the Munster fugitives were harboured in those parts, having before " burned all the houses and corn, diverted his forces into East Clanwilliam, where Pierce Lacy had lately been succoured, and, harassing the country, killed all mankind that were found therein, for a terror to those who should give relief to runagate traitors ; thence we came into Arloghe woods, where we did the like, not leaving behind us man or beast, corn or cattle, except such as had been conveyed into the castles."³

A French vessel having landed at Dingle laden with wine and munitions, which were sold to the Irish, measures were taken at the French court to guard against the recurrence of such relief.⁴ To prevent the money that came from England for the pay of the troops, and got into general circulation, from being used for the purchase of provisions from abroad, shillings worth only threepence were coined. They remained at such value on the hands of the Irish, while they could be exchanged in London for ninepence each by holders of a certificate of loyalty. This device was successful in hindering the importation of foreign corn, but it also disorganised the whole currency of the kingdom, and wrought general confusion and distress.⁵ While Ireland starved, the supply of money, troops, and munitions from England for the aid of the English army was constantly sustained.

The Earl of Desmond was at last betrayed by the White Knight ; Florence Mac Cartie was lawlessly seized, and both were sent to London. The President called a general session in Cork, and when the gentlemen of the district made their appearance, as usual on such occasions, he made the principal of them prisoners.

SECTION VI.

The proceedings of the deputy in Leinster and Ulster corresponded with those of Carew in Munster. Garrisons were planted along the frontiers of both provinces. A force was despatched to make a descent through Lough Foyle. All the packs of hell were loosed on the small poor creature of the wild. Treachery was sown among the O'Neills

¹ "Pacata Hibernia," pp. 154 and 175.
² *Ibid.*, pp. 208 and 219.
³ *Ibid.*, p. 190.
⁴ *Ibid.*, p. 141.
⁵ Fynes Moryson, p. 90. "Pacata Hibernia," p. 700.

and the O'Donnells. Some of the most active and trusted commanders of both families were induced to desert their country, and became, as usual with apostates, the fiercest partisans of her foes. Two attempts were made to assassinate Tyrone.[1] The garrisons of captured fortresses were massacred, and the English regiments were recruited with Irishmen, for the express purpose of having them slaughtered in the field. A quotation or two from the account written by the deputy's secretary will answer for a full detail. "Where other deputies used to assail the rebels only in summer time, this lord prosecuted them most in winter. This broke their hearts, for the air being sharp and they naked, and they being driven from their lodgings into the woods, bare of leaves, they had no shelter for themselves. Besides that their cattle (giving them no milk in winter) were also wasted by driving them to and fro, add that they, being thus troubled in the seed time, could not sow their ground. And as in the harvest time both the deputy's forces and the garrisons cut down their corn, so now in winter time they carried away or burnt all their stores of victuals in secret places, to which the rebels had conveyed them."[2]

The deputy, this writer tells us, stayed in Leix till the twenty-third of August (1600), fighting almost every day with the enemy, and as often beating them. The captains, and by their example (for it was otherwise painful) the common soldiers, cut down with their swords all the rebels' corn, to the value of ten thousand pounds and upwards, the only means by which, it is carefully noted, they had to live and keep their hired soldiers. It seems incredible, the writer goes on to say, "that by so barbarous inhabitants the ground should be so manured, the fields so orderly fenced, the towns so frequently inhabited, and the highways and paths so well beaten as the lord deputy now found them. The reason whereof was that the Queen's forces during these wars never till then came amongst them."[3]

Here we see the landless peasants of one island led by the example of their lords against their natural instincts to destroy the corn that God had grown for the food of the peasants of the other island. And here we may learn the meaning of the expression, barbarous people, when applied by certain English writers to the Irish. It does not mean a people incapable of manuring and fencing their fields, and making them richly fertile, or of keeping their highways in order, and their towns and villages populous and prosperous. It means a people against whom the epithet had gone forth as a sentence of condemnation anticipating all evidence, and forbidding the deductions of reason. The passage affords an instance of how English prejudice, penetrating to the mysterious and unknown substance of Irish character, has pronounced it to be evil, and all Irish accomplishments and virtues to be only worthless hypocritical accidents. It shows how the enemies of Ireland think it an easier thing to subvert the eternal moral law than to set Irishmen at discord with it. It demonstrates that Irish misery has always been caused by the presence of the queen's forces, and that their absence has

---

[1] Fynes Moryson's "Rebellion of Hugh, Earl of Tyrone," pp. 89 and 125.
[2] *Ibid.*, p. 50.
[3] Fynes Moryson, p. 77. Comp. p. 116.

always been rain and sunshine to Irish prosperity. And once again we have all through this war the refutation, written not by plough and reaping hook, but by sword and flame, destroying the hopes of a people's lives, of the reiterated statement that Ireland is not a corn-growing country, but meant by nature to be a land of pasturage. Nature made it corn-producing. Norman England destroyed the tilth of the land, as it afterwards destroyed the manufactures of the people; and to this day correctly interprets its own actions by reviling the Irish as incapable of manufacturing success, and condemning the fields to depopulation on the plea that they can only feed cattle. From the earliest times Ireland was a land of tillage and plenty. Districts afterwards covered with woods and bogs were golden plains of grain. The fuel of the country was procured from coal mines as it is now in England. The bogs are a modern formation, and were, many of them, caused by the devastation of tillage and tillers at this time of our history. The undrained and unpeopled lands accumulated moisture; outraged nature hid the scene of her disgrace under thick layers of moss, and fled from the vandalism of self-called civilisation to her ancient fortresses. When Swift recommended his countrymen to burn everything English except their coals, he did not know, or forgot, that the bogs of Ireland were true Norman manufacture.

The deputy, his secretary again informs us, arrived on Thursday, being Christmas day, at Phelim Mac Feogh's, so suddenly that his wife and eldest son were taken, "and himself hardly escaped at a back window, and naked, into the woods, where he kept a cold Christmas, while my lord lived plentifully in his house with such provisions as were made for him and his soldiers and kernes to keep a merry Christmas."[1]

An imposing excuse is found for the inhumanity of the Normans in Ireland, in the needs of English policy, and the devotion of the queen's courtiers. The Norman crown and nobles were contending for the establishment of principles against which the heart of Britain now instinctively throbs, and the purest intellect of Britain solemnly protests. They were struggling for the extension of those unparalleled laws that are day by day degrading the body of the English artizan, who cannot find a healthy home in his native land, and that are stunting the mind of the English farmer, who is not permitted to exercise his judgment, even in the disposal of his stubble. The zealous loyalty with which Mountjoy is credited was merely the cloak of treason. In the midst of his hostile operations, news came from England that Essex had been imprisoned for treasonable practices (1601). Mountjoy, who was a sharer in those practices, was thrown into a transport of terror.[2] He wrote passionate letters in terms of abject despair to Cecil, proffering his friendship and love. He withdrew all his private papers from his secretary, and ever after retained them. His plans for flight to France were ready on the slightest appearance of danger. The queen, who probably thought that a person in his circumstances was fittest for desperate work, wrote to him in assumed ignorance of his conduct.[3] His actual position resembled that of a condemned man allowed to live on

[1] Fynes Moryson, p. 87. [2] Fynes Moryson, pp. 89, 90. [3] Ibid., pp. 54, 89.

the condition of becoming executioner. In 1601 he marched to Ulster to complete his work, but was re-called by intelligence that Spanish troops were on their way to Ireland.

Section VII.

The Spanish general Don Juan De Aquila had entered Kinsale with three thousand soldiers. He was immediately surrounded on the land side by Carew and Mountjoy, who were joined by Clanrickarde and Thomond, with a large proportion of the lesser Irish chiefs. On the 6th of December, Tyrone and O'Donnell joined their forces at Bandon, and proceeded to Kinsale. The English, numbering six hundred and eleven horse and six thousand nine hundred foot, were now in turn enclosed by the Irish, who entrenched themselves in inaccessible morasses, and cut off all communication with the interior.[1] Tyrone, who had informed the King of Spain by letter that if he sent aid to Ulster, four or five thousand men would suffice, but that if he sent to Munster the army must be a very large one, strongly opposed an immediate attack, relying on the certain reduction of the enemy by their own chosen weapon—famine.[2] Victory, final and decisive, depended on allowing it to be won by the only man who was capable of winning it. Tyrone's position among the Milesian lords had always been an ambiguous one, and in this supreme moment the shadows of primeval jealousy darkened the counsels of the Irish army. The importunity of the Spaniards and the impetuosity of O'Donnell overbore all opposition, and a night attack by Spaniards and Irish was determined on. Brian Mac Mahon, a principal commander in the Irish army, whose son had been a page in England with the President, made the design known to him.[3] Preparations were made to surprise the surprisers.

When the night chosen for the attack arrived, three parties of the Irish, the O'Neills, the O'Donnells, and the men of Munster and Leinster, who had been exiles in Ulster, severally claimed precedence. They could agree only to march in three separate bodies. In the night march they lost their way, reached the English camp only at daybreak, found the English ready, and no Spaniards to aid, attempted to retreat, were thrown into confusion by an accidental explosion of gunpowder, and routed. Tyrone was wounded, and removed in a litter. The loss in men was inconsiderable, though Clanrickarde slew twenty kernes with his hand, but the loss of heart was irretrievable. Tyrone still insisted on the adoption of his own plan, which was as certain to redeem the failure as it would have been to prevent it. He pleaded in vain. The Spaniards surrendered (1602). O'Donnell went to Spain to seek further assistance. Tyrone returned to the North, assailed as he went by armed bands of Irish, and hooted by the peasantry, who saw in him only a disturber of their peace and a ravager of their fields. There is no more piteous scene in history than this Irishman raised prematurely

[1] The English force in Ireland at the time consisted of 1,198 horse and 16,000 foot. On the arrival of the Spaniards 5,000 additional men were sent from England.—Fynes Moryson, pp. 127, 150.
[2] *Ibid*, p. 178.
[3] "Pacata Hibernia," p. 414, and Fynes Moryson, p. 176.

from the expectant slumber of his race, vainly endeavouring to assert his genius in the council of his ruder fellow-countrymen, and suffering the unpopularity which their conduct deserved, and the shame of the defeat which their rashness entailed. The anger of the peasants affords an ever recurring instance of the true national element, that by Milesian chief and Norman lord was alike disregarded. The war forced on Tyrone was waged for Milesian supremacy rather than for Irish freedom. In later times champions of popular rights have travelled through Ireland with the price of the Government and the blessings of the people on their heads.

Carew and Thomond now addressed themselves with vigour to the task of quenching the scattered sparks of resistance. The Spaniards had held Dunboy Castle, and included it in their surrender. O'Sullivan, to whom it belonged, took it by surprise, and garrisoned it with a chosen body of men. The English set about a siege, unprecedented in the desperate courage of its defenders. The place was surrounded by land and water, and battered with cannon. Boats hovered near to kill those who might attempt to escape by swimming. The besieged, when the towers were beaten down, descended from loft to loft till they were driven to the vaults. Here, as the leader was about to fire the powder, he was seized by one of the assailing party, and held while another slew him. The survivors of the garrison were ordered to be put to death. No compunction, no generosity, no soldierly honour, no human misgiving arose to compete with the motives that governed the queen's soldiers. Tyrrel, a brave captain, offered any service in his power in return for the lives of his men. He was asked to play the part of traitor and refused. The men were hanged. Two, the commandant and an ecclesiastic, were reserved for prolonged torture. The first was hanged in chains at Cork; the other was hanged at Youghal, the town where he was born. Six or seven hundred horses, which could not be carried off, were slaughtered.[1] So intoxicated men drink on when a baser liquid is all that remains. This indiscriminate cruelty was no outburst of passion, no desperation of self-defence, or hate for a wrong, or vindication of liberty, or prosecution of a policy. It was the work of unprincipled men, done to please an aged and vindictive woman, who had titles and honours, a high social position and its attendant luxuries, to dispense.[2] Carew received a letter, addressed by Elizabeth to her faithful George, and ending with the invocation of God's blessing on him. He informed her, in reply, that her beauty adorned the world, and that her wisdom was the miracle of the age.[3]

Tyrone burned Dungannon, and retired into woods where no enemy could follow. The queen wrote to Mountjoy, giving him full powers to deal with the Earl. But, coquetting even in her vengeance, she hesitated between sparing and humbling her former favourite, now in her power. She concluded to demand his unconditional surrender, guaranteeing only his life. Cecil wrote at the same time, giving his own interpretation of her motives. Her resolution, he said, arose from a fear that Tyrone

[1] "Pacata Hibernia," p. 778.
[2] Mountjoy speaks of the Queen as "the Supreme Judge."—Fynes Moryson, p. 197.
[3] "Pacata Hibernia," p. 612.

would reply to any overture with insult and defiance, and he advised the deputy to come to terms with him for the very valid reason that England could not continue the war. Mountjoy, with whom a terrified self-interest was paramount, was more anxious to please the queen's pique than to follow the stateman's judgment. He made dispositions for surrounding Tyrone, set a price on his head, and laid the whole country desolate until he was able to tell the Council that nothing was to be seen but carcases of starved men and women.

The terrible details that are given in the accounts of famines suffered by the Irish and Anglo-Irish must be regarded as loathsome inventions or imaginations intended to illustrate the depth of their defeat and their helplessness, and at the same time to associate the unhappy people of whom they are told with thoughts of abomination and affright.[1] It is incredible that human beings could fling any living thing into a hell of torture, and then deliberately and complacently call on the universe to note the convulsions of its actual agony. Repeated modern experiences incontestably prove that Irishmen can endure this last trial of nature with dignity and self-respect.

It is enough for the general reader to know that everything that cruelty and craft could devise was unrelentingly done to starve the population of Ireland to death. It is also enough for Irishmen to know that all those efforts failed to quell the spirit of independence. The war continued and blazed out afresh in Connaught. Fears now began to be entertained, and on good grounds, that this obstinate resistance would encourage another Spanish expedition.[2] The spirit of Tyrone remained calm and considerate amid all agitations of his fortune. He advised that the Irish should resist or submit in a body, and he refused special terms of submission for himself. At last O'Conor and O'Donnell capitulated. Negotiations had commenced with Tyrone, and were proceeding, when the queen died (1603). They were hurried through by Mountjoy, who was now free from discovery, and only when they were completed, and lands and title were secured to the northern chief, was the intelligence of Elizabeth's death communicated to him. He burst into tears at the news. He had never forgotten her former kindness to him or wavered in his personal fidelity. He went to London, and on the journey was reviled and pelted with missiles by the countrywomen whose sons or husbands had been lost while massacreing and starving the Irish,[3] at the command of their Norman lords. Thus do the crimes of rulers evaporate in national hatreds. He was confirmed in his earldom, and Roderick O'Donnell, brother of Hugh, who had died in Spain, was created Earl of Tyrconnel. Mountjoy was made Earl of Devonshire,[4] and Carew Earl of Totnes.

[1] See Fynes Moryson, p. 271. Any reader who can force himself to read this horrible description will see in the fictions of forty years after the echoes of a maddened conscience.

[3] Ibid., p. 296.

[2] Ibid., p. 238, 240.

[4] Mountjoy's rule of conduct towards Ireland was "that all endeavours would be in vain if civil magistrates should think by fair means without the sword to reduce the Irish to due obedience, they having been conquered by the sword, and that maxim being infallible, that all kingdoms must be preserved by the same means by which they were first gained." Fynes Moryson, p. 297. From this rule of government the English and Irish equally have for centuries been struggling to escape.

Section VIII.

The war was ended, but the purpose for which it had been provoked remained unaccomplished. The men who had driven Tyrone to rebellion could not dissemble the fury of their disappointment when they saw him reconciled to the Crown and retaining his lands and title. The failure of their plans of robbery seemed to them a frustration of Providence and a surrender of the world to confusion. They moralised over it as a proof of the inconstancy of human affairs. The fact that the man for whose destruction they had undergone perils and privations was allowed to live in peace was an insult and wrong to them. They resolved on a new system of attack through espionage and legal artifice. We congratulate ourselves that the English language does not contain a word to express the action of a secret police. From this it is inferred that the thing itself does not exist among us. What we have is a police whose crimes are treated as open secrets. Tyrone was worried by ecclesiastical lawsuits, insulted by garrisons, and exasperated by a parade of spies. The strength of his character was subordinate to a sensibility that shrank from the kind of contest that was gathering round him. It was one in which he could only suffer and could not retaliate. He was truthful, and his adversaries knew language only as a thing to lie with. He had an Irish heart, and he had to deal with a generation that was all fangs. Every movement of his was commented on, misrepresented, and reported. He was heard to complain that he could not drink a glass of wine without it being known to the Council a few hours after. Rumours of a plot, in which he was said to be engaged, were mysteriously but sedulously circulated. O'Cahan, his hereditary Marshal, had been one of the first to make peace, and had received a promise of an absolute grant of his lands, which had always been held tributary to the O'Neill. When Tyrone submitted he received a grant of all the lands held by Con O'Neill, including those of O'Cahan. A dispute arose hereupon, which the Dublin lawyers decided by claiming the lands as the property of the Crown. It was announced that the king had assumed the settlement of the case, and would hear it in person. Tyrone was summoned to London. During his whole career he was as ready to trust the sovereign as he was cautious in dealing with inferior officers. This was the key to his life's purpose. He was now preparing to set out, when a letter reached him from the Continent, warning him that on his arrival he would be arrested. Moved by mingled disgust and apprehension, he resolved to leave his country and seek peace on some foreign shore. At the last moment the affection that was ever striking root in every nook and cranny of his tempest beaten fortunes predominated in his demeanour. His final parting from Chichester, the deputy, was marked by deep emotion. He next went to the house of Sir Garret Moore, at Mellifont, and wept as he took leave of the family, not omitting child or servant. He then hastened to Loch Swilley, and, accompanied by Tyrconnel, sailed to Rome. His enemies kept up a pretence of a conspiracy at Dublin. Lord Delvin was taken into custody. He was allowed to escape, and afterwards raised to the earldom of Westmeath.

A native lord still retained a small portion of Ulster. Sir Cahir O'Dogherty, Chief of Inishowen, was about twenty years of age. The deputy taunted him with being privy to the supposed plot. Paulet, governor of Derry, made the grounds of quarrel more secure by striking the young chieftain. O'Dogherty's rage at the cowardly insult, unheard of till his country lay helpless before its spoilers, blinded him to every consideration save redress of the wrong. Adopting the tactics of the enemy, he made the governor of Culmore fort his prisoner at a feast, and by threats of putting him to death compelled the garrison to surrender. Seizing the arms and ammunition, he suddenly attacked Derry, took it, and put the governor to death. The lives of the garrison were spared. He fell in battle a few months later.

Almost the whole six counties of Ulster, eight hundred thousand acres, lay at the disposal of the Crown. The deputy got the lands of O'Dogherty. The remainder was divided into lots of two thousand, fifteen hundred, and one thousand acres. The first portion was distributed among Englishmen and Scotchmen, the second among servants of the Crown in Ireland, the third among Irishmen. The first two classes were bound not to alienate their lands to the mere Irish.[1] Tanistry and Gavelkind were abolished, and the kind of land tenure that had lately been established in England was introduced. This wholesale outrage was not excused by a plea of policy, nor justified by even a quibble of law. If O'Neill and O'Donnell were traitors, that would not affect the right of the population who owned the soil of Ulster. Fraud and violence and wrong seized on the people's birthright, and called themselves law and order.

The war of Ireland for her independence under Milesian rule ended with the flight of O'Neill and O'Donnell.

[1] Carte, Vol. I., p. 33.

CHAPTER X.

THE CATHOLIC CONFEDERATION.

SECTION I.

RELIGIOUS reformation in England has been always more or less distinctly identified with the restoration of national liberties lost at the time of the Conquest. The people retained no reverence for a religion whose high places were filled by their tyrants. They now looked with jealous resentment on the Catholic nations of the Continent that would extend the Papal supremacy by force. Spain was most active amongst those nations, and as Spain was in alliance with the Irish chieftains, the religious hatred entertained towards that country was easily transferred to Ireland, to swell the ill-will caused by losses in war, and systematic misrepresentation. It was not taken into account that Catholicism in Ireland was not associated with absolute power in the Crown, that kings and chiefs were elected, and that the divine right was unknown there.

Immediately on the accession of James I. a Catholic conspiracy was formed to seize the person of the king, and a plot to blow up the king and Parliament with gunpowder soon followed. The English officials avenged those attempts of their own Catholic countrymen on the Catholics of Ireland. The latter had drawn up a remonstrance against religious persecution, and their delegates happened to present it on the day when the news of the Gunpowder Plot was published. They were committed to custody. On the other hand the extreme form of Protestantism that represented the Reformation in Ireland, and was in fact the hackneyed power of religion without its moral direction, became identified in the minds of Irishmen with cruelty and injustice.

A Parliament was called to give the semblance of law to confiscation and persecution. A majority was secured for Government by an arbitrary creation of boroughs. The outvoted Catholics complained before the king. James declared their remonstrance rash and insolent, and told them it was no affair of theirs whether he made many or few boroughs. When the attainders of Tyrone, Tyrconnel, and O'Dogherty were ratified, a bill was introduced revoking the old proscriptions of the native Irish, and admitting all to equal rights. The rights were admitted when there was little or nothing to be protected. Yet it may be questioned whether this empty privilege would have been vouchsafed had not the name of Catholic remained to take the outlawed place of that of Irishman. After the attainders had passed and a liberal subsidy was granted, some relaxation of the penal laws, by which Catholics were fined for not attending the Protestant service and excluded from all offices, was sought. The Parliament was immediately dissolved.

A convocation of the clergy at Dublin agreed to an ultra Protestant confession of faith, in which the absence of any intelligible rule of life was compensated for by declaring the Pope to be antichrist. Religious persecutions are generally connected with temporal endowments endangered by neglect of duty, or made uncomfortable by dishonest acquisition. The Puritans satisfied their consciences by reducing the men whose emoluments they had taken into their possession to the rank of idolaters.

The king attacked the property of his lay subjects in a similar spirit and with equal success. He appointed a commission of enquiry into titles, and by a lavish employment of fraud, perjury, and torture found that eighty thousand acres in Leinster belonged to the Crown. The supposed owners who held them from a long line of ancestors could not produce English title-deeds. The richest lands were portioned out to English settlers. He then directed his attention to Connaught. The landed proprietors of this province had surrendered their estates in Elizabeth's reign, and received new grants, but neglected to enrol them. In the 13th year of James's reign they surrendered again, and once more received new grants; but though they paid three thousand pounds to have them enrolled, the officer of the Court of Chancery omitted the form. James was about to take advantage of the flaw, when the landlords offered him ten thousand pounds. He died before he could make up his mind whether it would be better to accept this sum or avail himself of the absence of a technical formality.

Section II.

The accession of a new king raised the hopes of the Catholics. At a meeting, composed chiefly of members of that faith, an offer of a large contribution was agreed on as the price of security for their lands and freedom for their religion. The prospect of this offer being favourably received threw the Puritans into a phrensy of orthodox indignation. They drew up a protest against tolerating idolatry for money, and thus selling souls which Christ had purchased with his blood. The detestable profanity of their language was merely a new form of national arrogance directed under the pretence of intimacy with the secret ways of God at getting possession of the temporal goods of their fellow men. The king was in want of money, and for a sum of a hundred and twenty thousand pounds, to be paid in instalments extending over three years, granted the desired favour. The proposed articles covered the whole field of government, and aimed by wise and moderate measures at the liberty of the subject and the peace and prosperity of the nation. Lord Falkland, the deputy, summoned a Parliament to confirm those graces, as they were called, but omitted, in common with the Council, to send the requisite notification to England. The writs were declared illegal, the king withheld his interference, and the graces remained unconfirmed.

The resiliency of the Irish character awaited no formal ratification of the right to worship God as conscience dictated. With joyous alacrity, which to their sullen enemies seemed intentional insult, they resumed the public celebration of their religion, reconstructed some old buildings, and formed an academical institution for the training of priests. The same unquenchable spirit of devotion that had defied the Danes in former centuries now opposed itself to their degenerate successors, who, under the guise of religion, were endeavouring to destroy its restraints and monopolise its gains.

The unprincipled Council and the profligate Protestant clergy compelled Falkland to issue a proclamation forbidding Popish rites and ceremonies. The Catholics, uncheered by any sense of value received in return, complained that the sums they were called upon to pay were too heavy. A general discontent gave point to their dissatisfaction, and the Court was obliged to accept quarterly payments of five thousand instead of ten thousand pounds. When the king found that the graces were estimated only at their practical value, and that an unfulfilled royal promise was not considered equal to an accomplished engagement, he recalled Lord Falkland, and left the government in the hands of two lord justices, Loftus the Lord Chancellor, and Boyle, Earl of Cork. The former was son of the Archbishop, the other a forger, who had fled from England to a country where his abilities had greater scope. Both ascribed their rise in the world to God's immediate providence. The lords justices insisted on the attendance of Catholics at the Protestant worship, and proposed raising a revenue from the fines imposed on those who refused. The Catholics persisted in celebrating their own rites, having paid the stipulated price for the privilege of doing so. The Archbishop came upon them with a band of soldiers in one of their chapels, but the worshippers turned on their assailants and routed them. The matter was brought before the Council in England, and they ordered that fifteen religious houses should be confiscated for the king, and that the lately erected seminary should be handed over to Trinity College, which had been founded in Elizabeth's reign. The promised graces had neither been confirmed nor fully enjoyed : a reluctant half toleration was all that indicated their existence. Now when the money was nearly all paid, the king intimated to the lords justices that they were to be no longer taken into any account. He expressed his willingness to resort to fines for a revenue, but ordered this intention to be kept secret till the voluntary contributions were fully discharged.

Section III.

The quarrel between Charles and the Parliament was growing towards open war. The rebellion of the Commons was the struggle of an aristocracy against the absolute power of the throne. The House of Commons, after the destruction of the great nobles, was in all but title a House of Lords. The bond of union between them and the people was religion. But it was a mistaken bond. The religion of the masses was mainly an aspiration for the scriptural equality of all men. The risings of the English people had always been a protest in the name of primitive Christianity against the religion and policy of Norman rule. It was so in the time of Richard II., and in the time of Henry VIII., and it was so now. The leading Puritans consorted with their followers on equal terms in their religious exercises, and so led them to suppose that they were regarded as political brethren. But while the people used religion for the redress of their own social disqualifications, and the hardships imposed by their immediate lords, the members of the House of Commons employed it solely for the reduction of the royal prerogatives that bore with weight on themselves.

In 1632 Wentworth, who had deserted from the Parliament to the king, was appointed deputy, for the purpose of making the resources of Ireland available for the king in his contest with the English Parliament. He hated the Puritans, despised the lately arrived English who had raised themselves by infamous means, and looked on the Irish only as a conquered people. In England he would have been content to gain his ends by intrigue; in Ireland he used intrigue, but let it be known that force lay behind it. He urged the Protestants to compete with the Catholics in the alacrity of their contribution for the support of the king's army, intimating to them at the same time that their consent was only a matter of form. They agreed to his wishes, fearing the imposition of an annual charge on their lands. A Parliament was desired by all parties, but was at the same time viewed with apprehension by the king, since it would furnish an occasion of demanding a ratification of the graces. A plan was concerted that a Parliament should be held, that it should consist of two sessions, the second to take place at some indefinite period after the first, that subsidies should be granted at the first, and that the consideration of grievances should be postponed to the second. But this arrangement was kept secret, in order that the supplies might be granted quickly in expectation that the grievances would be dealt with immediately after. The Council, suspecting treachery, attempted to determine the matters that were to come before Parliament, on which the deputy informed them that the king sought one of two things—perfect compliance, or the grounds of a quarrel. A Parliament was called, and a large subsidy granted. The House of Lords made a stand for justice. They pressed for the fulfilment of the graces. One of these limited the king's claims on the land to a retrospect of sixty years. They particularly sought that this condition should be recognised. The deputy compelled the Council to pass a resolution that such limitation was inconsistent with the interests of the Crown.

The course was now clear for the confiscation of Connaught. The first swoop was made on Roscommon. The juries appointed to decide between the Crown and the present owners, consisted of persons from whom fines could be extracted if they refused to return the desired verdict. When they shrank from the ungrateful task, Wentworth assured them that all was done for their benefit, and that the king had paid them a high compliment in submitting his rights to their judgment. They found as was expected of them. Sligo and Mayo followed their example. The bias of the judges was secured by giving them four shillings in the pound out of the first year's rent of the lands, the titles of which proved to be defective.

The first resistance was made at Galway. The jury, impanelled to try the title of Lord Clanrickarde's estates, the same who had been so active at Kinsale, refused to give a verdict for the king. The sheriff was fined a thousand pounds, and each of the jury four hundred pounds; and sheriff and jury were committed to prison till they paid the fines and apologised on their knees. Clanrickarde died broken-hearted. All the other proprietors surrendered their estates and submitted to the king's mercy.

The absolutism that in England was contending against a faction, behind which lay a nation, tyrannised over the unsupported emissaries of the same faction in Ireland. Boyle, Earl of Cork, was forced to surrender the church lands which he had seized. With egotistic impiety he had erected a family monument near the high altar of St. Patrick's Cathedral. The deputy insisted on its removal. Lord Mountmorres was condemned to be shot for an equivocal expression at a dinner table. He was not executed, but made to suffer a hundred deaths by alternate withdrawals and renewals of his sentence. Chancellor Loftus was deprived of the great seal, and sent to prison for disobeying an arbitrary order of the Council. It is not severity that embitters a people so much as severity exercised with partiality. The people of Ireland for the first time saw arbitrary power equally administered over all.

Wentworth boasted to the king that the government was brought to a state of discipline and efficiency it had never known before, that trade was promoted, and manufactures were established. In no country could such gains as these, even if real, be a recompense for freedom and spontaneous growth. In Ireland they were not intended for the benefit of the inhabitants. The army was not organised for the protection of the country, but for the maintenance of past and the accomplishment of future confiscations, in the interest of the king. The manufactures were interfered with merely for the protection of English manufactures. The wool trade was a native production. It competed with the trade of England, and rendered Ireland independent of the ruling country in the matter of clothing. It was destroyed and an artificial flax trade substituted. Trade, religion, and people were to be alike plantations and were never to become indigenous.

For two years the country was quiet. In January, 1640, the deputy went to England, and was made Earl of Strafford and Lord Lieutenant of Ireland. He returned to the seat of his government, where he found Parliament in session and prepared to exceed his most sanguine expectations. They declared in language, if not feelings, unmistakably Irish, that their hearts were mines of subsidies for the king. Wentworth went back to England and proposed the example of the Irish Parliament to the English members. They refused to learn loyalty from Ireland, and separated without granting any supplies.

SECTION IV.

Wentworth had an army of eight thousand men in the north, intended for a descent on Scotland, which was now in rebellion against Charles. The Scots were first in the field and invaded England, where they were welcomed by the Parliamentarians. A change now came over the Irish Parliament. They declared the subsidies demanded by Wentworth excessive, and his mode of assessing them unconstitutional. They drew up a statement of the grievances they had suffered under his administration, and appointed a committee of sixteen to lay their remonstrances before the king. Wandesford, the Lord Lieutenant's deputy, vainly attempted to prevent their journey, and died of chagrin, Wentworth recommended Ormond as his successor, but the king, following the fatal advice of the Irish committee, assigned the government to Sir John Borlase and Sir William Parsons, two violent Puritans. The English Parliament, aided by the Irish committee, whose mission was strengthened by several Irish lords, now arraigned Wentworth for high treason, and brought him to the scaffold on the twelfth of May, 1641.

The king in a letter to the lords justices declared that his subjects in Ireland should henceforth enjoy the benefit of the graces, and on the twenty-sixth of July, the Irish Parliament, composed of Catholics and Protestants, resolved unanimously that the people of Ireland were a free people, to be governed by the common law of England, and statutes made in the kingdom of Ireland. Thus did a loyal Parliament, representing all claims, interests, and creeds, unite in asserting national rights and individual liberties, civil and ecclesiastical. There was no subject that concerned the welfare of the country, no institution that might be a source of future discord, to which they did not give attention. They were about to establish their work by measures of final confirmation, when the lords justices, before a single practical step in furtherance of liberty and conciliation had been taken, brought their session to an untimely and unwilling close, and set themselves to undo what had been effected, and to destroy the hopes of the future.

The island was strewn with inflammable materials. There was a multitude of dispossessed natives, who were despised and sneered at as beggared adventurers by the men who had left them homeless. The royal army was disbanded and added to the restlessness of the country, and was in turn made more dangerous by the unsettled condition that prevailed. The landlords of Connaught were kept in chronic torture by the terror of impending confiscation. Wrongs had been committed in the name of the Pope; wrongs had been committed by sovereigns claiming church authority; a faction now ruled that ascribed its basest acts of inhuman injustice to the immediate inspiration of the Spirit of God. Every wound that treachery, tyranny, and cruelty had inflicted on the unhappy land was still raw and bleeding, and was a perpetual source of scoffing triumph with the bigots, whose rage and rapacity were insatiable, while an Irish acre remained to be plundered and an Irish vein to be drained. Hatred of Catholicism exhausted in England found a fresh and ample storehouse of fuel in Ireland, where the Catholics of all classes were in a vast majority. Sir William Parsons openly declared that in twelve months there should not be a single Catholic seen in Ireland.[1] The dread of a general massacre began to vibrate through the Catholic community.

The king sent word to Lords Ormond and Antrim to rally the scattered army, and if necessary to employ it against the lords justices, and to unite the whole strength of Ireland in his cause.

An insurrectionary movement commenced prematurely. The families of the plundered chiefs had received a welcome and a home in every foreign court. Irish soldiers abounded in every Continental army. Irish priests were to be found in every branch of the Catholic Church. Among

[1] Comp. Carte's "Collection of Letters," Vol. II., p. 350.

those men the design arose of re-establishing Charles on his throne, and the Catholic religion in its ancient privileges. Henry O'Neill, son of Tyrone, held a high place in the Spanish army. His friend, Roger O'Moore, the exiled chief of Leix, came to Ireland and communicated the plan of a general rising, to commence in the month of October, to Lord Maguire and others. The enemy, who might have been the hatchers of the plot, so accurately were they acquainted with its details, assassinated the young Earl of Tyrone. The command devolved on Sir Phelim O'Neill, who, it was arranged, should initiate a general insurrection, while O'Moore, Maguire, and MacMahon were to seize the castle of Dublin. When the day for action arrived, of two hundred men who were to meet at Dublin only eighty appeared, and the attack was postponed. The lords justices, fully informed of all that was in contemplation from the beginning, but ascribing their knowledge to the sudden information of a Protestant named O'Conolly, took Maguire and MacMahon prisoners.

It had been agreed that the enterprise should be conducted with as little bloodshed as possible, and that the Scots should not be attacked. The Ulster insurgents were an unarmed tumultuous mob. In any kind of warfare men must be killed. The cause that has the misfortune to be defended by undisciplined troops, and that does not extemporise a mock tribunal to countenance its deeds, is always open to the charge of murder. The Irish took possession of several forts, and expelled the inhabitants of the surrounding country. Expulsion from their homes and lands had been their own experience during centuries. Now, when they took possession of their own fields, and drove out the intruders, a cry of cruelty and barbarism filled the air.

The Catholic lords of the Pale offered their assistance to the lords justices and were refused. When they renewed the offer, some of them were imprisoned, and others put to the torture. Letters were sent to London giving an alarming account of the success of the Irish Royalists, and news was spread through England that the Irish Papists, having destroyed Protestantism in Ireland, were about to invade England to carry out the same fell purpose there also. An army of ten thousand men and a grant of a hundred thousand pounds were asked for. The English Parliament at once acceded to the request.

The lords justices had refused to allow Ormond to go against the insurgent royalists. Assured now of aid from England they took more decided steps. They commanded the landowners of the Pale who were in the city to leave it in twenty-four hours, and they suppressed an order offering pardon on submission which the English Parliament had issued. To prevent any overtures towards a mutual understanding, they would have prorogued Parliament, had not the lawyers impressed them with the illegality of the proceeding.[1] They were compelled to allow the houses to meet for a single day (November 17th). After some difference between the Lords and Commons as to the terms in which the Irish in arms were to be described, the latter refusing to call them rebels, a deputation was appointed to receive from them a statement of their grievances. At the same time Lord Dillon was sent to the king

[1] See Temple's "History of the Irish Rebellion," p. 214.

begging him to appoint Ormond to the Lieutenancy, and to confirm the graces.

The lords justices despatched an agent to England representing that the course recommended by Lord Dillon was for the benefit of the Irish, whereas if the war was carried on by Englishmen and with English money the forfeited estates that must accrue would overpay the expense. Lord Dillon was seized at Ware by a warrant of the House of Commons, his papers were taken, and he himself was detained in prison.

Lords Gormanstown, Fingal, Slane, Louth, Dunsany, Trimblestown, and Netterville met the chiefs of the insurrection in December, and on learning their intentions agreed to join them.[1] The lords of the Pale were summoned to confer with the Privy Council on the affairs of the nation. They had good reason for apprehending a plot to seize their persons. They replied to the Privy Council that they had certain information from the language of Sir Charles Coote at the Council Board that a general massacre of the Catholics was contemplated, and they put forth a declaration that in common with the Ulster forces they had taken arms for the defence of the royal prerogatives and their Catholic liberties.[2]

Section V.

The lords justices had terrified and provoked the whole island into insurrection. All that now remained to be done was to rouse in the breasts of Englishmen towards Ireland a paroxysm of fury that could be allayed by nothing short of the annihilation or wholesale dispossession of her people. This was accomplished by devising and circulating the story of a massacre. Some reference to the notorious story of the massacre of 1641 is required, not because the account of it is true and is a part of history, nor because it is false and needs refutation, but because it is a State fiction, a falsehood with a purpose, and as such deserves mention as much as the levying of troops or the passing of laws. The record of the period is not the history of a massacre, but of the deliberate invention of a massacre. It is not the story of a massacre of Englishmen or Protestants by Irish Catholics; it is the concocted narrative of an attempted massacre of Ireland's reputation according to the tradition of her northern assailants from the earliest times. Accustomed to the infliction of legal atrocities under the laws of treason, such as unlicensed fancy never attributed to fiends in hell in the tortures of the damned, they were at no loss for pictures of loathsome and revolting cruelty. These they repeated and varied and multiplied in their kaleidoscope of murder until the heart of England was on fire, and the throat of England was parched with thirst for Irish blood. No word of massacre had been heard of in the first State document that referred to the so-called rebellion. The Catholic lords of the Pale would never have united their names and fortunes with those of murderers. The English Bishop Bedell, purest and honestest of men, drew up a remonstrance of convincing justification for the Irish: he never would have done so if their hands were red with murder. The royalists again and again urged in their treaties with their opponents that an investi-

[1] See Temple, pp. 237-241. [2] *Ibid*, 243.

gation of the cruelties committed on both sides should be made, and the proposal was always absolutely refused. Not only was room left thus for falsehood to flourish in, but special pains were taken that it should have the whole soil to itself, and that no germ of truth should be allowed to struggle with it for existence. Books were published giving a true account of the murders committed on the Irish by the Scots and the English. They were ordered to be burned, by the Parliament in London, and the Viceroy and Council in Dublin, and the printers and salesmen were imprisoned. One work out of many escaped destruction. Doubtless, the writer says, the Irish did in many places kill men, resisting them in their pillaging; but the report of their killing women, or men desiring quarter, and such like inhumanities, were inventions to draw contributions and make the enemy odious. Thousands of men, women and children were killed by command of the lords justices, he continues to say, while the Irish sent multitudes of English officers and soldiers, as well as women and children, in safety to the seaports and other places of security, so that while the Irish were called bloody inhuman traitors or barbarous rebels, their English opponents suffered themselves to be much excelled by them in charity, humanity and honour.[1]

What then are we to say of Hume's clotted rhetoric, and the grotesque horrors of Carlyle? They are the written lasting proofs of the fatal arraignment that it is the nature of the Norman to lash himself into the mood of outrage and robbery by imagining his own people as suffering them at the hands of his intended victims. It is against the whole tide of the Irish nature to commit massacre. It is the nature or the settled policy or habit of the Norman or his flatterers to ascribe massacre in fiction that he may retort it in reality. Accustomed in his unbridled selfishness to rob and murder without a throb of compassion long before he came into contact with Briton or Hibernian, by force of the same selfishness he wilfully believes and exclaims that the earth is deluged with blood if one of his fingers is scratched by the the rude weapon of an exasperated peasant. This policy of misrepresentation, which is not practised mainly by English writers, but by Irishmen and Scotchmen who wish to erect an altar of English injustice on which to sacrifice their Irish descent, wholly without justification when it is employed against a distant province, becomes the foulest domestic treason when directed against an integral part of the empire. Just as persons of indulged superstition deceive themselves at last into doing the acts which they ascribe to some occult power, so does the massacre-monger end by the procuration of crimes that prove his theory and support his policy. The massacre of 1641 was a massacre of Ireland's good name, perpetrated to justify unparalleled robbery and murder, and it is not to be expected that they who endorse or enjoy the robbery will deny the justification.

Systematic conquest is effected and continued by keeping the assailed people undisciplined and unarmed. It is no reproach to the Irish that a skilled commander and a trained army did not rise ready made from the soil. Sir Phelim O'Neill was wholly inexperienced as

[1] Prendergast's "Cromwellian Settlement," p. 71.

a soldier. He may have been—for we have no trustworthy proof—wanting in the self-control that merely economises hate in men of external refinement. The single fact which we know with absolute certainty concerning him is that when years after he had to make a choice on the scaffold between death and falsehood, he chose death.[1] While his forces were comparatively few, and observed some order, he was successful, and no excesses marked his course. But in a little time all those who had been driven out of their ancestral homes and fields, and had since been prowling like spectres around the scenes of their former happiness, gathered to his standard. For an army there was a confused crowd, and they were not armed even with pikes. Instead of a common purpose to defeat the enemy, each man was desirous to repossess himself of his own property. But no bloodshed stained their proceedings. Then the English gentry began to take concerted action, and fifteen hundred veterans, led by practised officers, were sent from England to their aid. The inevitable result followed. Discipline and arms were victorious in the formal fight, and the men who were not soldiers, but who were compelled to attack and defend themselves, enraged at their defeat, committed some inconsiderable deeds of violence. This is quoted as a massacre by those who calmly assume that any kind or amount of slaughter committed by men in uniform, or after a legal formality, is only a matter of course, and that extermination by famine and nakedness, if dignified with the name of policy, is a sign of ability to rule. The caparisoned huntsman goes to his sport in the pride of licensed enjoyment, but the poor hunted creature that in the phrensied struggle of its capture uses beak or claw is called treacherous and cowardly. The footstep of the invader is haughty and martial, but the writhing of trampled freedom is a proof of fiendish malice.

SECTION VI.

The English Parliament, really an aristocratic assembly, were contending against tyranny in Church and State, but their religious and political prospects alike never soared above earth, and were limited to their own party and class. In planting the machinery by which the throne was to be overturned, they used the English democracy only as a fulcrum, and they were ready to crush out the name and life of Ireland. They charged the king with favouring the Irish rising, and to render the charge more probable, instructed the lords justices to put every obstacle in the way of employing the royal army for its suppression. They had the additional motive that by keeping the management of the war in their own hands, they had a pretext for raising money which they could use to further their ends at home.

A large body of troops under Grenville and Monk came from England (1642), and were kept inactive till they began to mutiny. Ormond was then sent to relieve Drogheda, which was besieged by Sir Phelim O'Neill, but he was ordered not to cross the Boyne, and to return within eight days. By agreement with the English Parliament, who gave the whole conduct of the northern war to the Scotch generals, Monroe landed

[1] Carte's "Life of Ormond." Vol. I., p. 364.

with a large force at Carrickfergus, and occupied himself chiefly in exporting vast herds of stolen cattle to his own country. He varied this occupation by the slaughter of unarmed men and women, and the perfidious capture of the Earl of Antrim at an entertainment. Every engine of exasperation and terror was employed to drive those lords of the Pale who yet continued neutral, to join the confederate army. Lord Castlehaven offered his services to the authorities, was refused and imprisoned, made his escape and joined the confederates.

The lords justices in the meantime were busy in securing the conviction of all those concerned, or suspected of being concerned, in the insurrection, with a view to the forfeiture of their estates. The English Parliament proceeded to raise money by offering two million and a half acres of Irish land, prospectively forfeited, as security to those who would advance funds towards raising an army for the subjugation of the Irish loyalists. An army of five thousand foot and five hundred horse was raised by those adventurers, as they were called, but before they could sail for Ireland they were sent to meet the king's forces, and were defeated at Edge Hill.

The motive that men dare to avow, not that which really instigates them, becomes eventually, as it were, the flag around which their hosts rally, and on which their enthusiasm centres. The party cry that at this period united the enemies of Ireland at once inspired and sanctioned every crime. Hunger for other men's lands could not be openly acknowledged. Hatred of Irishmen did not go far or wide enough. The extermination of Popery covered the whole field of intended spoliation, justified every extremity of cruelty and fraud, and authorised robbery by a religious purpose. Papist and Irishman became convertible terms. The Dublin Parliament, reduced to a fragment by exclusions, demanded a vigorous execution of the penal statutes. The lords justices forbad the commanders of garrisons to hold any correspondence with Irishmen or Papists. Ormond was instructed not to receive submissions. New troops as they arrived insulted the old army as Irish. Another army raised by the adventurers, consisting of twelve hundred men under Lord Forbes, with Hugh Peters as his chaplain, was sent to Ireland with power to hang and shoot rebels, and divide among themselves whatever spoils they could seize. They disdained to unite with Irishmen however loyal, or with any who were not of the godly. They were repelled in their devastations at Kinsale, and distinguished themselves chiefly by digging up the graves and burning the bones of the dead of St. Mary's Church in Galway.

SECTION VII.

The royalist insurrection now began to organize itself into a governmental form. The Church took the lead. A synod was held, at which sentence of excommunication was denounced against all spoliations of Irish property, whether held by Catholics or Protestants, and all distinctions between new and old Irish were forbidden. This was followed by a national convention at Kilkenny, with an upper and a lower house, and a convocation of clergy. They renounced the authority of the government at Dublin, and in the name of God, the King, and the Country, made provision for the administration of justice throughout the island. Though recognising the original insurrection by meeting on its anniversary, they almost reversed its distinctive nationality. Owen O'Neill, who had lately arrived from the Continent, and been appointed by the northern Irish to the post previously held by Sir Phelim O'Neill, was nominated provincial general for Ulster, Preston for Leinster, Barry for Munster, and Burke for Connaught. No Milesian now held any position of influence in the confederation. O'Brien, Lord Inchiquin, who held the command though without the title of president, in Munster, was one of its most ferocious opponents.

All the pathos of circumstances marks the career of Owen Roe O'Neill. He was grandson of Matthew of Dungannon, and consequently not a true O'Neill nor a Milesian. He had distinguished himself in positions of high trust and great emergency in foreign service, and bartered when he came to Ireland the achievement of a great name on the world's stage, for a struggle among ungenial men and a place in an unread history. Without the attraction of a single selfish aim, without the compulsion of duty, he came to the land of his ancient race in its distress as a loving child would fly to its sick mother. His fame had preceded him, and his devotion excited the wonder of his enemies more than the admiration of his friends. The Earl of Leven, who took command of the Parliamentary troops in Ulster, endeavoured to dissuade him from his purpose by expressing his regret that a man of his reputation should act the rebel's part in Ireland. With him a rebel's lot was contemptible only when success seemed unlikely, and no brilliant prize awaited even on success. Owen replied that he had better reasons for coming to defend his country than Leven had for going to England to attack his king. The earl immediately afterwards handed over the command to Munroe, and warning him that O'Neill would certainly defeat him if he succeeded in raising an army, returned to Scotland. But the Irish general held victory only as a secondary consideration. With a sensitiveness that was singular where bloodshed was universal, his first act was the condemnation, and so far as he could, the punishment of the severities that had stained the cause before his arrival. Wisest and bravest, tenderest and truest of Irishmen, his name, when his country's noonday sun shall dispel the clouds of her stormy morning, will be a word of glory and guidance for all men. Till then it will safely live in the silent affections of his own people.

When the rebellion broke out in England every device was employed by the Irish Government to prevent the complaints of the army and the overtures of the confederates from reaching the king. Negotiations were, notwithstanding, commenced with the confederates, but, being impeded by the king's weak efforts to pander to Puritan intolerance, in the course of which he described the men with whom he was treating, and who were in fact fighting for his cause, as engaged in an odious rebellion; and by the perfidious double dealing of Ormond, who desired the failure of the confederacy more than the success of the king, and the advancement of his personal interests above all, ended on the 15th September, 1643, in a mere cessation of arms. This cessation stimulated the enemies of the king to great activity, put a stop to the progress of his friends without leading to a complete and cordial union with them, and ruined the cause of Ireland so far as it was represented by the confederates, who sought to accomplish for the Anglo-Irish nobles the same kind of independence which Tyrone had attempted on behalf of the Irish chiefs.

During the two years that the war had lasted, the troops of the confederacy had been making slow but certain progress. They were no longer disheartened by the occasional discomfitures that so constantly obstruct and so often prove ruinous to the early struggles of freedom. In Leinster, Preston, though twice worsted through the excessive impetuosity of his troops, by Ranelagh, president of the Province, and Ormond, took the next year several strongholds in Carlow, Kildare, and West Meath. In Munster, Purcel relieved Ross when besieged by Ormond; Barry repulsed an attack on his head-quarter at Kilmallock, and both generals decisively defeated Vavasour. In Connaught the surrender of Galway to Burke capped a series of successes. In Ulster, where the English power predominated, and Monroe had twenty thousand men, Owen Roe, having cautiously organised his recruits in a sequestered mountain region, marched towards the enemy, baffled and defeated an attempted surprise by Monroe, and carried off his men in safety from a superior cavalry force under Stewart. Again descending from the hills, he invaded Meath, and when attacked by Lord Moore and Colonel Monk, routed them, slaying Moore, and driving the future restorer of the monarchy back to Dublin. He then established his head-quarters near Lough Erne, took the castle of James' undertakers, and was planning further movements, when he was stopped short by the unwelcome intelligence of the truce.

Section VII.

A portion of the Royal army, left without employment in Ireland by the cessation, was sent to England, and joined the Chester garrison (1645). They were all Protestants, and most of them Englishmen. They were bound by a solemn oath to defend the Protestant faith and to fight against the Parliamentary party. Brereton, the Parliamentary commander in Wales, endeavoured to induce them to desert to him by dwelling on their common zeal for the Protestant faith. At the very same time he deliberately spread a report in which they were described as four thousand Irish rebels, reeking with Protestant blood, who had come to extend their barbarous massacres in England. Many of them went over to the enemy on the field of battle. All the principal officers, including Monk, were taken prisoners, and most of them were induced to adopt the cause of their captors.[1]

The Earl of Antrim, who had escaped from Monroe, was commissioned by the king to obtain help from the confederates. He sent three thousand men to reinforce Montrose in Scotland. Those regiments won the highest praise from their friends, and struck such terror into the foe

[1] Collection of Letters, by T. Carte, Vol. I., pp. 29-41.

that their progress was almost unresisted (1644).[1] The reputation of the Irish soldiery was at this time so high on the Continent that permission to levy recruits was sought by France and Spain from the confederacy.

The English Parliament passed an ordinance that no Irishman, or Papist born in Ireland, taken in arms on land or sea, should receive quarter or be included in a capitulation. The commander of one of their vessels took a transport containing one hundred and fifty soldiers of the king's army. He bound seventy of them who were Irish by birth back to back, and plunged them into the sea.[2] The Parliament presented him with a medal and gold chain.

Puritanism was a popular revolt against the claims of the throne and Church to exercise the vicegerency of heaven. Kings and priests had reigned in the name of God, and as representing the power of God. This power was now asserted to be a universal possession. Every man claimed the inhabitation of the Holy Spirit and a corresponding degree of divine omnipotence. Nothing less than the enthusiasm thus created could have overthrown the divine right of the throne and left a clear space for British liberty. Unhappily there was one element wanting to constitute the voice of the Puritan leaders the true utterance of the divine will. It was not the voice of the people, nor of justice. The prevalent notion concerning God's power always had been that it carried right with it. When the Puritans, therefore, now took the power of God into their own hands they supposed themselves invested with authority not to maintain justice against their unjust governors, but to follow the guidance of their own wisdom or their own passions as a light from above. While their efforts were unitedly directed against the tyranny that had provoked this fanaticism into being, the loftiness of their aim was sufficient to dignify the means they used. But when instead of opposing despots they undertook to rule men struggling for freedom, and instead of contending for the Commonwealth they sought each man his own interests, cruelty and greed wielded the sword of heavenly judgment. This was the attitude of Puritanism towards the Irish. Ireland was striving for the same object as England—a free Parliament. Catholicism was to Ireland the inspiration that Presbyterianism or Independency was to England. Puritan statesmen would acknowledge no rival to individual illumination. The Irish were seeking to regain or secure their possessions. Puritan adventurers demanded those possessions as the direct gift of God. The wholesale extermination of Irishmen by famine, by massacre, by expatriation, was openly proclaimed. The wholesale robbery of Irishmen by lying, by fraud, by perjury, was unblushingly practised. Ireland's unworldly Catholic zeal was not a match for the mundane fanaticism of the Puritans.

About this time Lord Maguire, who had been taken to London, was brought to trial for his share in the insurrection. He pleaded that the report of the massacre was false, and argued that there were not so many Protestants in the whole kingdom as were said to have been killed. He was found guilty. One of the points urged against him was that the confederate council had made a provision for his wife. He asked that

---

[1] Collection of Letters, by T. Carte, Vol. I., p. 73.
[2] Ibid, p. 49.

some minister of his own religion might be allowed to visit him, and was refused. He petitioned the Parliament that as a peer the manner of his execution might be altered. This was denied. In the last few moments before his death, notwithstanding his piteous requests to be allowed to compose his mind by prayer, he was harried by insulting questions. His pockets were searched, and a crucifix found there was taken away. He attempted to fix his attention on some devotional papers, which he carried in his hand, and he was compelled to surrender them. On one of these was written in the Irish language the fond farewell of some faithful adherent, "My thousand blessings on you, son of my soul." He was put to death with unnameable horrors, as a traitor against the king, though the party to which he was accused of belonging was then in league with the king; by men who were actually at the moment in open rebellion against the king, and some of whom afterwards suffered the same fate for the part they were then acting; and under a law devised for the defence of those royal prerogatives which his executioners were endeavouring to subvert.

SECTION IX.

A deputation of the confederates waited on Charles at Oxford, offering to place ten thousand men immediately at his disposal, and asking in return an independent Parliament, and an enquiry into all the acts of inhumanity committed on either side during the contest. The Protestants of Dublin were so eager to defeat this project that they outstripped the confederates in their journey, and made counter claims that amounted to the abject humiliation and civil extinction of the Catholics. They prudently declined an investigation into the cruelties committed in the course of the war. The king's efforts to secure the aid of the Catholics without alarming the prejudices of the Protestants led him into a series of secret engagements with the former, the unfortunate discovery of which covered him with confusion, and left him no resource but deeper burrowing in intrigue and more involved schemes of duplicity. He gave Ormond, whom he had appointed Lord-Lieutenant, full powers to conclude a final peace with the confederates on any terms. Ormond, forgetting the royal necessities, huckstered and held back about concessions to the Catholics. The king then employed Lord Glamorgan to enter secretly into any religious conditions by which he might obtain supplies. The battle of Naseby was lost, and in the king's cabinet, taken on the field, evidence was found of the authority given to Ormond, and of Glamorgan's commission. Glamorgan, though obstructed and delayed by Ormond, concluded a treaty. At this stage the Papal Nuncio, Rinuccini, arrived at Kilkenny. He objected to the treaty being kept secret, as the right to religious liberty would be dependent on the king's fortune and the life of Glamorgan, and to the peace which Ormond was negotiating, because it omitted freedom of worship. Meantime the Archbishop of Tuam was killed in battle at Sligo, and a copy of Glamorgan's treaty was found among his papers. This was sent to the English Parliament, who put it in print and circulation. Charles wrote a letter to the Parliament, in which he disavowed the treaty, but sent reassuring messages to Glamorgan. The latter aided the viceroy in his negotiations, and persuaded the Nuncio to consent to the immediate despatch of troops to England. They were about to sail when a printed copy of the king's letter to the Parliament reached the confederates. The embarkation was at once countermanded. Ormond concluded a peace, and an army was about to sail when news came of the king's flight to Scotland. The king's deceitfulness and Ormond's want of devotion to his master ruined all.

The English Parliament had agreed to a solemn league and covenant passed by the Scotch for the extermination of Popery, and in furtherance of its object appointed Monroe commander of all their forces in Ulster. Owen Roe appealed to the confederate council for aid. Fearing an invasion into the South by Monroe, they sent an army of six thousand men, but placed it under the command of Castlehaven, thus disposting the Irish general in his own province. Owen cheerfully bore the slight, and in the campaign that followed, if no brilliant deed was done, the enemy at least was prevented from marching into the Southern districts. The confederates offered the command of their united troops to Ormond if he would invade the North in the king's interest. He shuffled and evaded till the time of action was passed.

If Owen O'Neill had possessed the qualities of a Coote or an Inchiquin in addition to his own, he would have been a Cromwell. Without those qualities he would have won a greater name than Cromwell's in any land where the laws of peace and war were observed, or in his native land had he not been kept down in powerless subordination by inferior minds. As we see him now he stands alone on the scene of turbulence, patient, watchful, unwearied, calm amid the confusion, and instinctively seizing on the scanty occasions of success which his higher tactical genius was quick to discern and his purer morality could turn to account. The Milesian leaders disliked him, because he differed from them in character. The confederates were averse to him because he was an Irishman. They claimed the restoration of confiscated lands, but omitted Ulster. They were ready to sacrifice their cause to their jealousy. Just as Ormond preferred that the royal cause should be lost rather than it should prosper by the aid of the confederate Catholics, so the confederates preferred that the Catholic cause should be lost rather than that it should triumph by the genius of an Irishman. Owen's forces consisted of wandering herdsmen who, robbed of their lands, drove their cattle with them for a subsistence, and instead of quartering themselves on the enemy pastured their herds in his fields. The confederate council issued orders to resist this trespass by force of arms.

The Ulster chief was perhaps the only man in power who regarded the interests of Ireland. If there was another high official who was governed by a disinterested motive it was the Nuncio, who sought the restoration of Catholicism, and embraced as an ingredient in his scheme an independent Irish Parliament. Their partial identity of purpose, as well as the isolation of the two men in their respective positions, brought them into close alliance. Having obtained a supply of money from the Nuncio, Owen speedily collected and equipped an army of five thousand foot and five hundred horse, and marched towards Armagh. Monroe, who was meditating a descent on Kilkenny, hastened against him with six thousand foot and eight hundred horse. The two armies met at Benburb, on the banks of the Blackwater. Owen, typifying his country's destined triumph, kept the enemy in play till the sun revolved in the heavens and shot his dazzling beams from the Irish side. Then the moment for action had come, and Monroe's army was swept down as by a torrent. Three thousand eight hundred Scotch and English lay dead on the field, while the Irish lost only seventy men. The Lord of Hosts, Monroe wrote, has rubbed shame on their faces. He felt no shame in his heart when murdering Irish peasants, nor during his constant exportation of stolen cows to Scotland. The battle of Benburb was fought on the fifth of July, 1646.

SECTION X.

The Nuncio summoned Owen from his pursuit of the Parliamentary army to assist him in opposing the peace which Ormond was engaged on. He and Glamorgan, the king's confidential agent, required that the repeal of the penal laws and the suspension of Poyning's Act should be added to its terms. The confederates, instead of welcoming the victor, entered into an alliance with Ormond against him. Owen and Preston marched to the siege of Dublin, on which Ormond began to treat with the Parliament. A high command under Ormond was offered to Preston if he would abandon his ally, and Parliamentary forces reached Dublin. Owen, quickly aware of his danger, drew off his army by night. The aid sent by the Parliament was forwarded to Monroe, and Preston returned to his allegiance.

Owen was now forced to act an independent part. He proposed a cessation with Ormond if the latter would break off his treaty with the Parliament. Ormond consented. The matter was to be decided within fourteen days. A nephew of Owen's was sent to Kilkenny with the proposal. The Council kept him a prisoner until the period had expired. Ormond concluded his treaty with the Parliament, first of all securing from them indemnification for his pecuniary losses, and an annuity for his wife, surrendered Dublin to them, and soon after went to England, where he escaped imprisonment by flying to France. The Parliament assigned the government of Leinster to Michael Jones, and that of Ulster to Colonel Monk.

Preston, at the head of the Leinster army, attempted to surprise Dublin, and was disastrously overthrown by Jones. The confederates in self defence gave Owen the chief command in Leinster. The Irish general loved and handled his army as a skilful swordsman does his rapier, and never struck until he knew the blow would hit, nor sacrificed a single man to mere glory. Deriding Preston, not for being beaten, but for being compelled to fight, he declared that all the forces in England could not make him fight but when he pleased. He easily defeated every attempt of Jones to force him to a battle, until the Parliamentary general, tired out, had dismissed a portion of his army. He then marched to the very walls of Dublin, devastated the neighbourhood so that the inhabitants and troops were destitute of provisions, and having done the business for which he came, retired in safety before Jones could re-unite his forces.

Inchiquin, who because he had not been made President of Munster, had gone over to the Parliament, gained a complete victory over Taafe, the commander of the Munster army, near Mallow. He sent for Jones to aid him in taking Kilkenny, but O'Neill met the latter on his way and drove him back. The Nuncio proposed that the command of the Munster and Leinster armies should be given to O'Neill. The Council declared war against him instead, and made a treaty with Inchiquin, who, again feeling himself neglected, deserted the Parliament, and wrote to France urging Ormond's return. Owen marched to Kilkenny, and held his enemies under the sweep of his sword. But true Irishman as he was, he loathed bloodshed save on the battlefield. While he paused, master of the situation and of himself, Inchiquin and Preston[1] arrived with greatly superior forces. Then with his usual inimitable tact he eluded all their efforts to compel him to fight, and retreated to Ulster.

The Marquis of Ormond returned to Ireland and issued an address, in which he apologised for his surrender of Dublin, and declared his readiness to conclude a peace on behalf of the king. Charles meantime gave his written consent to an article prepared by the Parliamentary Committee, rendering null any peace concluded with the Irish without the consent of both Houses. He then wrote to Ormond instructing him not to take notice of this engagement. A denial that he had so written was wrung from him by the Parliament, when they were informed of Ormond's proceedings. Ormond concluded the peace (1649). By its terms the penal laws were repealed, and commissioners appointed to share authority with the viceroy. Before intelligence of the event reached London, Charles had been executed. By his former dilatoriness, and by his present penitent precipitancy, Ormond powerfully contributed to this catastrophe. The Nuncio privately embarked for France.

Ormond proclaimed Charles II. as king, and made an attempt to gain O'Neill over to the royal cause, which was frustrated by the perverse interference of the confederate Commissioners. Deep as was their severance from their Protestant countrymen, a far deeper chasm yawned between them and the Irish, which similarity of creed only thinly covered. Ormond sent Inchiquin, who had taken Drogheda and some other towns, to defend Munster against the apprehended arrival of Cromwell, and prepared himself to invest Dublin. The besieging army was attacked by Jones at Rathmines, and routed with great loss. Ormond fled with the remnant of his force to Kilkenny.

An effort to bring about an understanding between the Independents and the Catholics of England and Ireland, in which Cromwell had some share, was projected at this time.[2] Owen Roe made a cessation with Monk, who acted in this matter with the consent of his English employers, and even relieved Coote when besieged in Derry by the Presbyterians, who at the king's death declared against the Parliament. But the anti-Irish feeling which had been created now barred the path of compromise. Popular indignation burst out. Monk was compelled

[1] Clanrickarde, according to Carte, Vol. III., p. 381.
[2] Carte, Vol. III., p. 473.

by his soldiers to resign, and his conduct on his return to London was condemned by the very men who had prompted it. This treatment sank deep into his mind, and bore the fruit of heavy retribution in after years.

Humbled by his defeat, Ormond made more decided overtures to Owen,[1] who, on hearing of the action at Rathmines had determined to conclude a peace with him, but with punctilious honour waited till the cessation he had made with Monk expired.[2] The articles of the treaty were completed on the twelfth of October. Owen was suffering from severe illness at the time. He hastened his march, though he had to be borne on a litter. His sickness increased, and he died on the sixth of November, at Cloughouter in Cavan. While he lay dying he sent a portion of his army to aid Ormond with advice how Cromwell could be beaten without hazard. A banquet had been given in his honour at Derry, at which it was said he received his death from the use of a pair of poisoned boots, presented to him by a lady of the Coote family. A person named Plunket, at Louth, also laid claim to the credit of the deed. His health had broken down from a corresponding date. It mattered not now who lost or won: the soldier who sought victory for Ireland and could have won it, was dead.

He was dead, the Irishman who when his country was rent in body and soul by murderers and liars, never did an unjust or cruel act, nor made a false promise, nor cherished a personal jealousy, nor yielded to a selfish purpose. Towering above his contemporaries in military skill, he consented to serve under Castlehaven and Antrim for Ireland's sake. Seeking friends for Ireland he gave way to no antipathies or preferences under whatever name they sought shelter, but made alliances with Puritans and Catholics alike. All men looked up to him and respected him, and the Confederate lords hated and resisted him because they were compelled to feel his superiority. The Protestant soldiers of Inchiquin, indignant at their general's treachery, declared they would make their way to the camp of Owen Roe. The confederates dared not disband their superfluous forces, because they would flock to his standard. Prince Rupert knew that the royal cause was safer with Owen than with Ormond, and would co-operate only with him. He stood alone and apart, so that Irishmen may see in him the one peerless model for their imitation. He never changed. Inchiquin deserted the king for the Parliament, and the Parliament for the king. Castlehaven left the lords justices for the confederates, and the confederates for Ormond. Broghil forsook the king for Cromwell. Coote and Monk and Preston shifted from party to party. Ormond was faithful to no interest but his own. Owen was motionless, while all the rest were in motion. Yet he was the ally of the Confederates, the Parliamentarians, and the Royalists. But it was they who gave way to him, not he to them. He conciliated the bitterest foes of Ireland and Catholicism, and the rejection of his treaty with Monk met a Nemesis without parallel in history. While King and Parliament and Confederation, with the prestige of authority, and the national resources at their command,

---

[1] Comp. Carte's "Collection of Letters," Vol. I., p. 317.
[2] Carte, Vol. III., p. 423.

could scarcely maintain their troops or hold them together, and all in turn suffered defeat, Owen, by his superlative genius alone, during seven years, made and led an army that never wanted provisions nor mutinied, nor was forced to fight unless victory was secure, nor failed to force a victory when it engaged. It was the only strictly Irish armed and disciplined force that ever stood on Irish soil since the Anglo-Norman came, and by it only should the military powers of the Irish at home be judged. Led by Owen O'Neill, neither its courage nor its caution had ever encroached on each other. Had he survived it would have exhausted the resources and baffled the generalship of Cromwell. A single fragment of it sent him half paralysed from Ireland at last.

CHAPTER XI.

CROMWELL.

SECTION I.

ON the sixth of February, 1649, the government of England was vested in a Council of thirty-eight members, with Cromwell as President. The rebellion had been conducted to this successful issue in the name and by the power of religion. The army might be regarded as an embodiment of fanaticism. The problem before Cromwell now was how to move this concrete religious force towards the personal ends to which he had shaped the religious theory and conviction of his own soul. On the twenty-sixth of February a petition was presented by a portion of the army to Parliament, asking for a redress of grievances. This was treated as a breach of discipline. The soldiers then petitioned Fairfax, denouncing the Council of State as destructive of freedom. The petitioners were tried by court-martial and dismissed the army. Complaints arose throughout the country that two or three military grandees had usurped the Government. This was simply the fact; but it was not the turn that events had taken, but the discovery of it that was new. A landlord Parliament had entered into a contest against the prerogatives of the Crown on their own behalf. As the strife advanced it narrowed to a struggle for life. The leaders of the Parliament were haunted by the ghastly terrors of the treason law, which they knew the king would direct against them when he got the opportunity. They saved themselves for the time, and only for the time, by beheading him, and seized his power as their prey. The nation felt its hopes disappointed, but the Parliamentary leaders never had entertained the hopes of the nation.

In April a body of men known as levellers appeared in Surrey, inviting all to come and help them, threatening to pull down park pales, and declaring that the liberties of the people were lost by the coming in of William the Conqueror, and that ever since their forefathers had lived under tyranny. A few days after a mutiny broke out in the army. One of the leaders was executed in St. Paul's Churchyard. His funeral was celebrated with all the pomp of national mourning, and thousands of men in rank and file followed the hearse. In May several regiments mutinied and marched to Oxford. They were pursued by Cromwell, who seized and executed their leaders. Colonel Lilburne, who appealed to the country through the press, was lodged in prison. British and Saxon England was pining for freedom as the Irish people were pining for it, and was silenced as the Irish were about to be silenced.

Cromwell was appointed Lord Lieutenant of Ireland by the Parliament. Early in July a devotional meeting was held at Whitehall. Three ministers prayed, and Cromwell and others expounded scripture. On the same afternoon the Lord Lieutenant began his journey in such state and equipage as had scarcely ever been seen. He himself rode in a coach drawn by six whitish-grey Flanders mares. Several other coaches, containing the great officers of the army, accompanied him. His life-guard consisted of eighty gallant men, in stately habits, the meanest of them a commander or esquire. While this unparalleled pageantry dazzled the eyes of the crowd, their ears were stunned by continual blasts of trumpets.

In the middle of August the Lord Lieutenant landed at Dublin with eight thousand foot, four thousand horse, and a formidable train of artillery. On Sunday, the ninth of September, he began to batter the walls of Drogheda with his cannon. On Tuesday, having made a sufficient breach, his soldiers assaulted the place, and after two repulses offered quarter, and were admitted on those terms. The garrison, consisting of between three and four thousand of the king's best men, were English, and the governor, Sir Arthur Ashton, was an Englishman.[1] Learning from Jones that they formed the strength of the king's army, Cromwell ordered that no quarter should be given. The governor and chief officers had their brains beaten out in cold blood, and the soldiers and inhabitants were indiscriminately massacred. Multitudes took refuge in St. Peter's Church, and were killed there. When pursuing their victims up the galleries of the church, the assailants used children as bucklers to ward off the blows aimed at them from above. All the women of every rank had hidden themselves in the vaults, and were slaughtered when the work in the church was finished. One of them, a beautiful maiden clad in costly garments, moved a person named Wood, brother of Anthony Wood, a well-known author, to pity by her entreaties. He was helping her to escape, when a soldier ran his sword through her, and her protector took away her money and jewels. Every man, woman, and child within the walls were killed except thirty, who were sent to Barbadoes and sold as slaves. There is a special reason why an adequate conception should be made possible of the storm and massacre of Drogheda. It was intended, it is said, to quell resistance by one stern overwhelming blow, to appal by letting run a torrent of blood. If this design did not succeed, it must be shown that the cause of the failure lay in the souls of the men who could not be terrified, and not in any half measures on the part of the terrorists. Instead of spreading terror, the massacre of Drogheda planted an ineradicable and eternal spirit of defiance in the heart of Ireland to the act itself, and to every subsequent event nominally associated with it. It is a singular fact that the fiercest rage of indignation that Irishmen feel is excited by the murder of an English army, engaged in the cause of an English king, at the hands of an army of English rebels. The explanation is that they hear it continually avowed that this deed was done to crush the spirit and ruin the hopes of their country.

In his letter to the Parliament, giving an account of the storm of Drogheda, Cromwell says he is persuaded that the massacre was the righteous judgment of God upon those barbarous wretches, who imbrued their hands in so much innocent blood. It is very difficult to gauge the

[1] See Carte's "Collection of Letters," Vol. II., pp. 397, 403, 411. Memoirs of E. Ludlow, Vol. I., p. 301.

amount and the quality of the falsehood that is contained in this sentence. It was consistent to excuse murder by referring to an imaginary crime that was imagined for that very purpose. But Cromwell knew that the English garrison of Drogheda had no share in or connection with the Ulster insurrection. It cannot be pleaded for him that he was hurried away by a vengeance like that of the earthquake, which buries innocent and guilty alike, because it was by his special command that General Monk made an agreement with Owen O'Neill, the responsibility of which, when the Parliament would not tolerate it, he induced Monk to take upon himself.[1] He had been anxious for the alliance of that Ulster army, by contact with which the king's army, according to his own words, had imbrued their hands in so much innocent blood; and he actually made an attempt to win over Owen Roe to his party by flattering offers, which were rejected on the express ground of fidelity to the Crown.[2]

It is in vain to say that Cromwell used the extreme right of conquest. Was Ireland a conquered country? One of the charges that in England brought Wentworth to the scaffold was that he declared Ireland to be a conquered country.[3] One of the charges brought by the lords justices in Ireland against the confederates was that they denied Ireland to be a conquered country. And for whom are the privileges of conquest in Ireland claimed? Assuredly not for the man whose dead body was afterwards hanged by the public executioner as that of a traitor and regicide. Cromwell was not fighting against an Irish cause, but against the cause of an English king in Ireland.

It is the nature of civilised warfare that a smaller or worse armed force may meet a more powerful army, and suffer defeat without forfeiting to the conquerors the right to exist. All the chivalry of war depends on this understanding. A brave man is ready to fight under disadvantages, because it is assumed that those disadvantages signalise his soldierly qualities in proportion as they imperil his triumph. Conquered men are not criminals, nor conquerors executioners. A brave soldier would not condescend to contend with an army of hangmen. No consideration of this kind weighed with Cromwell. His was something more than the divine right of kings. "It was set upon some of our hearts," he writes to the Parliament, "that a great thing should be done, not by power or might, but by the Spirit of God. That which caused your men to storm so courageously, it was the Spirit of God, who gave your men courage and took it away again; and gave the enemy courage, and took it away again; and gave your men courage again, and therewith this happy success; and therefore it is good that God alone have all the glory."[4] It is certainly very convenient to have a god to whom we can ascribe the glory of our crimes, while we keep their solid fruits for ourselves. It did not occur to Cromwell to make his country's freedom an offering to God.

The model with which he satisfied his conscience was the slaughter of the Canaanites by the people of Israel. That barbarous episode in

[1] Gumble's "Life of General Monk," p. 28.
[2] Carte's "Collection of Letters," Vol. I., p. 208.
[3] See Pym's Speech against him.
[4] Comp. "Pacata Hibernia," p. 192.

the history of a nation that had misapprehended the Divine favour, and, as the result, was hastening to the worst slavery and the greatest crime that the world ever witnessed, has, with a perversity found only in religious subjects, been singled out for approval and admiration. It is an axiom in religious politics that the final catastrophe of Judaism exposed and condemned the whole previous history of the nation. The Jordan of Jewish life, it is seen, had been running into a Dead Sea. The only example it has left which has found imitators is the massacre of the Canaanites. The nations have been held back by this example almost in as great a degree as Christianity has led them forward.

Cromwell's hope lay not in his power to strike terror, but in spreading treachery and disunion among the king's forces, and in their want of a single competent or trusted leader. The soldiers had no confidence in Ormond or Inchiquin, who had already betrayed their cause. The Catholics, with good reason, regarded Ormond as their unrelenting enemy. The emissaries of the Parliamentary general were busy in corrupting the garrisons of the towns. He won the good will of the people, and secured provisions for his army by preventing plunder, and promising that everyone should enjoy liberty of religion.[1] There was nothing firm in Ireland to oppose him save the fragments of Owen Roe's orphaned army.

After some unimportant captures, Cromwell attacked Wexford, was treacherously admitted by Strafford, the Catholic governor of the castle, and made as great a slaughter as had been made at Drogheda. Some of the Ulster troops, heartbroken at the loss of their matchless general, now recruited Ormond. Cromwell moved towards Kilkenny, but the new army was at hand, and he changed his purpose. He attacked Waterford, but abandoned the attempt in disorderly haste when Ormond appeared.[2] He was at this critical moment joined by Lord Broghil, who obtained for him the adhesion of all the garrisons in the county of Cork, and provided comfortable winter quarters for his army.[3] The well founded mistrust of the Catholics forced Ormond to disband his troops. Eleven hundred Ulstermen, under Hugh O'Neill, nephew to Owen, entered Clonmel.

Cromwell once more took the field, and approached Fethard. So far was the garrison from being terror stricken that they fired on his trumpeter, and during a full hour refused to hear him. Some mutual acquaintances in both armies at last came together, and after a night spent in treaty, the town was surrendered on what Cromwell described as terms usually called honourable. The governor of Cashel yielded the keys of the town. The soldiers at Gouran mutinied and delivered up their officers, who were shot the next day. A few days before Castlehaven had taken seven hundred Parliamentary soldiers prisoners at Athy, and made a present of them to Cromwell, desiring, by letter, that he would return the favour when he had the power.[4] The king's forces were more hopelessly divided than ever. Some of the towns positively refused to admit Protestant garrisons. Others were garrisoned

[1] Carte, Vol. III., p. 489.
[2] Ibid., p. 508.
[3] Ibid., p. 513.
[4] Castlehaven's "Memoirs," p. 99.

by traitors, who submitted. Kilkenny, vainly assailed by treachery, was besieged, and though defended by only five hundred men, extorted honourable terms of surrender.

Clonmel was next invaded. Here, for the first time, Cromwell came into actual conflict with the soldiers of the dead northern chief. A breach was made, and an entrance attempted, but the Irish issued forth, and two thousand of Cromwell's murderers had the unmerited honour of falling before the veterans of Owen Roe. Cromwell did not venture another assault, but tried a blockade. Hugh O'Neill having spent all his ammunition and provisions, and seeing no prospect of relief, withdrew his garrison by night, and the townsmen keeping their secret made good conditions, and surrendered on the eighteenth of May, 1650. Cromwell returned to England, leaving his son-in-law, Ireton, in command. Wherever he met a remnant of the army of the north he was foiled. His spirit was broken in the last encounter at Clonmel. There is not a doubt but that if Owen Roe O'Neill had lived he would have saved Cromwell from the infamy of blood that will eternally attach to his name. Though dead he avenged it.

The importance of the siege of Clonmel as showing the failure of Cromwell's terrorism, and stripping his high-handed murder of the halo of omnipotence, is seen in the pains taken to suppress the facts. Ludlow, who explains the carnage at Drogheda as intended to discourage others from making opposition, is careful not to specify the opposition made at Clonmel. He only says that the Irish made good their breach till night parted the dispute, when the enemy, perceiving that the besiegers were resolved to reduce the place, beat a parley, and sent out commissioners to treat. He thus ascribes the capitulation to the courage of the attack, and represents it as having taken place on the night of, and in consequence of, the storm.[1] In reality the surrender did not take place for some weeks after the assault, and only when forced by want of food and ammunition; and in the meantime, as Leland[2] informs us, Cromwell, harassed and enfeebled by delay, made the most pressing instances to Lord Broghil to hasten to his assistance. Carlyle, who increases the number of Ulstermen present to two thousand from little more than half that number, is totally silent about the two thousand Cromwellian soldiers who fell, and quoting from a letter what he calls the solid account of an eye-witness and hand-actor, gives us to understand that the Irish were the principal losers in the conflict, and that the surrender took place the same night. This eye-witness and hand-actor dates his letter on May the tenth, and says that they entered Clonmel that same morning, after having stormed the town on the ninth.[3] Carlyle is very painstaking and ingenious in his efforts to establish a supremacy in blood-spilling for his hero. He further quotes his eye-witness as telling how they pursued the retreating Ulster soldiers, fell upon their rear of stragglers, and killed above two hundred, besides those they slew in the storm. In the storm they did not slay, but were slain, and the two hundred stragglers, brought in to swell the tale, were mostly women.[4] In prostituted

[1] "Memoirs of Edmund Ludlow, Esq.," pp. 303 and 307.
[2] Leland's "History of Ireland," Vol. III., p. 362. Comp. Carte, III., p. 538.
[3] Carlyle's "Oliver Cromwell's Letters and Speeches, with Elucidations," Vol. II., p. 147.
[4] "Contemporary History of Affairs in Ireland," Vol. II , p. 412.

enthusiasm, in brutal buffoonery, and in moral turpitude there is not throughout English literature a more monstrous and disgraceful production than the Irish portion of Carlyle's "Life of Cromwell." Froude, who suppresses all mention of Benburb, in which a purely Irish army contended against English and Scotch, and afterwards, in reference to the battle of the Boyne, a conflict of mingled nationalities, affirms that the English always defeated the Irish, also omits the siege of Clonmel. He is thus able to exalt the efficacy of murder by saying that the terrible blows at Drogheda and Wexford virtually ended the war.[1] We might imagine that Ludlow was ignorant of what occurred if we had not his own testimony to his vivid knowledge of the truth. When giving an account of the surrender of Limerick, he informs us how Ireton, on account of the blood formerly shed at Clonmel,[2] twice induced the court-martial to condemn Hugh O'Neill to death, and refrained from executing the sentence only in consequence of the dissatisfaction of some of his officers.

The manner in which Irish history has been written is an essential part of a true history of the people of Ireland. Murder is not God's thunderbolt. They who represent it so to be are authorising others to hurl it. The elaborate efforts that are made to represent the Irish as weak and contemptible prove that they who make them believe just the contrary, and only provoke the men thus falsely described to refute the error in the only language their opponents seem capable of understanding. Cromwell massacred the garrisons of Drogheda and Wexford simply to deprive the king's cause of so many soldiers. His success was not caused by terror, but chiefly by the death of Owen Roe, and then by the defection of Lord Broghil from the king, the desertion of Inchiquin's Protestant troops, the Catholic mistrust of Ormond, and the universal mistrust of Charles. He took his departure from Ireland beaten, it must be repeated, by a remnant of the only Irish army of the time. The cause that was lost was the royal cause, and the only soldiers who aided it by their victories and honoured it by their fidelity were men who, with the restoration of their king, sought an independent parliament and a free religion.

Section II.

Loyalty stands somewhat in the relation to patriotism that idolatry does to spiritual worship. In times of prosperity the warmth of personal interest, and in times of adversity disinterested zeal, blind the patriot to the occasional deformity of his idol. It is always too heavy a demand on the imagination of an Irishman to require him to love his country in the person of an English monarch, whom he knows only as the representative of the system that oppresses her. In subsequent times the political hopes and the poetical visions of the nation clustered round the ruined Stuart cause in undying verdure, but now the deformity of the idol was too apparent. The royal interest could not lift its leading supporters above their sectional motives. Rash and brilliant actions were performed, but they were without counsel or support. Heber MacMahon, Bishop of Clogher, raised to the command of the northern army for his popularity and not for his fitness, with far inferior forces, and from an inferior position, engaged Sir Charles Coote, was defeated,

[1] Froude's "English in Ireland," Vol. I., p. 127.
[2] "Ludlow," p. 374.

taken prisoner, and put to death. While Cromwell was blockading Clonmel, some troops coming to raise the siege were scattered, and the Bishop of Ross among others taken prisoner by Lord Broghil. His life was offered to him if he would advise the garrison of a neighbouring castle to submit. Being brought within hearing he advised the soldiers to hold out manfully, and was hanged. Teeroghan was besieged by Colonel Reynolds, and was gallantly recruited by a division of Castlehaven's army, who compelled the besiegers to make terms, allowing them to carry off half the artillery. Reynolds and Ireton, after the surrender, refused to perform the conditions.

The king's cause was lost for want of a leader single-minded in honesty or unscrupulous in self-interest. Ormond was devoted to his own objects, but he could not give his heart to an Irish or a Catholic alliance.[1] The Catholics believed, and with some reason, that he was treating with Cromwell. The towns preferred surrendering to receiving his garrisons.[2] There was a general disposition to make terms with the Parliament. News came that Charles II. had gone to Scotland, entered into an engagement with the Scotch people for the extermination of Popery, and annulled the peace of 1649.[3] Ormond left the country on the eleventh of May, 1650. He was offered a pass by Ireton, and his wife remained on her Irish estate till his return after the king's restoration. In September, 1650, the battle of Worcester was fought, and Charles was driven into his nine years' exile. Limerick and Galway obstinately refused to admit garrisons, and surrendered, the first on the twenty-seventh of October, 1651; Galway on the twelfth of May, 1652. Ireton died in the interval.

The disunion that prevented the Irish from defending themselves successfully is constantly quoted by inconsiderate prejudice as a vice peculiar to their country. It is forgotten that England surpassed Ireland in her divisions and in her subjugation. Why should Ireland be more united in the cause of an English king than England herself was? After Ormond had joined the king on the Continent, he was sent on a secret mission to England to promote a royalist insurrection. The result of his attempt will be best described in the very words of his biographer. He found in more than one party of men a great aversion to Cromwell's government, and a general inclination to serve the king, but such a mutual jealousy and animosity between those who wished well to the same cause, and desired His Majesty's restoration, that they would not so much as confer or correspond with one another.[4]

Ireland was at the mercy of the rebel army. Cromwell procured the appointment of Fleetwood, who had married Ireton's widow, to the Irish command. Ludlow and others were united with him in the civil government, with the title of Commissioners of Parliament. The punishment of those engaged in the pretended massacre was formally undertaken. Sir Phelim O'Neill was the only person found guilty in Ulster.[5] It was well known that the death of Lord Caulfield, with which

[1] Comp. Carte's "Collection of Letters, Vol. II., pp. 438-441, and comp. p. 443.
[2] See Carte's "Collection of Letters, Vol. II., pp. 426, 434, 452.
[3] Ibid., p. 443.
[4] Carte, Vol. III., p. 664.
[5] Ibid., p. 622.

he was charged, had taken place without his knowledge, and was punished by him when known. He was offered pardon on condition that he acknowledged having held a commission from the king. He refused to tell a falsehood, and was executed.

On the twenty-sixth of September, 1653, the war was declared ended, and the division of the spoil began. Those of the Irish landowners who were charged with participation in the massacre, if convicted, were to be declared incapable of pardon, and deprived of their lands. Those who took part in the war were to forfeit two-thirds of their estates. There were three sets of English claimants: the soldiers, who had been in service before Cromwell arrived, the adventurers who had advanced money on the understanding that they were to be repaid in Irish lands, and the army of Cromwell. A portion of Wicklow and its neighbourhood was assigned to the first, nine counties were divided between the second and third. Connaught was reserved for the Irish. The counties of Dublin, Kildare, Carlow, and Cork, and the lands of the bishops, deans and chapters, were kept at the disposal of Parliament.

The commissioners were proceeding in the adjustment of claims when intelligence arrived that Cromwell had dissolved Parliament, and been proclaimed Protector by a council of officers. His Protectorate was admitted in Ireland only by a majority of one vote. He sent his son Henry to take the guidance of affairs there. Henry found the expectants of land exasperated by the dishonesty of the commissioners, suitors oppressed and demoralised by the judges, and the nation laid bare and desolated by the cruel hate of the soldiery. A new method had been devised for the government of Ireland. The Parliament, reduced to thirty members, was for the future to sit in London with the English House of Commons. The commissioners proposed that the Irish members should be summoned by the Protector's writ. Ludlow, solicitous for the forms of liberty, insisted that the secret influence of the Government should be employed instead of the decision of one man.

Cromwell removed the commissioners and appointed Fleetwood deputy for three years. Henry Cromwell followed Fleetwood, and succeeded in winning a general consent to his father's government.

Between these stepping-stones of history, laid to secure a regular continuity of events, flows a sea of blood and tears which the eye cannot help seeing as we hasten on. Famine superseded or facilitated slaughter. When Ireton marched to Limerick in 1650, he went through tracts of thirty miles together in which scarcely even a beast was to be found, except wolves. The disbanded soldiers were eagerly sought for abroad. Between 1651 and 1654 thirty-four thousand men sailed from Ireland, and entered into foreign service. The long war and the departure of the soldiery left multitudes of women and children without protection. Government employed agents to seize them and transplant them to the English foreign colonies as slaves. The merchants of Bristol treated with Government for men, women, and girls, to be sent to the West Indies. A single instance will describe the traffic. A gentleman of Clare was transported for harbouring a priest. He had a wife and twelve children. The wife died of poverty and a broken heart. Three of the daughters, fair and delicate girls, were sent to Barbadoes. In four years four thousand four hundred men and women, boys and maidens, had been seized and carried out of the country. On the fourth of March, 1655, those proceedings were brought to an end by the Government. It was found that in the heat of the pursuit English victims as well as Irish had been entrapped and shipped off.

In this crisis of crime and misery the distinction between Anglo-Irish and Irish had vanished. There was on one side the rebel army of England, on the other the loyal Irish nation absolutely at their disposal. The descendants of former confiscators and exterminators were now compelled to give up their estates, and were transplanted into Connaught. The grandson of William Spenser, who had recommended the reduction of Ireland by famine, saw his estate, obtained by confiscation, confiscated afresh, and was banished to Connaught as an Irish Papist.

On the third of September, 1658, Cromwell died. He had ruled by Norman expedients, inhuman executions at home, and brilliant and barren victories abroad. At the end of that so-called Gospel reign no valley had been filled, no high hill brought low, no crooked way made straight, no rough way made smooth. All the resources of legitimate absolutism had been retained for the maintenance of usurped tyranny. The habitude of enslavement had been preserved unbroken, so that all classes were ready to submit to the old yoke the moment it was proposed for their acceptance. The popular hopes of freedom had been strained in long procrastination till their elasticity was lost.

In our modern love of biographies we confound the domestic virtues of the individual with the duties of his historical career. The two are not only unconnected but opposed to each other. The statue that stands apart in detached isolation does not resemble in any degree the image in bas relief that blends itself in the general structure. Recent writers set Cromwell's letters to his wife and children by the side of, and as elucidations of, his massacres. Love of family is often in inverse ratio to love of country or kind. It was love for his family that induced a man in our own day to embark explosive machines on board vessels containing hundreds of passengers on which he had effected insurances. The animal affection of a child for a parent, or of a parent for a child, is not a virtue. The human love of a father is the earnest desire to save his children from mean souls and tarnished names. Cromwell's letters to his children and his orders for the slaughter of the inhabitants of Ireland proceeded from unsophisticated and fanatical selfishness. This is the aspect of family life which Christianity in its profound knowledge of the individual soul, and ardent concern for the Commonwealth, calls on its adherents to hate.

Cromwell had the special vice of a ruler, that he ruled for himself. Being a usurper, his regard for self centred not in the enjoyment but in the preservation of authority. He maintained himself in his joyless state by the arts of royalty without its title, by the fervour of religion without its guidance or its comfort, and in the name of freedom without its confidence. No man ever betrayed his country with so small reward. He set aside a whole Irish county for himself,[1] but neither he nor any of his family ever possessed so much of it as to set his foot on. He waded through slaughter, and never reached dry land.

[1] "Continuation of Life of Clarendon," Vol. I., p. 386.

CHAPTER XII.

THE REVOLUTION.

SECTION I.

CROMWELL had ruled by his personal influence. He left the title of Protector to his son Richard, and the example of his successful usurpation to his generals. The yearning for free institutions that prevailed in the army was, in a great measure, quenched in Irish landlordism. The generals contended for the mastery. Monk, who commanded a large army in Scotland, declared for a free Parliament, marched to London, and re-established kingly power. The only condition imposed on the restored monarch reveals the nature of the struggle that was in progress. The rights annexed to feudal tenure were abandoned by the Crown. The landlord instinct fell like a ray of light on the troubled surface of the civil war, and after a hundred refractions, came out in its undeviating direction at the end.

The war in Ireland had been waged on the king's behalf. Owen O'Neill, whose word no man doubted, and who represented the only party that could be called national, in a letter to Lord Muskerry in 1648, wrote these words: "I do protest, swear and vow before Almighty God, that I never harboured the least thought of ambition in anything yet, but that which I assuredly thought and imagined to redound to the freedom, preservation and liberty of king, country, religion and nation, and that, during the remainder of my days, no private interest of my own, neither love, hatred, inducement, or suggestion of any will persuade me to the contrary." Ormond had kept the royal cause toppling on the verge of ruin by his calculating selfishness. Broghil and Coote had hurled it over by active co-operation with Cromwell. The instant that Coote saw the probability of a restoration he made secret offers of his services to Charles, and received from him a commission to act in his name. Jealous or apprehensive of Broghil's superior treachery, he expressly desired that his engagements should not be made known to him. Uncertain of the turn fortune was to take, the two traitors entered into communication with Monk. Finally they seized the castle on behalf of the king, who was soon proclaimed in all the great towns in Ireland.

The Catholics who had been true to the royal cause naturally expected the restitution of their lands. They had no means of personal access to the king, no friends at court, no money to bribe with. Their enemies had them all, and used them without scruple. The act of indemnity prepared on the king's return excluded all concerned in the rebellion; by which was meant in reality all those who had been fighting for the king against the rebellious English Parliament. This description embraced the whole Catholic party.

A commission was appointed for the disposal of the lands. An estimate was made which seemed capable, when the claims of the soldiers and adventurers were satisfied, of compensating the innocent Irish. The conditions that defined innocence rendered acquittal almost impossible. Residence within the quarters of the rebels (for so we are obliged to term the royal army) was to be considered conclusive evidence of rebellion. The lords justices had driven the landowners from Dublin on pain of death, and compelled them to live among the rebels.

In 1661 a Parliament was called. As the soldiers and adventurers were in possession of the lands, almost the whole House was composed of their party. They induced the chief justices to close the law courts until their titles were made good by a statute. They transmitted a bill disqualifying Catholics for seats in Parliament; and those men, belonging to the party which had brought the king to the scaffold, classed with the excluded Catholics, who had been fighting against them in the king's defence, all those who had pronounced sentence of death on the king. When this measure was deemed inexpedient in England, they spread rumours of plots and intended massacres, and covered with odium the men with whom they were to contend for their estates.

The Irish sent agents to London begging for some mitigation of the conditions of innocence, an dpleaded their services to the royal family, and the peace of 1649. They had to rely solely on the justice of their cause, and they were vindictively accused of urging its claims too boldly. Their requests were denied, and future petitions were forbidden.

The Duke of Ormond arrived as Lord Lieutenant, and gave the royal assent to the Act of Settlement. Its execution was assigned to English commissioners. In the first month thirty-eight Irish were declared innocent and seven nocent; in the second month fifty-three were declared innocent and seven nocent; and in the third seventy-seven were declared innocent and five nocent. The soldiers and adventurers cried out that England was sacrificed to Ireland, entered into communications with the discontented republicans, and plotted a general insurrection and the seizure of Dublin Castle. Power to tyrannise in Ireland or revolt against England were their alternatives. The House of Commons proposed to make the conditions of innocency so rigorous as absolutely to exclude the Irish from possible acquittal. When the Council declined, they passed a resolution binding themselves to obstruct the proceedings of the commissioners. Insurrectionary plots multiplied, and reached such a height that persons in important positions were openly canvassed to join the movement. On the day fixed for the seizure of the Castle, twenty-five persons were made prisoners, and a few of them were executed.

The king directed the viceroy and council to prepare a new bill of settlement. The claims of Protestants were accommodated to the dimensions of the spoil. It was provided that no Papist who had not been declared innocent should ever in the future be reputed so. Out of four thousand claims of innocency, not six hundred had been tried. The act was passed without a dissentient voice.

In such manner and degree was accomplished the end that for centuries had been longed and laboured for. Never did the vanity of human desires, and the fatal recoil of ambition, exhibit themselves in such retributory aspect. The lands sought by daring captains were secured by paltry money lenders and canting corporals. There was a scoffing parody in the new meaning of the word adventurer. The prizes that nobles panted for were given as bribes to save them from their ancestral serfs; and the unconscious craving of Briton and Saxon for their lost English land was baffled by the unexpected issue that took the men who might have redressed their wrongs from their side, and corrupted them with spoils torn from the peasants of Ireland.

SECTION II.

Charles was in the pay of the French king, and was concerting with him the conversion of England to the Catholic religion. The aid of the Nonconformists, who were seeking for their freedom, was relied on. Ireland was a fit subject for dangerous experiments. Ormond was recalled and replaced by Lord Berkley, a strong adherent of the Catholic interest. Peter Walsh, a Franciscan friar, had drawn up a remonstrance of the Irish Catholics, in which they openly disclaimed the authority or influence of any foreign power to interfere with their loyalty, or release them from their obligations. It was signed by a number of the lower clergy and lay lords. This declaration, which emanated from the native Church and expressed its spirit, was opposed by foreign ecclesiastics and the bishops, who were nominees of the Pope. On the arrival of Lord Berkley the remonstrants were deprived of their cures, and Walsh was excommunicated. Thus Irish Catholicism was compelled to avow the principles and bear the odium of the political Catholicism of England. Peter Talbot was raised to the Catholic Archbishopric of Dublin, asserted the Pope's unlimited authority, and boasted of the king's patronage. He celebrated mass with extraordinary splendour, and expressed the hope that Romanism would soon be the dominant religion. Catholics were allowed to hold commissions of the peace and were admitted to corporations.

An inevitable result followed: a number of Catholic lords and gentlemen began to hope for the recovery of their estates, and presented a petition on the subject. The occupants of the lands flamed into a phrensy of rage and fear. The English people, suspicious of the king's design, and justly apprehensive for their own liberties, turned their indignation on Ireland, which merely reflected without absorbing the Popery of the English rulers. Berkley was withdrawn. The English Parliament insisted on the maintenance of the Act of Settlement, and the removal of Catholics from corporations and magistracies. Ormond was once more sent as viceroy. About the same time William of Orange arrived in England, and was married to Mary, eldest child of James, Duke of York.

Titus Oates, supported by Lord Shaftesbury, invented a Popish plot for the subversion of Protestantism and the death of the king. A panic of alarm seized the Protestants of Ireland, who were but one to fifteen compared with the Catholics. The latter were disarmed, their ecclesiastics were driven from the kingdom, their convents and seminaries suppressed. Orders came from England to seize Richard Talbot, Lord Mountgarret, and Colonel Peppard. Lord Mountgarret was eighty years old, and no Colonel Peppard existed. Talbot was examined, but no evidence being found to warrant his detention, he was allowed to leave the kingdom. The Protestants proposed that the old dispossessed chieftains should be secured, and that all Papists should be expelled from the corporate towns, to which they had been admitted as a matter of social necessity. Ormond allowed the existing state to continue, but under limitations that rendered the native Irish tolerated aliens in their very homes. Still rumours were spread, hints were dropped, suspicions were sown, and a crop of informers sprang from the ground. Plunket, the Catholic Archbishop of Armagh, was taken to London, found guilty on some wildly impossible charge, and executed.

On the discovery of a plot to murder the king and the Duke of York, the king recovered his popularity, the duke's right of succession to the throne was allowed, and both began again to use Ireland for the furtherance of their plans. Ormond, who after two years' residence in London had just returned to his government in Ireland, was informed that he was to be removed, and Rochester appointed to succeed him. At this crisis Charles died.

SECTION III.

James was a Catholic. It was only natural that the Catholic Irish, who had been persecuted, robbed, and murdered by Protestant kings, should hope for better treatment from a monarch of their own creed. The situation was pregnant with wild hopes and fears, and bitter animosities. A Protestant rebellion broke out in England, and the Irish apprehended a massacre. James ordered the disarmament of the militia. Orders were issued that Catholic prelates should publicly wear the habits of their order. Controversy in Protestant pulpits was forbidden. Talbot, who was now Earl of Tyrconnel, and soon after became deputy, arrived as commander of the army with independent powers. Catholics were admitted to corporations, and the offices of Sheriff and Justice of the Peace, and several of them were advanced to high military positions from which Protestants had been removed. The Chancellorship and Attorney-generalship were filled by Catholics, and the corporations were compelled to take out new charters by which the numbers of Catholic and Protestant members were to be in proportion to those in the town or city.

In these changes we can neither discern concession to justice on the side of the king, nor assumption of undue power on the part of the Irish. James and Tyrconnel regarded the Catholic Church as the champion of the divine right of kings, and were promoting its interests in Ireland in that character. Judged by their intentions their conduct was oppressive and dangerous. But it is utterly unfair to judge the Irish Catholics by the motives of the men who restored to them what were simply the rights of all men, and of which it was an inhuman injustice ever to have deprived them. The ancient chiefs and Anglo-Norman lords had been robbed and reduced under the feet of Cromwell's soldiers in the name of religion. That the act had been done in the name of religion did not render it less iniquitous. That reparation was now made in the name of religion did not render it less just.

Tyrconnel proposed convening an Irish Parliament, and introducing a bill that would give the king power over a great portion of the lands. If this were unjust it was only in the same degree that all former changes of ownership of Irish land, after the first, made for the political purposes of England, were unjust. If it contemplated the restoration of the lands to the original owners its justice was as great as the injustice that despoiled them. Two commissioners were sent to lay this scheme before the English Council, who would scarcely give it a hearing. The populace followed the commissioners with mock honours, and held poles in their hands with potatoes on the tops. This display meant that the gentry of Ireland had been reduced to eat potatoes, and that they must continue to eat them, and that their destitution, so far from being a cause of pity, was always to remain a ground of triumph and derision with their enemies.

News arrived that William of Orange had landed in England, and that James, deserted by his subjects, had escaped to France. Letters were sent to various persons through the country, announcing an intended immediate massacre by the Papists. The Protestants poured into the cities for protection from the imaginary danger. Derry was a principal refuge for the fugitives. Tyrconnel had withdrawn its garrison on the first alarm of William's invasion. He now sent a force to supply the want. The citizens refused to admit them.

The Protestants of the North formed themselves into an association, and took the field. They were defeated, and sheltered themselves in Derry. Both Tyrconnel and the inhabitants of Derry were in doubt and despondency, when word came to the former from James, and to the latter from William, that they were soon to appear with large armies. On the twelfth of March, 1689, James landed at Kinsale with twelve hundred English soldiers and a hundred French officers. He raised Tyrconnel to a dukedom, and entered the capital in triumph. His first movement was against Derry, which he besieged. The men of Derry made a brave and prolonged defence. Relief came to them, and the enemy retired.

James returned to Dublin, where a Parliament of Tyrconnel's nomination repealed the Act of Settlement, gave complete freedom of religion, and asserted their legislative independence. All the Irish who adhered to William were attainted of high treason unless they surrendered within a given time. Acts were passed entitling Catholic ecclesiastics to all tithes payable by their own communion.

On the thirteenth of August Schomberg, William's general, landed at Bangor, in the county of Down, and laid siege to Carrigfergus. The garrison won terms of honourable surrender, and were allowed to march out with arms and baggage. This sight was more than the English troops could bear. They disarmed and plundered the garrison, and were with difficulty restrained from murdering them. Schomberg proceeded to Dundalk, where he encamped in unwholesome ground, and lost half his army by disease. James was at hand with his army, but made no attack. The English Parliament, which had retarded measures till the nation rose to the desired degree of impatience and exasperation, could now brook no delay. William was forced to go to Ireland and conduct the war in person. He arrived on the fourteenth of July, and won the battle of the Boyne over an army half his own in number. James, who long before the battle had made his preparations for flight, took the earliest opportunity that the alternating fortunes of the day afforded, and rode from the field, followed by his army in orderly retreat.

James left the kingdom. William remained master of the field and throne. The war of dynasties was over. The ordinary terms of pacification would have followed in any other country than Ireland. A proclamation of pardon was put forth, excluding the leaders. This was the work of officials, who at the same time obtained a commission for the seizure of forfeitures. They used this weapon so mercilessly, and the protection promised to the peasantry was so shamefully violated, that James' deserted party were compelled to continue the war. An army marched to Athlone, luring the peasants, through the whole journey, to surrender, and then plundering and murdering them. Failing to take Athlone, they joined William, who was advancing to besiege Limerick. Unsuccessful in this enterprise, William returned to England, leaving Ginkel in command. A time of lawlessness succeeded, deliberately prolonged, against the general's desire, by the great men on William's side. Athlone was taken after a desperate defence. Ginkel again wished to end hostilities by proclaiming pardon, but the Privy Council and the English nobles objected and obstructed.

Fresh troops arrived from France, under St. Ruth, and on the twelfth of June the French general was killed in the moment of victory at Aughrim, and the victory was turned into a defeat. Ginkel next attacked Galway. A treaty of capitulation was proposed. Ginkel, consulting for William's interests, overbore the opposition of the English officers, who had other motives to serve, and granted a free pardon to the governors and magistrates, with full possession of their estates and liberties. The Catholic clergy were allowed the private exercise of their religion. Catholic lawyers were allowed to practise their profession, and Catholic gentlemen to bear arms.

The strength of the Catholics collected at Limerick, which was next attacked. The confidence of the garrison increased as the siege proceeded, and Sarsfield, who was in command, contemplated aggressive movements. French aid was daily expected. A treaty was made, allowing the Catholics of Ireland the enjoyment of their religion as in the time of Charles II., assuring to those included in the capitulation the possession of their estates, and permitting all who chose to enter into foreign service. Those conditions were granted under no impulse of generosity on the one side or need of peace on the other. They were so far from being considered over favourable to the Catholics, that if the demand for the restoration of all forfeited lands had been pressed, the king's party must have yielded. A few days after the treaty was concluded a formidable French fleet arrived.

The contest thus ended was not a war for national independence. It was a contest between two English factions conducted on Irish soil. Because these foreign principles and foreign armies intruded their quarrel into Ireland, all the insolence of victory is exhibited towards that country, all the humiliation of defeat is supposed to attach to it. While the issue was uncertain, the events that occurred, the disaster or success, the gain or the loss, the daring or the suffering, were stamped with party hues that still disfigure them and unfit them for a detailed place in didactic narrative. They should be left in the tumuli of history for future generations to examine when the evil passions that still cleave to them have rotted away. Their premature and perpetual disinterments are poisoning the world.

SECTION IV.

No writer has contributed so much or so deliberately to the perpetuation of discord between England and Ireland as Lord Macaulay.[1] He has done a worse thing than even this in the prosecution of his purpose. He has taught his readers that all great qualities and accomplishments are to be acquired only by slave-owning. Men rise to higher things, according to his theory, on stepping stones, not of their dead selves, but of their living fellowmen. The mien is never so divinely haughty, the step is never so kingly in grace, as when the foot is planted on a human heart. There is no such thing as absolute excellence, or essential refinement. An ostentation of dainty artifice may be maintained by banqueting on corpses at night. There is no occasion here to show that every nation and every class that ever strove to exalt itself by sinking another nation or class, was only surely and steadily digging its own grave. There is no need to prove from profane history that the liberty which rested on social degradation by its side was the meanest form of dependency; or from sacred history, that the righteousness that throve on a community of sinners was a moral monster growth, compared with which the sin that contrasted with it was almost a virtue. It is sufficient to point out in the particular case with which this writer deals, that his mode of reasoning is incoherent confusion, that his armies of seigniors and slaves are mere visions projected from an obsequious fancy, and that in fact he is a gladiator on paper, slaying his fellow captive for the entertainment of the lords of the spectacle. We are astounded at the noise of his arguments until we discover that it is produced by the looseness of their construction. We admire the ease with which he wields his sentences, until we perceive that they are empty of facts. We applaud the steadiness of his measured tread as he crosses the stage, until we know that the blood of his antagonist has soaked through sand made from the shattered pillars of the universe.

His object is to make it apparent that the alleged misdeeds of the party that opposed William in field and cabinet, in the Irish campaign of 1689, were attributable to Irishmen exclusively. The Government and Parliament and army of the country, he would have us believe, were distinctively and aboriginally Irish. He then shows that it would be absurd to expect mercy or justice or wisdom from a class of men who

[1] Macaulay's "History of England," Vol. III., Chap. xii.

had gone through such a previous history as the Irish had experienced. Every thing they did, therefore, must have been unmerciful, unjust, and unwise. All the magnanimity, skill, courage, prudence, and victory were on the English side: all the slavish meanness, barbarism and discomfiture were on the Irish side. Ireland is despicably weak and hopelessly vicious. England therefore must rule her with a will of adamant and a rod of iron.

He proves that James's party were all Irish in the following manner. James, he says, had exerted his power for the purpose of inverting the relation between the conquerors or colonists, and the aboriginal population.[1] This means that James was placing members of the aboriginal population in command, and subjecting the conquerors or colonists to them. The person to whom he entrusted the execution of this inverting process was Lord Deputy Tyrconnel. Henceforth it becomes necessary to remind ourselves that Tyrconnel was a Talbot, not an O'Donnell. "In the autumn of 1688 the process was complete. The highest offices in the State, in the army, and in the courts of justice were, with scarcely an exception, filled by Papists." Aboriginal population and Papists are used as convertible terms. In a certain vituperative sense all Irishmen were considered and treated as Papists. But Lord Macaulay is not vituperating, he is reasoning solemnly, and for the purposes of argument he assumes that all Papists were aboriginal Irishmen. There is no figure of speech or loose declamation intended. He is seriously arranging premises from which momentous conclusions were to be drawn. He is about to charge the Irish Government with unprecedented weakness and wickedness, and he clears away all defences and prepossessions by exposing the members of it as aboriginal Irishmen, because they were Papists. He proceeds to specify his proofs. Fitton was Lord Chancellor; Nugent, Chief Justice of the King's Bench; Rice, Chief Baron of the Exchequer; Nagle, Attorney General; Keating, who was a Protestant, Chief Justice of the Common Pleas. These are all Norman, English, or Welsh names: there is not an aboriginal Irish name among them. The writer's implication is that the men were all unfit for office, inasmuch as they were aboriginal Irish, and he establishes the rule by its exception, Judge Daly, of the Common Pleas, the only Irishman whom he mentions, and whom he admits to have been a man of sense, moderation, and integrity.[2]

He goes on to the constitution of the Dublin Parliament. "The House of Commons consisted almost exclusively of Irishmen and Papists." He here destroys his former premise, admitting Irishman and Papist to be distinct terms, in order that he may bring on the members the double odium of being each a Papist and an Irishman at once. We must keep his purpose in mind. He intends to accuse this Parliament of the greatest enormities of crime and blunder that any Parliament was ever charged with. He is preparing a scapegoat, for which he means afterwards to prepare a desert. "Alone among the Irish Parliaments of the age," he says, "this Parliament was filled with Dermots and Geohagans, O'Neills and O'Donovans, Mac Mahons,

[1] P. 120.
[2] See King's "State of Protestants in Ireland," p. 72.

Macnamaras, and Macgillicuddies." If Lord Macaulay saw one man in an assembly towards whom he harboured a feeling of dislike, he might allow his mind to run on that one man more than on all the others, and so his mind would be filled with that one man. He could then say that, to him, that one man filled the whole assembly. In this way we may account for the sentence we have quoted. As a fact there were four Dermots or Macdermots, two Geoghegans, six O'Neills, three O'Donovans or Donovans, two Macnamaras, and one Macgillicuddy in the Irish Parliament of 1689. The names are evidently arranged with artistic skill, so as to terminate in a climax of cacophony. The Parliament consisted of some two hundred and forty members. Of these about forty were Irish; all the rest were Normans or Saxons. There were eight Fitzgeralds, seven Talbots, seven Butlers, five Burkes, and so on. The proportion of aboriginal Irish to colonists or Anglo-Irish was that which exists in the present united Parliament of Irish of all descents to English. The number of men with an O to their names in James's Irish Parliament was the same as in Queen Victoria's Parliament of to-day.[1]

This is no inadvertence or passing contempt. The writer intends to make capital of his assumption that all the members of the Dublin Parliament were aboriginal Irish. "James," he afterwards says, "was an Englishman. Superstition had not extinguished all national feeling in his mind." He was not a thorough Papist, and so he was not a thorough Irishman. Irish Catholics would probably say that, judged by this test, James's claims to be called an Irishman were far greater than their own. "He could not but be displeased by the malevolence with which his Celtic supporters regarded the race from which he sprang." [2] The most obvious fact to any impartial student of Irish history is that all the indignation and animosity, for "malevolence" is an inappropriate and evil word introduced for an evil purpose, that have ever prevailed in Ireland towards England have been always hottest among Irishmen of English descent. Again he writes, "The chiefs of the old Celtic families said publicly that if he did not give them back their inheritances they would not fight for him." The trait thus condemned by association is not Irish. And as the repudiation is not meant in praise, but censure, so when we say it is rather English we mean the ascription not in censure but in praise.

In describing the siege of Londonderry, Lord Macaulay is led to speak of the general character of the English inhabitants of Ireland. They were an "aristocratic caste, with a Castilian haughtiness of manner, and quite superior to their kindred in the mother country." He establishes this proposition, not by taking instances from the descendants of the Anglo-Normans or Cromwellians, but from the Northern defenders of Londonderry, who were Scotchmen, and like Lord Macaulay himself, indubitably descended from the aboriginal population. He forgets to state that the fury of resistance that saved Derry from capture was first roused, not by Irishmen or Englishmen, but by Lord Antrim's

---

[1] See "State of the Protestants of Ireland." Appendix, p. 374.

[2] Archbishop King gives a quotation intimating that James "not only hated the English Protestant, but also the English man."—*Ibid.*, p. 111.

highlanders, whose strange costume and fierce aspect terrified the Cameronian inhabitants by the recollection of the barbarities by which they had been driven from their homes in Scotland.[1]

Ominous hints are dropped about a coming repetition of 1641. A rumour was abroad that on a certain day a general massacre of the English was to take place. Tyrconnel contradicted the report with many oaths, but he was such a liar that his contradiction was equivalent to a confirmation. The timid took flight, deeming winds and waves less fierce than the exasperated Irishry whom they left frowning behind. The bold prepared to defend their lives. The Irish rose in a body. Never in modern Europe had there been such a rising of a whole people. A hundred thousand men rose in arms. Fifty thousand of them were soldiers. The other fifty thousand were violent and licentious banditti. Warlike ballads were sung in a hundred thousand cabins. Every smith, every carpenter, every cutler was at work on guns and blades. The very women were exhorted by their spiritual directors to carry skeans. Our blood runs cold as the awful Ides of March approach. While we hold our breaths and our hearts stand still, Lord Macaulay stalks majestically to his conclusion. No one would believe, he declares with elaborate asseveration, if it were not attested by witnesses unconnected with each other, and attached to very different interests, how those freebooters, who were accustomed to live on potatoes and sour whey, and had always regarded meat as a luxury reserved for the rich, killed fifty thousand horned cattle, revelled in beef and mutton, and actually devoured the meat without salt or herbs, and sometimes half raw, and sometimes burned to cinders.[2] Whether the historian carried his high-wrought mood into this battue, and imagined that he was describing a massacre by aboriginal Irish cannibals; or whether he adopted this covert method of conveying a wholly false impression of the numbers, nation, and arms of James's soldiers, who were comparatively few in number, very indifferently armed, and not one-sixth of them natives; or whether by a graphic account of savages gorging themselves with beef excessively or insufficiently cooked, he intended to divert attention from the fact that the inhabitants of Ireland, when their enemies, who had done them and theirs every wrong that man can do to man, were in their power, did not commit a single act of murder or violation, is not quite easy to discover. But there is one matter of historical importance involved in the narrative. The chief riches of Ireland, he tells us, consisted in cattle. Innumerable flocks and herds covered that vast expanse of emerald meadow saturated with the moisture of the Atlantic. More than one gentleman possessed twenty thousand sheep and four thousand oxen. As we read this luscious description, and recollect that beef was meant in Ireland only for rich men, the cause of the writer's indignation, and of his confusion of a massacre of men with a slaughter of cows, begins to dawn upon us. Ireland, in fact, was, as some men would again have it to be, in consequence of wholesale murders and famines, covered with wild cattle. The slaughter of those animals was nothing more than the

---

[1] 'State of the Protestants of Ireland," p. 115.

[2] According to Archbishop King, the slaughter of cattle was a stroke of Government policy.—"State of the Protestants of Ireland," p. 141.

slaughter of deer in Scotland at the present day by wealthy and refined Englishmen, for providing which pastime the same process that had depopulated Ireland was in full operation in his own country at the very time that Lord Macaulay was writing. Hundreds of cabins were echoing not to songs of war, but to the crackling of flames, and the moans of men and women expelled pitilessly from their homes and thrown on the wide world.[1] The scene of which Lord Macaulay wrote, and that which was occurring while he wrote, were closely connected with each other. In one case the people submitted meekly to their bitter lot, and he has not a sigh of commiseration for them. In the other case, the people resisted, are resisting, and will ever resist, till the occasion for resistance ceases, and all his powers of misrepresentation are marshalled against them. And in no other particular is he so far from the truth as when he ascribes violence as a distinctive mark to the aboriginal population. The peasants of Scotland who saw their houses wrecked, and went forth almost without a murmur to dwell or die by the wayside, or to seek a home across the ocean, were pure and unmixed Irish, true specimens of the aboriginal population. Therefore it was that they submitted too patiently and too silently. The peasants whom he reviles as aboriginal Irish and eaters of potatoes, owe their indomitable spirit of resistance to the fact that they are not wholly aboriginal Irish, but have Saxon and Norman blood mingling with Irish blood in their veins. The patience of the Irishman is there enduring as ever. And there too the vehemence of the Englishman, like the thunder-cloud, ever rolls against the tempest of tyranny. Be it known, then, that it is England, not Ireland, that Lord Macaulay assails and despises, and was rewarded for assailing and despising. He tells us of an Irishman who killed a cow merely to get a pair of brogues. The fable describes his own case.

It might be enough to show that the war of 1689 was one of Dutchman against Englishman, not of Englishman against Irishman, if every true Irishman as well as every true Englishman were not deeply concerned for the honour of the inhabitants of Ireland without distinction. It would be absurd, Lord Macaulay says, writing of James's Parliament, to expect mercy, justice, or wisdom from men abased by oppression, who in sight of fields and castles which they regarded as their own were glad to be invited by a peasant to partake of his whey and his potatoes. This is the key note of his condemnation of the repeal of the Act of Settlement, and of the Act of Attainder. It would be truly absurd to expect that men should continue to depend on the charity of peasants for a share of their meal of whey and potatoes, when they had it in their power to recover lawfully the fields and castles to which they were justly entitled. It is admitted that their property was taken from them unjustly; but was one injustice to be redressed by committing another more monstrous still? Exactly the same thing might be said of every execution of a murderer, if one chose to describe the execution as more monstrous than the murder. All the justice was with the natural owners of the Irish lands. The acts of England had nothing but violence and specially made law on their side. No appeal had been

[1] See Mackenzie's "Highland Clearances," p. 28.

made to justice, because none could be made. Yet the instant the Irish party attempted to right themselves by law, the name of justice is for the first time invoked, as if a few days' possession of stolen goods by one race gave a better title than an immemorial possession by another. The fact that compensation was provided for those persons who had purchased any of the lands is carefully withheld.

The Act of Attainder was a mere assertion of sovereign right according to established usage. The object was to vest the lands of the attainted persons in the Crown. It neither was nor was intended to be put in force. Yet the writer sprinkles his pages with quartering blocks, gallows, and innocent blood, as if Ireland really did the things which she had only suffered. "This law," he says, "was without parallel in the history of civilised countries." We sincerely trust we are paying Lord Macaulay no undeserved compliment when we say that he was ignorant of the history of civilised countries. A precisely similar Act had been passed a few days before by William and Mary's London Parliament.[1]

In literal truth, for patriotic forethought and large-minded religious toleration, the proceedings of the Irish Parliament are without parallel in the history of all civilised countries except Ireland. Ireland is the only country that never retaliated religious persecution, when it had the power. Hanging Catholic bishops and priests had been a kind of jest with Protestants at all times, just as one might provoke a laugh by a travesty of Scripture. There was no thought of vengeance. In James's House of Lords there were only six bishops, and all of them were Protestants. All this was nothing new. The same thing had occurred in Mary's reign.

With regard to the characters of the two armies a couple of short quotations will suffice. Story, a Protestant chaplain in William's foreign army, writes: "The poor Protestants were now in a worse condition than before, for they had enjoyed the benefit of the Irish protection till our coming thither." Dr. George, Schomberg's chaplain and secretary, is more emphatic. "Can we expect," he says, "that Sodom will destroy Babylon: or that debauchery will extirpate Popery? Our enemy fights against us with the principle of a mistaken conscience; we, against the conviction of our own consciences, against him."

Dire as are the woes with which God afflicts willing, and only willing slavery, they are inconsiderable compared with the penalties which He has attached to unjust rule. The cost at which England kept Ireland in subjection has been often estimated in money. Who shall measure the loss in outraged reason, violated truth, degraded intellect, subverted morals, falsified standards? The philosopher must accommodate his system to an exception which he dares not examine. The orator must stammer and hang his head when he reaches his noblest theme. The novelist must add falsehood to fiction. The historian tempted by the rewards of divination must deliberately restrict himself to partial views in order that he may curse where it is his interest to curse, although he has received the divine command to bless. Even with the loftiest

[1] The fact is referred to Matthew O'Conor, and the details are given in "Leckey's History of England."

inspiration of genius the maddening fumes of national prejudice will mingle, and by the side of the immortal glory will stand the immortal shame, the pitiless indelicacy, the brutal calumny, the tricked and dramatised slander, leaving men of later days no alternative save to turn their backs in reverential humiliation, or to look with shameless boasting on the nakedness of their great forefather.[1]

[1] See Froude's "English in Ireland," Vol. I., p. 7, where it may be observed the blow aimed at the mere Irishman falls on one of English descent.

CHAPTER XIII.

PARLIAMENTARY DEPENDENCE.

SECTION I.

THE war that had now come to an end was not waged by the original Irish, nor for Irish freedom. The rebellion in England had become settled government. The base metal treason had passed through the crucible of success, and had been transmuted into the gold of a constitution. Ireland was not intended to derive any benefit from the transmutation. The base metal was to be accepted by her, not because it had been changed to gold, but merely because her master willed it. She was expected to receive the Revolution as she had been expected to receive the Reformation. The cloud of heaven adapts itself to the inequalities of earth's surface. The cloud of foreign rule demands from Ireland an instantaneous conformity of her surface to its own changing figure.

The troops of King James, including a large number of Protestants, arbitrarily handled by foreign generals, and forsaken by the king, did all that could be reasonably required of them, when they ended the contest by a treaty which allowed them to enter into a distant service, and secured the liberties and properties of those whom they left behind. The mass of the people were weary of a war in which they were not concerned. Like the people of England during the Parliamentary war, they saw their fields trespassed on, their goods taken from them, and their farming operations interrupted, by two parties, in neither of whom they felt any vital interest. The end of the struggle was to them simply a return to the occupations of peace. What had occurred at every interval of repose from foreign disturbance occurred now. Within a fortnight after the English left Limerick, a man might travel alone throughout the kingdom without fear of injury.

A peaceful and a united Ireland was not the object the English Parliament had in view. Under the common understanding between them and William each had separate designs. William had his wars of ambition to prosecute. The Parliament had personal interests to advance. During war laws are silent, is an adage of history. During peace, it may too often be said, laws speak and justice is silent. Two months after the Treaty of Limerick the English Parliament passed a bill imposing the Declaration against Transubstantiation on members of the Irish Houses. When the Irish Parliament met in 1692 no Catholic could take his seat. Thus was the protecting power of the treaty destroyed, Protestants put in sole legislative possession, and the commencement made of that penal code which robbed the vast majority of the Irish people of every social and political right, and violated the most sacred privileges of nature. Those laws were not enacted from any love of truth or hatred of error. The Catholics were by far the more numerous body, and they had been deprived of their lands. Earnest and constant efforts have been made to prove that this deprival was a just and a legitimate measure. It would have been an incalculable blessing for Ireland if the men who were gainers by it were sincerely of this opinion. The conscience of the day spoke in another voice than that of modern advocacy. It was the haunting sense of their morally indefensible position that inspired the legislature of Ireland to pass the penal laws. Their design was not only to prevent the Catholics from ever recovering their properties, but to make them appear undeserving of ever having possessed them. They not merely excluded them from Parliament, and deprived them of the right of voting and the possession of arms, but they endeavoured to prevent them from growing in intelligence, or even retaining the mental powers that would qualify them for those privileges. If this end were gained their ill-got properties would be safe and their usurpation justified. As there is no more terrible dispensation among the mysteries of life than that law by which the slave and the victim of wrong are miscreated by their sufferings into criminals or weaklings, no longer fit for the rights they have lost, so there is no guilt on earth comparable with that of those who deliberately make use of it to maintain their injustice. Victims themselves to the circumstances in which the crimes of their rulers had placed them, the Protestants of Ireland strove by long repression to dwarf every faculty, to numb every energy, to stifle every aspiration of the Catholics, and to leave only the trunk of a soul behind. For a time the scheme, its results being considered inevitable, furnished an excuse for acting as if it had succeeded. At the present day we see actions of the past prejudged on the ground that they were done by men who were vitiated by slavery. "It is no reproach," Lord Macaulay says, writing of the Irish Parliament of 1689, " to the Irish nation to say that, of all the Parliaments which have met in the British islands, Barebone's Parliament not excepted, the assembly convoked by James was the most deficient in all the qualities which a legislature should possess. The stern domination of a hostile caste had blighted the faculties of Irish gentlemen."[1] It was no reproach to Irish gentlemen that they were degraded and demoralised, because they were only sufferers under the influence of successful oppression; and it was no reproach to the oppressors that they had done the work, because it was a desirable political consummation, successfully accomplished. This gives us the clue to the meaning of the current depreciation of Irishmen. The penal laws were not meant to abolish Catholicism, but to debase the Irish Papists. They were so administered that the Catholic religion, legally banned and socially ostracised, was allowed to smoulder in obscurity, while the laws that beggared the Catholics were rigorously enforced. Catholics in other countries persecuted to convert. Protestants in Ireland persecuted to enslave and debase. The political descendants or supporters of these men unconsciously enter into their views, and triumph in their assumed success. No one at this day would

[1] Comp. Archbishop King's "State of Protestants in Ireland," p. 24. The poverty of the plundered Catholics is given as a reason against their holding office.

avow that he was about to despoil another man, and then degrade him with the express view of making him fit only for further despoiling and degradation. Yet that is what was done, and what is indirectly advocated with regard to Ireland. Thus we come at the meaning of the terms of contempt and contumely heaped by Lord Macaulay on the Irish people. He knew that the system of repression was essentially atrocious. But the vilest system may be lauded if it have succeeded in producing certain ends supposed to be patriotic. If the penal system in Ireland failed it would stand by itself in unrelieved hatefulness. It is taken for granted, therefore, that it succeeded. But its success implies that the Irish were pariahs, Hindoos, and swine, to use the epithets of Lord Macaulay.

The penal laws did not succeed. No nation ever won a better victory than Ireland won, when after her long entombment she came forth with her love of freedom keener than ever, and her faith intact. It is no dishonour to us that our ancestors failed in crime. England of to-day is not answerable for all the guilty expedients that may have aided the Revolution. Least of all is she identified with the conduct of the levellers who became aristocrats and tyrants in Ireland. She has little in common with their Protestantism, and nothing with their politics. As a man who in the tumult of thoughtless strife has smitten another to the earth, and standing horrified at his deed, discerns with joyful relief signs of returning animation, so should England view Ireland's wildest struggles for liberty, and rejoice that her hands are not stained with soul-murder.

Section II.

The common enemy, the Catholics, being reduced to impotence, the two Parliaments remained confronting each other. Ireland, when no longer to be feared as an enemy on the field of warfare, rose in a new character as a rival in manufactures and commerce. English rents, from several obvious causes, had suffered very considerable diminutions. Some landowners ascribed the falling off to the importation of Irish cattle. So early as 1663, a temporary Act was passed prohibiting the importation of fat cattle from Ireland. In 1665 a bill was brought in perpetually prohibiting the importation of Irish cattle of all kinds. It passed the Commons, but a prorogation took place before it had time to pass the Lords. In the meantime the fire of London occurred, and contributions were made to meet the calamity. It was proposed by the deputy and adopted by the privy council and gentry of Ireland, that assistance should be sent to the sufferers. The only wealth of the country consisted in cattle. Thirty thousand beeves were subscribed. This act of sympathy was interpreted in England as a contrivance for defeating the threatened prohibition. The bill was resumed, and in its preamble the introduction of Irish cattle was described as a nuisance. In the Lords an attempt was made to alter nuisance to detriment or mischief; but the Commons insisted on their own term. Lord Ashley proposed that the importation should be called a felony or a premunire. The Chancellor suggested the word adultery as appropriate. The Duke of Buckingham insisted that no one would oppose the bill except such as had Irish estates or Irish understandings. This was almost literally true, and may serve to explain a thousand similar sayings. Men with Irish estates were no doubt the persons whose understandings would prompt them to oppose a bill ruinous to their estates. Lord Ossory, a son of the Duke of Ormond, assuming an Irish understanding, and exhibiting a sensitiveness usually ascribed to the aboriginal population, challenged Buckingham. The latter complained to the House, and Ossory was sent to the Tower. The Scotch Parliament improved on the English precedent, and prohibited the importation of Irish cattle, beef, and corn.

Home manufactures were the natural remedy for the loss occasioned by the exclusion of raw material from the English market. Woollen manufactures were long established at Clonmel and Carrick, and five hundred Walloon Protestant families were brought from Canterbury to promote their success. At the commencement of William's reign sheep had become abundant in both countries, in consequence of the turning of the lands on which the peasantry formerly lived into pasturages. Manufactures in wool were in consequence an important branch of industry. In the competition that ensued, the Irish manufacturers were able to undersell their English rivals in foreign markets. The two Houses addressed the king, and argued that some remedy must be found against this intolerable interference with the trade of England. The Lords besought him to declare to his Irish subjects in the most public and effectual way, that the growth of woollen manufactures was looked on with great jealousy, and if not remedied, would occasion strict laws for its total prohibition and suppression. The king replied that he would do all that he could to discourage the woollen trade in Ireland. A Parliament was summoned in Dublin for the express purpose of destroying a flourishing branch of Irish industry. The lords justices brought the subject forward, and urged the lower house to encourage hempen and linen manufactures instead of woollen, of which England desired the monopoly. The Commons endeavoured to avert the coming blow by placing some additional burthens on their trade, but nothing short of total extinction would suffice. A law was passed in 1699 prohibiting all export of Irish woollen goods, except to England and Wales, from which countries they were practically excluded by heavy duties. Even the export of wool was restricted to a single English port. The navigation laws had long prohibited all direct trade between Ireland and the colonies. No colonial produce could be carried to Ireland till it had first been unloaded in England. Those laws had been repealed under the Parliament of James II. in 1689, but they came into force again when the Stuart cause fell. The promised encouragement of a linen and hempen manufacture could never have proved a compensation for the loss of an established trade, and was not intended even to alleviate it. Wentworth had before destroyed the Irish woollen trade under the engagement of a similar substitution. The linen trade promoted by him never throve, and perished in the Revolution. England now took the whole manufacture of woollen into her own hands, and at the same time continued her manufacture of linen without giving Ireland any legislative encouragement till she was so sunk in weakness that she could no longer make use of it.

It was computed that twelve thousand Protestant families were maintained in Dublin by the woollen manufacture at the time of its destruction, and thirty thousand throughout the rest of the country. For half a century after this period the history of the Irish people is a history of famines in which they were compelled to eat grass, and died of hunger by countless thousands. Ireland could not be said to have a Parliament. The country and the nominal Parliament it possessed were absolutely in England's power.

Section III.

When the true nation, Catholic Ireland, passed out of account, the faction that usurped its place began to assume airs of independence, and to speak the language of patriotism. The design of the first settlers from England had been the establishment of an independent kingdom. This design always grew or subsided according as the distinct power of the native population diminished or increased. It was a seed that waited for a favourable season to germinate. Such a season had now apparently been brought by the political extinction of the Catholics. The subsequent history of the country, to the time of the Union, is that of a continual struggle for independence made by the English colony, always frustrated by disunion artificially infused into their ranks, and by the presence, felt but scarcely acknowledged, of a nation under foot waiting for its resurrection.

The desire for independence was not the growth of mere pride or sentiment. We have seen how ready and ruthless England was in destroying the prosperity of Ireland when it competed with her own, and how lightly she regarded the Protestantism, by whose aid and in whose name she held the country in subjection. By Poynings' Act every Irish bill should be submitted to the English Privy Council. They might reject it or alter it and send it to the Irish Parliament, who, in the latter case, might reject but could not alter it again. The Habeas Corpus Act did not exist in Ireland. The English Minister made the appointments to all the great Irish offices. In the Church and the Law the principal officers were always English. The mistresses of Charles II., James II., William III., and George I., were all pensioned on the Irish Treasury. The Irish Parliament had strong provocations to lay claim to greater freedom. The changing condition of circumstances afforded them legitimate means of asserting their authority. The royal hereditary revenue was derived from Crown and quit rents and excise duties, and had become insufficient for the increasing expenses of Government. It became necessary to apply to Parliament for supplies, and for this end the more frequent assemblage of the Houses was required.

In 1692 two money bills which had not been first transmitted from Ireland, but had originated in England, were sent over to be passed or rather registered. The Irish Commons declared their right to prepare the heads of bills for raising money, and passed one of the two, an excise bill, with the proviso that their action was not to grow into a precedent. The deputy warned them that they must quickly finish their work or the session would soon close. The excise bill was passed, but the other was rejected on the ground that it had not its rise in the House. The deputy prorogued the Parliament, rebuked the members for their ingratitude to the king in thus entrenching on his prerogative, and had a protest against their assumption entered in the journals.

The check which England possessed over the Irish Parliament lay in her power to regulate their treatment of the Catholics. The Irish Parliament wavered between the yearning for freedom and the craving for greater power to tyrannise. They would gladly identify the two, if it were possible to bind heavier chains on the Catholics without having to own a greater dependence on England at the same time. This was the problem that was to work itself out. Sydney, the viceroy, was unpopular because he pressed the claims of English supremacy, without countenancing the further degradation of the Catholics. Complaints were made in England of the oppressions occasioned by the liberty which the Catholics were allowed to possess, and evidence was given of the loyalty of the Irish Parliament. Sydney was recalled, and Lord Capel, who was known to hold very different sentiments, was appointed to succeed him. He summoned a Parliament in 1695, reminded the members how the king had won for them the supremacy of their religion, and the possession of their estates, told them that further provisions for their security were about to be made, and urged them to exhibit a suitable liberality. The Commons, bartering freedom for delegated power, and recognising only a relative freedom at best, passed such money bills as were required, and then entered on the measures intended for their further security. The king had been successful in his Continental war, and the disposition and opportunities of oppression were enlarged.

It had been a question for some time how far the articles of Limerick were to be considered binding. The doubt arose from no ground of uncertainty in the terms of the articles. Their meaning was plain, and wherever the language was loose it only left room on the side of a more liberal interpretation. They were questioned because they tolerated Popery and guaranteed a few Catholics in the possession of their rightful estates. A million acres had been confiscated in the previous war, and somewhat more than a quarter of these had been restored to Catholics adjudged by the commissioners to be entitled to them by the articles of Limerick or Galway. The special object of the legislation now and afterwards directed against the Catholics was to lower their position as landowners, to break up their estates into fragments, and to deprive them universally and finally of all property in the soil. Petitions poured in from all quarters, and were referred to a Committee of Grievances. The mayor, sheriff, and aldermen of Limerick complained that they were greatly damaged in their trade by the large number of Papists residing there. Edward Skragg and others, porters of Dublin, were indignant and outraged because one Darby Ryan, a Papist, employed porters of his own persuasion. Catholics were already excluded from the Legislature, from Corporations, and from the liberal professions, excepting that of medicine. They were now disarmed, debarred from educating their children at home, or sending them abroad to be educated, forbidden to possess a horse worth more than five pounds, and prevented from intermarrying with Protestants. The clergy were all banished, and Catholic labourers or servants were compelled to work on the holidays of their Church.

The Parliament then passed an Act for the Confirmation of Articles, not *the* Articles, of Limerick, or so much thereof as may consist with the safety and welfare of the subjects of the realm. Three gentlemen, named Cusack, Segrave, and Eustace, petitioned to be heard by counsel in defence of their rights as affected by these laws, and their petition was unanimously rejected. Twelve members of the House of Lords protested against the bill confirming the Articles on the ground that the title contradicted its contents. The king knew how much he owed to the Treaty of Limerick. He had sent instructions to the lords justices before it was made to assure the Irish of much more favourable terms than were afterwards obtained. The justices did not make these terms known, but the king knew them. Two days after the treaty was signed eighteen ships of war, six fireships, and twenty great ships of burthen, with a large quantity of arms, two hundred officers, and three thousand men arrived from France in Dingle Bay. In addition to the express articles of the treaty, it contained—what should have bound the king more firmly than any distinct engagement—an understanding that William should summon a Parliament in Dublin and procure such further securities for the Catholics as would preserve them from any disturbance on account of their religion. The whole treaty had been ratified by their Majesties' letters-patent. The king, notwithstanding, now gave his assent to acts which not only ignored the treaty, but made the burthen heavier where he had stipulated to make it lighter.

SECTION IV.

A saying of our times to the effect that England's difficulty is Ireland's opportunity, has given prominence to a one-sided view of truth, and caused resentment where a full statement would produce sympathy. Periods of adversity in war have been most fortunate for England and Ireland. The prosperity of aristocratic England in arms has always been a source of unrelieved suffering to the masses at home. In England the deluded people, drunk with glory, have always immolated their liberties before the Juggernaut of triumph. In Ireland, whither the warmth of victory could not extend, the winter of persecution, freezing men's blood to ice, had no assuagement. The reign of Queen Anne was the time of Marlborough's victories, and of additional and more grievous statutes against the Catholics of Ireland.

The English ruling class was divided into Whigs and Tories, modified continuations of the Roundheads and Cavaliers of a former day. Tory was the name by which ruined adherents of King James, who lived in a state of outlawry in the wilds of Ireland, were known. It was applied in derision and insult to those who inclined to hold the divine right of kings. Whig, a term denoting an opposite class of men in

Scotland, but similarly circumstanced to the Irish Tories, was applied in the same manner to persons who leaned towards the political views of nonconformists. The rivalry of the two parties was personal, and in its aim did not reach beyond their common class. They were both equally ready to employ the artifices of private intrigue, and the éclat of public policy, in order to gain office or power. Each of them was prepared to advocate foreign war when it seemed likely to win popularity, and to condemn it when the rival party used it for their own ends. Nations are preserved in their integral continuity, not by identity of interests or opinions, but by geographical boundaries; just as the waters of a stream are held together, not by mutual attraction, but by the banks. England's insularity brings her more completely than other countries under the influence of this simple law. Her rulers, wedged together at home, indulge their rivalries, and contend against each other, in foreign wars and in the management of Ireland. But it is remarkable that at the time of which we are now writing, the two English parties were unanimous in their passionate policy of oppression towards the sister island. The large principle of popular rights that has animated our modern politics, and compelled party leaders to make Ireland as well as England the scene of its admission or denial, and so identified the interests of the people of both countries, had not yet been developed. The royalists and parliamentarians were opposed to each other as if they were two distinct nations, yet they were in perfect agreement in their disregard of Irish rights. The Duke of Ormond sacrificed the interests of Charles I. to his jealousy of the Catholics. Another Duke of Ormond, who was plotting for the establishment of the Catholic Pretender, came now as viceroy. He was afterwards attainted for his fidelity to the Stuarts, and yet his hate of the Irish Catholics must have been stronger than his love of the cause for which he ruined his fortunes.

We are about to behold the moral vivisection of a nation. The designs of the operator are of greater importance to us than the sufferings of the subject. The victim has survived. We have only to watch the devices of tyranny—the exquisite nicety of her processes, and the extremities to which she is willing to carry them. We need not fear that any tremor of her hand will endanger the life of the sufferer. She will mangle every nerve, but never touch the life.

Catholics were already almost wholly plundered of their lands. They were excluded from every honourable or lucrative office or profession. They were not permitted to carry a single weapon by the very sight of which the instinct of manly self-defence is kept alive, or the sense of superiority over the wild creatures of wood and mountain is retained. Ormond was presented by the Commons with a bill to prevent the future growth of Popery, in order that he might obtain for it the authority of the great seal of England. This bill provided that if the son of an estated Papist conformed to the established religion, his father should be incapacitated from mortgaging or selling his estate, or disposing of it by will: it ordered that if a child though ever so young professed to be a Protestant, it should be taken from its father, and placed under the guardianship of the nearest Protestant relation: it rendered a Papist incapable of purchasing any landed estates, or holding any lease for a term exceeding thirty-one years, or even in the case of such leases of enjoying a profit greater than one-third of the amount of the rent, otherwise his right must pass over to the first Protestant who made the discovery: it imposed the oath of abjuration of the Pretender as a qualification for voting at elections: it ordered the estates of Papists not having Protestant heirs to be gavelled, or divided in equal shares among all the children: and it deprived the Catholic citizens of Galway and Limerick, except day labourers, of the right to live in these towns and carry on their trade there, which had been guaranteed to them by the treaty. The viceroy promised that he would recommend the bill in the most effectual manner, and do everything in his power to check the growth of Popery.

The English ministers, who had just addressed their ally, the Catholic Emperor of Austria, on behalf of his Protestant subjects, added to the Irish bill against Catholics another clause imposing the sacramental test on all Protestant dissenters taking office in Ireland. It has been alleged that they hoped by this addition to secure the rejection of the whole bill. Their sincerity is sufficiently established by the fact that they had only just passed through the Commons a severe measure against Nonconformists.

When the bill was returned to Ireland a number of Catholics, all of English descent, prayed and were allowed to be heard by counsel in opposition to it. Three Catholic lawyers—Sir Theobald Butler, Counsellor Malone, and Sir Stephen Rice—themselves protected by the Treaty of Limerick, appeared at the bar of the House of Commons. They pleaded that the Articles of Limerick were agreed to not as a concession, but for the most valuable considerations, and that the honour of the kingdom was pledged to their observance. They represented the grievous hardship that a Catholic must suffer if, after acquiring an estate by his labour and industry, his son could deprive him of all disposal of it by becoming a Protestant. They besought the Parliament not to tempt their children, whom they loved more than their lives, to become their plunderers. They begged them in the name of the divine Being to do as they would be done unto. The Protestant legislators made their calculation that by doing thoroughly now they should avoid all danger of being done unto at any time, and passed the bill without a dissentient voice. The dissenters made no noticeable remonstrance. They were willing to bear the light end of the load that crushed the Catholics into the dust. The grounds on which the Parliament justified their course were that since the Treaty of Limerick the Papists had not declared their fidelity to the Crown; that they might recover the rights the bill took from them by conforming; and that the treaty only put them in the state in which they were in the reign of Charles II., at which time there was no law in force which hindered the passing of any law that seemed necessary.

Mr. Froude justifies the Parliament on a general principle. "The appeal" (to the treaty), he says, "was not conclusive, for no treaties can bind eternally, when conditions change."[1] The eternity of the minor premise in this argument lay between 1691 and 1703. That in

[1] "The English in Ireland," Vol. I., p. 306.

which the validity of the treaty expired in the estimation of the English Parliament, owing to change of conditions, could be measured by weeks. The change of conditions that had taken place was the departure of the Irish army to France and the return homewards of the French fleet. This writer seems to labour under a strong feeling of indignation, which he almost unconsciously exhausts in the wrong direction. He apparently thinks that any blow became Irish the moment it fell on the body of Ireland. Any wrong that England did to Ireland he regards as an Irish wrong in the active sense. He shifts the word Irish from the sufferer to the doer with such rapidity that a superficial reader is more than bewildered. Writing of the resumption of forfeitures in William's reign, the management of which the English Parliament had usurped from the Irish Parliament, and conducted through agents of its own appointment, he says that "an attempt to control the affairs of Ireland on principles of probity and uprightness, was abandoned as hopeless."[1] The impression cursorily conveyed is that Irish affairs could not be managed on principles of probity and uprightness : but the real textual meaning is that England could not manage the affairs of Ireland with probity and uprightness. Again in reference to the Penal Code he says : "Ireland appeared to the English ministry to be a country where honour, conscience, and common sense were words which had no application."[2] The narrative shows the meaning to be not that Ireland was destitute of honour, conscience, and common sense, but that England was destitute of those qualities in dealing with Irish affairs. The real cause of the writer's indignation is the discovery in an unexpected connection that tyranny must be unjust, a rule which he only exemplifies in his attempt to conceal it.

The chief particular in which the Irish penal statutes differed from the English Popery law, passed three years before, and from which most was hoped, was the clause by which the estates of Catholics were to be equally divided among the children. The want of a provision to this effect rendered the English Act inoperative.[3]

The weakness of this bill for the transfer of land from Catholics to Protestants consisted in the humanity and virtues of the whole people. In an independent State an attempt to maintain a law that offends the conscience of the community must finally be surrendered. In a country situated as Ireland is, the attempt may be prolonged till the situation ceases, or the public virtue fails. English soldiers in the time of Elizabeth cut down the crops of the Irish peasants only when compelled. Policemen to-day are convulsed with grief as they enforce the atrocious law of eviction. The Protestants in Anne's time were not soldiers or policemen, and they refused to volunteer in ruining the fortunes, scattering the families, and breaking the hearts of their Catholic neighbours. The remainder of the reign was occupied in efforts to overcome their repugnance. A struggle commenced between social treachery and mistrust inculcated by Government, and the virtuous instincts of human nature. All the guiltless efforts at escape on the part of the sufferers, all the shrinkings of high-minded honour from the

[1] Froude's "English in Ireland," Vol. I., p. 277.
[2] Ibid, p. 306.
[3] Burnet's "History of his own Time," Vol. IV., p. 101.

revolting office to which the law tempted them, on the part of the Protestants, were carefully watched, weighed, and prevented. A few days after the Act passed, a resolution was unanimously come to by the Commons, that all magistrates who neglected to put it in execution were betrayers of their country's liberties. To nullify nature's disgust at treachery, it was resolved that informing against Papists was an honourable service. Denied the exercise of their religion and the practice of commerce, the people held fairs at their holy wells on the annual festivals of the patron saints to whom they were dedicated. Similar customs grew into great national institutions on the Continent. A fine of ten shillings, and in default of payment, the punishment of whipping, was imposed on every person who attended these meetings; and a fine of twenty pounds on everyone who should erect a booth for the sale of commodities at them. In 1708, a law was passed forbidding any Papist to serve on a jury, if a sufficient number of Protestants could be found, and giving the plaintiff or prosecutor in trials for offences charged on Papists, a peremptory right to challenge any Papist returned as a juror. In 1709, the Earl of Wharton was viceroy, with Addison as secretary. A bill was proposed and passed by which Papists were declared incapable of holding annuities for life; parents whose children conformed were compelled to discover the full value of their properties to the Chancellor, who was to make an order for the independent support of the converts, and on the parent's death, appoint for them such a share of the property as he might think fit; jointures were secured for Catholic wives who chose to desert their husbands; Papists were prohibited from teaching even as ushers to Protestant schoolmasters; and a graduated scale of prizes was offered for the discovery of Catholic archbishops, bishops, vicars-general, priests, and schoolmasters. In 1713 the Commons ordered that an address should be made to her Majesty to desire that she would be pleased not to grant licences to Papists who had gone abroad, to return into the kingdom. In the same year an order was made that the Sergeant-at-Arms should take into custody all Papists that should presume to come into the galleries of the House of Commons.

It was as Irishmen, not as Catholics, that the people were thus depressed and weakened. The Tory party leaned towards some of the tenets of Rome. There was real religious animosity in their persecution of the Nonconformists of the north, whose principles they hated. Ireland itself the landowners and manufacturers of England regarded as a Norman pirate used to regard the field of his forays. The savage delight of carrying off the peasant's scanty meal by violence was more tempting to them than the quiet acquisition of a larger booty. The owners of the vast estates which confiscation had accumulated were absentees. The lands were let to sub-tenants in manifold succession, each of whom naturally thought that he had as good a title to live at home in idleness, as the chief landlord had to live in a foreign country. The suppressors of commerce and manufactures reduced the products of the soil to the simplest form,—wool for the English market and potatoes for the labourer. All between these two was imported. Little or no corn was grown. When the potato crop failed there was always a famine. The whole country was being turned into pasturage for sheep. The average size of farms was nearly a thousand acres. Tillage was forbidden in the leases. In the beginning of the next reign the Irish Parliament sent the heads of a bill to England, in which the cultivation of a small proportion of each farm was made legal, and a trifling bounty on corn grown for exportation was recommended. The English manufacturers preferred that Ireland should grow wool for them, and the English farmers and landlords did not approve of bringing Irish corn to compete with their own, and the bill was in effect declined.[1]

Under the pressure of the penal laws the wealthier classes conformed. Those of them who did not were gradually beaten down to the lowest level. The loutish pride of the Cromwellians and adventurers held the place of honour. The truest men of Milesian and Norman descent, the pick and choice of the aristocracy of both countries, who were true to their religion and their sense of right, became labourers and mechanics, and mingled with the aboriginal people. They carried their Christianity with them—its form is a matter of minor importance—and as in the time of St. Patrick, the peasantry began to be the religious teachers and moral rulers of the nation. Through their priests, men of their own blood, they governed their bishops, who had no great laymen to fall back upon.

On the suppression of the woollen trade a tide of emigration set towards America, which ran undiminished for many years. Irishmen were foremost and most efficient among the founders of American independence. At a later time vaster floods of more strictly political emigrants have gone to occupy the fields which their fathers freed. Religion is the claim and the right to pronounce judgment on law and government. In an age when God's name is dwindling to an echo of man's voice from the clouds, when the authority of natural conscience is studiously killed, when arbitrary human government is the only standard of right, and is represented to the multitude only by the law's lowest officers, and when all educational influence is passing from men who strove to sway the powers and passions of the soul to men who know only of nerves and tissues, it seems a providential over-ruling of evil that the children of the penal time, with their instinctive religion and their indestructible love of justice, should remain and abound to reanimate the earth.

A distinction between Irish Protestants began to appear about this time. The old settlers were identified with the honour and welfare of the country, and held their estates without any feelings of uneasiness. The possessors of the lately confiscated lands threw all their terror of dispossession, all their pride in their upstart station, all their fanatical religion, and all their perverted zeal for liberty into political worship of King William.

The effect produced on character by laws that entered into all relations of life, and forced men to be magnanimous or mean can be easily conceived. A Catholic could not legally possess a horse worth more than five pounds. A Protestant walked up to a Catholic who rode a splendid horse on a racecourse, offered him five pounds, and arrogantly ordered him to dismount. The gentleman dismounted, drew out a pistol, and shot his horse through the brain.

[1] Froude's "English in Ireland," Vol. I., p. 398.

Another seized the bridle of the horse he wished to possess, and proffered the legal price. The rider felled the man to the earth. When brought before a magistrate his conduct was justified, because though the man might demand the sale of the horse, he had no right to take possession of the bridle.

The Parliament met again in 1697. The deficiencies of the revenue, and the need of strengthening the Protestant interest and encouraging Protestants to settle in the country, were brought before them. A grant of a hundred and fifty thousand pounds was made, and bills were passed forbidding the return of Irish exiles, and for the better suppression of ejected landowners and disbanded soldiers who had not left the country and were known as rapparees or tories.

No pandering to their fears, no gratification of their jealous animosities, sufficed to quench the instincts of independence in the Irish Parliament. A bill was passed in England relating to the oath of supremacy, expressly meant to have effect in Ireland. The Irish Parliament re-enacted it as if it were otherwise invalid, and repudiated the claim involved in the term "imperial crown of England" by using the expression "imperial crown of Ireland." In 1698 Molyneux, one of the members for the University, published a work on Ireland, in which he maintained the perfect and reciprocal independence of the two kingdoms. The English Commons declared this book to be dangerous to the subjection and dependence of Ireland on England, and ordered it to be burned by the common hangman.

The motives of all oppressors are identical when carried to the last analysis. The Irish Parliament reduced the Catholics under their power, and the English Parliament the Irish, in order to fill or save their coffers. William was constantly importuning his Parliament for grants of money to carry on his wars. In 1693 they had presented an address, requesting an enquiry into the manner in which the lately forfeited estates had been disposed of. The king evaded the request by a prorogation. They now by an unwarrantable encroachment on the province of the Irish Parliament appointed a commission to enquire how far the Irish forfeitures had been made available for the public service. The commissioners reported that some of those lands had been restored to Catholic proprietors, and others granted by the king to his personal friends. A grant of ninety-five thousand acres had been made to the Countess of Orkney. A bill of resumption easily passed the Lower House, and was sent attached to a money bill to the House of Lords, where it met with much opposition. It was finally carried, and unwillingly assented to by William. Those who had purchased any of the estates were left to recover their money in the best way they could. The lands were placed in the hands of trustees for sale, and though they were worth fifteen hundred thousand pounds they produced little more than a third of that sum. The proceeds were swallowed by the expenses. Petitions were presented against the proceedings of the trustees, but the Parliament declared them false and malicious.

The isolated supremacy of the Protestant party in Ireland, and their extrusion from all share in England's commercial prosperity, led them at this time to propose a union with England. It was not a union of the two nations that was contemplated, but a union between the Irish Protestant faction and the English House of Commons, whereby the former would give the latter a closer fellowship in their own ascendancy, and receive in return a share of their gains. The English Parliament were quite satisfied with the ascendancy they possessed, and had no desire to have a partner in their profits, so they rejected the proposal. Perhaps they preferred to superintend the suffocation of Irish Catholicism from a greater legislative distance.

SECTION V.

George I. came to the throne in 1714. Parliament became supreme in England, the Whigs in Parliament, and the territorial interest in the Whigs. Trade and manufactures flourished under a landlord Parliament by monopoly and continued encroachment on the rights of the rural population, and the value of land increased with the increasing wealth of trade. The people had as yet no voice to make heard. In Ireland the people were the Catholics, and the ruling class was united against them by the animosities of religion which supplied the lack of coalescing industrial interests. In the Parliament of 1715 the lords justices recommended in their speech to the Houses that they should advocate such unanimity among themselves as "at once to put an end to all other distinctions in Ireland but that of Protestant and Papist." The Catholics were described in the same speech as "the common enemy," and all who sympathised with them as "enemies of the Constitution."

Jonathan Swift, a churchman, who had filled an unofficial position of the highest importance in the party contests of England, but an Irishman by birth, and so, as he believed, excluded from all high preferment, was Dean of St. Patrick's. He was the intimate friend of the English statesmen who had intrigued for the restoration of the Stuarts, and was consequently supposed to be a partner in their plot. When he returned to Ireland, after the proclamation of the new monarch, he was hooted and pelted by the mob of Dublin, and his life was put in danger by an Irish nobleman, who attempted to ride him down on the public highway, and threatened him with a pistol. Burning with rage against the injustice which the misfortune of his birth brought upon him, and the defeat of his political friends had confirmed, despising the country on account of which he suffered, and incensed with the country which, while acknowledging his great abilities, refused to honour them in one born in Ireland, he threw himself into the ignoble struggle that flickered round him, and raised it by his genius to the magnitude of a national contest. He had no love for his country, and he never entertained, or at least expressed, the idea that the demands of justice applied to the persecuted Catholics. He assailed only secondary grievances, but as he mused the fire kindled, and the darkened heavens that covered the land like a dome were reddened by the glare of his rage. It may be that he acted on calculation when he kept the wrongs of the great majority of the nation out of sight. There are usurpations so monstrous that to seek their redress by direct appeal would be an insulting and exasperating exposure. There are sordid and interested hatreds so fixed that the tongues of men and angels inspired by love would provoke only a deadlier rancour against victim and advocate alike. Swift seemed to concur in the legal degradation of his Catholic countrymen. He knew that the penal laws were cruelly enforced, that the administrations of their clergy were denied to a stripped and starved people, that the chalice of mercy was dashed from the nation's dying lips. It did not seem to move him. He fell in with the political axioms of the day that the Protestants were the nation, and that the Catholics were exceptionally recognisable for exaction, but invisible and imponderable for mercy and justice. For it was a settled fiction of law that the Catholics were non-existent. Lord chancellors and chief justices pronounced from the bench that the law did not suppose such persons to exist as Irish Roman Catholics. Swift, in an address to the whole people of Ireland, speaks of the Papists in the third person. This, as has been said, may have been only prudence. A mountain of tyranny lay on the country, and he grappled with the nearest granite points that crushed into her vitals. But to understand the history of the country we must be aware of the fact that Swift reasoned with and counselled Protestants only, well knowing that all power and all responsibility was with them. His first pamphlet on Irish affairs, his Proposal for the use of Irish Manufacture, was written in 1720. In the previous year an appeal had been made from the High Court of Exchequer to the Irish House of Lords, and the decision of the former reversed. An appeal was made to the English Lords, who confirmed the original judgment, and an Act was passed by the English Parliament enacting and declaring that the King, Lords, and Commons of England had the right, full power, and authority to make laws to bind the people of Ireland, and that the Irish House of Lords had not any jurisdiction to affirm or reverse any sentence given in any court in that kingdom. Swift takes no direct notice of this enactment. He says that the landlords, that is, the Protestant landlords, were everywhere by penal clauses absolutely prohibiting their tenants from ploughing, one effect of which was already seen in the pro-digious dearness of corn, and the importation of it from London, as the cheaper market, and that those politic gentlemen of Ireland had depopulated vast tracts of the best land, for the feeding of sheep. He speaks of the smuggling of wool to France as if it were a perfectly legitimate trade, altogether sanctioned and established by the necessities of the case against the unjustifiable usurpations of England. "Our beneficial traffic of wool with France hath been our only support for several years past, furnishing us with all the little money we have to pay our rents and go to market." He expostulates with the country landlords who, by unreasonable screwing and racking their tenants all over the kingdom, had already reduced the miserable people to a worse condition than the peasants in France, or the vassals in Germany and Poland; so that the whole species of substantial farmers would in a few years be utterly at an end. It was pleasant, he says, to observe these gentlemen interfering with the bishops in the letting of their revenues, at the very instant that they were themselves letting their own land to the highest bidder upon short leases, and sacrificing their oldest tenants for a penny an acre advance. He makes it quite plain towards the end of the tract what class he addresses, what was their sin, and what was the cause that tempted it. "I know not how it comes to pass (and yet perhaps I know well enough) that slaves have a natural disposition to be tyrants, and that when my betters give me a kick, I am apt to revenge it with six upon my footman; although, perhaps, he may be an honest and diligent fellow." The Protestant rulers and landlords were slaves to England, and therefore they tyrannised in a sixfold degree on the Irish Catholics, who very probably were honest and industrious men. "Whoever travels," he adds, "this country, and observes the face of nature, or the faces and habits and dwellings of the natives, will hardly think himself in a land where law, religion, and common humanity are professed." The remedy he proposes is that the House of Commons should pass a resolution against wearing any cloth or stuff in their families which was not of home growth and manufacture; and in order to do this, to exclude all silks, velvets, calicoes, and other female fopperies; and that the ladies should be content with Irish stuffs for the furniture of their houses, for gowns and petticoats for themselves and their daughters. He mentions with approval a current observation that Ireland would never be happy until a law were made for burning everything that came from England, except their people and their coals, and goes on to say that as to the former he would not be sorry if they stayed at home, and as for the latter he hoped in a little time there would be no occasion for them.

The whole point and value of this tract depends on its close application to the class for whose instruction it was written. It was not written for the Catholics, because they were not the landlords of the country, nor did they compose the Parliament; nor was it written for the peasantry, because they did not use stuffs for their furniture, nor silks and velvets, nor staylaces, nor scarlet and gold lace. Swift meant to imply that the country was in the hands of the Protestant Parliament and landlords, and was ruined by their neglect. They were the men who, although they were slaves to England, had it in their power to deal mercifully with their tenants, and encourage home manufactures. Yet the interpretation and comment of Mr. Froude[1] is that the whole people of Ireland, and chiefly the peasantry, were altogether in fault, because they did not rise above repressive laws, and maintain a voluntary independence and prosperity by moral forces only. He commences by asserting that wherever any signs of good cultivation can be seen in the country it may be assumed that they are the work of English colonists. But the majority of them became reckless, and "the peasantry took to whiskey drinking and Whiteboyism." "Fettered with restrictions, robbed of her markets, blockaded round with prohibitions, he (Swift) saw that, if her people were worthy of her, Ireland might still be sufficient for herself, and, out of her own resources, might develope her own industry. England might lay a veto on every healthy effort of Parliamentary legislation; but England could not touch the self-made laws which the conscience and spirit of the nation might impose upon themselves. By their own energy the Irish might still, if they chose, rise superior to their miseries, and, by their success, inflict the bitterest humiliation on their

[1] "English in Ireland," Vol. I., p. 499.

tyrant. England might close their ports, reject their tillage bills, discourage the legislative efforts for the better management of their lands; but she could not prevent them from ploughing their own fields, wearing their own frieze jerkins, and buying and selling among themselves."[1] Swift did not write of the nation or the Irish, including the peasantry, when he recommended native industry. He referred only to the Protestant landlords and legislators. He knew well that the tenants could not possibly thrive without the consent of the landlords. He did not propose that they should give up silks and velvets for home stuffs. What he said of them was that they were rack rented, sacrificed for a penny advance in rent, and on the eve of annihilation. Yet Mr. Froude not only includes the whole nation in the responsibility, but throws the special onus on the tillers of the soil whom England could not prevent from "ploughing their own fields, wearing their own frieze jerkins." Why, Swift had just complained that they were prevented from ploughing their own fields, not by England, but by their Protestant landlords; and rack-rented to rags and starvation, not by England, but by their landlords, who were content to be slaves to England on the express condition that they were allowed to be tyrants to their miserable, suffering, and hopeless Catholic tenantry. Mr. Froude means to insinuate that the Irish peasantry of the present day might by industry and energy triumph over unfavourable conditions, just as the peasantry of Swift's day might have done. But it is perfectly clear, from Swift's own words, that the peasantry of his day could not possibly do anything of the kind; that the greater their energy, the greater the certainty of their being ejected from their farms; and that in fact they were sixfold more slaves to the landlords than the landlords were to England, if earth can contain a more abject slave than he who plays the tyrant by delegated power.

This habit of violently introducing the alleged vices of the peasantry to avert the blow of condemnation from the responsible classes, constantly appears through Mr. Froude's pages. Its exposure is all that is required to render his history a most valuable one. With a sensitiveness for which every allowance must be made, he recoils from striking the guilty, and as his anger is so great that he must strike somewhere, he strikes the innocent. Looking on the miscreations of Ireland, magnified by his remorse, he says in his heart that England's adverse legislation has the power of a curse, and that his country may create evil for her glory. England's truest sons and best friends repudiate such a glory, and deny such a power. In a previous chapter he distinctly and justly distributes the blame of Irish misgovernment. "This responsibility for the mismanagement of Ireland must be divided equally between England and the Irish colony. With a perversity of misunderstanding, whatever salutary measure England recommended the Irish Parliament thwarted. When the Irish Parliament saw their way clearly, England was wilfully blind, or deliberately cruel."[2] After the responsibility had been thus equally divided and exhausted one would suppose the matter was at an end. But, no; "The Irish peasant was indolent." The so-called indolence of the peasant, which was merely his standing wearily in the

[1] Froude's "English in Ireland," Vol. I., p. 500.
[2] "English in Ireland," Vol. I., p. 393.

market place till somebody hired him, is thus at one time treated as an ancestral vice, and at another as a dependent consequence, until the confusion runs into the flattest of self contradictions. "They grew up in compulsory idleness, encouraged once more in their inherited dislike of labour." If they disliked labour, their idleness could not be compulsory. There is no less indolent a being on earth than an Irish peasant. His only utterance through cycles of misrule is a prayer that he may be permitted to labour. His only request now is that he may have something to labour on, that will prove his labour by its fruits. He does not like to spend his life winding a prison crank, or turning a treadmill for victims with whom he may at any moment be called to change places. He never settles into a contented tramp. When he goes to a climate where the blossom labour is the joyous prelude to the fruit reward, on the instant, like Aaron's rod in the tabernacle of witness, he brings forth buds, and blooms blossoms, and yields almonds. When men from other lands where industry is encouraged settle in Ireland, where industry is always discouraged, they cannot compete with the love of labour that has never slumbered in the native peasant's arm. In the beginning of the eighteenth century several small colonies of German and French Protestants were brought over by a few landlords, aided by government grants. Sixty years after, Arthur Young describes their settlements. "They had houses built for them; plots of land assigned to each at a rent of favour, were assisted in stock, and all of them with leases for lives from the head landlord. The poor Irish are very rarely treated in this manner; when they are they work much greater improvements than common among these Germans." The Irishman's love of labour is so intense, he strikes his spade so deep into the soil, he seems so much at home in his work, and surrounds himself with such evidence of his power to replenish the earth and subdue it, that he is a challenge and a terror to the man who claims his farm and the heavens above it as his exclusive property.

But is it true that a people can defy prohibitive laws, and flourish in spite of enactments made expressly to prevent them from flourishing? Can prosperity be smuggled like wool or brandy? If so, what is the use of governments? And if a bad government may be ignored as unable to do evil, a just government may still more be dispensed with as needless to do good. Such is the conclusion which the logical desperation of the advocacy of injustice suggests. It suggests this, or the alternative conclusion that England's impatience of bad laws, her desire for good laws, her watchful struggles for religious freedom, her fight for reform, have been all useless labour, since her greatness might have been achieved by the self made laws of conscience. Such is the lesson that is taught to Englishmen by the defenders of mis-government in Ireland.

An address to the Roman Catholic clergy of Ireland was sent forth by Bishop Berkley in 1749.[1] It abounds with the harshest censures and the most contemptuous invectives against the "aborigines" of Ireland. We are reminded as we read it of the "Hibernionaces" of St. Patrick's time and the "conquest-privileged Scoti."[2] The bishop throws all the

[1] "A Word to the Wise." Berkeley's Works, Vol. III., p. 437.
[2] See p. 17.

blame of the woes that devastated the country on the indigenous indolence of the natives. This most amiable and virtuous of men has furnished a pretext by the authority of his name, for unlimited prejudice and injustice. With scarcely needed caution he commences with a proviso that "whatever is said must be so taken as not to reflect on persons of rank and education," or on the inhabitants of the northern parts of the kingdom. The Irish were driven out of their homes and reduced from rank and wealth to penury, and Berkeley rebukes them for not dwelling contentedly in their cabins, and for not instantly conforming in spirit to their altered circumstances. He ascribes their wandering propensities to their Scythian descent, and their pride to their Spanish descent. He introduces a saying of negroes in the English plantations that if "negro was not negro Irishman would be negro." The negroes had seen youths and maidens kidnapped and torn from Ireland, as they themselves had been kidnapped and torn from Africa, and treated as they were treated, and they found a kind of comfort in the reflection that their wrongs were not attributable to their colour, since if black men did not exist there were white men whom their white masters would capture and chain and flog. It was no doubt concealed from them that Englishmen were enslaved[1] indiscriminately with Irishmen, or they might have given a keener point to their proverb by carrying it a step farther.[2] Berkeley applied the saying that denoted the cannibal omnivorousness of the slave owner, to the abject condition of the slave; as if the negro would assert his own abjectness. Mr. Froude represents the saying of the plantations as "the world's bye-word."[3] There was not a court, an army, or a university in the world except in England, Ireland, and the plantations, where the name of Irishman was not held in honour. Berkeley calls on the Catholic clergy to rouse their people from sloth in return for "the lenity and indulgence of the government." "There is small encouragement, say you, for them to build upon another's land, wherein they have only a temporary interest. To which I answer that life itself is but temporary." Life is short, and therefore the Irish tenant should employ each shining hour in gathering honey for his master, in order to hasten the stifling termination of his toils. "It will be said, the hardness of the landlord crushes the industry of the tenant. But if rent be high, and the landlord rigorous, there is the more need of industry in the tenant." Such are the Bishop's arguments and incentives to industry. He was one of those who maintained that absolute unlimited non-resistance, or passive obedience, was due to the supreme civil power wherever placed in any nation. Human laws must be allowed to produce ruin or misery, because God does not change his laws, although they produce plague, famine, inundations, and earthquakes.[4] This view he either published on behalf of the Hanover line, or if he meant it in support of the Stuarts, he accepted a bishopric from their supplanters. It is hard to have to call Berkeley a time-server, but it would be harder still to call his time-service truth.

---

[1] See Macaulay, Vol. I., p. 645.
[2] Carte's "Collection of Letters," Vol. I., p. 177.
[3] Froude's "English in Ireland," Vol. I., p. 508.
[4] "Works," Vol. III., p. 167.

His amiability was confined to his class, and his virtue took the lower range of censuring the defensive vices of the slave, and not the higher one of condemning the aggressive vices of the tyrant. He took exactly the opposite course to that of his Master. And yet in one softly whispered sentence he refutes and recalls all his charges. "If the same gentle spirit of sloth did not soothe our squires as well as peasants, one would imagine there should be no idle hands among us." The whole truth is here told, but it is muffled to a lullaby. Laziness, for which no epithet is savage, no description disgusting, enough, when it haunts the beggared Irishman, is transformed into an ethereal spirit when it floats with moveless pinion over "our squires." The sentence is pronounced on one side, the punishment is inflicted on the other. Unhappily men are more impressed by the penalty than by the guilt.

Civilised and advancing countries differ from ignorant and stationary ones, mainly in the refusal of the subject classes to bend before increasing exaction, and to toil the harder in proportion to the ever-increasing burthen laid on them. Where labourers accept the will of their lords as final and unquestionable, neither lord nor labourer has any margin for progress. Turkish or Chinese stagnation is the result. There are two natural methods by which opposition may be made to the perpetual absorption by landlords and others of the increasing productiveness of toil—active resistance and idleness. The idleness of the people of which Berkeley complained was the single obstacle to the eternal and irredeemable degradation of the whole of the upper and middle classes. In England the same conditions had long existed. The peasant first resisted the Normans by assassination. He afterwards resisted by sturdy beggary. He now resists by organised strikes. When Berkeley wrote the cost of relieving the poor in England was more than half a million : when the century closed it was over four millions.

Section VI.

In 1723 an occasion offered that called forth and permitted the full exercise of Swift's power. The country had been for some time inconvenienced by a scarcity of copper coin, and applications to England for liberty to supply the want by a fresh coinage were unsuccessful. An Englishman named Wood proposed to contract for the coinage of a hundred and eight thousand pounds worth of halfpennies and farthings, and by the assistance of the Duchess of Kendall, his proposal was accepted. The two houses voted addresses to the Crown charging the patentee with fraud, and complaining that the circulation of the debased coin would be highly prejudicial to the revenue and commerce of the country. The entire current money of the kingdom amounted at that time to four hundred thousand pounds. The proportion of copper to gold and silver would be so great that the former would enter into all payments, and displace the latter, while the baseness of the metal rendered it easy and cheap to be counterfeited. Swift snatched at the opportunity, and making Wood's halfpence the symbol of the authority from which they emanated, insisted that they were about to cause the country's ruin.

He wrote a series of letters known as Drapier's Letters, from the signature which they bore, in one of which he solemnly declares that he will suffer the most ignominious death rather than submit to receive those coins, unless they be forced on him by the law of his own country. In another he boldly states that this was a grievance beyond the power of the English minister to redress, that the remedy was in their own hands, and that they are and ought to be as free a people as their brethren in England. Throughout the controversy he carefully avoids making common cause with the Catholics. He expressly disowns their co-operation. Yet he immediately became the most popular man in Ireland, and the authorities as speedily saw in his popularity a tendency to a reconciliation of Catholics and Protestants. Warnings were sent to England that intimacies were springing up between Jacobites and Whigs, who before had no correspondence with each other, and Swift, who for some time had been subjected to the spy system, was watched with stricter espionage during a visit which he paid to England about this time. A cry arose against the Catholics: a number of resolutions against evasions of the penal laws, and a bill rendering priests liable to castration, were passed. The English Parliament rejected this bill on the remonstrance, it is said, of some great foreign ecclesiastics.

On the accession of George II., Catholics either feeling the incipient stirrings of civil life, or remembering the consequences of their neglect in the commencement of Queen Anne's reign, presented a humble congratulatory address testifying their unalterable loyalty. Its receipt was not acknowledged, nor was it ever known whether it reached its destination. This faint symptom of vitality, added to the threatened union of the Catholics with the Parliamentary party who asserted the rights of the country, roused the fears of Government. A bill was rapidly passed through both Houses and received the royal assent, enacting that no Papist should be admitted to vote at the elections of members of parliament, or at the elections of magistrates for cities or corporate towns.

The Earl of Clanrickarde, who had conformed in the reign of Queen Anne, petitioned for the restoration of his estates, and was graciously heard by the king. The friends of the English interest in the Commons voted an address to his Majesty, in which they assured him that they would be always ready to defend his right to the crown with their lives and fortunes, which nothing could enable them so effectually to do as the enjoyment of those estates which had been the forfeitures of the rebellious Irish Papists, and were now in the possession of the Protestant subjects of the kingdom. The force of so significant a remonstrance was felt, and the king assured the Commons that he would for the future discourage all such applications. Soon after a similar claim was made by Lord Clancarty, and was similarly defeated. The loyalty of the Protestants was given on the stipulation that they were allowed to retain the estates of the Catholics. In 1727 certain Catholics applied to the king for the reversion of outlawries which reduced them to beggary. In preparing the documents putting forth their claims, legal assistance had necessarily been employed. A bill was sent to England, and in 1734 was passed into law, that no one should practise as a solicitor who had not been a Protestant from his fourteenth year, or unless he had been five years articled to some clerk in Chancery in England or Ireland.[1]

The deeper and more established was the depression of the Catholics the better use could Swift make of them in his ambiguous style of reasoning. The dissenters petitioned for some relief from the disabilities to which they had voluntarily submitted rather than embarrass the Government in its measures against the Catholics. Swift assuming the prostration of the Catholics to be as much an immutable principle in English government as the author of the Analogy assumes the laws of natural religion to be in the divine government, conclusively showed that there was not a single plea that could be put forward on behalf of dissenters which could not be urged with far greater force on behalf of Catholics. Several Catholic writers have supposed that he was seriously arguing on their side. There is no doubt about his meaning when he describes the actual condition of the country. The wanton destruction of timber, making the sites of ancient forests bare and desolate; the exorbitant raising of rents in proportion to the improvements made on the lands, reducing the tenants to the condition of slaves; the prevalence of absenteeism; the turning of large tracts of country into sheep pastures, were all exposed by him with bitterest condemnation. In 1729 he wrote a Modest Proposal for relieving the miseries of the poor, by disposing of their children, and taking them off their hands. He calculated the number of the children of poor parents, and asks how they are to be reared and provided for. "We cannot employ them in handicraft or agriculture," he says, "since building houses in the country, or cultivating land, was a thing not practised." He proposes, therefore, that a hundred thousand of them should be offered for sale to persons of quality and fortune throughout the kingdom to be killed, cooked and eaten. He grants that this food will be somewhat dear, but it will be on that account the more fit for landlords, who, as they have already devoured most of the parents, seem to have the best title to the children. As to the aged, diseased, or maimed, there was no need for uneasiness, because it was well known that they were every day dying and rotting by cold and famine, and filth and vermin; while the young labourers could not get work, and consequently were pining away for want of nourishment to such a degree that if they were accidentally hired to common labour they had not strength to perform it. The advantages of the measure he proposed are, he says, obvious. The number of Papists who stay at home to help the Pretender while so many good Protestants leave the country will be greatly lessened, and the poorer tenants will have something valuable of their own, which by law may be made liable to a distress, and help to pay their landlord's rent, their corn and cattle being already seized, and money a thing unknown.[2] In anticipation of objections he observes that his remedy is calculated for the one individual kingdom of Ireland, and for no other that ever was, is, or can be, upon earth. Therefore, he says, let no one talk to me of other expedients, of taxing our absentees at five shillings a pound; of using neither clothes nor household furniture,

---
[1] Froude's "English in Ireland," Vol. I., p. 577.

[2] See Arthur Young's "Tour in Ireland," Vol. I., p. 68.

except what is of our own growth and manufacture; of utterly rejecting the materials and instruments that promote foreign luxury; of curing the expensiveness of pride, vanity, idleness, and gambling in our women, and of introducing a vein of parsimony, prudence, and temperance; of learning to love our country, in the want of which we differ even from the Laplanders and the inhabitants of Topinamboo; of quieting our animosities and factions, nor acting like the Jews, who were murdering one another at the very moment their city was taken; of being a little cautious not to sell our country and consciences for nothing; of teaching landlords to have at least one degree of mercy towards their tenants; lastly, of putting a spirit of honesty, industry, and skill into our shopkeepers, who, if a resolution could now be taken to buy only our native goods, would immediately unite to cheat and exact upon us in the price, the measure, and the goodness. The design of the treatise is shown in the enumeration of those expedients, among which, it may be observed, the increased laboriousness of the peasantry has no place. They furnish the only alternative to his present proposal. He concludes by requesting those politicians who dislike his overture to ask the parents of beggars by profession, and the farmers, cottagers, and labourers who are beggars in fact, whether they would not, at this day, think it a greater happiness to have been sold for food at a year old, and thereby have avoided such a perpetual scene of misfortunes as they have since gone through, by the oppressions of landlords, the impossibility of paying rent without money or trade, the want of common sustenance, with neither house nor clothes to cover them from the inclemency of the weather, and the most inevitable prospect of entailing the like or greater miseries upon their breed for ever.

The opposition of Swift compelled the cancelling of Wood's patent. A victory was won over England, but of more moment than the victory was the tendency to union between Catholics and Protestants, and the bolder spirit of independence that had been developed in the course of the contest. The dawn of a policy of a separate and corrupting conciliation of Protestants and Catholics by England may soon be perceived.

SECTION VII.

Three distinct threads of struggle may be discerned appearing and reappearing in the confusion of Irish affairs. The peasants were clinging desperately to the land for their lives. The educated Catholics were seeking for relief and a recognised place in the constitution of their country. The Protestant Parliament was growing towards independence. The Parliament gained its special object in 1782, sold it in 1800, and left the larger quest of freedom to mingle with the strife of the peasants and the claims of the Catholics. The latter won the principle of their religious liberty in 1829, and carried it to complete success in 1869. The struggle of the peasants still continues.

The land monopoly had now for some time been drawing lines of defence around its original violent occupation. From the time of the Norman invasion of England it had obstructed the discussion of its claims by the invention of a barbarous jargon, the knowledge of which was declared to be indispensable to the proper comprehension of its merits. Whoever strove to master it lost all comprehension of the real subject, and was only introduced into a labyrinth of legal subtleties and counterfeit rights. He entered into a dark cavern, in whose intricacies he went astray, and growing accustomed to the artificial light, which shone brighter in his eyes as he forgot the light of heaven, he became the slave of the darkness which he hoped to dissipate. We have seen how the landlords of England, in the reigns of Henry VIII. and Edward VI., made themselves exclusive owners of the soil, by a short and summary process, undelayed by the endless tortuosities without which the reversal or modification of the procedure is now said to be wholly impossible. Having seized the right to exact whatever sums of money they pleased for the use of lands in the production of the food of the country, from the toilers who had been the true owners, they got rid of their own obligations to the Crown in the reign of Charles II., by paying in lieu of them a grant of one hundred thousand pounds, which was to come not out of their own purses, but from the general excise. In the reign of Queen Anne they passed a law enacting that no person should be deemed qualified to represent a county in Parliament unless he possessed an estate of six hundred pounds a year, or a borough, unless he possessed a qualification of half that sum. The design of this bill was to exclude traders from the House of Commons, and to lodge the legislative power with landowners only. They thus got possession of the land, and of the only authority by which that possession could be affected.

In Ireland the Protestants got the land into their hands through confiscations and the treacherous violation of the Treaty of Limerick. They introduced the English land laws, with their unlimited power over the tenant, and their all but nominal evasion of the dues of landlords to the Crown. They guarded themselves in their unjust tenure by passing penal laws, which rendered the Catholics legally incapable of transmitting or acquiring estates. When the Catholics endeavoured through the justice of the monarch to obtain the revision of outlawries, and employed lawyers of their own persuasion to prepare the necessary papers, the Commons, by laws of continuously increasing severity, forbade Catholics to practise as lawyers. Men were still found to struggle for their properties. Eighty-seven suits were commenced for the recovery of lands unjustly confiscated. The Commons passed a resolution denouncing all those proceedings as a disturbance of the common weal, and declaring all who instituted such suits, or acted in them as lawyer or solicitor, to be public enemies. Such were the methods by which the sanctity of the rights of landlords was created.

Yet if the land question be regarded apart from the intentional obscuration of lawyers, its natural rights are as simple as those of the Christian to worship his God in freedom, or of a nation to be governed by its own laws. Whenever there has been a relaxation of the powers of government in England or Ireland there has not been what is commonly understood by anarchy, or spoliation of other men's goods. The characteristic resort has been to the quiet tilling of a piece of land which the cultivator considered his own, with an instinct like that of the child who plants a flower in a border and calls it his garden. To plant and sow comes next to the right to breathe. They who deny the right of men to till the soil of England or Ireland also formally and practically deny their right to breathe the air of England or Ireland. They bid them to go and breathe in some other part of the universe. Swift's straightforward common sense, though he spoke in words of savage irony, saw right through the unnatural claims of landlords, as through empty space, when he beheld the people dying of want. Title deeds did not obstruct his vision. Bishop Berkeley, when he put his views in the form of queries, had no difficulty in discerning the causes that desolated his country with famine and pestilence. He asks whether there be upon earth any Christian or civilised people so beggarly, wretched, and destitute as the common Irish? Whether, nevertheless, there is any other people whose wants may more easily be supplied from home? Whether, if there was a wall of brass a thousand cubits high round this kingdom, our natives might not nevertheless (he meant therefore) live cleanly and comfortably, till the land and reap the fruits of it? Whether a foreigner could imagine that one half of the people were starving, in a country which sent out such plenty of provisions? Whether it is possible the country should be well improved while our beef is exported and our labourers live upon potatoes? Whether trade be not then on a right footing when foreign commodities are imported only in exchange for domestic superfluities? Whether the quantities of beef, butter, wool, and leather exported from this island can be reckoned the superfluities of a country, where there are so many natives naked and famished? Whether a great quantity of sheep walks be not ruinous to a country, rendering it waste and thinly inhabited? Whether the creating of wants be not the likeliest way to produce industry in a people? And whether, if our peasants were accustomed to eat beef and wear shirts, they would not be more industrious?[1]

Neither Berkeley nor Swift held Socialistic views—they only knew that land was intended by Providence for the production of food, and not for the mere production of rent; and they saw that when rent reached its highest point the true use of the land was most completely and iniquitously frustrated. The whole body of tenant farmers felt these same convictions, not as speculative opinions to be disguised in figures of speech, but as the voice of reason and manhood bidding them seek a remedy or perish. They sought a remedy, and are still seeking it. An English tourist, writing in 1775, describes the landlord and tenant system as it then existed: "The landlord of an Irish estate, inhabited by Roman Catholics, was a sort of despot who yielded obedience in whatever concerned the poor to no law but that of his own will. A long series of oppressions, aided by very many ill judged laws, had brought landlords into a habit of exacting a very lofty superiority, and their vassals into that of an almost unlimited submission: speaking a language that was despised, professing a religion that was abhorred, and being disarmed, the poor found themselves in many cases slaves even in the bosom of written liberty. A landlord in Ireland could scarcely invent an order which a servant, labourer, or cottar dared refuse to execute. Disrespect of any kind he might punish with his

[1] "The Querist." Berkeley's "Works," Vol. III., p. 355.

cane or horsewhip with the most perfect security." The writer then gives an instance of landlord exaction scarcely reproducible on the modern page, though by no means without parallel in modern practice, and adds that he had heard "cases of the lives of the people being made free with without any apprehension of the justice of a jury."[1] This account carries us back to the condition of Ireland under Turgesius the Dane.[2] We see an invasion of barbarism, and the landlord and tenant system, as introduced into and maintained in Ireland by England, produce exactly the same effects. Landlordism, in fact, is the prolonged and organised sack and pillage of conquest. It always, because of its absolute power, exceeds and cannot but exceed detailed compact, and so far as it does so it carries the tenant outside the regions of law to meet with it man to man. This is the result of all England's efforts to get Ireland into her power. This is the end that justifies murder, and famine, and falsehood; the violation of treaties, and the prostitution of laws.

Yet Mr. Young, while exposing the abuses of landlordism, never seems to think that the system itself needed any amendment. In his preface he condemns monopoly in commerce as tending to reduce Europe to beggary; but with Ireland worse than beggared under his eyes, it never seemed to occur to him that almost every evil he saw was directly or indirectly traceable to monopoly in land. When he expressed his surprise at the severity of the Popery laws to Chief Baron Forster, he was informed that though severe in the letter they were seldom executed. This statement brought to his mind Burke's admirable expression in the House of Commons that connivance is the relaxation of slavery, not the definition of liberty. Yet in the same page he quotes with approval an opinion of the Chief Baron that the raising of rents universally quickened the industry of tenants, but that if carried too far it deadened instead of animating it, without perceiving that good or prudent landlordism as it existed in Ireland is liable to the very same objection as the mild administration of the Popery laws. It holds the slave with an easier grasp, but keeps him still a slave, dependent on change of mind and change of master.

A cattle epidemic had exorbitantly raised the prices of beef, cheese, and butter in England. The law forbidding the importation of Irish cattle was suspended for five years (1758). The landlords having absolute disposal of the agricultural customs, turned whole baronies into grazing lands, bringing total ruin on tenants and labourers. At the same time financial distress, caused by the drainage of the country's revenues to meet increased military expenses, paralysed trade, and acting with the laws which forbade Catholics to exercise any lucrative industry in corporate towns, rendered the people more and more dependent on agriculture. Pasture land had been exempted from tythes, by a resolution of the Commons in 1735, and the greater part of the burthen was thrown on the tillers of the soil and their scanty potato fields. The exactions of the tythe proctors, persons who farmed the tythes of the parish rectors, grew more searching and more cruel in proportion as the narrow resources of the people grew narrower. A

[1] Young's "Tour in Ireland," Part II., p. 40. [2] See p. 31.

remnant of the ancient tribe ownership of the land survived in the form of right of commonage, which the tenants enjoyed as some alleviation of the extreme severity of their rents. The landlords now began to enclose the commons. All these causes combined to drive the tenants to resistance. The enclosure of commons afforded an object of attack. In Waterford, Cork, and Tipperary the sufferers assembled in crowds and levelled the fences. They soon formed themselves into societies, bound themselves to each other by secret oaths, extended their opposition to tythes and excessive rents, made their excursions by night, and, from the dresses they wore on those occasions, became known as Whiteboys.

The Whiteboy disorders were represented and treated by the Government as a Popish rebellion, fomented by France, and aiming at the restoration of the Pretender. Here the testimony of Mr. Young may be taken as conclusive. He states that he made many inquiries into the origin of these disturbances, and found that no such thing as levellers or Whiteboys can be heard of till 1760, which was long after any French expedition was contemplated; that no foreign coins or arms of foreign construction were ever seen among them; that they began their work in Tipperary by pulling down fences of enclosures of commons, and were first known by the name of levellers. They afterwards set up to be general redressers of grievances, punished all obnoxious persons who advanced the value of land, or hired farms over their heads, and were guilty of many acts of violence and cruelty. From other sources we learn that these tumults were connived at by several Protestant landlords, who looked on tythes as a diminution of their rents, and, disgusted with the manner in which Church affairs were administered, were glad to see public odium transferred from themselves to the clergy. The Whiteboys declared themselves to be followers of Captain Right. Five of those unhappy men were executed in 1762 for having been present at the burning of a cabin, on the information of an associate, himself the very person who applied the fire. They all, immediately before the execution, publicly called God to witness that in all those disturbances it had never entered their thoughts to do anything against the Government.

Religious parties or factions are not what their names express, or their origin suggests, but what the rival party that oppresses them, or is oppressed by them, causes them to be. Catholicism has an avowedly human side that links itself to political institutions. Protestantism is wholly spiritual, and whenever it looks up to an earthly patron or leader, it can scarcely distinguish him from its god. The Protestantism of Ireland has in the main been that which is implied and exemplified in the later title, Orangeism. As the Catholicism of Ireland is not to be judged by the Catholicism of other countries, so the Protestantism of other countries is not to be judged by the Protestantism of Ireland. The men who claimed to hold the orthodox faith had robbed the Papists, and to hide or excuse the robbery wished that the quarrel should be regarded as a religious quarrel, and their supremacy only as a religious supremacy. The actual condition of affairs was now revealing itself as legalised plunder effected through the merciless abuse of a falsely gained advantage. The Protestant Parliament and local magistrates were determined that this revelation should not proceed. They must make an agrarian discontent appear to be a Popish treason. Any person who took the part of the enslaved tenant must be branded as disloyal.

The Reverend Nicholas Sheehy was the parish priest of Clogheen, a village in Tipperary. When he saw his parishioners weighed down by rents and tythes, and an arbitrarily appointed tax of five shillings for every marriage celebrated by a priest, and deprived of their right of commonage, his heart was troubled for them. He publicly denounced the imposts that left them without the means of subsistence. He became from that moment a marked man. A special commission was appointed for the trial of some Whiteboy prisoners, and was presided over by Sir Richard Acton, the lord chief justice. The proceedings were conducted with strict impartiality. The magistrates and grand jury raised such a clamour against the excellent judge that he was forced to leave the Irish bench and accept an inferior appointment in England. A military force fixed its head quarters at Clogheen and killed great numbers of the insurgents, as they were called, in the neighbourhood. A half-witted man named Bridge was arrested, and under examination by torture charged several respectable persons, including Father Sheehy, with being present at a nocturnal meeting of the Whiteboys. The priest was taken into custody, but was liberated for want of sufficient evidence against him. Bridge disappeared, the rumour went abroad that he was murdered, and though his body was never found, the grand jury offered a reward of fifty pounds for the discovery of any person concerned in the murder. The priest was continually menaced with prosecution, until at last in apprehension of being taken, and despair of a fair trial, he hid himself. A proclamation was issued charging him with high treason, and five hundred pounds were offered for his apprehension. He immediately declared his desire to give himself up on condition that he should be tried, not at Clonmel, but at Dublin. His terms were accepted, and he surrendered himself to a Protestant gentleman named O'Callaghan. Mr. O'Callaghan did not treat him with sufficient severity, and he and Lord James Cahir, a partner in his lenient conduct, were denounced as suspected persons, and forced to fly from the country to save their lives. The priest was tried for treason at Dublin and acquitted. He was then taken to Clonmel, tried for the murder on the evidence of the same witnesses who had sworn against him at Dublin, found guilty, hanged, drawn and quartered. He died declaring his innocence. During his trial a Mr. Keating, a man of property and credit, gave evidence that the prisoner had lain in his house the whole of the night of the supposed murder. The Rev. Mr. Hewitson, a magistrate, rose up and informed the court that he had Mr. Keating's name on his list as one of those concerned in another murder. His evidence was thus rendered useless. He was immediately hurried off to Kilkenny gaol, and after lying some time in a loathsome dungeon, loaded with irons, was tried, sworn against by the same witnesses who gave evidence on Sheehy's trial, and acquitted.

Q

The priest's declaration of his innocence raised a doubt as to the correctness of the conclusion which the Protestant faction wished to establish. It was also a kind of moral triumph, the last consolation that remains to the victim of criminal power. Three Catholic gentlemen were taken up and arraigned at Kilkenny for the murder of a soldier. The evidence broke down; on which they were sent to Clonmel, charged with being concerned in the murder of Bridge, and convicted on the testimony of the witnesses who had failed to obtain credit at Kilkenny. Previous to their execution they were visited by the Rev. Mr. Hewitson, another clergyman, and an emissary from the grand jury, who offered them pardon on condition that they made useful discoveries, implicating men of weight and fortune, of an intended rebellion and massacre, aided by the French, and especially if they swore that the priest had died with a lie on his lips. They all indignantly refused. They were young men in the prime of life, in prosperous circumstances, moving in good society, husbands and fathers. The wife of one of them hurried to the Viceroy to beg for mercy, but the faction had been first in the field, and threatened a social revolt unless the executions took place. The distracted wife flew back to her husband, but found that he had left the gaol on his long pilgrimage to the place of execution, a distance of ten or twelve miles. She overtook the melancholy procession, burst in the phrensy of agonised love through the ranks of soldiers, and threw herself on her husband's bosom. On the scaffold the three men solemnly declared their innocence of any participation in the murder or the proceedings of the Whiteboys.

The ordinary liar or murderer for the most part risks his fate on one attempt. Privileged liars and murderers aim at success by constant repetition. Successive batches of fresh prisoners were brought to trial on the same charge. The characters of the witnesses were seen in the light of truth from the lips of dying men, and convictions could not be obtained. Still the ascendancy party could not desist from their purpose of attaching a false origin to the popular discontent. Several gentlemen of high social position were accused of treason and aiding the Whiteboys. One of the witnesses, who had given evidence in all the former trials, was seen while being led by the most active of the magistrates to a door in front of the dock in order that she might be able to identify some of the prisoners whom she had never seen before. A friend of the persons thus indicated sent them word of what had taken place, and advised them to exchange their coats. They did so, and the witness singled out the wrong persons, which led to their being all acquitted: not however without open denunciations and secret threats against the judges from the baffled faction. Once again they returned to the charge. In September, 1767, seven persons were tried for high treason. The chief witness in the former trials gave evidence differing from what he had already sworn, and the judge ordered an acquittal. One mode of falsification still remained. The Tipperary grand jury passed complimentary resolutions to the magistrates for their spirit and good conduct. The grand jury of Dublin also presented them with their thanks, and stated their conviction that those late riots in the south were fomented as well by foreigners as by domestic enemies of our happy constitution in church and state, in order to overthrow the same. The magistrates, in reply, heartily concurred in the opinion that the troubles in the southern districts were not owing to pretended grievances, but to a settled intention of overthrowing our present happy constitution in church and state.[1]

If any extrinsic proof were required that these Whiteboy disturbances had no political motive, it would be found in the fact that similar outbreaks occurred among the Protestants of the North, whose loyalty to the Government was never questioned. The Oakboys rose against the Road Act, which threw the burthen of making roads that benefited only the landed proprietors on the poorer ratepayers. The Act was altered and peace was restored. The Steelboys were chiefly the ejected tenants of Lord Donegal, an absentee landlord, who, when his leases expired, let his lands to two or three rich merchants of Belfast, on the payment of large fines, and thereby depopulated a vast district. Other landlords were in the habit of advertising their farms in the newspapers, and letting them, with the confiscated improvements of the previous occupants, to the highest bidder. The peasantry banded together, and imitated the practices of the Whiteboys. Several of them were tried on the scene of their transgressions and acquitted. An Act was passed for the removal of the trials to Dublin, where acquittals were again recorded. Tranquillity was produced by the repeal of the Act, and the emigration of large numbers of the evicted tenantry to America. The successful competitors for the advertised lands were most commonly Catholics. The rivalry thus fomented was pregnant with future mischief.

Mr. Froude's version of Father Sheehy's story is marked by his habitual misapplication of guilt. In one sentence he speaks of the unchangeableness of the Irish disposition;[2] in the next he says that had the English treated the Irish as human beings their prejudices would have given way. By the unchangeableness of the Irish disposition, therefore, he means the unchangeableness of Norman tyranny. He does what three Catholic gentlemen died rather than do. He charges Sheehy with having died with a lie on his lips, that he might leave a stain on the law which condemned him.[3] He says. the same thing of another priest of a later date.[4] The simple fact is that Mr. Froude is so blinded by his anger that he cannot appreciate the motives of Christian men in their dying moments. He only feels that no retaliation whatever would have been unnatural or undeserved in their circumstances. The terrible charge which he makes is really levelled against an infamous system of misgovernment. Sheehy, he says. kept the oath of secrecy which he had sworn as a Whiteboy. But the question at issue is whether he was a Whiteboy. The writer assumes the man's guilt in order to prove it. He grows coarse and vindictive in his remorse. "Father Sheehy," he says, "was as deep a criminal as ever swung from a crossbeam." But we now know the true application of Mr. Froude's anger.

[1] Madden's "United Irishman," Vol. I., p. 87.
[2] "English in Ireland," Vol. II., p. 19.
[3] *Ibid*, p. 31.
[4] *Ibid*, Vol. III., p. 321.

SECTION VIII.

It is not considered to be within the historian's province to pronounce an opinion on the credibility of the religions that come under his notice, or the sincerity of their professors. The truth of Christianity, as compared with other religions, is a conventional understanding between writers and readers in Christian countries. But while the truth of Christianity is nominally admitted, its falsehood is practically assumed, and it is never expected of rulers to act according to its laws. The history of Ireland cannot be understood unless we suffer the light of an immortal hope to shine on its pages, and judge the representatives of the rival churches, if not by the soundness of their creeds, at least by the comparative appearances of sincerity which they exhibit. Christ declared that the success of His Church depended on the display in its individual members of courage and steadfastness, as exemplified in the character of St. Peter. The Church that builds itself on those qualities, without perfect orthodoxy, is more sincere, and more likely to endure than the Church that trusts to its orthodoxy without them. A nation that was destined to pass through the most pitiless storm of persecution that ever beat on the souls of men could not find an example more suitable for their contemplation than that of the Apostle, whose title reminded them of a rock. History does not contain a character more inconsistent with their position and claims than that of Him whose mere name Irish Protestants have forcibly substituted for the qualities of His apostle. Prosperity and adversity are only the accidents of a Church. Dogmas are mostly mere symbols. Righteousness or justice is the unchanging and only test. Christ's kingdom is essentially the kingdom of righteousness. Irish Protestantism was founded on injustice and cemented by worldly interest. It became a servile ecclesiastical aristocracy with a feeble doctrinal theory, a false spirituality, and the solitude of its usurpation for martyrdom. It was an exact reproduction of the supercilious and sensitive Pharisees supported by the Roman Government, withholding knowledge from the people, calling them accursed because of their ignorance, working heaven and earth to make a single proselyte, and rendering him when made tenfold more the child of hell than themselves.

There were, of course, true Christian men in the Protestant Church. It was as necessary to set them aside in the distribution of power as it was to silence conscience in the souls of those who used the name of religion to enslave and despoil the country. A sincere believer was more embarrassing to the Castle authorities than a Catholic. Through the reign of George II. the Government was virtually conducted by two Englishmen who successively, at a short interval, held the primacy of Armagh. Primate Boulter, appointed in 1724, governed by intrigue and corruption, sowing divisions among Irishmen, and stopping up each remaining crevice through which Catholic freedom gasped for breath. On his death in 1742, it was thought that the virtues and learning of Berkeley entitled him to the succession. Berkeley himself knew that being an Irishman was an insuperable obstacle to his promotion. Hoadley, brother of the English bishop of that name, was appointed, and was soon succeeded by George Stone, who was notorious for unnameable vices, and turned his residence into a brothel for the seduction of the youth of Dublin.[1] In the same reign Bernard MacMahon, the Catholic primate, lived in a farmhouse, and performed the duties of his office in secrecy, and at the risk of his life. The priests were generally the sons of the dispossessed gentry, accustomed from their early years to the comforts of wealth and the society of educated companions. They now lurked in caverns and bogs without proper food or clothing, and watched for opportunities of consoling and instructing their otherwise forsaken countrymen. Many of them returned from the safety of foreign lands to live in peril and privation. To adhere to the Catholic religion was to accept poverty and contempt. Protestant England regarding Ireland in her religious character condemns her as superstitious, and viewing her politically despises her as unfortunate. A people who abandon lands and houses for their religion should be considered exclusively in their religious character, and those who are gainers by their abandonment should put the profit only to their political account. Wearing the martyrs' spoil is no proof of having the martyrs' spirit. The earth which meekness is to inherit means conquered hearts, not conquered lands. Protestantism has inherited the lands in Ireland, Catholicism the hearts. The poverty of Ireland is attributed to her Catholicism. There is, no doubt, a close connection between Irish poverty and Irish Catholicism, but it is made altogether by Protestant law. Protestants boast that they possess the truth. Christ has promised victory not to truth but to sincerity. Christianity is recommended to the world by the devotion, not by the profession of its followers, and as the world's true welfare and right progress are dependent on the maintenance of Christianity, it must not be forgotten that Ireland is the only nation that, as a nation, has practically testified to its truth.

"From superficial views of combining artificers in a metropolis," says a Protestant preacher, referring to the lower classes of his countrymen, "and avaricious complaint of those who would have much work for little wages, idleness has been accounted one great feature in their national character. In the north of Ireland, where an established manufacture exists, is there any grounds for this complaint? In the south, what part of the trade it was possible for them have they not drawn into their hands? Do not the day labouring class repair even to a different kingdom in search of opportunities of industry? In other countries are not their occupations of the most laborious kind? and in this, when paid according to any other standard of computation but that of time, are not their exertions great? When landlords have been wise enough to give them an encouraging tenure of that waste land, which no gentleman could reclaim but at an expense exceeding the total value, has not industry changed the face of the soil, called plenty forth from the dreariness of the damp desert, and opulence from the bowels of the rock? The alterations which are known to have happened in consequence, alterations in their comfort, the demeanour, and even the dress of the

[1] Gordon's "History of Ireland," Vol. II., p. 220.

people, clearly show with whom it lies to remove many of your national faults."[1]

In exact proportion to the ruinous effects on the temporal fortunes of the Catholics produced by Protestant ascendancy, was the spiritual ruin that recoiled on a portion of the Protestants themselves from the same source. Not a famine of bread was sent among them, but the deadlier famine of which the soul perishes. They hated as Protestants instead of loving as Christians. They regarded their ascendancy as the beginning and the end of their religion. During the rebellions of 1715 and 1745 the Catholics did not make a single motion in favour of the Stuarts, yet in the apprehension of a French invasion of England, the usual method of inflaming the passions of the English interest had been so sedulously pursued that a serious proposal is said to have been made in the Council to massacre the Catholics. The proposal was rejected, but a conspiracy to the same effect was entered into by the Protestants of Lurgan, and frustrated by its accidental discovery.[2] Yet those men, swollen with earthly pride and fired by the basest passions, vaunted themselves as the upholders of the Bible. What atonement can England make to Ireland for producing this misshapen offspring of hell and heaven? The distress and the disquiet will pass away, and a pure religion will again shine on the earth, but the half immortal child of political adultery, with the evangel on his lips and the mark of Cain on his brow, will long walk among men. "In one particular," says another Protestant preacher, they (the Catholics) are certainly more successful than it is in our power to boast. Their places of devotion are at some periods of the day resorted to by all who join in their Communion. This, it will be said, is the effect of superstition, denouncing the punishment of damnation against all who absent themselves from what is called the sacrifice of the mass. But what is this but to acknowledge that the voice of superstition is more powerful with its votaries than all the injunctions of our pure and reformed Church, urging and inculcating the commandments of God to those who take a pride in being members of that Church. Well, indeed, might they take a pride in this. It is a proud distinction. It is approaching nearer that sublime and perfect form of religion contained in the Gospel, and professed by the primitive disciples of Christ, than is elsewhere to be found in the Christian world. But to take a pride in the name, to be ready to spill their blood for the distinction, and yet to yield to no one impulse of the spirit it breathes, and yet to neglect and appear to contemn every duty and every ordinance it prescribes, is among not the least striking paradoxes of these strange days."[3]

Every artifice of ingenious tyranny, every outrage of savage force, had been employed to crush the Catholics to a depth of degradation and despair in which they could no longer be moved by a sense of their wrongs. The failure of the attempt exhibits one of the greatest triumphs in the cause of human progress. The particular religion was a matter of accident. Had England remained unreformed, and had Ireland

[1] Sermon preached before the Association for Discountenancing Vice, in St. Mary's Church, Dublin, on the 5th of March, 1795, by the Rev. Robert Burrowes, D.D., F.T.C.D., p. 39.

[2] Matthew O'Conor's "History of the Irish Catholics," p. 228.

[3] Sermon preached before the Association for Discountenancing Vice, in St. Peter's Church, Dublin, on the 22nd May, 1798, by the Right Rev. T. C. O'Beirne, D.D., Bishop of Ossory, p. 25.

accepted the Reformation, all that has occurred would have happened under different names. It was the Irish people, long oppressed by falsehood and violence, who now arose to appeal to public opinion, and proclaim justice. Time had been ripening the harvest for them, and their eyes watched every mellowing tinge of its maturity. Too frequently the natural decay of tyrannous authority is attended with a corresponding declension of spirit in the enslaved people. There are instances where the slave has battled desperately for his degraded lord. Ireland had not sunk to this depth. Protestant ascendancy was left without a social atmosphere. Catholics, it was soon found, were needed to till the lands, to carry on wars, to keep up the value of estates in the market by their competition. As the ancient Irish had become the traders of the country, after the Scotic invasion, so now the Catholics, excluded from all civic employments, and the possession of lands, threw their energies into mercantile enterprise. The dominant faction aimed at loosening the chains of the Catholics only in such a degree as would render them more efficient ministers to their wants. The Catholics took every concession as a right, and as an instalment of a complete emancipation. The historical falsehoods by which Protestants defended their ascendancy were shamelessly repeated and published. The growing intelligence of the nation at last surrounded them like light.

The so-called massacre of 1641 was the subject of annual sermons. On the 23rd of October, 1746, a young girl passing through the Castle yard, with looks of horror and uplifted hands, was heard to ask two ladies whom she accompanied if there were any of those bloodthirsty Papists still in Dublin. A physician named Curry, the descendant of an ancient Irish sept, attracted by the exclamation, traced it to a sermon which had just been delivered. From that day he devoted himself to the vindication of his country and his religion. A work by Sir Richard Cox, full of insults and slanders, stirred Charles O'Conor, a member of the ancient royal family of Connaught, to a similar undertaking. A third co-operator appeared in Thomas Wyse, the descendant of a family which had followed the Earl of Pembroke to Waterford, whose efforts as an organiser gave stability to the literary efforts of his companions. The fates of those three men are characteristic. O'Conor and Curry were patient and moderate, and their lives were passed to old age in comparative tranquillity. The third provoked the bitterest application of the penal code, and died broken-hearted, enjoining on his children in his will to sell their property, and fly to some country where they could worship God in peace.

A Catholic association was formed in 1756. The chief Catholic nobility, in ill-grounded and unreasonable pride, stood aloof. The bishops, fearing to compromise themselves, and clinging to the doctrine of divine right, would give no hearty countenance to a movement that appealed to the House of Hanover. A knot of commercial men, who had enriched themselves by their industry, were its chief supporters. In 1759, when a fresh Jacobite invasion was apprehended, they resolved to address the Government. The gentry and clergy resisted this measure with obstinacy, and the body was divided into two parties, known as addressers and anti-addressers. The Committee persisted in their intention. The address was drawn up by Charles O'Conor, and was signed by four hundred of the most respectable citizens of Dublin. A difficulty arose about its presentation. The Catholics were not supposed to have a civic existence. In such a case rights must be assumed before they are allowed. The Catholics waited on the Speaker, and read their manifesto. The Speaker took the document in silence, and bowed the delegates out. After a few days the Viceroy had the address printed in the Dublin Gazette; the Speaker then sent for the two delegates, ordered one of them to read it to the House, and expressed his pleasure in serving so respectable a body of men as the signers of that document. Such was the first official recognition of Catholics. This small success hurt the pride of the anti-addressers so deeply that they wholly seceded. In 1760, the association was re-established on a representative basis, allowing non-members a right to deliver an opinion at its meetings, but not to have a vote. The attempt to embrace the whole country failed: only the representatives of Dublin and a few gentlemen elected for the counties met in committee. On the accession of George III. they drew up an "Address to the King." The lords and clergy held a separate meeting and passed a separate address. The Catholics now prepared a statement of their grievances for presentation to the throne. It was impeded by the intolerant arrogance of Lord Trimleston; and the association melted away in 1763. A new organisation was attempted in 1773, which fell under the control of Lord Kenmare. The American revolution commenced, and in 1778 a bill was carried in the Irish Parliament, enabling Catholics to take leases for nine hundred and ninety-nine years, and to dispose of their lands as other subjects could. In 1783 the Belfast Volunteers instructed their delegates, at a convention held in Dublin, to support the equal admission of Catholics to the rights of freemen. Lord Kenmare issued a disavowal, on the part of the body to which he belonged, of any wish to be restored to their lost rights, and some time after, with sixty-eight followers, withdrew from the association. In 1791 some Catholics attempted to form a society for the removal of religious prejudices. "We are willing," they said, "to forget that any besides the present race ever existed on this island. We have long been willing to forget it, if our recollection were not kept alive by what we suffer, and by the celebration of festivals memorable only as they denote the era of the events from which we date our bondage." In 1793, the Catholic association was founded on a more strictly representative principle, and Wolfe Tone was appointed its secretary. It was resolved to send five deputies to the king, without using the Irish administration as a medium, to ask in the name of three millions of his subjects that the equal enjoyment of the blessings of the constitution should be extended to Catholics. The deputies in their journey passed through Belfast, where the horses were taken from their carriage, and they were drawn on their way by the people with loud acclamations. The king graciously received them and accepted their petition. On their return the leaders of the party were tampered with by Government, and induced to declare themselves satisfied with a compromise. Meantime a Militia Bill, a Gunpowder Bill, and an Act for the Suppression of Tumultuous Assemblies were hastily passed. On the ninth of April, 1793, the Catholic Relief Bill received the Royal assent. It removed the fearful burthen of the Penal Code, and gave Catholics the elective franchise : but it excluded them from sitting in Parliament and from the offices of Lord Lieutenant, Lord Deputy, and Lord Chancellor.

Every concession was the product of circumstances, but there was an organisation in readiness to improve the occasion. The weakness of this organisation was that its leaders had not been absorbed into the more popular element. The people, indeed, did not exist as a power. Aristocracies under all conceivable vicissitudes will sympathise with one another. The Protestant bishops always shrank from aiding in the depression of their Catholic brothers. The Catholic lords and bishops, particularly since the French Revolution, dreaded friends of the popular class more than foes of their own.

The Protestant landed interest knew exactly where to stop short in their concessions. While they had been spending their means, the Catholics had been making and accumulating money. They were willing that this money should be put into general circulation and enhance the value of their lands by making them purchasable to its owners. But they were determined to keep the final control in their own power. After their independence was won from England in 1782, they passed a law formally excluding the Catholics from the legislature. They were excluded previously only by the law of William III., which imposed the oath against Transubstantiation. The grant of the franchise to Catholics caused a very great increase in the competition for farms. While only Protestants had the right to vote for members of Parliament the landlords felt it their interest to have Protestant tenants. The possession of the franchise made Catholics equally eligible. Rack rents, tithe exactions, and the turning of tillage lands into pasturages had displaced numbers of Protestant families in Armagh, a large proportion of whom emigrated to America. Their places were filled up by Catholics, who for the sake of dwelling in the homes of their fathers were willing to pay higher rents and work for lower wages. A stronger impulse was now given to this movement. The Protestant population conceiving themselves injured by the competition, burned the houses and ill-treated the persons of the Catholics. In 1795 they formed themselves into a regular body, and were known as Peep-of-day boys, Wreckers, and Protestant boys. The Catholics combined for self-protection, and called themselves Defenders. Unarmed and leaderless, they were defeated by their privileged opponents, and then persecuted and imprisoned by magistrates and soldiers. Thirteen hundred of them were taken out of prison without any form of trial, and sent on board ships of war or transport vessels.

SECTION IX.

The laws by which God wills the government of nations to be conducted are almost as simple as the physical laws which he has impressed on matter. He has made of one blood all nations, and determined the bounds of their habitation. He has given men indestructible instincts of local affection and political right in accordance with this elementary condition. The inflexible rule by observance of which one man or nation may claim to govern another man or nation is that the governor must not seek his own gain, but sacrifice it, or life itself, for the good of the governed. Men and nations are anxious to rule because they do not recognise this law, that is, because they lack the primary qualification for ruling. The more determined a nation is to rule another nation, and the more peremptory is the expression of its determination, the greater is that nation's inability and unfitness to rule. The height of this unfitness is reached when the attempt is persistently made to displace the love of country by fear of foreigners. This is the constant policy of Norman England. She sets up the hangman as a rival to God, and the gallows as his altar. On the thirteenth day of September, 1882, the public prints announced how one man was hanged in Ireland and another in Egypt, not because they were guilty but because the terror of England's laws must be displayed. And we read how the populations of the two countries made saints and martyrs of the two executed men, not with any reference to their innocence, but in assertion of the right of which no nation can divest itself, that each nation is exclusively entitled to pronounce on the guilt or innocence of its own children.

It is a merciful arrangement that we can never adequately realise the crimes of tyrants. If we had been endowed with faculties capable of comprehending the fulness of the horror, our souls would recoil from earth in renunciative detestation. But if we are unable to appreciate misrule in action, we can at least examine the grounds which it assumes for self-defence in theory. "From the beginning of Anglo-Irish history," says a modern apologist, "there can be traced, in the leading spirits of the island, a particular notion of the meaning of the word liberty. True liberty means being governed by just laws, laws which are in harmony with the will of the Maker and Master of the world. It is the worst curse of injustice that it leads men to look for redress, not to better government but to none, and to regard their own consent as the measure of the restraint to which they may rightly be submitted. Liberty, the Irish said, and even Swift lent his authority to the definition, liberty consisted in the being ruled by laws which men made for themselves; tyranny in being ruled by laws made for them by others. If this be true, the minority in every constitutional state lives under a tyranny, for it lives under laws against which it has formally protested."[1] Every canon of ethics and common sense is ruthlessly violated in this extraordinary medley of paradoxes. It is valuable, because it is the philosophical reflection of the misgovernment which it defends. True liberty does not mean being governed by external law, just or unjust. It means being governed from within. Where the spirit of righteousness or justice is, there is liberty. He is the true freeman whom the truth makes free. These are not religious sayings. They are political principles, and as such they were intended. It is true they are goals, not starting-posts, but the legislation that does not aim at them and contemplate its own final extinction in their accomplishment, is at war with the will of God

[1] "English in Ireland," Vol. I., p. 604.

and the happiness of man. True liberty, then, does not mean being governed, as the word is commonly used: it means being not governed, because men have the law written on their hearts and rule themselves. And analogous to this definition of individual liberty is that of national liberty, which means being governed by the nation's own laws, or the national conscience. The Maker of the world made England and Ireland two distinct islands. When we appeal to him, therefore, our course is clear. Yet when the Irish say that liberty means being ruled by the national conscience, it is replied by the very writer who appeals to the laws of the Maker of the world, that if this were so the minority in every state must live under a tyranny, thus defying the Maker of the world by representing the inhabitants of one distinct country as being to the inhabitants of another distinct country, what the minority is to the majority in one and the same country. The fact that injustice leads men to look for redress not to better government, but to none, shows how by the constitution of our nature, good and bad laws equally direct man to the true solution of his difficulties, the minimisation of government. It would be for the advantage of rulers only, and would be an encouragement to them to rule unjustly, if men sought a multiplication of rulers in proportion as injustice prevailed, and increased their reverence for law according as it contradicted the end for which it was designed. "The consent of man was not asked," we further read, "when he was born into the world; his consent will not be asked when his time comes to die. As little has his consent to do with the laws which, while he lives, he is bound to obey." The latter clause of the first sentence is not true. Man's consent to his continued existence is asked each day of his life, and not one man in fifty but consents, after due warning given, either directly or indirectly, to his own death. But it is quite true that no man's consent to his being born is asked before he is born. On the ground, then, of this magnificent generalisation it is seriously put forward that when a band of disciplined and armed ruffians, too idle to do honest work, and too vicious to remain quiet, come on a weaker people and subdue them, that people are bound for ever to give their men and women to the will of the conquerors.

It might be supposed that the object of this writer was to charge the Irish, or rather the Anglo-Irish colony, for it is with them he is concerned, with insubordination to just government, that he was preparing an indictment against them for not being thankful when they were ruled with leniency and justice. He is doing nothing of the kind. He speaks of good government in order, apparently, that when he accuses the Irish of resisting bad government, his readers, confused by his language, may condemn resistance to the bad as if it were resistance to the good. "Let a nation be justly governed, and if it is wise it will not quarrel with its destiny, which has provided for it the greatest of earthly blessings." Then follows the application. "English misrule in Ireland reached a point at which its grasp relaxed, and weakness compelled a surrender of a power which had been so scandalously misused; not, however, through any rising virtue on the part of the oppressed Irish, or through any divine aspirations after freedom and self-government, but because wrong had borne its necessary fruit in the feebleness of the oppressor." Just government is the greatest of earthly blessings; the Irish delivered themselves from unjust government; therefore they deserve no credit. The fact was that the Irish volunteers forced their independence from England in 1782, and rather than allow the inference that they were right in doing it, or able to do it by inherent power, Mr. Froude describes England as corrupted and enfeebled by her own tyranny, whereas in reality all her strength was engaged in a war with America and France.

We constantly hear it asked, What do Irishmen really want? What do they mean by home rule, repeal of the union, and all the rest of their vague demands? It may be asked, in return, What does England ask or expect from Ireland? What are the conditions or circumstances under which she expects her to be satisfied? We may now form some idea on the subject. It is expected of Irishmen to own (not by all Englishmen, or this history would never be written, but by a class of Norman Englishmen), that the Maker of the world blundered when He made Ireland a separate island; that true liberty consists in being governed by foreign laws; that, because man's consent was not asked to his being born by God, he should never expect to have his consent asked by the fellow mortal who aspires to be his ruler; and that, because to oppose just rule would be ungracious, resistance to English misrule can never be a mark of rising virtue, or a proof of divine aspiration after freedom and self-government. English and Irish demands are in direct opposition, and England protests that she will never yield. It is a matter of rational calculation whether the demands that are in unison with nature and the world's increasing purpose, or the demands that defy nature and history, are likeliest to endure and to triumph.

The Irish House of Commons consisted mainly of landlords. There were several lawyers, some of whom rose above their profession, while others were ready to sink below it. There were a few true patriots, and there was a still smaller number of able men, possessed by a demon of ambition, who sought a wider field in which to display their powers by uniting their country with England. The usual encroachments of government gradually provoked opposition. Public debts were incurred, and the administration was charged with extravagance. An attempt was made to change the annual vote for the discharge of the national debt into a grant for ever or for a number of years. A warm debate ensued, and the parties were nearly balanced, when a member named Tottenham came hastily in his riding dress, contrary to the etiquette of the House, and gave a majority to the anti-ministerialists. "Tottenham in his boots" became a standing toast of patriotism.

In 1749 Ireland had a surplus revenue to dispose of. It was claimed as of right belonging to the Crown. The Commons transmitted a bill to England, applying it to the liquidation of the national debt. A message came back that the King would consent to this appropriation of the money. The Commons passed a bill disposing of a portion of it, and omitted the word "consent." The Minister reinstated the word. In 1753 the same scene was expected, but the patriots went to a division, and won by a majority of five. On this, as on every occasion when the national dignity was asserted, the joy of victory was felt by none more acutely than by the excluded Catholics. The Viceroy took the surplus revenue by virtue of a royal letter. Boyle, the leading patriot, was removed from the Privy Council; Malone, another of the same party, was deprived of his title of precedence as prime serjeant; and Lucas, a Dublin apothecary, who had fought the battle of the corporation, and was now asserting the sovereignty of Parliament, was compelled to fly to the Isle of Man. The significant cry was raised in England that the Irish majority was Popish. Lord Kildare, who had been active on the national side, laid with his own hands a memorial before the king, and explained his action by declaring that remonstrances addressed through ordinary channels were systematically intercepted. This bold step excited a universal ferment. The Government changed their tactics. Boyle was made Earl of Shannon, with a pension of two thousand a year; Malone, refusing the Chancellorship of the Exchequer, accepted its profits; and several prominent members of the opposition were placed in lucrative employments.

The enormously-increased list of pensions on the Irish establishment was a subject of deep-seated discontent. A bill vacating the seats of members receiving pensions or places of profit was thrown out by a majority of eighty-five to fifty-nine.

In 1757 the English Whigs contemplated a union with Ireland as an accession to their own strength, and even calculated on the aid of the Catholics in support of the measure. The very rumour of a union roused the Protestant mob of Dublin to a state of fury. They surrounded both Houses of Parliament with loud outcries, and proceeded to such extremities that the Speaker came out and solemnly assured them that no union was intended. They stopped the members as they entered, and forced them to take a pledge against the union. They seized Lord Inchiquin, but when he told them that his name was O'Brien, they loudly cheered him. The military were at last called out, and the loyal Protestants were ridden down and scattered. Some ascribed this disturbance to the Catholics. Pitt insisted on imputing it to the failure of a bank.

Septennial Parliaments had been in existence for some time in England. In Ireland each Parliament was elected for the lifetime of the king. In the new Parliament that assembled on the accession of George III., Lucas, who had returned from exile, took his seat as member for Dublin. He and his friends saw that the extravagance and corruption of Government could be remedied only by making the Parliament more immediately responsible to the people, and began to agitate for septennial elections. In 1767 a Septennial Bill was transmitted, and altered to an Octennial one by the British Cabinet, in the hope that their interference would ensure its rejection. The Irish Parliament, however, accepted it. As might have been foreseen, while the electoral basis remained unaltered, it only afforded the proprietors of boroughs opportunities of more frequent sales.

The government was carried on by bribing a few great families, and making them the distributers of bribes to a large number of dependents and supporters. Those magnates began to assume airs of independent authority. The office of bribing was taken from them and exercised immediately over the wider surface. A period of sixteen months was allowed to elapse between the dissolution of the old and the meeting of the first octennial Parliament. This interval was busily employed by the Viceroy in completing his influence over the members according to the new system. There were certain lengths to which the Parliament refused to be bribed. They would not allow the English council to originate money bills. The Commons would not even suffer the Viceroy to enter his protest against their claim in their journals. He redoubled his efforts to render the members more compliant, made another attempt and was more decisively beaten. An English newspaper condemned the conduct of the Irish Parliament as a daring insult, and advised that the English Legislature should directly vote the Irish supplies, inasmuch as the Parliament of Great Britain was supreme over its conquests. The Irish Parliament ordered the paper to be burned by the common hangman. The Viceroy postponed the meeting of Parliament by a series of prorogations till 1771, won over Mr. Perry, one of the more conspicuous patriots, by a promise of the Speakership and a peerage, distributed money and honours lavishly, and secured a majority, who passed a vote of thanks to him for his just and prudent administration. There were other victories that were beyond his power. He was besought to save a Catholic gentleman who was about to suffer death unjustly: "They are resolved to have his life," he said, "they may as well have it now."

The war carried on by Pitt had involved England heavily in debt. Some relief was sought by taxing the American Colonies. The Americans resisted, the king and his ministers would not withdraw their demands, and the war of American independence began. No event in history can so forcibly impress us with a sense of the danger to mankind arising from oligarchic rule, as the reflection that if the American contest for freedom had been postponed until the engines of modern warfare had been invented and perfected, the war party of England might have triumphed, and the hopes of the world been crushed for many centuries. No greater misfortune can befall the people of England than the reduction of Ireland to such a condition of servility that her inhabitants may be relied on to prosecute those foreign conquests by which the heaviest burthens of domestic tyranny are supposed to be balanced. The natural recoil from so base an employment justifies every Irish revolt.

The exports from England to Ireland were two millions and a half annually. Ireland besides supported a large standing military force; armies of placemen, pensioners, and absentees spent her money in England. Her linen trade with America, the only branch that remained to her, was at an end. An embargo had been laid on the exportation of Irish provisions in favour of English contractors. Some trivial concessions were now made, such as allowing the exportation of clothing for regiments on the Irish establishment employed abroad. When due acknowledgment had been rendered for this boon, the Viceroy informed the House of Commons that the situation of affairs required the sending of a force of four thousand men to America, which his Majesty meant to replace by an equal number of foreign Protestant troops. The departure of the Irish force was allowed, but the introduction of foreign troops was decisively negatived as an insidious method of enslaving Ireland at the cost of England, which could afterwards be used to enslave England at the cost of Ireland. The House in an address to the king stated that with the assistance of the government they might be able to exert themselves so as to render aid unnecessary. A money bill was altered by the Privy Council, and in consequence rejected. These symptoms of independence alarmed the government, and Parliament was dissolved. An unprecedented number of promotions and creations of peers took place in one day. The new Parliament was formally convened in June, 1776, and repeatedly prorogued to October, 1777. In this month General Burgoyne surrendered his army to the Americans at Saratoga. The next year France declared for America. French and American privateers were sweeping the channel. The Irish Parliament passed a militia bill for the defence of the country. The people of Belfast, dreading an invasion, applied to the Irish secretary for assistance, and were informed that only a troop or two of horse could be spared. They commenced enrolling themselves as volunteers, and the whole country quickly followed their example. The arms intended for the militia were given by the Viceroy for their use. Their number soon reached seventy-five thousand men. Government discouraged, but could not prevent their enrolment. On two sides the institution was weak. It was commanded by noblemen, and it excluded, or admitted only by connivance, the Catholics. It placed the unnational nobility at its head and refused the basis of the nation. A letter from Lord Tyrone to one of the Beresfords is extant in which he says that the Catholics were forming themselves into distinct companies, but that seeing the consequences which would attend such an event he had stopped the movement. The Catholics looked with pride and sympathy on the proceedings of their Protestant brethren. Denied a personal share in the enterprise, they helped it with their money. A better feeling gradually grew between the two religions.

The English Parliament beheld what was taking place with angry bewilderment. They were beset on both sides.. They preserved a monopoly in trade, and they were ready to beggar all their colonies and dependencies, and to create fresh colonies and dependencies with the view of beggaring them, for the aggrandisement of manufacturers and traders whose success gave them security, and increased their importance and their wealth. One of Ireland's demands was a right to compete with England in trade on equal terms. She had now an army to back her demand. In March, 1779, the subject was introduced in the English House of Commons, but had to be abandoned through fear of raising a rebellion in the Lancashire towns.

When the volunteers saw that nothing could be obtained from English justice, they carried the volunteer principle into trade, and entered into combinations to use home manufactures and exclude British commodities. England claimed the government of the country, but could neither afford them an army to defend their shores, nor allow them a trade to support their people. They had their own army, and they determined to have their own manufactures. On occasions like this men forget the language of diplomacy, and ascribe conduct to ordinary human passions. The freemen of Dublin at a public meeting, resolved that the opposition of Great Britain to Irish commerce originated in avarice and ingratitude. This was quite true, but it was not seen that commercial avarice was a secondary and artificial affection. The traders of both islands were driven into rivalry by the great lords whose interests were identical. The citizens of Waterford formally determined to use Irish manufactures, and not to deal with any merchant or shopkeeper who offered foreign goods for sale. Great irritation was produced in England. The volunteers were described in the House of Lords as an angry mob, and the press denounced Irish encouragement of their own manufactures as the policy of savages.

When the Irish Parliament met in October, it was moved in an amendment to the address that temporary expedients were insufficient, that law must establish effectual relief, and that free trade was the only means of saving the nation from ruin. The streets of Dublin were lined with volunteers with "Free-trade or—" labelled on the necks of their cannons. Ministers were compelled to yield, and the resolution passed. The next day votes of thanks to the volunteers were carried, with a single dissentient in the Lords, through both Houses. The country was now in their hands. They instructed the Opposition to vote the supplies only for six months. An amendment to this effect was carried in November. The English ministers yielded, but with a bad grace. In February, 1780, a bill was passed giving Ireland liberty to export woollen goods, and to trade with the British colonies. It was accompanied with the declaration that it was a boon from the English Parliament resumable at pleasure.

A free Parliament was indispensable for the protection of a free trade, and forthwith became the object of general desire. In April, Henry Grattan, the chief orator of the Nationalists, moved that the King, Lords, and Commons of Ireland are alone competent to enact laws to bind Ireland. The motion was not pressed to a division; but the nation's rights had been embodied and uttered in ringing words. The English Minister could no longer prevaricate. His next step showed how exactly the occasion was understood and provided for; and how fully the Irish Parliament was relied on to contend for its own and the country's enslavement. The bill for preventing mutiny in the army was transmitted to England with its usual duration of six months. The Privy Council made it perpetual, and the Irish Commons passed it in that form.

The contest, be it ever remembered, was not between England and Ireland. It was between all that was true and just in both countries, against all that was selfish, tyrannical and dishonest. A large party in the English Parliament, and in England, supported America and Ireland in their struggles. A purchased majority in the Irish Commons battled obstinately for aristocratic England against the genius, the arms, and the rights of Ireland.

The Viceroy had incurred a debt from which he now laboured to extricate himself. He had promised peerages, pensions, or places, to nearly a hundred persons, and he found on submitting his engagements to the English ministers, that they would not be made good. The king took on himself to confer a certain number of peerages. The Viceroy was soon after recalled.

Throughout 1781 several vain attempts were made to repeal Poyning's law and amend the Mutiny Act. The Parliament and the nation were in open opposition. In the debates the country was exhibited on one side as the most flourishing on earth, so that nothing was wanting to the people but resignation to the government; on the other, it was represented as the most wronged country under heaven. At last the volunteers felt that the time was come to cut the knot. It was resolved that delegates should be sent from all the Ulster corps to Dungannon on the fifteenth of February. The representatives of one hundred and fifty-three corps assembled on the appointed day, and resolved that the claims of any body of men save the King, Lords, and Commons of Ireland, to make laws for Ireland, are unconstitutional, illegal, and a grievance; that the ports of Ireland are rightfully open to all foreign countries not at war with the king; that a perpetual Mutiny Act is unconstitutional and a grievance; that the independence of judges is essential to the impartial administration of justice; that the right of private judgment in matters of religion is equally sacred in others as in ourselves, and that they rejoiced in the relaxation of the Penal Code as fraught with happiness and prosperity to the inhabitants of Ireland. Those resolutions were adopted by the whole country. Grattan brought in a motion declaring the national rights. It was lost by a majority of one hundred and thirty-seven to sixty-eight.

Lord Cornwallis was forced to surrender at Yorktown, in America. Lord Rockingham and Fox came into office. The American war was at an end. An Irish war was prevented. Delays were sought for to instigate enquiries, but the volunteers would brook no postponement. In the month of April, 1782, Fox communicated to the Commons of England the king's recommendation to take the discontent of Ireland into their serious consideration, in order to such a final adjustment as might give mutual satisfaction to both kingdoms. On the seventeenth of May it was carried unanimously in the two Houses at Westminster that the Act of 6th George I., entitled an Act for the better securing the dependency of Ireland on the Crown of Great Britain, should be repealed. On the twenty-seventh Poyning's Act was repealed in the Irish Parliament. Ireland was free.

The words Protestant and Catholic are only names of political parties in Ireland. A few Protestants succeeded in usurping the lands and the government of the country, and maintained them by fomenting sectarian hatred among their co-religionists. They insist on the truth and purity of their doctrines. What greater calamity can befall true Christianity than its identification with glaring wrong? The Catholic people represent the indefeasible national rights. The Lords and Bishops of both religions agree in politics. It is the people of both persuasions who in the name of religion are kept in constant political warfare. In the history of Ireland, and particularly in that portion of it through which we have been rapidly passing, Catholic means nationalist. The Catholics always look with delight on any step that is taken for what they consider the good of their country, quite apart from the religion of

R

those concerned in it. They are as ready to follow a Protestant leader as a Catholic if his politics agree with theirs. They applauded and aided the volunteer movement, though they were not permitted to join in it. When Protestants asserted the rights of Ireland, the friends of English supremacy always reviled them as Papists or Catholics, thus admitting that Catholic was the same as patriot. As the volunteer movement grew to national proportions, and assumed national sentiments, Catholic and Protestant lost their political meanings, and stood only as religious denominations. The moment they did so the Protestants recognised the Catholics as fellow-Christians and fellow-countrymen, and demanded their deliverance from the political penal code. When Catholics attain estates and a share in the Government they are as apt to become zealous supporters of the supremacy of England as any Protestants can be. The real motive of the exclusion of Catholics from juries in state trials is not the apprehension that Catholics could not be found who would give verdicts for the government, for it is well known that they could be found as easily as Protestants, but the desire to keep the religious feud alive, and to infuse mutual mistrust and offence between Catholics and Protestants, by pretending that the Catholic must be the unchangeable political enemy of the Protestant.

False and dazzling lights have been cast around the history of Ireland's independence by friends and foes. A passage from a writer whom we have often had occasion to refer to is resplendent with warning. "Nations," he says, "are not born on the floors of debating societies, nor on the parade ground of volunteers. Freedom must be won on the battlefield, or it is as perishable as the breath that boasts of it. In truth and fact, Ireland, bound to England by situation, and inhabited by a people who would howl for liberty but never fight for it, had snatched from the embarrassments of her neighbour what she could neither keep nor use worthily while it was hers."[1] If the writer's intention was to goad and irritate the Irish people to insurrection he could not find language more suitable for his purpose. Similar taunts are not unfrequent in a portion of the English press. Addressed to a people for whom the possession of a gun or an attempt at drill would be instant imprisonment and penal servitude, they are only a provocation to what would be called murder and massacre, and be retaliated upon by real and wholesale murder and massacre. That freedom can only be won on the battlefield is a commonplace of poetical oratory which one does not expect to find just after a denunciation of eloquence. What countries unaided have ever delivered themselves from the grip of their conquerors on the battlefield? What shred of freedom did England ever win on the battlefield from Hastings to Peterloo? Freedom is the birth of time, the growth of events. The English people could not get even the repeal of the laws that kept them without bread for their children until famished Ireland held out her skeleton hand like a menace from the grave. They will not shake off the hold which the Norman conqueror keeps on their lands until America undersells their produce. If they attempted to win them back on the battlefield they would be slaughtered as they were before, and instead of German or Italian

[1] Froude's "English in Ireland," Vol. II., p. 330.

troops, as in former times,[1] Irish regiments would, if necessary, be ordered to do the work.[2] Freedom comes in the order of God's government of the world. The independence of Ireland in 1782 was not gained either by orators or armed men, not on platform or parade ground. It was brought about by a cause that is liable to recur at any moment. Volunteering may be prevented, and oratory may be stifled, but the unseen march of events cannot be arrested. The circumstances that placed freedom within Ireland's reach a hundred years ago may always start into being before the course of a week is run from what may seem settled security. No foresight can anticipate this, no power can avert it. If English statesmen be wise they will provide against it in the only possible way in which it can be provided against, by making Irishmen friends to England. How is that to be done? No idler question was ever asked since the Pharisee, after professing that his duty was to act fairly to his neighbour, inquired, "Who is my neighbour?" Only a prejudiced Jew, full of national or sectarian hatred, could propose such a question. A Samaritan would act on the instant. Ireland lies stripped and wounded by the way side.

[1] See p. 120.
[2] "The 21st Regiment of Foot (Irish) was ordered to proceed by forced marches. On their arrival some of them were heard to declare that they would now have revenge on the Sutherlanders for the carnage of their countrymen at Tara Hill and Ballenamuck."—Mackenzie's "History of the Highland Clearances," p. 12.

CHAPTER XIV.

PARLIAMENTARY INDEPENDENCE.

SECTION I.

THE Irish Parliament in declaring their freedom had merely obeyed the instructions given to them by the British Minister. The eloquence of Grattan had not influenced a vote or altered an opinion. The Parliament and the Minister yielded to circumstances, and waited with unchanged minds, till the pressure was withdrawn, to recover the ground they had lost. The displays of oratory that signalise any historical crisis are an expression of enthusiasm proportioned to the intellect of the nation. They are in most cases more a consequence than a cause. When the ultimate appeal to arms is impending they are less than a cause, they are a hindrance. The excessive brilliancy of Grattan's eloquence misdirected the atttention of his countrymen. They imagined the country was saved by an orator, and they assigned to him almost all the importance that belonged to the two facts that England was without an army, and that Ireland had an army. The volunteers numbered a hundred and twenty-four thousand men. They were commanded by men of position, and disciplined by retired British officers. Their sergeants were chiefly veterans who had served in the American campaigns. Their drill and discipline were continued without intermission. Their artillery was exercised daily in Phœnix Park. They were prepared to take the field at the first sound of the trumpet. The Catholic nation lay behind them ready to rush in and unite for ever in their ranks. The thought of bringing the forces which Great Britain had at her disposal into collision with the volunteer army of Ireland never entered into the dreams of the wildest English enthusiast. The position which the two countries had occupied for centuries was exactly reversed. England did not then say that freedom was to be won only on the battlefield. It was the very thing she did not wish to be even hinted at. Now when things have gone back to their former state, when England has an army and Ireland has none, and when all the world knows that England holds Ireland by keeping her unarmed, and that a month's opportunity would give Ireland an army which the English army, itself half Irish, dare not meet in the field, and bring into inseparable combination Catholics and Protestants, Orangemen and Fenians now kept in artificial discord by foreign influence, it is, to say the least, not befitting the dignity of England, that it should be said in her name by paradoxical historians, or recreant Irishmen of the London press, that freedom must be won only on the battlefield.

All eyes were fixed on Grattan. English Ministers helped the delusion. An Irish member proposed that a hundred thousand pounds should be granted to him by Parliament for his services. The proposal was immediately supplemented by an offer on the part of the Viceroy of the viceregal palace in the Phœnix Park to be settled on him and his heirs for ever. A grant of fifty thousand pounds was eventually made. The generosity of Grattan's nature was overcome. The concession of England and the gratitude of Ireland, melted into a confused emotion that rendered him incapable of vigilance or mistrust till it was too late.

Flood, Grattan's rival in oratory, who had held office for some years, and only lately joined the national party, strove to provide guarantees for the liberty which he had not been most prominent in effecting. His efforts were not seconded, or rather were resented, by Grattan, and two men whose abilities if united might have established the happiness of their country, only entertained the world, and delighted the enemies of Ireland, with specimens of unexampled personal invective. Flood insisted that Irish liberties were not secure until England not merely repealed the laws which bound Ireland, but positively renounced the right to bind her by legislation. Grattan considered that this would be an ungenerous suspicion of British sincerity. Flood's discernment would be fully justified by the publication of written correspondence of high officials at the time. But he was not left to his powers of penetration and to inferential conclusions. Fox had plainly stated in the English Parliament that some future irrevocable arrangement between the two countries was yet to be made. A member of the English Commons, who held office in Ireland, had declared on the repeal of 6th George I. that the English Parliament had not power to pass such a bill, and that the king had no authority to relinquish the inherent right of the British legislature to make laws for Ireland. A bill was introduced into the House of Lords which stated that since the kings of England were masters of the seas that surrounded Ireland, for eighteen centuries, the British Parliament had the sole right to regulate the commerce of Ireland. Those were growlings that indicated what the temper would be when the fangs were regrown. The country saw that Flood's precautions were demanded by circumstances. The two opposing parties began to marshal their respective forces. The Irish government brought all their resources of corruption into play. The volunteers beat to arms through the country, and made every hill resound to the tramp of their men, and the strains of their music. The British Cabinet did not say that England's renunciation of the right to bind Ireland must be sought for on the battlefield. On the contrary, knowing that then it could certainly be won on the battlefield, they submitted and passed a statute unequivocally renouncing all future right to legislate for Ireland, basely and dishonourably purposing in their hearts, when the necessity had passed away, to belie their own formal and solemn enactment.

During the progress of this controversy a coolness sprang up between Grattan and the volunteers. The lawyers' corps appointed a committee to enquire into the question, and they reported in favour of Flood's view. The Dublin corps, of which Grattan was colonel, requested him to support the decision of men so well qualified to judge. Without resigning his colonelcy, he intimated to his regiment that they might decline to re-elect him. He was re-elected, but the seeds of distrust were scattered and soon grew to maturity. Dissatisfaction with the volunteers involved a preference for some other military body. It seems incredible now that Grattan could have mistaken the cause to which his country owed its freedom. When England and Ireland rivalled each other in ascribing to his genius the revolution that had taken place, it can scarcely be wondered at that he over-estimated the value of his efforts in comparison with other agencies. He supposed that England had yielded to reason. It was a natural corollary to this most mistaken idea to imagine that the coruscations of his fancy had stricken light, and the vigour of his antithesis carried conviction into the British Cabinet.

SECTION II.

Had the Irish demanded a complete separation it would have been yielded without resistance. It would have been better had it been. The two countries would have immediately joined on terms of equality and of mutual confidence and respect. But the more the English Cabinet gave way the less were the Irish disposed to press their advantage. A feeling of warm attachment to England rapidly took the place of distrust. There never existed in Ireland so sincere and friendly a spirit of spontaneous union with England as at this moment, when the formal bond of union was almost wholly dissolved.

From the moment when England made a formal surrender of her claim to govern Ireland a series of inroads commenced on the various interests supposed to be left to their own free development by that surrender. Ireland had not, like England, a body of Cabinet Ministers responsible to her Parliament. The Lord Lieutenant and the Irish Secretary held their offices and received their instructions from the English minister. There was greater need than ever before for a bribed majority in the Irish Commons, and the machinery for security and managing it remained intact.

The Perpetual Mutiny Bill had been repealed. A Police Bill, which took the powers of local government from mayors and corporations, and handed them over to paid magistrates, was proposed. The pretexts provided for carrying this measure, betraying at once the unscrupulousness of the means, and the nature of the concealed object, are described in the speech of one of its opponents. Sir Edward Crofton said that the accounts of disturbances in the country calling for interference were extremely exaggerated and misrepresented. Camps and cannon were spoken of, and fortifications were said to have been erected. It was also rumoured that the Roman Catholics were in open rebellion. This was an insidious, infamous, and false report calculated to cast an undeserved reflection on a body of men remarkable for their loyalty to their sovereign and their known attachment to the constitution. It was an illiberal and an infamous attack on a people distinguished for their peaceable demeanour, and was intended but to serve the purposes of this more infamous bill. The speaker continued to say that he was himself at first imposed on by those reports, and that having property at stake, he made every possible enquiry, and found that the only basis of so much exaggeration was a drunken brawl in which there had not even been a broken head. The bill was denounced by several other speakers as intended to take away the constitution under the specious pretence of giving police. The ominous accusation was made that the government created disturbances in order to procure its being passed. Several adverse petitions were presented and were received only with contempt. One was forwarded by the freeholders of Dublin. The Attorney-General moved that it be rejected as an insult to the House. His motion was passed by a large majority. The bill was carried.

At a subsequent Parliament the question of retrenchment was introduced with especial reference to the reduction of the army. The true point at issue was whether the British army or the Irish volunteers were to garrison the country. Grattan, staggering under his load of gratitude for the concessions of 1782, could not advance an inch beyond the conditions that then existed. It was a matter of compact, he said, that the regular force should remain at the standard settled at that time. It did not seem to have occurred to him that it was also necessary to provide for a similar permanence of the volunteer body. On this matter he quarrelled beyond hope with Flood, and severed his connection with the men who, if his eloquence had not carried the contest into the field of debate and intrigue, might have definitely established and preserved their country's independence.

The freedom of trade which had been won did not produce the advantages which were expected from it. Free trade did not then mean the importation or exportation of goods free of duty, but the right of Ireland to have those duties imposed, and her commerce generally regulated by her own Parliament and in her own interest. England, while she had the power, had prevented Ireland from sending her manufactured goods either to the British shores or to the colonies, and had kept all the trade of the islands in her own hands. By this means she had established the superiority of her own manufactures, got possession of the markets of the world, and acquired vast wealth. All those advantages were gained by excluding Ireland from competition with her, when she might have competed on equal terms. Ireland was bound at the starting post, while her rival ran the race. When the right to manage her own commercial concerns was attained the race was over, the prize was won. Giving Ireland control over her trade in 1782 was the same thing as permitting a starved Irish dealer to open a shop in his native village, and win to himself if he could the customers, including his landlord, of the palatial warehouses of London. England had gained her superiority by excluding Irish goods from her ports, and keeping Irish ports open to her own goods, and underselling Irish rivalry by the greater skill and wealth which monopoly had thus obtained for her. When Ireland in the early volunteer days had attempted to do, by the operation of the national will, what England had done by law, and encourage her own manufactures, the English press had denounced the Irish as barbarians. But they were only fairly protecting themselves by the same method, though not passed into a law, by which England had unfairly got for herself the trade of the two countries. In fact, it was by protection that England had acquired her wealth and her manufacturing supremacy, and it was only in the dockyard of protection that Ireland could now, at the eleventh hour, lay the keel of her commercial enterprise. All English manufactures were imported at a trifling per centage into Irish ports, while duties amounting to prohibition were imposed on the importation of the produce and manufactures of Ireland into England, excepting linen.

In April, 1784, the member for Dublin moved for the imposition of a duty on woollen goods imported into the country. Free trade, he argued, would be only a name unless the freedom was made use of to promote trade. This must be done by supplying home consumption, and exporting the redundancy. But it was impossible to undersell other nations in foreign markets, while England undersold them in their own. They could not expect to cope with England, who had the advantage of long established trade, of large capitals and extensive credit. While Irish ports were open to the exportation of raw materials, and the importation of British manufactures, no benefit from the extension of their commerce could be expected. He censured the conduct of those who took from the Irish the field and motive for labour, and then ridiculed them as idle. He challenged the House to specify an instance in which the people were indolent where the laws of their country protected them in their endeavours. Before the laws encouraged agriculture a great proportion of the inhabitants of the country lived on imported corn. No sooner was encouragement held out to the plough than a large quantity of corn was annually exported. In the linen trade, although they were compelled to yield an established manufacture in woollen, and engage in another against a country that had arrived at great perfection in it, yet they had prospered, simply because they had not been interfered with. He proposed, therefore, that they should adopt the conduct of England and France, and other countries, and protect their home manufactures. The proposal was rejected by a vast majority, and the whole system of protecting duties was ridiculed as visionary and pernicious. The disappointment of the people of Dublin was so great, and so hotly expressed, at this failure, that preparations were made by the authorities to meet an insurrection. Before the session closed an address was voted by the Commons to the king, praying for a more advantageous system of commerce between both countries. Soon after a mutual understanding was come to between the British Cabinet and Irish Commissioners appointed for the purpose, the result of which was laid before the Irish Commons in February, 1785, by Mr. Orde, in eleven propositions. The spirit of these propositions was an equalisation of duties between England and Ireland. They passed the Irish Parliament. They were not immediately brought before the English legislature, and in the interval a vehement torrent of opposition rolled from Lancashire, and other great seats of English trade. A cry was raised that the English operatives would be thrown out of employment by the competition of Irish labour. The merchants and manufacturers, knowing how the danger would be averted, and the advantage which they possessed over Ireland maintained, insisted on a legislative union with Ireland as the real remedy. Lord North roundly asserted that Ireland had no right to a share in the British markets, which ought to belong exclusively to the British manufacturers. He also declared that the union of both countries under one Parliament was the only satisfactory mode of settling and confirming

England's claim with respect to Ireland. A new and totally different set of propositions, twenty in number, one of them giving England absolute commercial control over Ireland, was brought before the Irish House of Commons in August. It was carried by so small a majority that Mr. Orde declared he would not proceed with it that session; and it was never afterwards revived.

The fears of Irish Protestants and English manufacturers are a singular comment on the contemptuous charges of indolence and want of enterprise brought against the people of Ireland. The Protestants would not permit the Catholics to purchase land, because they argued, if they had the power the whole country would come into their possession. The English manufacturers would not allow the Irish to compete with them lest they should be beaten and undersold. And this at a time when the limbs of the Catholics were benumbed with chains, and the habits of trade had been destroyed in Ireland by commercial restrictions, and by accomplished and completed English monopoly.

We must perpetually remind ourselves of the elements of British history. The Conquest was not merely an ancestral tradition tinging the line of descent: it was a perennial fact, never ceasing to exercise its original potency, and infuse its lawless spirit. England was held by the real or political descendants of the Normans, who gratified their instincts and supported their power by the acquisition and spoliation of foreign territory, and fostered a fierce and unscrupulous system of trade. The extent and the uses of conquest may be seen in the careers of Clive and Hastings. The Nabob of Oude employed Hastings to conquer a territory which he dared not assail with his own numerically superior forces, and paid him four hundred thousand pounds for the job. The Rajah of Benares offered him a bribe of twenty thousand pounds to escape a tribute of fifty thousand. Hastings took the money, changed his mind, paid the sum to the Company, fined the rajah ten thousand pounds, and demanded half a million from him in one sum. The unhappy prince offered two hundred thousand pounds. Hastings deposed him and acquired the command of that sum annually. The House of Lords gave those acts the sanction of their acquiescence. The trade that Norman prudence encouraged may be instanced by the slave traffic. In 1783 an action was brought to recover the amount of an insurance on a hundred and thirty slaves who had been thrown overboard under an unfounded apprehension of scarcity of water. Damages were obtained by the plaintiff of thirty pounds for each slave. They were treated as mere chattels. Such were the rulers and such the traders who sought union with Ireland, instead of an independent Irish Parliament and equal commerce.

Section III.

While the rulers of England were plotting for a forced and formal union with Ireland on their own behalf, tendencies towards a true identification of the aims and interests of the people of the two countries were working to the surface. The volunteers were taking the Catholics into their body, and the doctrines of the English reformers were spreading to the sister country. The struggle of Ireland has always been human rather than national. Hidden in remote obscurity, her efforts have appeared wild and purposeless, or directed to some narrow and selfish end. To lessen her claim to sympathy on such pretences would be like saying of some brave soldier whom the enemy had singled out and cut off from his companions, that no account was to be taken of him because he was fighting to save his own life. Ireland is fighting for her own life, but she risked her life in the cause of everything that makes life precious to all men.

The House of Commons consisted in a great measure of nominees of the Lords, and a few territorial magnates. A thorough reform of Parliament was imperatively required. The volunteers met by their delegates in June, 1783, and resolved that a more equal representation of the people could alone perpetuate the possession of a free constitution. Similar resolutions were adopted in every part of the country, and a general meeting of volunteers at Dungannon was appointed to be held in September. The delegates of two hundred and seventy-two companies assembled and passed resolutions in favour of extension of the franchise and shorter Parliaments. The mutual aid of English and Scotch citizens engaged in the same great enterprise was sought for. It was arranged that a convention of delegates should be assembled in Dublin in November to digest a plan of Parliamentary reform. It met and drew up a scheme which was presented in Parliament by Flood. The proposed changes were moderate, aiming at the extension of the franchise and the exclusion of pensioners from seats. The opponents of the bill directed the whole debate to the alleged indignity of yielding to the dictation of armed men. They preferred the dignity of corruption. It was urged that boroughs were sold like an ass or an ox. This only pithily and practically described a state of things which the salesmen wished to be continued. A line of denunciation followed by Fitzgibbon, a true Norman of that type which won Lord Macaulay's reverence,[1] of exterior refinement, but coarse-minded and conscienceless, deserves particular notice. He was devoted to the service of the English minister in hope of reward. His pride, his hope, his glory, was to annihilate his country in the Nirwana of Union with England. Yet he made it an indelible and unanswerable reproach against his reforming countrymen, that they were in league with English reformers. He ascribed the desire for reform to certain system-mongers in England, and traced its origin to the London Constitutional Society. He saw in England what he saw in Ireland, lords and slaves. He saw two Englands—an England of privilege, and an England of privation—and he launched it as a poisoned missile against the Irish advocates of purity of election, that they made common cause with the struggling commonalty of the sister country. The Irish Parliament of aristocratic nominees had been compelled to recover their rights from the aristocracy of England, but it would be an insufferable degradation to compel them to join the democracy of England in winning freedom and prosperity for all. The motion was overwhelmingly defeated.

The volunteers in vain awaited for tidings of success, and at length adjourned in silence. Lord Charlemont was their chairman. The Hon.

[1] Macaulay's "History of England," Vol. I., p. 11; Vol. III., p. 193.

Robert Stewart, father of Lord Castlereagh, was a chairman of a sub-committee. A meeting of those leaders and their friends was held at Lord Charlemont's, and peace was unanimously decided to be the first object. The convention met on the first of December. Lord Charlemont repressed the rising spirit of indignation, adjourned the meeting, and at their next assemblage, the day after, dissolved the convention. They let the opportunity pass and never had another. There were divisions among them on Catholic emancipation. A company at Belfast attended a Catholic chapel to signalise their unqualified devotion to the country. But numbers of them, and chiefly Lord Charlemont and Flood, were bigoted in their opposition to Catholic claims. A fresh source of dissension was now introduced. Those in favour of Parliamentary reform adopted a resolution that they would not associate with any regiment which continued under the command of officers opposed to it.

An attempt was next made by Flood and others to call a national congress. The Sheriff of Dublin was fined and imprisoned in an arbitrary manner for exercising his official power in the election of representatives. Printers and publishers of obnoxious newspapers were similarly treated. The congress, however, met; Flood attended and explained his plan of reform. It omitted the consideration of Catholic emancipation, and met in consequence no support. Flood withdrew and the congress died away. The Ulster volunteers, in an address to Lord Charlemont, condemned aristocratic tyranny, and suggested union with the Catholics as the surest method of protection. The earl discountenanced the notion, and received the thanks of the corporation of Dublin.

The project of the national congress seriously alarmed government. It was severely censured in Parliament. Grattan on this occasion directed attention to a change that was taking place in the constitution of the volunteers. The lowest classes of the populace, he said, were now under drill. The volunteers originally represented the property of the nation, they were now becoming the armed beggary. He spoke as if armies were always composed of rich men. The volunteers, thwarted in their aims and abandoned by their leaders, were drifting with a new tide into a wider expanse, over which darkness yet brooded. The organisation lingered for a few years and died away.

Section IV.

When the Parliament met in 1789, a bill was passed to facilitate the suppression of tumultuous meetings. Fitzgibbon enlarged on the excesses that prevailed, and ascribed them to the miserable condition of the peasantry, who were ground to the earth by extortionate rents. Several landlords plainly retorted that the disturbances were fomented by government emissaries in order to supply a pretext for striking down the constitution of the country. Every attempt to put a limit to pensions was denounced as a democratic interference with the prerogative of the Crown, and hopelessly defeated. Grattan vainly endeavoured to pledge the House to a future consideration of tythes. The weight of misery that a united people were preparing to shake off resumed its pressure as they grew disunited, and produced mutual exasperation.

The French people, from the depth of oppression, rose against their king and nobles. The kingly governments of the Continent and England combined on behalf of threatened monarchy; and liberty, in wild self-defence, committed for a moment the deeds by which despotism is uniformly maintained. The splendour of Burke's imperious fallacies drove things to extremities, broke up the Whig party, and confounded in the language of the designing, and the minds of the unthinking, the efforts of Englishmen to emulate French democracy with those of Ireland to rise to the level of the British constitution. The atheism and republicanism of France alienated the heads of the Irish Catholic Church. There was an obvious concert between government and the bishops on the Catholic relief bill, the practical effect of which was to detach the more influential members from the community.

Glaring exposures continued to be made in Parliament of the systematic corruption that was at once working and justifying the enslavement of the country. Peerages were openly sold, and the money used to purchase seats in the Commons. New offices with new salaries were created. The men who did these things were pronounced to be public criminals. So we say of great conquerors that they were public murderers. The accusation of crime is diffused and lost in the magnifying epithet. Policemen under government orders were stationed through the country. Laws giving magistrates power over meetings were enacted. Soldiers were multiplied. The coasts were lined with military stations. Disturbances were fomented, and crimes of a sensational character were committed. Protestants were armed. The leading Catholics being in a sense made prisoners by conciliation, every device was used to throw discredit on Catholics generally, and to provoke Protestants against them.

The English ministers and their Irish agents were plotting openly against the life of Ireland. The scarcely concealed purpose was to replace the volunteers by soldiers, to disunite Protestants and Catholics, and to conquer the country afresh. After the sacred engagements that had been made and were now disregarded, all appeals to law and order were impious profanations. Ministers had power, but law was on the people's side. Everything that government did was done in contemptuous violation of a compact that, if words have any meaning, could never be dissolved.

In 1791 Theobald Wolfe Tone, the son of English parents, a Protestant, a man of rare simplicity and earnestness of character, capable of inspiring confidence in holders of other creeds, which he never betrayed, and winning love from the staunchest enemies of his cause, which never forsook him, founded the institution of United Irishmen in Belfast. Their object was to balance the weight of English influence by uniting all the people of Ireland for the achievement of a complete Parliamentary reform. A similar society was immediately formed in Dublin. More than two-thirds of the leading men were Protestants, and nearly all, Protestants and Catholics, were of English descent. The objects of the United Irishmen were legitimate and their proceedings public. In

1793 two members were fined and imprisoned by the Lord Chancellor for complaining of the inquisitorial conduct of a committee of the House of Lords. In 1794, Archibald Hamilton Rowan was prosecuted for a seditious libel published two years before. The prosecution had been postponed in order to complete the new machinery for a conviction. A fitting sheriff was appointed, a jury was packed, a perjured witness was provided, and Rowan was found guilty. This was the commencement of packed juries and paid witnesses. A few months after, a meeting of the United Irishmen was dispersed by the police and their papers seized.

England in this year needed pecuniary assistance from Ireland. Earl Fitzwilliam was appointed Viceroy, and came with full powers to emancipate the Catholics and purify the Government. He began by making changes in the public offices. A sum of a million and seven hundred thousand pounds was asked for and granted. One of the displaced officers, named Beresford, rushed to the king with his complaints and was received with favour. Earl Fitzwilliam was recalled in 1795. The powers of reform which he claimed to possess were denied, and he was charged with a betrayal of state secrets in claiming them. The correspondence relating to his appointment and recall was asked for in the English Lords and Commons, and refused by large majorities. A grant of ten thousand pounds was made to Maynooth.

The United Irishmen, driven from constitutional courses by the lawlessness of the authorities, adopted extreme views, and like all men who find relief in the knowledge of the worst, exulted in the unrestricted political prospect that opened before them. They formed themselves into a secret society, and aimed at the establishment of a republic. Their hopes of success rested on the assistance of the Catholics. The Court faction sent agents to Armagh, and under their instructions, in order to prevent the union of Irishmen, the Peep-of-day Boys took the title of Orangemen, and formally entered into a league for the destruction of Irish Catholics. The first Orange lodge was formed on the twenty-first of September, 1795.

The French Directory sent a Protestant clergyman, named Jackson, to report to them as to the readiness of the English and Irish people to receive an invading force. He made his mission known in London to a person who communicated the knowledge to Mr. Pitt. The minister set his informant as a spy on Jackson, while he disseminated treason and manufactured victims for the gallows. The two men went to Ireland, where, after some feeble efforts, Jackson was arrested, and, being found guilty, poisoned himself in the dock, that his little property might not pass from the possession of his widow. Tone, who had been implicated in Jackson's proceedings, was permitted, through the influence of his friends with the Government, to emigrate to America, from whence he went to France, and formed an alliance between the Irish Union and the French Government. Lord Malmesbury was sent by Pitt to France, where he took measures that frustrated the French and Dutch attempts to assist Ireland in 1796 and 1797.

Lord Camden came over as Viceroy, and Parliament met in January, 1796. The Attorney-General introduced measures indemnifying magistrates acting in excess of their legal powers, and giving them increased authority to search for arms, prevent meetings, and send suspected persons on board the fleet. Grattan and others showed how the Orangemen were committing greater atrocities in Armagh with impunity than anything laid to the charge of the Catholics in the south; how they were driving thousands of Catholic weavers from their homes, murdering them, or turning them as beggars on the world. All remonstrance was in vain. The proceedings of which Grattan complained were part of the Government plan, and were only recommended by the condemnation of the friends of the country. As the summer advanced military outrages increased in the south; houses were burned down, and the inhabitants maimed or murdered on the suspicion of a landlord. In October the Habeas Corpus Act was suspended.

In May, 1797, the question of Parliamentary reform was brought forward once more. It was the last effort of reason that stood between the country and ruin. The Government declared that the people must be subdued before they could be relieved. This inseparable condition of Irish redress meant that rulers were irresponsible, that they chose to rule by terror and not by confidence, that the people were worthy of punishment for discontent, even though they had good grounds for exhibiting it, and that Government must be carried on by men and not by laws, by the passions of tyrants and not by the equity of the Constitution, by the despicable malice of affronted official pride and not by the humanity of justice. Grattan closed the debate by telling the minister that he knew the offer of peace would be rejected, and that having no hopes of persuading or dissuading them he would trouble them no more. He knew now that it was not his oratory that had won the victory of 1782. He did not offer himself for re-election after the dissolution that took place at the end of the year.

Relief having been refused, the subjection that must precede it was forthwith applied. The soldiery were let loose on the peasants.[1] In the Irish accounts of what ensued no blame is attached to the English regiments. The native yeomanry, Germans, and a regiment of Welsh volunteers, known as the Ancient Britons, led by the officious and misplaced loyalty of Sir Watkin Wynne, were the chief actors. It was boasted by officers of rank that within certain large districts no home had been left undefiled. The bayonet was used to force compliance. There are men who have the shameless audacity to complain of excesses committed by the peasantry in the insurrection that followed.

On the twenty-second of November the Earl of Moira declared in the British House of Lords that he had seen in Ireland the most disgusting tyranny that any nation had ever groaned under. He had seen the most grievous oppression exercised on the presumption that the objects of it were in hostility to the Government, and this in a part of the country as quiet and free from disturbance as the city of London. He had known men to be tortured almost to death on mere suspicion, houses, thirty in a night, to be burned, and other more aggravated facts over which prudence must draw a veil. The newspapers, he added, dared not make these things known lest they might share the fate of the *Northern Press*, the offices and property of which had been destroyed

[1] "Memoirs of the Whig Party," by Lord Holland, Vol. I., p. 113.

by a party of soldiers in the open day. Lord Granville, in reply, confidently appealed to the House whether measures of concession and conciliation had ever been abandoned? During thirty years his Majesty's Government had been distinguished by the same uniform tenderness of regard, the same adherence to the principles of a mild system.

In all other experience the mirage appears in the distance, and recedes as we advance. In Ireland we are always in the present told that the barque of state gently heaves on a placid lake, and that palm trees of peace surround the scene. The tract that yesterday was similarly described is to-day admitted to be a savage desert, as to-morrow that of to-day will be allowed to be.

The Government had spies among the United Irishmen, some of their most active and trusted members, who reported everything that occurred or was intended to occur. A journalist who recommended assassination was in their pay. On the twelfth of March, 1798, the leaders were made prisoners. New leaders, including two brothers named Henry and John Sheares, were appointed. On the twenty-first of May the Sheares's were seized and convicted on the testimony of an informer who had sat at their board and fondled the children of one of them. When the verdict was found they clasped each other in their arms. Henry, who had a wife and six children, in broken accents, begged for a little time to settle his affairs. The Attorney-General asked that execution should be done the next day. The court ordered it so. Heartbroken letters were written to procure a commutation of Henry's sentence. His conviction was in fact illegal. A niece of the Viceroy knelt at her uncle's feet, beseeching for mercy. Fitzgibbon, who was now Lord Clare, hindered her success. An interview was arranged for a sister of the condemned men with the Viceroy, but Lord Clare's creatures prevented it. When the brothers met on the morning of the execution they again rushed into each other's arms. When the sheriffs arrived, the prisoners entreated them to be the bearers of a supplication for a short respite. The message was carried to the Castle, and a respite refused. A new entreaty was made for a respite for at least one of them till Monday. The sheriff went, and returned with a denial. The authorities had subordinates worthy of them. When fitting the rope on Henry's neck the executioner did his work so roughly that he drew an exclamation of anger from the unhappy man. With halters round their necks and caps drawn over their faces, they tottered out on the platform, holding each other's hands. Before the drop fell the executioner hauled up John until his head and face came into violent contact with the block of the tackle, and held him suspended above for nearly a minute. At last the platform fell.

Lord Edward Fitzgerald, another member of the directory, when betrayed resisted his captors, killed one of them, and died in a few days of the wounds he received in the struggle. Neilson, a Northern United Irishman, was surprised whilst examining the prison in which some of his friends were confined, with a view to their rescue. He fought till his body was covered with gashes. On his trial he appeared in the dock loaded with irons. He defied the judges, and refused to engage counsel for his defence. Ultimately he was exiled.

When the chiefs were in prison or executed the peasantry were goaded by merciless burnings and tortures till they rose in the sheer instinct of self-defence. Leaderless and unarmed, they almost carried off in triumph the bait of freedom that was held out to lure them to their country's ruin. They failed only because they did not know how to improve on their repeated victories.[1] At Arklow they attacked a disciplined army in the field, were winning the day till their ammunition failed, and the battle was a drawn one. At Ross, after ten hours' incessant fighting, they stormed the town, gave themselves up to drunkenness, and were butchered. They always succeeded in their ambuscades, and had they confined themselves to desultory warfare they would have cleared the land of its foes. The smaller their body the more certain was their success. When they fought in large numbers they could not calculate on each other's movements, and they had no general. At Vinegar Hill, though attacked by twenty thousand regular troops, with ordnance, they defended themselves for several hours, suffered but little loss, and retired unpursued. They lost fifty thousand men, chiefly killed in cold blood. They slew twenty thousand of their enemies in the field. The Ancient Britons were slain to a man. This was the work of a few counties in Leinster. What would the result have been had there been a general rising? The rebellion of 1798 is a warning to statesmen not to venture on such a crime again.

When the insurrection was over, the native tyrants, who were still reeking from the slaughter of their unarmed countrymen, had an opportunity of encountering regular troops. The French effected a landing with less than a thousand men at Killala. Bishop Stock happened to be there at the time; he published an account of the event, in which he bore testimony to the unexceptionable conduct of the French and the Irish, and thereby forfeited his promotion. The royal army fled before them like a mob, infantry and cavalry mixed, leaving all their artillery behind them. The French at last surrendered when surrounded by twenty thousand men. Wolfe Tone had accompanied them as a commissioned officer. He was condemned to be hanged by a court martial. He begged for the death of a soldier, and was refused. He escaped the pollution of the hangman's touch by cutting his throat. The wretches would have hanged him while expiring had not a legal process disputing the legality of his conviction intervened.

One or two instances of cruel massacre, as at Scullabogue barn and Wexford bridge, are quoted as descriptive of the whole insurrection. The constant reiterations of Scullabogue prove its exceptional character. The frequency with which it is repeated is intended to serve for frequency of occurrence. Had the Irish retaliated by extermination they would have liberated their country. Who are those men who claim a right to murder Irishmen, and scream like children or women when a blow is struck in return? Scullabogue was the one spot that reverberated to a thousand massacres. A nation, like an individual, in vulgar estimation becomes great when the solitary murder swells to multitudinous proportions. In very truth it is not the magnitude of the Scullabogue slaughter that is condemned but its contemptible littleness. Had the

[1] "Memoirs of the Whig Party," Vol. I., page 111.

flame raged far and wide, had unflinching vindictiveness, and iron-handed system gathered all enemies of Irish happiness under one vast roof, and extinguished them in blood and smoke, the deed would be accounted heroic, and would win the plaudits of those who now hiss the incompleteness of the tragedy. The admirers of wholesale gigantic massacre are the men who revile the achievements of pigmies in the murderer's trade. Vigorous swimmers in the ocean of blood, they vituperate the scanty driblet that fails to stain the sole of the Irishman's foot.

This plea is not made for the sake of native or Catholic Irishmen. A large number of those who perished at Scullabogue were Catholics. The whole insurrection was Protestant and English. The Wexford men were of pure Saxon descent. Two of those prominently associated with the massacre bore the names of Devereaux and Fitzhenry, and were descendants apparently of the Earl of Essex and King Henry I. The general of the Irish was a Saxon. His successor was a Norman. No Milesian name is noticeable in the insurgent ranks.[1] Lord O'Neill fell fighting on the English side. An O'Brien was the chief informer against the United Irishmen.

The Irish severities were the retorts of natural justice. They piked some German prisoners for having wantonly shot a lady, the wife of a royalist. In the higher region of human conduct they won a victory which more than redeems their defeat. No priest who fell into the hands of the soldiers escaped a cruel death. The Irish did not kill a single Protestant clergyman. The military burned fifty or sixty Catholic chapels. The Irish burned one Protestant church. They did not insult even one woman. No friend of Ireland or freedom need blush or fear for 1798.

The United Irishmen movement was the Irish aspect of a general agitation, inspired from France, that was passing over the three kingdoms at this period. It was repressed in England and Scotland by laws forbidding public discussion, the conviction of printers, and the introduction of foreign troops. Some of the most prominent leaders were tried and acquitted in England. A jury's verdict in that country is the last decision, and is generally taken as expressive of the people's indisputable will, even when it is contrary to law. In Ireland, unless it slavishly echoes the English minister's policy, it ranks with the alleged crime which it refuses to condemn. The spirit of reform was however extinguished for the moment even by the confidence in public institutions, which the allowed verdict of an independent jury diffused. The people themselves, as in Ireland, were divided. In Birmingham the mob wrecked the houses of the principal reformers. In Scotland the reformers were persecuted with extreme severity. The judges, in referring to the claim of universal suffrage, said that the landed interest alone had a right to be represented. The rabble had nothing but personal property, and what hold had the nation on

[1] Arthur O'Connor, whose name occurs prominently in the history of these times, was the descendant of a London merchant named Conner or Conyers. Fergus O'Connor was of the same family.

them?[1] In the navy alone the demand for reform triumphed. The sailors mutinied, and as they had power to enforce their requirements, they were appeased by the redress of their grievances, the dismissal of tyrannical officers, and a full indemnity.

SECTION V.

Before the English minister had quite killed he hastened to take possession. While the insurrection raged a pamphlet proposing a Legislative Union was published. With all the strength that remained to it the nation lifted its arm to ward off the blow. Meetings of the Irish Bar, of the mayor and citizens, of the bankers and merchants, of the fellows and scholars of Trinity College, protested against the project. The Chancellor of the Exchequer and the Prime Sergeant were dismissed for their opposition. On the twenty-second of January, 1799, the Viceroy recommended to Parliament the consideration of the best means of consolidating into one fabric the resources of the British Empire. A union was resisted in both Houses as beyond the power of Parliament. The Lords, with the exception of sixteen, who protested, voted the question an open one. In the Commons an amendment to the address was moved declaring a resident Parliament to be the birthright of Ireland. It was lost by a majority of one. This majority was obtained by buying in the sight of the House the vote of a member who was holding out for high terms, and inducing another member to refrain from voting on the false plea that he had resigned. On the twenty-fourth the address was defeated by a majority of six against Government.

Meetings continued to be held protesting against the union. The military under pretence of keeping order stifled discussion. Districts that showed an anti-unionist spirit were proclaimed. All the machinery used for suppressing the insurrection was kept in motion to promote the union. Hands wet with the people's blood were laid on their constitutional liberties. The Press was purchased to admit only one-sided publications. The Post Office was employed to circulate only unionist writings. Sheriffs were instructed to prevent the sense of the counties from being collected at public assemblies. Publicans were punished with loss of licence if they allowed their houses to be used for obtaining signatures to anti-unionist addresses. The Viceroy fondled the heads of the Catholic Church. The fact that the most violent opposers of the union were Orangemen cooled the enthusiasm of the masses. The Dublin Catholics who were immediately interested held a meeting at which Daniel O'Connell, a young lawyer, defended his co-religionists from the charge of favouring the union, and declared that they would prefer throwing themselves on the mercy of their Protestant fellow countrymen to acquiescing in the political murder of their country.

---

[1] Irish agitation is often contrasted with the peacefulness of the Scotch. They made a desert and called it peace (see p. 195). Slavery, pure and simple, existed in Scotland so recently as 1799.—See "Memorials of His Time," by H. Cockburn, p. 76. In criminal cases the presiding judge selected the jury.—*Ibid.*, p. 384. An instance in the political trials of 1793 epitomises the history of the period. One of the prisoners was arguing that all great men had been reformers, "even our Saviour Himself." "Muckle he made o' that," chuckled Braxfield, the judge, "he was hanget."—*Ibid.*, p. 117.

The ministry took their measures undismayed. They had received instructions from Pitt to make certain of a majority of fifty. There was no variety possible in the established methods of bribery and bloodshed. A party of soldiers was marched into the streets of Dublin, and without any provocation fired a volley of balls among a crowd. Lord Castlereagh publicly offered as compensation for loss of patronage, to every nobleman who returned members to Parliament, fifteen thousand pounds for each member so returned; to every member who purchased a seat, the return of his purchase money; to all members and others who should be losers by the union, the division of a sum of a million and a half. In addition, over a million was given in bribes out of the secret service fund. Forty new peerages were created and given as bribes. Ten bishoprics, one chief justiceship, six puisne-judgeships, were similarly bestowed.

On the fifteenth of February, 1800, the union was carried by a majority of one hundred and fifty-eight to one hundred and fifteen. A guard of cavalry paraded round the Parliament House during the debate. On the thirteenth of March it was moved that the king should be requested to convoke a new Parliament before any fresh arrangement was made. This motion was lost by a majority of forty-six. The Union Bill received the royal assent on the first of August, 1800.

It is impossible that the union of 1800 can be considered as a final settlement. It is impossible, not so much because Ireland could not be contented under it, as because the nature of it is such that England cannot or will not take the steps necessary to make her contented. She feels that she holds her ground by fraud and force, and can maintain it only by those means. To submit to it on Ireland's part would not be yielding to England's superiority, but bowing before the omnipotence of evil. Irishmen believe in a God and love justice. To consent to the union is to them the denial of a God. All the might of England's empire, and all the height of England's pride, are as froth against this rock. The objections are not merely that the measure was constitutionally and intrinsically invalid, or that it was carried when the country was swooning with loss of blood, and confronted by the bayonets of a hundred and thirty-five thousand soldiers, or that it was won by bribery and false promises. Those are only technical invalidations of a technical enactment. The time and the manner have left not merely obstacles which reason discovers, but instinctive shudders and revolts of conscience. If the contrivers of the union had waited till the sword was sheathed, and the corpses had rotted from the gibbets, and earth had covered her slain, so that the two countries had met in the innocencies and sympathies of nature, the union might have been an incorporate one. But when they were forced together, compressing between them unsoaked blood and unslaked hate, and unburied rottenness of flesh and spirit, they enclosed a barrier of mutual repugnance from whose contact Ireland, and whose consideration England, violently recoils. The islands must be disjoined by open debate for a space that the filth and corruption that separate them may be cleared away. Their union to be peaceful and permanent must be honourable.

If fairly initiated and conducted the union would be the best settlement. The manner in which it was obtained prevents it from being fairly carried out. It is maintained as it was achieved. The tyrannical temper and determination, the insulting airs of superiority, still remain. What a man has gained by fair argument he will never think of declaring he will retain though all argument should be against him. England did not enter on the union as equal uniting with equal. It was a union forced on an inferior. The citizen of a small but free state can assert himself as on equal terms with the subject of the greatest states. His plainness of living, his unadorned attire, his poverty, he may boast of as his national customs : and he may take pride in contrasting them with the luxurious ways of a wealthy country, just as the citizen of a Republic can boast of his democratic simplicity. The native of a poor country united by violence to a rich country cannot act in this way. Irishmen have naturally those virtues of poverty that stand unabashed before wealth. No Irishman feels it a loss to his dignity that he has not a retinue of menials to wait on him. Irishmen in consequence do not conduct themselves with awe-struck humility in the presence of wealthy or titled Englishmen. Why should they not? it will be asked. An Englishman of humble circumstances behaves accordingly towards an English superior. Why not an Irishman? Because the Irishman belongs to a distinct nation, in whose ancient traditions wealth has no claims to worship, and it is only by a legal fiction that he is of the same country as the Englishman. Attempts were formerly made to educate the sons of Milesian chiefs into Norman distinctions in London. When they were brought home, they confounded their tutors by meeting their tribesmen and shaking hands with them, as equal meets equal. The wider the separation grows between rich man and poor man in England, the wider grows the moral severance of the Islands.

The wisdom and expediency of the union must be proved. It never can be satisfactorily proved while it is said that its continuance does not depend on proof but on the will of the stronger. The refusal to argue the subject raises the question whether the Irish Parliament had the power to pass a measure that precluded future discussion. If the measure was passed because it was for the best, that argument must always remain open. If we may not discuss the union, no legal union exists. There must be a problematical separation before there can be a sincere union.

The man who avows that he will not reason, nor listen to reason, is he who observes neither honour in peace, nor humanity in war, and who compels his opponent to follow him to the extremities to which his principles inevitably lead. He is in a region where right and wrong have no meaning. When English writers assume Irish independence to be an impossibility, they only gratify their pride, and insult those who think differently. The Irishman who otherwise would not consider a real union an impossibility is roused to take that position, and to insist that Ireland's independence was once a fact, and under similar circumstances, would, after past experience, become an eternal fact.

The restoration of the Heptarchy is always given as the parallel of repeal of the union. To this most singular argument it may be answered that the restoration of the Heptarchy is a domestic affair in which Ireland has no right to interfere. In the growing impotency of Parliament, and the increasing concentration of populations, it may be that the restoration of the Heptarchy in a certain degree would be a great blessing. But Irish independence has as little relation to restoring the Heptarchy, as the union has to the reconquest of America. "Repeal the Union!" some one said, "you might as well talk of restoring the Heptarchy." "Eternal Union with England!" the Irishman may answer, "you might as well talk of bringing back the American Colonies."

A union to justify the name should entail equal opportunities of honour and power. The Sovereign should reign over England from Ireland as well as over Ireland from England. The Parliament should legislate in Ireland for Irish interests, as in England for English interests. The present so-called Union seizes on the advantages of a material junction for England, and imposes the disadvantages of a foreign conquest on Ireland. When arguing for a union Clare or Castlereagh would never have ventured to say that the intention was to make Ireland a grazing farm for England. Such a thought would have been utterly inconsistent with the stated aim and condition of the compact. It was a union of Englishmen with Irishmen and not with Irish cattle that was proposed. The inferiority of Ireland and Irishmen that is now practically asserted, was never a matter of stipulation. The mocking alternative offered to Ireland is to be the mother of herds for England or to be sunk under the sea. This latter saying, as old as Spenser, is a mark of that insanity of impious ownership which a Milesian long ago charged on the Normans. Irishmen have an opinion in the matter. It would be better for each individual Irishman to find his way speedily to an honourable grave than to suffer the kind of slavery, which some Englishmen, or more often Irishmen assuming airs of Norman rule, desire to impose. It would be better for Ireland to be sunk under the ocean than that she should fatten cattle for the Norman tyrants who are making England half a palace and half a poorhouse, and filling the earth with violence that eventually, unless the sons of God keep aloof from the daughters of men, will drown the world in a deluge, not of water, but of blood.

A brief reference to an insurrectionary attempt made by Robert Emmett in 1803 may be made here. Like the rebellion of 1798, it sprang from the contagion of the French Revolution, and was a local, and almost individual, outbreak of the general aspiration for reform that found expression about the same time in the conspiracy of Colonel Despard in England. The object of this secret movement was the independence of England and Ireland, and an equalisation of civil, political, and religious rights. Government were fully aware of all the proceedings of the conspirators, and prompted some of their actions through spies. After six months' close watch Despard was taken, tried, and hanged in February, 1803. Emmett made his arrangements for the commencement of his attempt on the twenty-third of July. The traitors or spies who gave information of his plans to the authorities are not known. There is not even any positive proof that treachery existed in his case. There is only circumstantial evidence. With the silent, steady, unerring operation of some impalpable machinery, everything he did was undone, every preparation he made was frustrated. Undismayed and undiscouraged he went on with his undertaking. On the morning of the appointed day a division arose among his followers, some of them proposing a postponement of the attempt. Emmett must either totally abandon the project or immediately proceed. He decided on proceeding. The design was to seize the Castle. Chosen men were awaiting the summons in several counties. The persons appointed to give the order to the Wicklow men never left Dublin. The Kildare men came, were informed that the enterprise was deferred, and returned home. The Wexford men were in Dublin ready to act, but received no commands. Another large party was assembled watching for a rocket that was to be the signal; but no rocket appeared. Emmett found himself with eighty men baffled and disheartened. A messenger rushed in announcing that the military were coming on them.[1] Without waiting to ascertain the falsity of the alarm, they issued forth, and as they swept tumultuously along, Lord Kilwarden, passing in his carriage, was caught in the disorderly train that followed, and murdered. The character of this incident belonged to those who instead of preventing an insurrection reduced it to a riot.[2] Emmett was taken and hanged. Those who were acquainted with his plans, and capable of giving an opinion on them, affirm that if they had been worked out success was almost certain. This means that success was certain if the whole affair was not in the hands of Government agents. It is ungracious to criticise the prudence of a man who gave his life for his country. But the right of any person to embroil his country in a desperate struggle because he is ready to sacrifice his own life, may be questioned. There are mightier tides of feeling in which all such calculations are lost. The desire to win a place among the martyrs for freedom and the sympathy of the world, is a temptation to which some young and enthusiastic minds will always yield, and rulers must be held accountable if they create the occasions. He who resists unjust power, unjust not according to the judgment of those exercising the power, but of all mankind besides, and ventures his life in the deed, will secure the admiration of all time. Emmett's uninscribed tombstone is more eloquent than all the graven marbles in Westminster.

. . . .

Near the town of Castleisland, in the county of Kerry, there is a remarkable formation in the limestone soil. In the midst of a plain country, a deep declivity sinks into the earth like a fragment of a valley blocked at either end. Its sides are formed of massive rocks, sloping banks, and broken surfaces all veiled with trees, festooning shrubs, and luxuriant herbage. At one end a copious river springs upward from the earth, rushes across the length of the sunken space, and loses itself in a cavern in the rocks. At a little distance a similar depression in the earth is found, and the river is seen flowing from the hollow cave at one end and entering another cave at the opposite extremity. The river rises once more into daylight after a subterraneous flow of more than a mile, runs with increasing volume by hamlet and town, washes the

---

[1] See "Memoirs of Viscount Castlereagh," Vol. IV., p. 323, and comp. pages 331-3-4.
[2] "Annual Register for 1803," p. 315.

walls of the castle where Desmond's knights were put to death for their fidelity to their chief, passes under the arches on which stand the ruins of Castlemaine, the last fortress gained for Elizabeth by Carew, and flows onward till it joins the sea in which the streams of the neighbouring island mingle. This river symbolises the career of the people of Ireland. They spring from an unknown source, cross the abyss of history in the purity of their unstained origin, burst into view for a bright and romantic moment, and then after being lost to sight so completely that men walk the fields of siege and treaty and battle without being aware of their existence, they rise, assert their right to a place and an enterprise, associate their name with the chivalry of the past, and with unerring and inevitable purpose struggle onwards to the level sea of freedom in which the people of England are likewise seeking to purge away the defilements of their long and suffering serfdom. When the two peoples thus meet there will be a union.

CHAPTER XV.

CATHOLIC COMMITTEE.

SECTION I.

THE first united Parliament met on the twenty-second of January, 1801. The main argument for the Union had been the impossibility of obtaining full emancipation for the Catholics in an Irish legislature, and the understanding that it was to be an early measure in the Imperial Parliament. A rumour went abroad that Pitt was about to resign. The reason given for this course was that the king refused to consent to emancipation, and that Pitt felt bound to retire from an office in which he could not fulfil his engagements. The truth was that peace with France was imperatively demanded by the country, and that the pride of the minister would not allow him either to negotiate its terms or to admit his unwillingness to do so. The compliment was therefore paid to Ireland of letting it be understood that a regard for her interests caused a change of administration. Mr. Addington took office pledged to refuse emancipation, and with the promise of the support of his predecessor in his refusal. Twelve months after, Pitt, having insured the renewal of war, resumed his place as Prime Minister, and solemnly engaged to the king that the claims of the Catholics should never again be mentioned.

Meantime the system of raising false alarms by disseminating rumours of vague danger, which seemed to come from all quarters of the heavens, only because they were not limited by real existence to any special direction, was kept in sedulous activity. The report of a secret committee represented the united kingdom as overrun with Jacobinism. This was the exasperating name under which the popular longings for human happiness were to be suppressed. England was said to be honeycombed with secret associations impregnated with French principles, and the Irish rebellion was continually mentioned in connection with English discontent, to bring discredit on the yearnings of freedom, to inflame the minds of the foes of progress, and to justify the suspension of the Habeas Corpus Act—an Act which Ireland knows only by its suspensions—and the continuation of martial law in Ireland. Emmett's insurrection, which was allowed, with studied abstention, to run its unarmed and impotent course, was made the pretext for the multiplication of spies and arbitrary arrests, and the infliction of inhuman barbarities at the bidding of personal malice.

It is true that a number of expatriated Irishmen, chiefly Anglo-Irish and Protestants, were using every means in their power to procure the aid of France for the deliverance of their country. An Irish legion was formed by Bonaparte's instructions, and preparations were made for an invasion. When the armament was ready it was diverted to other purposes. It had been carefully stipulated by the Irish that the intended interposition was to be for the liberation, not the annexation, of Ireland. The French were to assist the Irish as they had assisted the Americans. This endeavour to escape from a Union that had been avowedly passed to prevent Irishmen from competing with Englishmen for the means of existence; from a nobility who gained their titles by selling their country, and paraded them by spending the produce of its toil in distant lands; from anniversary celebrations that never allowed the healing waters of time to bathe their wounds; from a public debt that was incurred in purchasing their independence and quenching the principles whose prevalence was their only hope; from religious suppression and political extinction; from yearly famines and hourly insults, must be taken into account when the case of Ireland is estimated. The unhappy land made every effort that a nation could make to escape from the alternative of death, or a struggle that was only less terrible than death, that lay in the future. It had argued with the eloquence of an angel's voice, it had appealed with the tenderness of a woman's heart, it asked for the reform of notorious abuses, it pleaded for the removal of acknowledged wrongs, it rebelled, it sought for foreign aid. If it made a single effort less, it might so far be held accountable for the events of its later history. There was nothing left but willing annihilation in accepted slavery, or the exercise of a deathless spirit in perennial civil commotion. It is Ireland's glory that she chose the latter course. It was the only glory that remained to her, and it is greater than any glory ever won by hireling armies in the field of war. There is no conceivable crime—assuming, yet indignantly denying, that Ireland has committed crime—no rancour so unappeasable, no agitation so prolonged, as that it is not to be put on the side of virtue if it be the only escape from the conscious corruption of living national death. Blinded by centuries of enforced darkness, and debarred from loving his native land, the Irish peasant has had in a sense to contract his affections to his circumstances, and fight for his farm and his chapel, as under happier fortunes he would have fought for his country.

Pitt's departure from his undertaking to satisfy the Catholic claims could be concealed only by preventing them from being pressed. The Catholic Committee either was worked by petty official usurpers for their private ends, or languished under aristocratic patronage. The seductions of the Castle were played on Lord Fingal, who was at this time one of its leaders. The Catholics, however, met and prepared a petition. A deputation waited on Pitt, who plainly informed them that he must resist it, although they had only begged that it might be laid on the table of the House with the assurance that the immediate adoption of its prayer was not urged. The delegates then applied to Fox. One of the speakers in the debate that ensued suggested the compromise of a veto by the Crown on the appointment of Catholic bishops by the Pope. The Whigs soon after came into office. The grant to Maynooth was increased on the avowed principle of connecting the Irish Catholics with the State, and hindering the education of their priests in France. In a similar spirit a bill enabling Catholics to hold commissions in the army and navy was introduced. Its operation, it was pleaded, would be to increase enlistments in Ireland, and so place a salutary check on the superabundant population of that country. The bill was read a first time, and immediately a violent ferment arose both in England and Ireland. The University of Oxford and the Corporation of Dublin petitioned against it. The king called on his ministers to resign. They proposed to withdraw the bill, but the king insisting on their giving a pledge that they would never again bring forward any measure affecting Catholics, their resignation was tendered and accepted. A No-Popery ministry, in which Spencer Perceval was the ruling spirit, came into office.

It was proposed at a meeting of Catholics held in Dublin in 1808 to petition Parliament for a repeal of the remaining penal laws. Charles O'Conor, in despair of success at such a time, moved the adjournment of the meeting. O'Connell counselled perseverance and stirred to agitation. A petition was prepared and forwarded, but because of a technical informality was not received. It was sent back to Ireland, and Lord Fingal, who had charge of it, remained in London, where he was induced to bind the Irish Catholics to the acceptance of the veto if emancipation was granted. The concession did not secure the expected result. The petition was carried back, presented, and its prayer rejected by a majority of a hundred and fifty-three. A national synod of the Irish Catholic prelates met in Dublin and decided against the veto with only three dissentients. O'Connell and the lay Catholics vehemently protested at public meetings against the measure. A motion for the admission of Catholics to the governorship of the Bank of Ireland was defeated. The Maynooth grant was reduced. Eighteen new police magistrates were created. Corruption in elections continued as before the Union, and no one was more busy or more efficient in its management than the Irish Secretary, Sir Arthur Wellesley.

In 1810 the subject of the veto was revived. The English Catholics were willing to receive it as the condition of emancipation. The Irish, lay and clerical, opposed it. A new proposal of a state provision for the Catholic clergy of Ireland was advanced. The king's reason had been for some time affected. The malady became hopeless. The Prince of Wales was appointed Regent. He had publicly announced himself as the friend of emancipation. Influenced, it is said, by one of his mistresses, he signalised his advent to power by the prosecution and imprisonment of two members of the Catholic Committee for violation of the Convention Act, which forbade the assemblage of representatives. O'Connell had specially guarded against the danger, but a packed jury defeated his precautions. English influence was brought to bear on the Pope, and his consent to the veto was obtained. The English Catholics warmly concurred. The Irish universally continued their opposition to what they considered the enslavement of their Church, even when recommended by the Pope. They formally resolved that in such a matter as this their feelings must not be influenced by any determination of his Holiness. Their conduct was in exact accord with the genius of their religion from the most ancient times. The union of ecclesiastical and temporal power in the same hands has always been the desire of kings and the danger of peoples. Wherever it has prevailed the instincts of freedom have been pronounced rebellion against God, and the worst vices of humanity have been familiarised to mankind as a licence from heaven. Virtuous women would have considered it a kind of sin to resist the advances of the profligate Prince Regent. The mixture of political and religious elements has its height in the Throne, its depth in Orangeism. This baleful institution was never so active as at this period. Secret as Satan, and hot as hell, it multiplied its lodges and nursed its hate.

The contest between the vetoists and the anti-vetoists grew to mutual recriminations. There was no place for compromise. The people became self-assertive; the aristocracy withdrew; the Committee or Board was suppressed by proclamation, dwindled in numbers, waxed noisier in debate, and was drowned in the acclamations of Waterloo.

SECTION II.

The victory of Waterloo raised the United Kingdom of Great Britain and Ireland to the pinnacle of glory. The loftiest aspirations that could be formed by the most powerful country for earthly triumph were gratified to the full. Ireland had an ample share in the achievement of this success and the erection of this unprecedented greatness. The general who conquered Napoleon was Irish;[1] the commander who won India was Irish; the statesman who presided over the country's fortunes was Irish; the writer and orator who inspired the nation to resist France was Irish. The force that served under Wellington at Waterloo was nearly one-half Irish. It is true that captain and statesman did what they could to conceal their nationality. It is also true that of the two motives with which the enlistment of Irish soldiers in the British army was encouraged by the great statesmen of the day, the evil one, the desire to diminish the Irish population, was more active and more consciously present than the prudential willingness to accept of Irish aid, and that Ireland was not considered as entitled to any share in the public joy; still we may take the facts as they existed, and looking at the glory of the occasion as equally of English and Irish accomplishment, we may consider the condition of the two countries on which the sun of victory shed such sultry beams.

We have to remember, in judging the whole case, that the course of foreign conquest on which Republican France entered, and the subsequent and consequent betrayal of her liberties by her victorious general, were forced on France by the wanton opposition of the surrounding nations, in which England took a leading part; that the opposition was commenced to prevent the spread of French freedom, and that only its spread to other countries was prevented, inasmuch as France, though baffled in external war in the person of Napoleon, remained in full possession of all the real objects and advantages of her revolution. France lost only in glory. Glory was the only gain of the United Kingdom. Everything that France had done or suffered was rewarded. The theories of philosophers, the dreams of poets, the schemes of statesmen,

[1] Richard Cowley of Castle Carbery, County Kildare, took the name of Wesley or Wellesley in the last century. He was ancestor to the Duke of Wellington. The name Cowley was old Irish, and was originally written M'Cowolly.

the crimes, victories, and disasters of war, were only accidental to the substantial fact that France remained self-possessed, that the people of France continued to hold the lands of France free of rent or tax. The nation had conquered its domestic tyrants, and abolished for ever the usurpations of conquest. The battle of Waterloo was fatal to Napoleon and to the people who conquered him, for the same train of events that left the French masters of France left the English and Irish people serfs in England and Ireland.

When England was brought to apparent ruin by the loss of her American colonies, the inventions and toils of her people in Lancashire raised her to solid prosperity, won for her honest wealth, and enabled her to add incalculably to the comfort and happiness of mankind. What was the condition of the English people after Waterloo? The great landowners appointed the House of Commons. Seats were sold and bought. The increase of wealth stimulated the traffic. In a few large towns where the choice was free, bribery, drunkenness, and murder disgraced the elections. Pensions and peerages were lavished without any other discrimination than the exclusion of merit. Game laws were in force that set the life of a hare or rabbit above the life of a peasant. Every landlord on his own domain was as absolute as William the Norman had been in the whole island. Legislation was mainly directed to such a regulation of the price of corn as would keep up the rents. During four centuries after the Conquest the exportation of corn was entirely prohibited. It was afterwards allowed when the price fell below a certain sum. When the price rose above the fixed sum it was allowed on payment of a duty. Then when its price fell below the fixed sum a bounty was paid on its exportation. In the ten years ending in 1751 a million and a half pounds were paid in such bounties. The Church existed for the advantage of the Bishops, who were the relations or dependents of noblemen. That larger portion of the population who worked for their bread lived on the verge of famine. Poor-laws were administered not to relieve the poor, but to reduce wages. The production of labourers was regulated like the production of corn. The parish had the right to apprentice the children of the poor to any trade, and masters were compelled to receive them. Children were sent in waggon loads from London to Lancashire, separated for ever by fresh settlements from their parents, and left absolutely at the disposal of persons whose only object was to coin their toils into gold. At the age of seven or five they laboured fifteen, often seventeen, hours a day. Apprentices were frequently murdered for the sake of fresh premiums. There was no difference between poverty and crime. The pauper might be imprisoned indefinitely. In prison the felon and the debtor shared the same yard, and often the same bed. It was a capital offence to steal to the value of five shillings from a shop, or forty shillings from a dwellinghouse. The peers and judges would not hear of changing the punishment to transportation. In 1813 it was seriously proposed to punish fraudulent debtors with death. More people were hanged in England than in all Europe besides. The *Quarterly Review* wrote in 1816 : " We have our professors of humanity like Robespierre, who propose to abolish capital punishment." The extreme penalty was inflicted wholly to cow the people, and was not determined by innocence or guilt.[1] The caprice of the judge decided. In 1815 a married man committed a capital offence, and was transported. His wife committed the same offence that she might join him, and was hanged. Rewards were paid for the detection of felony, and the training of crime till it reached felony became a trade among the police. It was well known that innocent men were brought to the gallows by police officers for the sake of the reward. So absolutely was the war glory of the time a class enjoyment that the common soldiers were treated as slaves while in the service, and left to destitution and contempt when out of it. They were drawn from the very lowest class, often from the hulks. Such is a very faint picture of the condition of things that the French war was waged to maintain in England. The very soldiers fought for their own degradation.

The artificial prices of commodities caused by the war ceased with it. The farmers in large numbers resigned their farms, and none could be found to take them. The fact was a condemnation of the English land tenure. The cultivation of the soil and the cultivation of the mind are the only industries that are pursued for their own sake. The maintenance of the race and the progress of thought are thus ensured. The method of holding land that prevails in England makes agriculture a mere money-getting traffic. When it ceases to be lucrative the farmer abandons it. The condition of the farm labourers, who have a natural love for their work, became deplorable. They had not even a voice with which to express their sufferings.

The introduction of machinery into manufactures, stimulated by war prices, had increased the wealth of the capitalists at the cost of the workers. The fall of prices complicated by the resumption of bank cash payments caused severe distress. Labour is the only unprotected vested interest. The propertied class demanded the removal of the income-tax, and it was removed. But the labourers could not find employment. This was inevitable, it may be said. But it is also inevitable that the man who lives by his toil should consider his trade or calling as sacred as the landlord considers his estate. A bad harvest and a famine occurred. Agitations arose throughout the country for reform in land laws, corn laws, and representation. The Ministry treated all expression of suffering as treason, encouraged emigration, suspended the Habeas Corpus Act, suppressed public meetings, and silenced the press.

In Ireland it seemed to be felt that the sowing of disunion between the inhabitants was the only mode of preserving the union with England. The part which the Protestants had taken in 1798 was to be prevented in the future at any cost. There was at once a safety and a danger in Orangeism. It might be relied on to destroy Catholics, but its tendency was towards insubordination, its loyalty being conditional, and its institution in fact being intended to act independently of Government. The vain effort, therefore, was made to keep it tame by satiating its hungry hatred. The Protestants as a body leaned towards conciliation. The Dublin University could not be prevailed on to petition against the Catholic claims. The Protestant inhabitants of nine counties had petitioned in their favour. O'Connell, in after years, always said that

[1] See " Lord Ellenborough's Diary " Vol, I., p. 155

rather than remain in the union he would be satisfied to repeal Catholic emancipation, and trust himself to his Protestant fellow countrymen. Against those dispositions Orangeism must be fostered, as it had been created by Government. All that was needed was to give it legal strength, and let it follow its own will. It was supplied with congenial magistrates and arms. In June, 1808, a number of men, women, and children were amusing themselves round a bonfire near Newry. Eighteen yeomen, commanded by their sergeant, approached, and fired several volleys at them, killing one man and grievously wounding many. The Viceroy, when appealed to, would give no redress. The corps to which those murderers belonged soon after fired a volley in defiance as they returned from parade, over the house of the murdered man. In this same year fifty unarmed men of the King's County militia, who had volunteered into the line, were marching through Omagh. A party of three hundred Orange yeomen, who were celebrating the battle of Aughrim, encountered them. One of the yeomen knocked off the regimental cap of a militiaman because it was bound with green, and trampled on it. The men resented the insult, and the whole body of yeomen made an assault on the fifty unarmed militiamen. The latter retreated to the barracks, and being there supplied with arms defended themselves, and shot four of their assailants. One of them was tried for the murder of these four men, and found guilty of manslaughter. In Mountrath the Orangemen murdered a parish priest, and the next year a Catholic named Cavanagh, without ever being punished or even questioned. Those are isolated instances of a practice that was almost universal. One other case may be quoted to show the common feeling that pervaded Orangeism and the Government. Patrick Spence, a private in the county Dublin militia, was thrown into the black hole because, being a Catholic, he would not attend the Protestant worship. He wrote a letter to his major excusing his conduct. This letter was pronounced to be mutinous, and he was sentenced to receive nine hundred and ninety-nine lashes. He was offered the choice of going into foreign service, and accepted it. On a representation to the Viceroy, an order came that the man should be liberated and join his regiment. He was imprisoned, and discharged from the army. The letter on which he was condemned was often called for and always refused.

The rents had been raised during the prevalence of the war prices, and were not reduced when they fell. The population now amounted to six millions. The increase that was apprehended from prosperity came with greater certainty from habits engendered by insecurity and want. The policy that resorted to suppression, modified by mild encouragement to emigration in England, broke out into undisguised extermination in Ireland. A new constabulary force was organised, and a series of cheap Ejectment Acts passed in 1815, on the recommendation of Mr. Robert Peel, who was Irish Secretary. Two more cold-blooded and deadly blows were never aimed at the spirit and the body of any nation that ever existed.

The impunity accorded to Orangemen had a very real meaning. The dominion of England could not be maintained for a day in Ireland without their aid. To have to acknowledge this fact would have been a bitter humiliation. It would be an admission that English power was not supreme in Ireland, that the conquest was further than ever from being accomplished. An appearance, therefore, of subordination must be obtained. In 1808 the Viceroy made a tour through Munster, and ordered that no Orange displays should be made in his line of progress. This desire was communicated to the Orangemen of Bandon, with the qualified proviso that it extended only to the present occasion. On their next parade day they appeared all decorated with orange lilies. The Earl of Bandon then ordered them to remove those emblems or ground their arms. They amounted to about six hundred men. With the exception of twenty-five, they threw down their arms and accoutrements rather than obey the command of Government issued through their officer. They only exhibited an abnormal form of the indestructible national spirit.

SECTION III.

In 1816 a committee to inquire into the state of Ireland was moved for, and successfully resisted by Peel. There were occasional acts of violence, but these were the convulsive movements of starving men. An enquiry would reveal this, and recommend reform instead of coercion acts. England was in a similar state. The importation of corn, till it reached a famine price, was forbidden. The constitutional demands for reform were cruelly repressed. The people assembled in lawful meeting were massacred in Manchester by a body of troops. The next year, 1820, Arthur Thistlewood and several desperate men conspired to assassinate the ministry. An act was passed prohibiting the possession of arms, the assembling of more than fifty persons together, and what were called "blasphemous and seditious libels," by which was meant comments on the proceedings of Government.

A bill for Catholic Emancipation was introduced in 1821, and was vehemently opposed by Peel. The same year the king visited Ireland. By special request all political dissensions were laid aside, and the people were silent in eager hope. The famine of 1822 was the fulfilment, and the people became wild as they saw their grain and cattle shipped to England, while they starved.

Is it possible for an English statesman to pause, and ask himself what it is he expects from Ireland? What was expected at this time was that her people should forego all their rights as mortal and immortal beings, toil as slaves without the protection of slaves, without the privilege of the ox that treads out the corn, and die without a complaint when at last they were driven from their homes, and all this for the sake of men who hated and despised them. English ministers did not pause—they only saw that Ireland resisted, and were determined to quell the resistance. An Insurrection Act was passed, and the Habeas Corpus Act suspended. This was the last exploit of Lord Castlereagh. He died immediately after, removing by his own hand an enemy of the human race. A milder policy began to appear. The Marquis of Wellesley was Viceroy, and showed a conciliatory spirit towards the suffering people. The Orangemen threw a bottle at him in a Dublin theatre. Neither a grand jury would find a true bill, nor when the Attorney-General proceeded, *ex officio*, would a jury return a verdict of guilty against the perpetrators of the outrage. The Orange party were resolved to show who were the rulers of the country.

In 1823 O'Connell and Richard Lalor Shiel met by accident at the house of a common friend in Wicklow, and planned the Catholic Association. O'Connell had already acquired a high place as a successful lawyer and popular leader. He possessed a combination of qualities that singularly fitted him for the emergency. The ancient race and its earlier conquerors met in him. He was a dark-haired Milesian. To the physical audacity of the Scotic blood he added the varied mental resources and the religious fervour of the Iberian. The pride of the aristocrat mingled in him with the surging spirit of democracy. A constitutionalist by nature, and shocked in the dawn of his manhood by the sight of the revolutionary excesses in France, where he was educated, he chose moral agitation as the medium of his country's deliverance. But his peaceful struggle was conducted with the shout and onset of the warrior. He roused, united and informed his countrymen. He inspired one soul into Ireland. He taught the people their power and lifted them to a height of courage and consentaneous action from which they have never fallen. He made them one mass, inspired by one mind, and capable of following one chief. At the same time he powerfully appealed to the reason and sympathy of Englishmen, and contributed to the growth of English liberties. The tyrants of both nations he dared and defied. The sacred impostures and impious manifestoes with which they triumphed over the consciences of men he burned in the public places in the fires of his eloquence. His gait as he trod the streets was a challenge to men who claimed a servile demeanour as their due. We can scarcely now estimate his towering character, as he stood alone in the valley white with the skeletons of centuries, and prophesied upon them, and covered them with flesh and sinew and skin, and called the breath of freedom from the four winds to breathe upon them, till they stood on their feet an exceeding great army. The magic of his sonorous voice, pealing over a desert, is lost to us who knew of him only when his accents were drowned in the million echoes they had created. We can form some notion of his style of oratory, by comparing it with that of Shiel, his fellow labourer. Shiel composed orations, moulded perfect forms of art; O'Connell breathed oratory, poured forth its materials in a fused and burning flood. Shiel produced photographs; O'Connell shone as the sun. The dangers to which he exposed himself and his personal intrepidity under them endeared him to the multitude. A member of the Dublin Corporation, a man of French extraction, challenged him. He knew that his life was sought for political ends, yet he deliberately aimed at only disabling his adversary, though the wound unfortunately proved fatal. He was met on his return from the field by a troop of dragoons on their way to protect the man who it was supposed had slain him. Peel sent him a challenge some months after, conceiving himself insulted in a speech, but information reached the authorities from different sources, and O'Connell was dogged by detectives, and arrested and bound over to keep the peace.

The Catholic peers gradually joined the association. The bishops followed. O'Connell instituted penny subscriptions, and they soon averaged five hundred pounds a week. The people were thus organised, and the priests came with the people. A new and closer relation sprang up between the clergy and their flocks. Emancipation was made not a purely religious or sectarian question, but a principle that affected man's rights, and the liberty of the human conscience. The Pope, bishops, and peers regarded the subject as one of expediency, and would submit to the veto: O'Connell, with the mind and voice of the people, proclaimed a universal principle, and demanded for every religion absolute spiritual freedom. The Presbyterians of the north and the reformers of England became his natural allies. The intellects of England and Ireland found a common platform.

Parliament first tried the vulgar method of repression. The association was declared illegal. O'Connell's legal knowledge enabled him to steer the bark of his country's hopes clear of those artificial rocks. A bill was then, during Canning's ministry, brought in admitting Catholics to Parliament and Municipal Corporations, but accompanied, for Ireland, with the disfranchisement of forty shilling freeholders, and the endowment of the Catholic clergy by the State. O'Connell was at the time in London on a deputation concerning a bill for the suppression of unlawful assemblies. The occasion produced two noticeable incidents. Under the influence of friendly intercourse, and separated from his Irish supporters, O'Connell was willing to receive the two "wings," as they were called, of the Emancipation Bill. The measure, however, after passing the Commons, was thrown out in the House of Lords, chiefly through the opposition of the Duke of York. The second incident was an angry outburst of feeling on the part of Peel towards O'Connell, showing how narrow personal jealousies could lurk under his cold aversion.

The Association turned its resources to the return of Liberal Protestants to Parliament in the general election of 1826. The Beresfords in Waterford, the Fosters and Jocelyns in Louth, were defeated at the poll. The Orangemen plied their unfailing antidotes to the spread of light and the triumph of opinion in the celebration of the anniversaries of conquest. Some Protestants, mistaking the march of a nation for a religious procession, took the apparently more reasonable course of preaching a new reformation. Several polemical discussions took place, with the usual result of each party claiming the victory for its own champion. Men even still fail to see that Catholicism is much more than a religion to Ireland. As a spiritual empire it supplies the room for organisation and free thought which the loss of political freedom took away. It is in vain to tell the Irishman that he is in spiritual bondage when he knows that his communion with Rome is the only real freedom he possesses. What Romanism did for Europe, at an immature political stage, it still does for the country whose political growth is restricted.

The Duke of Wellington became Premier and Sir Robert Peel Home Secretary in 1828. The Irish Catholics sent a petition signed by eight hundred thousand of their number praying for the relief of Protestant dissenters from the tests that excluded them from holding office. A measure to this effect was proposed by Lord John Russell and
T

carried. The Association had pledged themselves to oppose the election of every supporter of Wellington's administration. The member for Clare accepted office and offered himself for re-election. Lord John Russell wrote to O'Connell, suggesting that the Association should depart from their rule in this instance. O'Connell's desire to make common cause with English reformers would have led him to consent, but he was overpowered by the general vote. He offered himself as candidate to give the people an opportunity of indicating their will. He was opposed by all the great landed interests, Milesian and Norman. The O'Briens and Mac Namaras united with the Vandeleurs and Fitzgeralds in resisting him. He was returned by an immense majority.[1] The ministry yielded and granted the Catholic claims, but mingling the petulance and malice of individuals with the solemn act of the State, they suppressed the Catholic Association, disfranchised the forty shilling freeholders, and so worded the Act that it deprived O'Connell of his right to sit as member for Clare. Catholic Emancipation was not a triumph of Irishmen for Irishmen, nor was it sought as such. It was a triumph of principle, and as such sufficed for those who won it. Peel could not grant it, but O'Connell could accept it on large impersonal grounds. It brought no respite from suffering to the Irish people. It made their lot worse, because on them fell the vengeance of the defeated faction. O'Connell was one of the army of advanced thought, and his country, though seemingly engaged in a contest with England, was in reality moving with the great tide of revolution that swayed the nations, contributing to its volume and modifying its progress. The object of the Tory party was to keep things at the level which they took after Waterloo. Ireland in the meantime had invented, in direct intentional opposition to the violence of the French Revolution, a new method of moral agitation, and had seen it succeed. The French now again arose, overthrew the system which the rest of Europe had laboured to perpetuate, and appointed their own manner of government. England caught the contagion, but adopted Irish tactics. An association was formed at Birmingham on the exact model of the Catholic Association in Dublin, and reform was eventually won, O'Connell giving it all the assistance in his power. But each nation discharges its duty towards the aggregate of nations, not merely by contributing to the general warfare, but by fighting perseveringly its own individual battle. We find O'Connell accordingly at one and the same time contending strenuously with England when she opposed justice in Ireland, and co-operating with her heart and soul when she struggled for the deliverance of her own people, or for human rights in any part of the globe. The true glory of those times was not that of Wellington and the English and Irish soldiers who fought under him at Waterloo; it belonged to the people of England who conquered the conqueror of Napoleon on a far more difficult field than that of war, and wrung reform from him; and to the people of Ireland who compelled him to grant Catholic Emancipation.

[1] See "Lord Ellenborough's Diary," Vol. I., pp. 157-162.

CHAPTER XVI.

Repeal of the Union.

Section I.

In 1833 the Church Temporalities Act, by which ten bishoprics and church rates were abolished, was passed. The people gained no material advantage, but the axe was nearer to the root of the tree. The next year O'Connell brought the question of repeal of the union before Parliament. Queen Victoria's accession to the throne in 1837 was inaugurated by a poor law. The object of poor laws in England had been the punishment of houseless poverty, on the ejection of the people from their lands and the suppression of monasteries. The object of the Irish poor law was exactly and unmistakably the same. It was moreover meant to facilitate and encourage ejection. In 1838 tythes were converted into a charge on the land, and were paid by the landlord, who, of course, exacted them from the tenant. In 1840 a Municipal Reform Act gave the inhabitants of towns the right to elect town councillors. O'Connell was elected first Catholic Lord Mayor of Dublin. The Irish Act differed in one essential particular from the English usage. In England the Corporation chooses the sheriff. The Irish Act gave the appointment to the Viceroy.[1] The sheriff had charge of the jury lists. Of those liberal measures it might be said that they brought no solid or immediate relief to the people. But they were diminutions of usurped privilege, and as such were desperately contested. They were Irish contributions to the general cause of free government. O'Connell worked vigorously with the Liberal party while they were in office, and held Ireland's peculiar claim in reserve.

In 1841 Sir Robert Peel became prime minister, and O'Connell immediately started the Repeal Association. The movement towards freedom is identical in England and Ireland. When it is obstructed by the party of privilege it takes different forms. The people of England were starving, while abundance was prevented from flowing in by a duty on corn that protected the landlord's rent. In Ireland the people were starving, while corn and cattle poured in a great river from her shores to produce the absentee landlord's rent. England was asking for a repeal of the corn laws, that corn might come freely into the country. Ireland asked for a repeal of the union, that sufficient corn might remain in the country to feed the population. England has two labouring populations, the agricultural and the manufacturing. The demand for repeal of the corn laws was made in reality for the sake of the manufacturing population. When the demand was granted, the change did not affect the condition of the agricultural labourer. Ireland demanded a repeal

[1] By an Act passed in 1876 the Corporations of Dublin, Cork, Limerick, Waterford, Kilkenny and Drogheda appoint the sheriffs.

of the union, because she had only an agricultural population. The manufacturers of England were seeking deliverance from a distinct, and in some manner, a rival interest on their own soil. The only way in which Ireland could obtain deliverance from Irish landlordism, whose chief strength lay in its union with English landowners, was by home legislation. No common law could protect both countries from the power of landlords. The victory which the free traders won in England did not extend to Ireland. Landlordism and its cognate interest, in the two countries, have only one object in reference to Ireland, and that is, to make it a grazing farm or cornfield for England, and to treat its population in entire subserviency to this design. In 1843 three million quarters of grain, and a million head of live stock, were exported from Ireland to England. It might be argued that this was a sign of prosperity. Prosperity to whom? The price of all those exports was exported also in the form of rent. Five millions rental left Ireland this year for England. At the same time the population was emigrating at the rate of a hundred thousand a year. The nature of this emigration may be inferred from the advertisements of emigration agents, which offered gentlemen who wished to send out their surplus tenantry credit for six months. The landlords in Ireland were sole judges of what constituted a surplus tenantry, and they formed their judgment not in reference to Ireland, from whence their rents were drawn, but in reference to the United Kingdom, which meant England, where their rents were spent. Sir Archibald Alison, writing in 1833, stated that the emigration from Ireland in 1831 amounted to eighteen thousand. "No reason," he added, "can be assigned why it should not be a hundred and eighty thousand."[1] Can any fair-minded Englishman wonder that O'Connell wished to have a Parliament in Dublin who might deliberate, not leaving the decision altogether to Sir Archibald Alison, whether or not a reason could be assigned?

O'Connell acted on the belief that if an overwhelming demonstration of popular sentiment was made, its requirements would be conceded as a matter of course. He moved a resolution in the Dublin Corporation for a petition to Parliament, demanding a repeal of the union. It was carried by a majority of forty-one to fifteen. He then began a series of vast meetings throughout the country, consisting of hundreds of thousands of men. Government sent bands of armed constabulary to be present on those occasions. They could only be a provocation to the multitudes, who always kept the most exact order. Other and more direct incentives to violence and sedition were secretly and lavishly employed, and employed altogether in vain.[2] The most marked character of O'Connell's agitation was its impregnability to detective influences. Peel declared in the House of Commons that if all the members for Ireland were unanimous for repeal he would not grant it. If one were to answer a fool according to his folly, the answer to this statement would be that if Ireland was unanimous in demanding repeal, no English Minister would be able to refuse it. But the wiser answer is that no

[1] "Blackwood's Magazine," Jan., 1833.

[2] A well-known writer for the English press stated in a letter to the *Morning Chronicle* that he saw men at the Irish meetings who had been hired to create disturbances at the Free Trade meetings in England.

English constituency ever authorised its representative to utter such a sentiment; and that Sir Robert spoke the language only of personal petulance. No more unstatesmanlike words were ever spoken in the most reckless flight of Fenian oratory. An Arms Act, requiring that all arms should be registered and branded by the police, was introduced. Mr. Smith O'Brien, a member of the Inchiquin family, in which the title was at the time extinct, proposed as an amendment the appointment of a committee to enquire into the cause of Irish discontent. The House refused the enquiry, and passed the Arms Bill. Fresh troops were sent to Ireland, gun-boats were anchored in the rivers, and cruised round the coast, and barracks and police-stations were loopholed. There were several gentlemen holding the commission of the peace among the members of the Repeal Association. They were insultingly superseded. O'Brien, who was not a repealer, resigned his commission, and several magistrates followed his example. O'Connell appointed courts of arbitration, in which the dismissed magistrates settled disputes voluntarily brought before them. He spoke of inviting three hundred gentlemen to assemble in Dublin as the basis of the future Parliament. The public meetings continued and were attended by increasing numbers. A meeting intended to be the last of the season, was appointed for Sunday, October 8th, 1842, at Clontarf. Late on Saturday a proclamation was issued, forbidding it. O'Connell and his committee instantly countermanded the assemblage, and all Saturday night was spent in laborious and exhausting efforts, from the effects of which some of those engaged in them died, to prevent the multitudes from coming together. On Sunday morning the troops were marched to Clontarf, but found the ground vacant.

Had the people assembled in their usual numbers, and had a collision taken place, it is impossible to determine what the result might have been. O'Connell was perfectly sincere in his strict adherence to moral displays in urging the concession of a native Parliament to his country. Among the motives that conduced to this determination, besides his natural repugnance to bloodshed, his knowledge from yearly experience of the inability of a mob or crowd of men to stand the onset of a few armed and drilled policemen or soldiers, must have had a place. The constabulary force organised by Peel, unless some alteration takes place in its management, will bring some fatal calamity even on England. Policemen have almost succeeded in driving all manly independent action from the habits of Englishmen. Coroners' juries constantly append to their verdict a severe censure on some one who quietly stood looking on while a prolonged brutal murder was committed. Men dare not interfere with what is supposed to be policemen's work. If a policeman were seen in the streets offering the most cruel ill-treatment to an unoffending prisoner, any passer by who interfered merely in remonstrance would be dragged before a magistrate and sent to prison.[1] Men accustomed to being cowed and browbeaten by policemen at home, are in danger of crouching before a display of authority or determination wherever they are confronted by it. The servile fear is not expelled by wearing a soldier's uniform. We remember the events of the African

[1] See Serjeant Ballantine's "Some Experiences of a Barrister's Life," Vol. II., pp. 16-32.

war. When the late Egyptian campaign commenced, some of our soldiers were seized with a panic at the first appearance of the enemy. The fact was denied and concealed; but all the reconnoitres that so long tantalized public expectation were really nothing more than a prudent seasoning of the soldiers before they were committed to an actual engagement. Everything depends on accident in collisions between a crowd and soldiery. Small bodies of policemen had frequently about this time routed hundreds of peasants in Ireland. On one occasion, when the police shot the first man, the peasants, instead of being dismayed, became infuriated, and slew all the policemen on the spot. On another occasion the people had exhibited the most undaunted courage in a conflict with soldiers. Something of this sort might have happened at Clontarf.

A state prosecution was the next step. O'Connell and eight others were indicted for conspiracy. By conspiracy was meant open combined constitutional action to gain an end. Meanwhile the repeal agitation went on unchecked. A new hall, which had been erected as a meeting place, was opened amidst enthusiastic promises of support from increasing and influential quarters. O'Brien joined the movement. The weekly contributions rose to a very large sum. The arbitration courts continued their labours. Government were compelled to proceed with their prosecution. They had attempted to use the soldiery in destroying the liberties they are enrolled to protect. Foiled in that intention, they deliberately exposed law to eternal detestation and universal distrust by setting it against the order for the sake of which it exists. And all that they did was done not to preserve the union, but to preserve England, as in the most ancient days, from the contagion of Irish freedom; and to maintain the obligation on the multitude in the two islands of pining on scanty fare, or starving outright, for the sole pre-eminence of a class.

The trials began in 1843. Everything depended on the formation of the jury. The jury list was specially revised, and Catholics excluded wherever a pretext could be found. Yet a large number remained in the list. A slip containing sixty-seven Catholic names disappeared. Out of forty-eight names taken by ballot from the list thus exhausted, the jury was to be chosen; the Crown and the prisoners having the privilege to strike off twelve each. The first twelve of the remaining twenty-four that answered when called constituted the jury. Of the forty-eight eleven were Catholics. The Crown struck them all off, as well as several Liberal Protestants. During the trials the professional letters of the agents of the traversers, as they were called in legal parlance, were read in the Post Office. When the grand jury had found against the prisoners, they used a wrong term in describing the charge; on being corrected, they replied that they found for it "whatever it was." The Chief Justice, when summing up, described the counsel for the traversers as the "gentlemen on the other side." A verdict of guilty was returned. The traversers were ordered to come before the court in May for sentence. From the day of Clontarf the conduct of the authorities was that of men not punishing for illegality, but endeavouring to intimidate from legal courses by illegality. The Liberal leaders in Parliament strongly condemned the conduct of the Irish law officers. A banquet was given to O'Connell in Covent Garden Theatre, to show "on the part of Englishmen their admiration of his constant advocacy of the rights of Irishmen." He appeared in the House of Commons, and exposed the lawlessness of the means by which the verdict had been procured. Government must proceed or confess themselves to be criminals. The traversers were sentenced to a year's imprisonment and a fine. The judgment had been appealed against, and was reversed by the House of Lords. The jury who found the verdict were all Conservatives in politics. One of the Irish judges, a Liberal, gave his opinion against the formation of the jury. Those of the English judges who were Liberals were for quashing the proceedings. Finally in the House of Lords, Lyndhurst, a renegade Irishman, and Brougham, a Scotchman, both Tories and personal enemies of O'Connell, decided that the verdict was good; Denman, Cottenham, and Campbell, all English Liberals, decided that it was contrary to law and justice.[1]

O'Connell was never so powerful as on his release. The people never for a moment doubted his ability to defeat his enemies. But all through the struggle the hope that held them together was not deliverance from England, but deliverance from their landlords. O'Connell had always placed fixity of tenure among the first results of repeal of the union. It was angry terror at hearing their absolutism assailed, and not injured loyalty, that inspired the landlords to oppose him. A Landlord and Tenant Commission, consisting wholly of Irish landlords, was appointed and commenced its labours in 1844. In one portion of Ireland a custom prevailed that practically solved the problem of the nation's distress. In Ulster what was called tenant right, a remnant of the old tribal system, kept the north prosperous and contented. The want of it kept the south distressed and disturbed. The commission of landlords condemned tenant right, and recommended consolidation of farms and emigration. Sir Robert Peel brought in a bill substituting a principle of compensation for tenant right, promoting the "removal of a vast amount of labour," and proposing the employment of a part of it on waste lands. The tenants of Down declared at a public meeting that this bill would deprive their class in Ulster of a million and a half of money. The landlords did not wish to have their waste lands meddled with, and they revolted from the idea of compensation. The bill was thrown out.

Eviction was the grand remedy of the landlords. They would defend the union by lessening its human materials on the Irish side. Their plea was that large farms were most productive. The farming that is most productive is not necessarily best. A lesser productiveness that benefits many, morally and physically, is better than a greater productiveness that benefits a few materially and demoralises all. Land is for food and food is for men : the farming that increases productiveness by diminishing men has lost its way. If higher productiveness were the sole test, it might appear in the course of time that Ireland would produce more by getting rid of the landlords, as well as of the tenants. Ireland would produce most for England by being cultivated by machinery under a small number of agents.

"[1] Life Lord Campbell," Vol. II., . 186.

The Government increased the Maynooth grant; induced the Pope to order his clergy to confine themselves to their religious duties, and refrain from politics; and endowed three secular colleges, thereby producing much bitter controversy between the friends of education generally, and those Catholics who are in favour of educating Catholic youth separately.

The Repeal Association continued to supply the want of a native Parliament so far as the discussion of public topics, and the formation of a cultivated and intelligent public opinion, could accomplish that end. The aid and sympathy of American slave owners were indignantly rejected by O'Connell as wholly incompatible with Irish aims.

Some late writers have disparaged O'Connell's work in winning emancipation, and have pronounced his repeal agitation a failure. They arrive at those conclusions by regarding him merely as a Irish leader. He was more than this : he was a soldier in the great army of progress, and his efforts are to be judged as contributions to its final success. The idea that emancipation would come spontaneously is a delusion. When an instalment of right is made we assume that the concession arises from an increased sense of right, and that it is accompanied by a general loosening of all wrongful tenure. On the contrary, the grasp on what remains becomes tighter, and the defiance of right more conscious in proportion as the tyrant is compelled to disgorge. Justice prevails by extortions, not by concessions. There must be a man able to extort. The masses have been wronged, and they are becoming aware of it. That is supposed to be a wider spread of the love of justice. The intellectual growth of right is a distinct movement far in the rear of events.

In agitating for repeal of the union O'Connell made his country potentially a nation. He gave it the power of rising to the voice of one man. It was he infused the spirit that keeps the pulses of Irishmen in all parts of the globe beating to one measure. He helped to preserve the integrity of the American Republic, by teaching Irishmen what side to take in the war against slavery. He took the cause of independence out of the hands of a faction and made it the life of the country. In 1810 the Orange Corporation of Dublin passed a resolution against the union by a majority of thirty. The Grand Jurors of Dublin sent a requisition to the sheriffs to call a meeting for considering the necessity that existed of petitioning for a repeal of the act of union. The freedom they sought was for the privileged few. O'Connell delivered a speech at the meeting that made the demand for repeal his and Ireland's.

Section II.

A party which became known as Young Ireland had grown up within the Repeal Association. It was composed of a number of young men who were impatient of O'Connell's constitutional method, and of his limited aim. They were seeking for some independent line of action when their leading spirit, Thomas Davis, died, and a fearful famine fell with the suddenness of a thunderbolt on the land. Landlordism had encroached on the produce of the people's toils till nothing but potatoes was left to them to live on. It continued its merciless exactions till the soil was compelled to yield a cheap, degenerate, and unhealthy root, and the peasantry, as their rents increased, became dependent on it for their subsistence. Man might bear this strain, nature would not bear it. The earth refused to be a partner in such inhuman tyranny. God's nature revolted against man's injustice. The potato crop failed. If Ireland had possessed a native Parliament, the national resources would have been applied to meet the emergency. If there were a real union with England the resources of the United Kingdom would have run to Ireland just as water seeks its level. Heaven presented Sir Robert Peel with an occasion of illustrating the union as sincere and equal from the English side. He might have furnished the friends of the union for ever with an argument in England's considerate care for her suffering sister. The people of Ireland suggested the very measures which, if adopted, would have told against their demands for independence in after years. Their suggestion explained what they had been saying in their secret souls, while repeal had been on their lips. They had hitherto spoken in the pride of coveted nationality. God now put them to the torture and they spoke the very truth. They did not whine for alms, nor offer to die as irreconcilable enemies. The Corporation of Dublin asked for an early assemblage of Parliament, and the employment of public money in public works. The men who had petitioned for a separate Parliament a little time before, now showed what their motive was in seeking for it, by their expectations from a united Parliament. The Duke of Leinster, the Lord Mayor, O'Connell, and others waited on the Viceroy and recommended the opening of the ports to foreign corn, the stoppage of distillation from grain, and similar measures. If common sense or common humanity could enter into the councils of rulers those steps would have been immediately taken. But instead of sense or justice, the self-justifying spirit of the individual, and the crooked pedantry of statesmanship, which has done for government what theology has done for religion, ruled the Cabinet of England. Ireland must be humbled and depopulated. The whole management of the famine was kept in the hands of Government. Sir Robert Peel, who had changed his mind on the corn laws, took advantage of the occasion to propose their repeal. His ministry broke up in dismay, but he returned to power again in 1846, on the failure of the Liberals to form a cabinet. The corn laws were repealed, Peel was defeated in an attempt to carry an Irish Coercion Bill, and Lord John Russell came into power. A division immediately took place in the Repeal Association. O'Connell, following the tenour of his life, gave his support to the Liberal administration. The Young Irelanders, led now by O'Brien, formed themselves into the Irish Confederation and separated from O'Connell. Their avowed object was armed insurrection in opposition to O'Connell's moral force.

English Liberals act towards Ireland from principle as regards the just demands of Ireland, and from expediency as regards the prejudices of their own country. It is an essential part of their principles to satisfy Ireland's legitimate demands, but it is an indispensable part of their policy, if they would ever hold office, to maintain that attitude of mastery over Ireland which is supposed to be required by the dignity of England. The Tory or Conservative party could at any time succeed in exasperating almost all England with a fury of resentment against their rivals if they could charge them with conniving at what they call treason in Ireland. This is a natural infirmity and a party weakness which every Irish political leader should make allowance for. The Young Irelanders could make no allowance. They were driven mad by the sights that surrounded them, and by the English mode of dealing with their cause, for which England was partly accountable. The removal of two millions by death or emigration was provided for by the nature of the remedial measures that were adopted. The necessity of maintaining England's supremacy will be pleaded in excuse. It was landlordism that brought on the crisis, and it was the supremacy of landlordism that was upheld. The Liberals had an uneasy consciousness of this fact, and they gave utterance to it when out of office, but when they held the reins of power their whole attention was given to the management of the team. A Coercion Bill was passed, which made the police masters of the persons, houses, and thoughts of the peasantry. Its extreme severity measured only the impression made on the imaginations of the ministry by the poetry of the Young Ireland writers, and on their consciences by their arguments. A group of talented young men, most of whom won the highest distinctions afterwards in other countries, and who, if their own country were healthily governed, would have found ample scope for the exercise of their abilities in the forum or the field, had not space large enough for their sweep of pinion save in the unlimited region which even the aspiration for freedom affords. But they aspired only in print and on platform, and in frequent scenes of festivity, a species of patriotic entertainment in which O'Connell never indulged. They rejoiced in refuting and reviling England. They triumphed in cutting parody and defiant rhetoric. They provoked the English Press to undignified retort, and the authorities to insulting personal reprisals. They were not quite to blame. They only misused the occasion: and the occasion was produced by the men who perpetrated the union, by the brutal pride of the Tories, and the party necessities of the Liberals.

John Mitchell, a northern Protestant, was hampered even by the moderation of the men for whom O'Connell was too pacific. He started a newspaper, which soon outran the other national Press in the race for popularity. He, O'Brien, and Meagher, the orator of the party, were charged with uttering seditious language. O'Brien and Meagher were tried first and acquitted by the refusal of a single juror in each case to convict. The country was seized with a delirium of joy, and Government with something like terror. In reality the contest was one of mutual insults and provocations. The Young Ireland clubs went through the streets of Dublin in military array. Pikeheads were publicly exhibited for sale. All was done in derision and defiance. Any calm spectator might have seen that an insurrection was quite out of the question. There was no stern purpose. All passion evaporated in excitement. On one of the days of O'Brien's trial Meagher walked at the head of his club on the quay opposite the Four Courts. He was supposed to be a captain at the head of his regiment. As they marched along a loud shout arose in the neighbourhood of the Courts from which O'Brien had just emerged. Meagher's regiment broke up, stormed an iron toll-bridge which spans the river at the spot, and rushed to the newest attraction. Meagher vainly strove to retain even the companion on whose arm he leaned, and was left alone abashed and confounded. This was the kind of military force the authorities had to fear. But the authorities were also seized with the joy of the conflict. They were carried away by a spirit of retaliation. An Act was passed making seditious language felony. Mitchell was tried under this Act on a new charge, and convicted by a jury from which the national element had been carefully removed. The tones of the Crown Solicitor, as he ordered the challenged jurors to "stand by," were full of mockery and scorn. The judge's face, as he emphasised "fourteen years' imprisonment," blazed with exulting triumph. A young girl who sat in the sheriff's box, beamed with light smiles, save when she looked towards Mitchell, when she gazed as she might at a wild beast in a cage. The prisoner, in a short speech, declared that he was found guilty by a packed jury, a partisan judge, and a perjured sheriff. He might as certainly have foreseen this as experienced it. He said that he was surrounded by men who would follow his example. John Martin, his friend to death, Meagher, and others, who sat round the dock, started to their feet in confirmation of his words, and a scene of wild confusion arose. He was removed, and hurried on board a war vessel. He expected a rescue. He tells us in his *Jail Journal* how when he found himself shut up in his cell, he burst into tears of wrath and remorse.

All Mitchell's great abilities were perverted and marred by his violent and indiscriminating hatred of England. There is an England, as there is an Ireland, to be hated, execrated, fought against with brain and sinew by every man who believes in a God and a destiny for the human race. It is the peril and the holy dread of seeing Ireland made the instrument of this England in accomplishing its odious projects of enslavement, that more than justifies the demand for repeal, and the wish for separation, or union with France or America, or any other country under the sun. But Mitchell forgot, or could not see, that there is an England to be loved and died for by any Irishman who, unblinded by his country's wrongs, perceives that they are only one item in the long catalogue of sorrows which this England is striving to erase. He did not reflect that in his own time a wide and earnest struggle was going on in England, a battle for peace and equal rights, in which the great heart of O'Connell had mingled without one throb less for his own country,[1] and that this great cause had also its physical force advocates, who were suppressed with as great severity as he had suffered. He did not remember or rightly estimate the fact that it was his own countrymen who struck him down; that the judges, law officers, and jury were Irishmen; that the police, whose bearing insulted him in the streets; that the spies who read his letters and cast their shadows on his hearth, were Irishmen. He did not reflect that the readiness of

---

[1] O'Connell seconded in 1833, the first proposal made in the House of Commons, for the repeal of the Corn Laws.

Irishmen to be bought, not the untainted and unpurchaseable Irish peasantry, but Irish professional men, secretaries and committee men, has been not so much an agency for the malice, as a temptation to the virtue of England.

Young Irelandism was in a great degree a social insurrection against the insolent airs of the official garrison, and the loyal aristocracy of Dublin. Had they confined themselves within the proper lines they could have triumphed in their real superiority. But when they talked of force they changed the nature of the fight. Bands of police held the streets. Two men could not speak for a moment on the footway without the interference of a constable. Poets, orators, and editors were seized and imprisoned for a word. Newspapers were cut down, and fresh crops sprang up to tempt the sickle. The war was waged as if the publication of a new journal was a triumph of Ireland, the suppression of it, England's glory. But under this airy tournament a real work was going rapidly forward. Whole estates were under process of clearance, hamlets were dismantled, crowds of starving wretches, whose limbs sank under them in the dock, and whose eyes had the terrible famine glare, were sentenced to transportation. If an Irish newspaper hinted at the little sympathy the portly justice showed for the fainting prisoner, the English press gravely lectured their Irish brethren on their want of good taste. And all through this time of noisy word-war and famine, and ruthless extermination, the corn of the country was floating to England, and—unfailing mark of delegated rule—Dublin and the provincial capitals were ablaze with balls and gaiety.

Insurrections are made when men look each other in the face, and understand the common purpose in the lines of the forehead and the pressure of the lips. The Young Irelanders were only rehearsing an insurrection before an audience. The Habeas Corpus Act was suspended and warrants were issued against O'Brien and Meagher. They went into the country to commence resistance. To O'Brien was conceded the leadership. He was an honest aristocrat, whose vanity had been hurt by the rejection of his remedies for allaying disaffection. He joined the patriots, and was celebrated in print and speech as the model of an honourable and humane gentleman. That he was by nature, but he was now acting the part consciously, and with the sense that all men were watching his actions. The peasantry flocked round him, but he would not give them anything to do. He resembled a timid rider who instinctively pulls in his horse as it rises to the leap. He seems to have been mastered by the expectation that the enemy would yield to his influence, and that no blood need be shed. His party was scattered, and he was taken prisoner by an English policeman at a railway station. Meagher and some others came to an understanding with the authorities that they should not suffer capitally, and gave themselves up. Their dock speeches were made and listened to with this knowledge. They and O'Brien were transported. O'Connell died in May, 1847. The famine killed him. At the close of 1848 the editors of two of the national newspapers were tried before Protestant juries and convicted. Charles (now Sir Charles), Gavan Duffy twice escaped by the disagreement of his jury. It was rumoured at the time that he was the only man whom the authorities wished to hang. The Encumbered Estates Act, a desperate attempt to introduce a new race of landlords into Ireland, by violating all the sanctities of landlordism, utterly failed in its purpose. The Queen visited Ireland in 1849, and was received peacefully. The population had fallen, through death or emigration, from about eight millions and a quarter to six millions and a half. During the twenty years between 1849 and 1869, Parliament authorised the expenditure of nine millions, to come out of the lands, in assisting the poor to emigrate, and so lessen the poor rates. Only a hundred and nineteen thousand pounds were actually spent. The people were left to do the work for themselves. Within the same period thirteen million pounds were remitted by the Irish in America to their friends at home, of which nine millions were spent in emigrating.[1]

SECTION III.

Efforts of the most generous character were made by the English people to relieve the distress in Ireland. They were impeded materially and morally. Government got hold of the supplies of food, and influenced their management. A portion of the English Press openly triumphed in the diminution of the population, and Lord Carlisle spoke of Ireland as a future grazing farm for England.

In 1850 the Irish Tenant League was formed. Duffy and Frederick Lucas, an Englishman, were its chief journalists. Lucas wrote to a friend in 1852 of the Irish peasantry in these words: "The limited intercourse I have had with them has left on my mind a very strong impression that there is not in the world a people—I refer to the unsophisticated portion of the country people—for whom a man of any heart or conscience would sooner lay down his life. The wrongs they continue to endure fill me with a passionate indignation, which I hardly know how either to express or repress, and I would give every hope I have in this world to alleviate them a little."[2] Fifty Tenant Right members were sent to Parliament, pledged to oppose all Governments that did not allow the principle of Tenant Right for all Ireland. Two of their number, James Sadlier and William Keogh, took office under Lord Aberdeen. The bishops supported them, and obtained an order from Rome, prohibiting parish priests from attending political demonstrations. Lucas was sent with an appeal to the Pope. The long delay, usual in such cases, caused his death. Duffy went to Australia. Sadlier was exposed as a swindler, and committed suicide.

The fall of the League made room for a secret organisation calling itself Fenian, from the name of the soldiery of ancient Ireland. It deserved the term secret only in one respect. Its leader was James Stephens, who had escaped to France in 1848. He returned and connected himself with a club known as the Phœnix Society, in Skibbereen. Suspicions were aroused, several members were taken up, pleaded guilty, and were released. Stephens continued to enrol members,

[1] "North American Review," April, 1882, p. 356.
[2] "Frederick Lucas: A Biography," p. 108.

and in 1863 started a newspaper—the *Irish People*—in Dublin, and employed his resources in vigorously opposing all the legitimate proceedings of the nationalist party. In 1865 the American war ended, and a large number of disbanded Irish soldiers came to Ireland and joined the conspiracy. A confidential agent of Stephens' was in government pay; on his information the staff of the *Irish People* and all the private papers of the society were seized. Stephens was soon after taken at his house with the remaining leaders, the money, and complete lists of the organisation. He was imprisoned in Richmond gaol. The Castle raised a question with the prison board about the expense of the military guards of the prison, and they were withdrawn. Stephens escaped by the connivance of a warder whom the Government did not prosecute on this charge. The Fenian leader never afterwards had the confidence of the Irish.

In 1864 negotiations were entered into to effect an alliance between Irish and English Liberalism, and the National Association of Ireland was founded for the disestablishment of the Irish Church and the alteration of the land laws. Mr. Gladstone spoke, and Mr. Bright wrote, words of encouragement. An instance of the manner in which the prejudices of the English people are roused against Ireland here presents itself. In an article on Ireland, in a magazine of wide circulation, the name of O'Connell is thus introduced without any apparent appropriateness: "When the famine was at its height, and the splendid subscriptions of the English were pouring into the country, we chanced to pay a visit to what was termed, as if in irony, Conciliation Hall. Presently Daniel O'Connell entered. He was then an old man, and wore a shabby red wig, forming a disagreeable contrast with his wrinkled face, a face with the same fixed smile noticeable in that of Pio IX. Over his broad shoulders hung the red robes of a Lord Mayor. His speech was not calculated to make him find favour in our eyes. It turned on the famine. . . . At last he said, 'And these subscriptions—these thousands of pounds they are sending to you, and of which we hear so much. Do you think these English men and women—these Protestant English—care for your trouble? . . . Do you think there is one iota of pity or sympathy in what they are doing? There is not a man in England cares in his heart one straw whether you live or rot. Shall I tell you why they send you this money? It is for this reason, and none else—*they are afraid of you.* Yes, the English are afraid of the Catholic Irish, and that is why they send money to stop your mouths. You are seven millions strong.'"[1] O'Connell was never Lord Mayor except in 1840. At the time referred to he was dead or dying in a distant land, and the Irish were far from being seven millions strong.

In the summer of 1866 Mr. Bright was entertained at a public banquet in Dublin. The Conservatives instigated the Fenians to make a disturbance. The Church was seen to be on the verge of its fall.

On the deposition of Stephens his place was taken by a man named Kelly, who had planned his escape from Richmond. He was denounced as a traitor to the Fenian Committee. They laid a plan for the

[1] "Fraser's Magazine," October, 1865, p. 412.

assassination of the man who denounced him. The attempt was made in the presence of detectives, yet none of the assassins were prosecuted.[1]

About the same time an informer named Massey was in the hands of the Dublin authorities. Orders were given by the commander of the Fenians in Dublin that he should be rescued while passing in a cab, unescorted, at a specified hour from the prison to the Castle. He himself had sent an account of the particulars. Some persons who doubted his honesty informed the Government that a rescue was to be made. If the Government on this information sent him through the town well guarded they intended to rescue him. He was driven through the streets accompanied by two policemen in plain clothes. The Government attempt to get up a rescue failed in this case. Fenian trials were in progress at the time, but the counsel for the defence could not be induced to use those facts in evidence.[2]

Kelly went to Manchester, and was taken by the police, armed and making a disturbance in the streets at midnight. Warning was given to the authorities that he would be rescued while being conveyed from the court-house to the gaol. An escort of twelve policemen was sent with him; but they were quite unarmed. The rescue was made, a policeman was shot, three men were hanged,[3] and Kelly was heard of no more. An attempt was soon after made to blow down the wall of Clerkenwell prison with gunpowder, in order to release a Fenian prisoner. This was prompted by a spy who prosecuted his victims to the gallows. When the English public cooled and began to see what had taken place, a reaction began. In 1869 the disestablishment of the Irish Church was completed, and the first blow at landlordism was struck.

The Home Rule movement commenced in 1870. The Irish Nationalists and the English Liberals were never on more cordial terms than during its continuance, and the hopes of Ireland were never nearer fruition. The organization in England suddenly got into the hands of the enemy. Home Rule officials from Ireland declared in public meetings in English towns that the Irish discarded the Liberals and preferred Tory assistance. The policy thus initiated culminated in the imprisonment of the Irish Parliamentary leaders. When they showed a disposition to retrace their steps, Lord Frederick Cavendish and Mr. Burke were murdered in open day, almost in sight of policemen who refused to interfere.[4] Murder was loosed, and the flash of the

[1] "Blackwood's Magazine," April, 1882, p. 460.

[2] "Fortnightly Review," March, 1882, p. 397.

[3] A Committee was appointed to seek a commutation of their sentence. The attempt was controlled by police agents. Some of those prominently concerned in it immediately left Manchester. In the endeavour to drive away another of them, the greatest crime known to the law was committed or simulated. A few years after an Irishman named Habron was condemned to death in Manchester for the murder of a policeman. A meeting was called by advertisement, at the Clarence Hotel, Spring Gardens, to petition that he should not be hanged. A person was stationed on the stairs at the hotel, who told those who came that the meeting was postponed for an hour. When they returned at the end of the hour they found that the meeting had been privately held. Habron's sentence was changed to penal servitude for life. Afterwards Peace, the notorious burglar, confessed that it was he who killed the policeman. The persons who prevented the public meeting knew Habron's innocence; yet they would have suffered him to be hanged had not the people of Manchester asked for an enquiry, and they would have left him in confinement all his life had not Peace confessed.

[4] Evidence to this effect, given at the coroner's inquest, was subsequently withheld at the trial of the assassins.

assassin's dagger was followed by the thunder of coercive legislation in London. But the Liberals were true to their principles, and passed a further measure of land law reform.

*　*　*　*　*　*　*

A short time ago two strangers from England visited the Phœnix Park Zoological Gardens. Their attention was caught by an eagle in an iron cage, which flapped its wings continuously as if in flight. They attempted to attract its notice, but its eyes remained fixed on the horizon, and the movement of its wings never ceased. They went through the other portions of the gardens, and on their return the bird was occupied as before. As they departed they again and again looked back, and to the last the eagle was winnowing the air with its pinions, and gazing into the far distance.

INDEX.

	PAGE
Act of Attainder	196
Act of Settlement	180
Adrian, Pope	56
Aidan	24
Alba	13
Alexander, Pope	71
Alienated patriotism	96
America	209, 227, 233, 285
Ancestry	2, 4
"Ancient Britons"	254, 256
Apparel sought	79, 123
Armada	140
Armagh, See of, founded	18
—— Synod of	64
Armoric St. Lawrence	80
Arms Act	277
Armour not used by Ancient Irish	59, 77, 82, 90, 113
Aryans	4, 8
Assassination	132, 133, 147
Assumption of Irish names	93
Attacotti	9, 13
Attempt to unite Catholics and Independents	173
Bagnal, Marshal	130, 144
Bards	22, 35
Barons in England	94
Battles—Ardee, 38. Tara, 40. Sulchoid, 40. Clontarf, 43. Hill of Victory, 76. Athenry, 90. Faughard, 92. Stoke, 113. Knocktow, 115. Lough Swilly, 134. Kinsale, 151. Yellow Ford, 144. Benburb, 172. Boyne, 190. Aughrim, 190. Waterloo, 267.	
Battles with unarmed peasants misunderstood	73
Bentus	15
Belgæ	7
Berkley	215, 228
Berkley's persuasives to obedience	216
Blount (Lord Mountjoy)	148
Boarian tribute	11
Boyle (Earl of Cork)	158, 160
Browne, Archbishop	123
Bruce, Edward	87, 92
—— Robert	88
Bull, Papal	56, 68, 70, 71, 91
Burke	72
Cade	106
Carew, President of Munster	147, 153
Carlyle	180
Cashel, Synod of	68
Cathaldus	15
Catholicism falsely associated	126
Catholic Association	231
—— Relief Bill	232
Cattle, Importation of, from Ireland forbidden	200
Celestius	15
Celestinus, Pope	15
Chieftaincy disintegrated	104
Character of people, how composed	12
Church Temporalities Act	275
Civil war	109
Class rule and race rule	53

	PAGE
Claudian	13
Clonmel	180
Coercion before redress	254
Columban	180
Columbkille	20
Commercial towns founded by Ancient Irish	35, 39
Confederation of Kilkenny	166
Conversion of Irish, Peculiarities of	17, 19
Confiscations	130, 155, 159, 183
Connection between Catholicism and poverty	220
Conquest of Henry II. was over his own rebellious subjects	64-9
Conquest	2, 9, 32
—— perennial	249
—— systematic	164
Contest not between England and Ireland	240
Contrast between North and South	135
Convocation of Clergy	156
Corn-producing, Ireland	149
Cornwall	13
Cromwell	176
Dalcassians	30, 41, 45
Danans	6, 8
Dathi	13
Davis, Thomas	280
Dawn of Reformation and Revolution	101
Debasement of coin	148
Declaration against Transubstantiation	198, 233
Defenders	233
Delusion of English people	70
—— concerning object of Henry II.	105
Despard, Colonel	261
Divisions of Ireland	7, 8, 11
Drogheda, Siege of	177
Dunboy Castle taken	153
Eber	8
Emmett, Robert	261
England's duty to Ireland	105
English parties	205
English and Irish Catholics	187
Enmity, Origin of	54
Erigena	37
Erimhon	8
Essex, Earl of	136
Eugenians	30, 45
Evil of partial concessions	233
Failure and new plan	146
Famine, Descriptions of	153
Famine, Potato	281
Fiana, Rules of	19
Fitzgeralds	57, 72, 90-93
Fitzgibbon	250, 255
Fitzstephen	57, 59
Fomorians	6, 7
Fostering	29
Free Trade	238
Freedom—How fought for	77
Freedom of early Irish thought	27
Froude	197, 206, 213, 227, 234, 242

U

INDEX.

Gallus 26
Gaveston 87
Germanus 15
Golden Age, Meaning of 43
Grattan and Flood 245
Gunpowder Plot 156

Harold expels Normans by Irish aid 54
Hasculph 64
Heresies of Irish Church 68
History, Proper subject of 2
History, Irish, Mystery of 49
— not traced by reigns of kings 125
Hobbes English 97

Iberi 3
Invaders, Advantage of 7, 83
— imagine they are seizing their own 85
Invasion of Ireland viewed politically 69
Iona 21, 23, 31
Ireland, Ancient names of 5, 6, 7
Ireland's struggle more than national 250
— a place of refuge from England and Wales 54-56
— not allowed to be prosperous or loyal .. 129
Irelands, Two..6, 9, 17, 36, 43, 49, 77, 81, 89, 92 122
"Irishman would be nigger" 216
Irish reformers condemned for acting in concert with English reformers 250
Irish pensions 202, 237
Irishmen, Disparagement of, What it means. 199
Irishmen's work and reward 269
Irishmen's alternative 265
"Ireland sunk in the sea" 261

Jackson, Rev. W. 253
James lands 189
John lands 72, 79
Justice prevails by extortions, not concessions 280

Killala 256
Kilwarden, Lord 262
Kings (English):—
Oswald and Oswin, 24. Harold, 41, 54. Henry II., 56, 58, 64, 67. John, 79. Henry III., 80, 82. Edward I., 84, 85. Edward II., 87. Edward III., 95. Richard II., 98. Henry IV., 102. Henry VI., 106. Henry VII., 111, 113. Henry VIII., 121. Mary, 125. Elizabeth, 126, 128. James I., 156. Charles I., 157. Cromwell, 176. Charles II., 185. James II., 188. William III., 190. George I., 211. George III., 232.
Kings (Irish):—
Erimbon, 9. Moran, 10. Tuathal, 10. Niall, 13. Dathi, 13. Malachy, 33. Hugh Finlath, 34. Flan Sionn, 34, 37. Donchad, 38. Congal, 39. Donnal, 40. Malachy, 40. Brian Boru, 42. Malachy, 45. Regency, 46. Murkertagh, 47. Terence O'Conor, 47. Roderick, 48. Crovderg, 75. Hugh, 83. Manus, 86. Felim, 87. Henry VIII., 123.
Kings, Four, Knighted 99

Land Laws 220
Landlordism 222
Land Tenure, Changes in 120
Leaders killed 82, 90, 92, 255
League and covenant 171
Legitimation of children 29
Lesson from the past 50
Liberty 235
Limerick, Treaty of 100, 203
Livery 29
Lucas, C. 237
Lucas, F. 285

Macalpine, Kenneth 13

Macaulay, Lord 77, 101, 199, 250
MacMurrough, Dermot 48
— Art 100
Maguire, Lord 162, 169
Manchester rescue 287
Massacre, an old charge against resistance to tyranny 10
Massacre of Spaniards 130
Meath 10
Mildness of Irish laws 84
Milesian or Scotic rule ends 155
Misrepresentation, Instance of 286
Missionaries 14, 26
Mitchell, John 282, 283
— his error 283
"Modest Proposal" 219
Monk, General 163
Monroe, General 163
Mountmorres 59
Moran 10
Motives of oppression 210
Murders, Accounts of 35
Murkertagh 38

Nathan's parable 19
Nemedians 7
Nesta 57
Norman abuse of Irish laws 93, 94
— superiority 51
— religious policy 39, 90, 121
— intestine quarrels 94
— rule 52-3, 208

O'Brien, 44, 66, 75, 110. Earl of Thomond, 123. Lord Inchiquin. 167, 257. Smith, 277. The Informer, 257.
O'Connell, Daniel 258, 286
— condemned and acquitted, according to political party of judges 278
O'Conor, Charles 231
Octennial Bill 237
O'Doghcrty, Sir Phelim 155
O'Donnell, Earl of Tyrconnel 153
O'Neile, 30, 33. Con, Earl of Tyrone, 123, 131. Shane, 131. Hugh, 139. Sir Phelim, 152. Owen, 167. Lord, 257.
O'Neile's letter to the Pope 91
Orangeism 224, 230, 253, 258, 267, 270, 280
O'Ruark 48, 70
Orde's Propositions 248
Organising power of Irish 81
Ormond, Duke of 170, 173
O'Toole, Lawrence 63

Packed juries 253
Pale, Irish, disturbed, 11, 29, 44, 50, 69, 78, 85, 105
Palatinates 93
Palladius 15
Papal power always on side of England, 90, 112, 114
Parallel between England and Ireland, 78, 94, 108, 121, 182, 275
Parliament, 88, 98, 106, 160. Of James, 192.
Parliament supersedes the Church 109
Parties, Religious 224
Partholan 6
Patricius 15
Peace, Irish, disturbed, 11, 29, 44, 50, 69, 78, 85, 105
Peep-of-day boys 233
Peasantry described 215, 285
Pelagius 15
Pembroke, Earl of 58, 72
Penal laws 198, 205
Perkin Warbeck 114
Persecution, No 125
Picts 13
Police 246, 277, 287
Poynings' Act 114

INDEX.

	PAGE
Prendergast	60, 66
Principles at stake	150
Progress, Marks of	217
Prosperity for whom?	276
Protestant testimonies	229, 230
Protestants, Distinction of	209
Puritanism	159, 161, 169, 176
Race, Distinctions of	3, 4
Rebel, Force of word	139
Rebellion, Seeds of	59, 78
—— of Desmond	130
—— of Silken Thomas	117
—— of 1798 deliberately fomented	254
Reformation in the two islands	122
Reformation, Opposition to	124, 129
Reform, Spirit of, common to both islands	249
Regeneration, Irish	77
Repeal Association	275
Religion—of Aryans, 4; of Ancient Irish, 5, 11, 16; of Northmen, 29; Essentials of, 19, 228	
Religious hate only a pretence	208, 230
Religious reformations connected with civil liberty	156–8
"Restore the Heptarchy"	261
Right of conquest newly stated	129
Rinuccini	170
Rising of 1641 forced by Government	161–2
Rollo	31, 52
Royal consecration	22
Rulers, Two classes of	10
Rule, True idea of	121
Savage, Sir Robert	94
Schomberg	189
Scotland	13, 21, 22, 43, 87, 132, 134, 165
Scythi or Scoti	7, 12, 17, 20, 30
Scotch reformers	257
Scotia, ancient name of Ireland, transferred to Alba	13
Sedulius	15
Separate interests of England and Ireland	79, 99
Sermons on 1641	231
Scullabogue	256
Sheil, R. L.	272
Sheares's, The	255
Sheehy, Rev. N.	225

	PAGE
Spaniards at Smerwick	130
—— at Kinsale	151
Septennial Bill	237
Slavery abolished	64
Spies	154
Statute of Kilkenny	97
Stilicho	13
St. Leger, Charge against	124
Stonehenge	6
Strathclyde	13
Swift	211, 217, 219
Tara	10, 20
Talbot (Lord Furnival)	103
—— Earl of Tyrconnel	188
Tenant Right	279
Tenants, English, fly from Norman Lords	93
Terrorism	53, 62, 92, 234, 268
Threefold struggle	220
Tone, T. W.	252, 256
Turgesius	31, 38
Union	210, 237, 248, 258, 268
United Irishmen	252
Unnatural laws	208
Veto	265
Virgilius	27
Volunteers	239
—— Weakness of	239
Wales	13, 56
Wars of Milesians, Anglo-Normans	137
Waterford taken	63
Wentworth	159
What does Ireland want	236
Wellesley	266, 274
Wexford attacked	59, 69
Whitby, Conference at	24
Whiteboys	222
William III.	190
Windsor, Treaty of, assured the monarchy to the O'Conors	71, 75, 79, 80, 82, 83, 86, 90
Wolsey	115, 117, 122
Wreckers	233
Young, Arthur	215, 223
Young Ireland	280

PRINCIPAL AUTHORITIES.

Annals of Loch Cé. London, 1871.
Annals of the Four Masters. Dublin, 1848.
Keating's *History of Ireland.* Translated by J. O'Mahony. New York, 1866.
Wars of the Gaedhil with the Gaill. Translated by Todd. London, 1857.
Todd's *Life of St. Patrick.* Dublin, 1864.
Curry's *Manners and Customs of Ancient Irish*, with Introduction by Sullivan. London, 1873.
Maine's *Early History of Institutions.* London, 1875.
Giraldus Cambrensis. London, 1863.
Regan's *Fragments of History of Ireland*, in Harris's *Hibernica.* Dublin, 1770.
Thierry's *Conquest of England.* London, 1847.
Moore's *History of Ireland.* London, 1835.
Leland's *History of Ireland.* Dublin, 1774.
Plowden's *Historical Review of the State of Ireland.* Philadelphia, 1805.
Pacata Hibernia. Dublin, 1810.
Fynes Moryson's *Rebellion of Hugh, Earl of Tyrone.* London, 1617.
Carte's *Life of Ormond.* Oxford, 1851.
Contemporary History of Affairs in Ireland, from 1641 to 1652. Dublin, 1880.
Gilbert's *History of Viceroys of Ireland.* Dublin, 1865.
Earl of Castlehaven's *Memoirs.* Waterford, 1753.
Memoirs of Edmund Ludlow. Switzerland, 1698.
Life of Clarendon, with continuation. Oxford, 1857.
Prendergast's *Cromwellian Settlement.* Dublin, 1875.
Burnet's *History of His Own Time.* Oxford, 1823.
King's *State of Protestants of Ireland.* London, 1692.
Life of Tone. Washington, 1826.
Mitchell's *History of Ireland.* Dublin, 1869.
Barrington's *Rise and Fall of the Irish Nation.* Dublin, 1843.
History of Irish Catholics, by Matthew O'Conor. Dublin, 1813.
History of Catholic Association, by Wyse. London, 1829.
Taylor's *Civil Wars of Ireland.* Edinburgh, 1831.
Madden's *United Irishman.* Dublin, 1857.
Richey's *Lectures on History of Ireland.* Dublin, 1870.
Lecky's *History of England.* London.
Gardiner's *Fall of Monarchy of Charles I.* London, 1882.
Sullivan's *New Ireland.* Glasgow, 1882.
Russell's *Kett's Rebellion in Norfolk.* London, 1859.
Mackenzie's *Highland Clearances.* Inverness, 1883.
Strype's *Memorials.*
Carte's *Collection of Letters.*
Temple's *History of the Irish Rebellion.* Cork, 1766.
Neander's *History of the Church.* Edinburgh, 1855.
Cambrensis Eversus. Dublin, 1848.
Cloney's *Narrative of 1798.* Dublin, 1832.
Memoirs of Viscount Castlereagh. London, 1848.
Lyttelton's *History of Henry II.* London, 1769.
Borlase's *Reduction of Ireland.* London, 1675.
Gumble's *Life of General Monk.* London, 1691.

www.ingramcontent.com/pod-product-compliance
Lightning Source LLC
Chambersburg PA
CBHW030819230426

43667CB00008B/1286